CHALLENGING U.S. APARTHEID

CHALLENGING

WINSTON A. GRADY-WILLIS

U.S. APARTHEID

ATLANTA AND
BLACK STRUGGLES
FOR HUMAN RIGHTS,
1960–1977

DUKE UNIVERSITY PRESS
DURHAM AND LONDON
2006

© 2006 Duke University Press

Printed in the United States of America on acid-free paper

Typeset in Quadraat and The Sans

by Keystone Typesetting, Inc.

Library of Congress Cataloging-in-Publication Data appear

on the last printed page of this book.

FOR DAD

CONTENTS

Acknowledgments ix

Prologue xiii

Abbreviations xxiii

PART I: NONVIOLENT DIRECT ACTION

1 The Committee on Appeal for Human Rights and
Phase One of the Direct Action Campaign 3

2 Phase Two of the Direct Action Campaign and the
Fall of Petty Apartheid in Atlanta 33

PART II: DEMANDING BLACK POWER

3 Bridges 59

4 The Atlanta Project of the Student Nonviolent Coordinating Committee 79

5 Neighborhood Protest and the Voices of the Black Working Poor 114

PART III: THE QUEST FOR SELF-DETERMINATION

6 Black Studies and the Birth of the Institute of the Black World 143

7 The Multi-front Black Struggle for Human Rights 169

Epilogue 206

Notes 213

Bibliography 265

Index 281

ACKNOWLEDGMENTS

I owe a profound debt of gratitude to many who have provided support and moral sustenance as I have written this book. Anyone familiar with the struggles waged by those who hold the field of Africana Studies near and dear realizes that the responsibilities and burdens concomitant with that field require collective commitment and work. I have been fortunate to be a part of such a collective group of teaching scholars and dedicated staff members in the Department of African American Studies at Syracuse University. In particular, Micere Githae Mugo and Milt Sernett have been valued mentors. I am especially grateful to Micere for her comments on an earlier draft of this book, and for her relentless work on behalf of the field. Janis Mayes provided an important professional opportunity at a key moment. I owe a great deal to Linda Carty, who assumed the most difficult job at virtually any academic institution—chair of an Africana department—with both tenacity and grace. Linda is a scholar whose integrity can only be matched by her commitment to the fields of Africana Studies and Women's Studies.

The women and men who consented to be interviewed are the driving force behind many of the pages of this book: Benjamin A. Brown, Joseph E. Boone, Herschelle Challenor, Beverly Guy-Sheftall, Mukasa Dada, Jualynne Dodson, Jan Douglas, Gene Ferguson, Sandra Hollin Flowers, Larry Fox, Vincent Harding, Beni Ivey, Lonnie King, Joyce Ladner, Emma Jean Martin, Ethel Mae Mathews, Silas Norman, Fay Bellamy Powell, Gwendolyn Zoharah Simmons, Michael Simmons, William Strickland, and Columbus Ward. (Although we never conducted a single formal interview, I also thank Dwight Williams for several informal discussions of the Atlanta Project.) Beginning with Ms. Mathews, I will be forever grateful to these grassroots community organizers, feminists, radical nationalists, and engaged intellectuals for being so incredibly giving of their time. Interviewing these activists has underscored the importance of lifting up the living history of Black human rights struggles.

This particular journey began at Emory University and in the Black neighborhoods of Atlanta. I will be forever in debt to Dan Carter, Leroy Davis, and Mary Odem for their guidance and support throughout the entire dissertation process. My doctoral studies were also influenced by the teaching, scholarship, and support of Beverly Guy-Sheftall, James Roark, Kristin Mann, and

Leslie Harris. Alton Hornsby and Mozelle Powell made life as an instructor at Morehouse College a true honor. Charles Jones has been a valued mentor as a Panther scholar and an institution builder in the field of Africana Studies. Akinyele Umoja's principled work as an activist and scholar go practically unmatched. The friendship and support of Talibah Mbonisi (academe still awaits you), Bobby Donaldson, Uche Egemonye, Bill Carrigan, Dan Aldridge, Margaret Storey, Jonathan Heller, Amy Scott, and Belle Tuten were invaluable. Although my connection to Alternate ROOTS, the progressive performing artists' service organization, was essentially a spousal one, I could never overstate how important many of its members have been to me. Finally, Atlanta would have been a lot less hospitable without the friendship of Ralph and Carol England, and their children Brian and Steven.

A number of others have supported this project in direct and more indirect ways. I owe readers of the manuscript (some anonymous and others known to me) a sincere thank-you for their thoughtful criticisms. In particular, Rhonda Williams has been a godsend, a meticulous scholar who always goes beyond the call of duty. The scholarship of several individuals has influenced my own work, including Carol Anderson, Robin Kelley, Brenda Gayle Plummer, and Barbara Ransby. I continue to be influenced in profound ways by the scholarship and example of Cornell faculty members James Turner, Margaret Washington, and Robert Harris Jr. Several others have provided advice and friendship along the way, including Scot Brown, Byron Tatum, James Hunter, Stephanie Smallwood, JacQuie Parmlee-Bates, Dineo Khabele, Marcellus Blount, Quandra Prettyman, Geraldine Gregg, Lisa Wilson, Anthony Browne, Lisa Hazirjian, Alethia Jones, Jaribu Hill, Aishah Sales, and Bill Sales.

Several individuals made the process of fashioning this book much easier: Diana Lachatenere and Andre Elizee of the Schomburg Center for Research in Black Culture; Karen Jefferson and Antoine James of the Robert Woodruff Library at Atlanta University; Skip Mason and Hasan Crockett of Morehouse College; Harry Lefever of Spelman College; Danielle Parisi and Tracey Robin-son of Industrial Color Labs. I certainly owe a special thank-you to the editors and staff at Duke University Press, but in particular to Raphael Allen and Miriam Angress for their early faith in the possibilities of the book when my own was in short supply.

Some say that teaching gets in the way of research. I have been blessed, however, in that classroom teaching and interaction with students have helped fuel and inform my research in tangible ways. Connecticut College students who enrolled in courses that I taught there as a visiting professor remained engaged with each passing week, especially Jessie Vangrofsky and Daniel Raffety. So many students at Syracuse University have influenced my work that frankly, mentioning some by name is a recipe for trouble. But I will take my chances. Practically every student who enrolled in the graduate and upper-division undergraduate seminar in Black women's history contributed to making life incredibly satisfying on the day of the week on which it was held. In addition, I offer special thanks to the following students: the undergraduates Aaron Bell, LaToya Burton, Antoinette Carr, Rasheedah Cooperwood, Rachel Clay, Le'Mil Eiland, Andrea Ferrand, Jason Grant, Gaynor Hall, Jennifer Hall, Ajua Kouadio, Krishna Kranen, Veronika Levine, Cynthia Lully, Shanell Manning, Sondra Mastrelli, Nicole Mayo, Temi Noah, Kayt Odlum, Joseph Perez, Colin Seale, Joy Smith, Christopher Tamburrino, Gregory Williams, Nikea Williams, and Heather Yenawine; and the graduate students Ayesha DeMond, Sharon Dunmore, Henia Johnson, Nicole Jones, Tina May, Joy Mutare, Moushumi Shabnam, Cheryl Spear, and Demond Thomas.

Of course, none of this would have been possible without the support of an incredible family. Despite enduring racism and sexism in the workplace, Lisa Grady-Willis has continued to expose a number of students to the importance and vitality of Black Theatre. On a more personal note, of course, Lisa has been nothing less than an inspiration and guiding light for our children, Bakari Wyn and Emi Alis, and for me. Thank you, Sunshine. My mother, Verlean Willis, in addition to making every sacrifice, made certain that her young sons visited the neighborhood public library often. Although our brother Malcolm, who is autistic, may not have benefited directly from this experience, Noel and I certainly did. Noel, you have made your big brother very proud! My grandmothers Bernice Mayfield and Thelma Sylvester did more to nurture the historian in me with their stories of Black life in the rural South than any childhood classroom experience could accomplish. My stepmother, Harriet Palmer-Willis, and my mother-in-law, ancestor Ruby Grady, have been indelible influences. Unlike a sobering number of Black folk, I have also been blessed to have three important men influence my life: my father, Leon Willis; my father-in-law, Henry Grady; and my maternal grandfather, John Henry Sylvester. In their own way, Dad, Papa G, and Granddad have done more to define what it means to walk with integrity than I can convey in words.

Whenever schoolteachers questioned the authenticity of my work my father came to school the very next day to demand an explanation. He and his colleague Dave Butler (Damani Camara) lost their jobs in defense of integrity in the early days of the Black Studies program at the University of Colorado, Boulder. To this day, no one has been more interested in the progress of this project than he has. Dad, this book is dedicated to you.

During the first five decades of the twentieth century, a small circle of elite Black clergymen, attorneys, and business figures had come to know limited influence in their dealings, almost always informal, with Atlanta's powerful Whites. As a result, individuals such as Rev. William Holmes Borders of Wheat Street Baptist Church and attorney A. T. Walden of the local chapter of the NAACP enjoyed support from their constituencies even as they advocated a gradualist approach. "You don't want to be drawn into any trap that might hurt all of us," Borders cautioned Black bus riders following a 1959 court decision desegregating public transportation. "You've got to have sense enough to take a victory in stride without irritating anybody." Yet inhabitants of Atlanta's Black neighborhoods were growing impatient with such modest victories in the quest to desegregate the city. A stinging blow the following year—a rezoning defeat that kept Blacks virtually hemmed-in—served to remind these established leaders that the city's White power brokers simply had no respect for their influence.[1]

It was precisely during this rude awakening of early 1960 that many of the city's Black elder statesmen were forced to confront the rise of a group of young activist professionals who sought to make their own impact on the racial politics of the Georgia capital. Led by Atlanta University professors Carl Holman and Whitney M. Young, fourteen of these younger middle-class activists formed the Atlanta Committee for Cooperative Action (ACCA). The ACCA raised its share of eyebrows with the January 1960 publication of *A Second Look: The Negro Citizen in Atlanta*. The groundbreaking sixteen-page pamphlet, which had been underwritten by the Black-owned Atlanta Life Insurance Company, provided a well-researched and judiciously argued analysis of all facets of segregation in the city. The members of the ACCA acknowledged that Atlanta was "generally forward-looking" and "potentially a great city." Yet, in tempered language directed as much at the old guard as to White leaders, they contended that people in high places should "take a long, hard, honest look at some problems which will not simply go away if we wink at them."[2]

The activists pointed to significant impediments to the quality of life for the city's African American population in education, health, housing, employment, transportation, recreation, public policy, and the criminal justice system. The ACCA's indictment of education at the local and state levels deplored the prevalence of double sessions, the absence of textbooks, and the tracking of Black high school students toward teaching while their White counterparts could receive "advanced training" in medicine and engineering. The study noted that research expenditures at the graduate level for the segregated institutions of the University of Georgia system totaled over six million dollars while Black colleges received a paltry thirteen thousand dollars. The contrast between Atlanta's Blacks and Whites was as stark in the area of health. The fourteen general hospitals and nine related institutions in the city provided only 430 beds for Blacks; three private hospitals catering to them offered but 250 beds. Only 157 of the city's 2,500 graduate nurses were Black and a mere thirty-eight of the Fulton County Medical Society's nine hundred physicians were Black. It came as no surprise, then, that the death rate for Blacks was 11.7 for every one thousand compared to 8.3 for every one thousand Whites.

Although the authors of A Second Look acknowledged that housing for Blacks in Atlanta was "better in many respects than will be found in many northern communities," they correctly asserted that the overall picture was dismal. Blacks had to contend with paying a proportionally higher percentage of their income than did Whites when purchasing or renting property. What made matters worse, however, was that Blacks bought "generally lower quality property." Furthermore, Blacks had been "blocked and hamstrung" by zoning restrictions. The ACCA pointed to a report published by the Metropolitan Housing Commission the year before that indicated that Atlanta's "nonwhite population," which accounted for 35.7 percent of the city total, lived on 16.4 percent of the developed residential space. While 70 percent of units occupied by Whites were held by owners, only 29 percent of Blacks owned their housing units. Among renter-occupied dwellings, 80 percent of those held by Whites had a private toilet and bathroom with hot water, while only 45 percent of residences held by "nonwhites" had such conveniences.[3]

Employment opportunities for Blacks in the city continued to be extremely limited. Despite being over one-third of the population, Blacks continued to be boxed out of most occupations other than domestic, menial, and blue-collar jobs. The White-to-Black ratio of employment was nine-to-one, two hundred-to-one, twenty-to-one, and thirteen-to-one for social welfare, bookkeeping, electrical, and general white-collar work, respectively. The ACCA also noted that many of the more than three thousand national firms located in Atlanta often openly discriminated against Blacks. The paucity of employment extended to the criminal justice system, an area with which many Atlanta Blacks had daily contact. Of the city's eight hundred policemen, only thirty-one were Black, and but four of those were detectives. The City of Atlanta employed no Black attorney, and only one of twenty-six lawyers in the Fulton County Solicitor General's Office was an African American.

The ACCA activists realized that the grossly inferior position Blacks occupied in socio-economic terms had been inextricably bound to their virtual absence in important policy-making positions even as they continued to make some modest gains as an electoral bloc in Atlanta. No Blacks served on the Atlanta Board of Aldermen, two on the sixteen-member City Executive Committee, and one on the Atlanta Board of Education. This lack of representation had been compounded by the absence of Blacks in the Atlanta Chamber of Commerce, Atlanta Real Estate Board, Georgia Educational Association, and "larger trade unions."[4]

The juggernaut of statistics provided by the ACCA provided ample evidence for the existence of both petty and full apartheid structures in the city. Brick by brick, and supported by the mortar of violence, custom, and law, White business and political leaders had erected these structures since the beginning of the Jim Crow era following Reconstruction.[5] The ACCA activists publicly called attention to petty apartheid—the most visible form of white supremacy, evidenced by separate and decidedly unequal public facilities—in a straightforward and explicit way. Yet, the group went further still by crafting an analysis of institutionalized discrepancies between Blacks and Whites in practically every facet of daily life. Subsequent Black activist struggles in Atlanta and beyond challenged these apartheid structures, serving to refashion and in some cases destroy them. More important, such activism signaled to the world that a fundamental concern of the Black freedom struggle was in securing human rights, and that principal among them was the right of self-determination.[6]

This book seeks to illuminate what self-determination meant for particular groups and individuals by charting the landscape of Black activist politics from the student-initiated nonviolent direct action movement that ended petty apartheid, to various efforts to grasp and realize the meaning of Black Power, to the reemergence of explicitly Black women-centered activism. This study contends that the work of Black activists on several key fronts in Atlanta was central to the development of late twentieth-century Black freedom struggles, as well as to our understanding of those struggles. From Martin Luther King Jr. to Toni Cade Bambara, some of the most influential activist personalities of the period did incredibly important work in the city, both theoretically and practically. As a result, Atlanta provides a fluid baseline for studying the transition from the nonviolent direct action phase to the Black Power phase of the larger Black human rights struggle.

One scholar with a particular interest in the city's early history spoke of Atlanta as a palimpsest of modern streets, highways, and neighborhoods that followed the paths of earlier railroads and streetcar tracks, the railways themselves built to conform to the ridges of the area's topography.[7] In much the same way, the city has represented for several decades a key point of convergence for overlapping and contested lines of Black political thought and action. Several organizations concerned with the Black struggle for human rights anchored themselves in the city. As a result, a talented and eclectic group of Black activists flocked to Atlanta from throughout the country. The city also provides an important lens through which to view the various and often contested ways that Black folk—old and young, men and women, middle class and poor—sought to define and engage in struggles for a more humane world. With each subsequent effort by particular Black activist constituencies to define the terms of struggle and envision a different world, new sites of struggle and self-determination emerged. As a result, Atlanta was emblematic for the expression of particular intraracial struggles revolving around interrelated issues of class, gender, generation, and ideology.

■ ■ ■

Challenging U.S. Apartheid has benefited from the elaboration of several interpretive frames. The first concerns the assertion of *human rights* in discussing the contemporary Black freedom struggle in the United States. Scholars have long used the term *civil rights* in chronicling the efforts of Black activists to obtain national democratic citizenship rights and an end to institutionalized racism through legal and nonviolent direct action strategies. However, this tendency is problematic for two key reasons. One, Black activists who risked their lives within the crucible of frontline struggles both north and south of the Mason-Dixon Line did not perceive their efforts in such narrow terms. Instead, such activists spoke in broader and more transcendent terms, embracing less confining descriptors such as *freedom struggle* and *rights struggle*. Two, the term *civil rights* implicitly privileges state measures such as the Civil Rights Act of 1964 over the grassroots agency that fueled the decades-long direct action movement.

Some scholars of U.S. history have discussed the significance of employing a human rights frame, usually within the context of the rise of groups such as Amnesty International during the mid-1970s. These human rights organizations have tended to focus on the abusive practices of governments and corporations overseas. As scholars such as Carol Anderson have demonstrated, however, revisiting the Black freedom movement in the United States from the perspective of a human rights frame complicates this discussion.[8] What scholars have often termed a distinction between Civil Rights and Black Power politics and activism can be better explained as a transition between the nonviolent direct action and Black Power phases of a broader contemporary Black struggle for fundamental human rights. In 1960, Black college students who coordinated the sit-in movement to end lunch-counter segregation in Atlanta founded the Committee on Appeal for Human Rights. They did so precisely because they understood that institutionalized white supremacy represented an assault on human dignity and threatened the pursuit of African American self-determination in political, economic, and cultural terms.

The second interpretive frame that drives this book is the explicit use of the term *apartheid* in describing the scope of institutionalized white supremacy in the United States, and specifically within the Deep South. The ruling Afrikaner elite in South Africa brought the term *apartheid* into familiar parlance in 1948 following the decisive victory of the Nationalist Party. However, scholars of South African history have treated the entire period of institutionalized "separate development" from 1910 until the collapse of the Pretoria regime in the early 1990s within an apartheid context. I contend that a parallel development took place in this country following the demise of Reconstruction. The term *Jim Crow*, particularly rife with folk meaning, does not adequately portray the scope and severity of the complex apparatus of terrorist violence, disfranchisement, segregation, labor control, arbitrary racial classification, and social custom that constrained the lives of Blacks from the late 1870s until the mid-1960s. Atlanta University professor and community activist Jan Douglas later recalled that in her lectures "I didn't say 'segregation,' I said 'apartheid'" when discussing the history and practice of institutionalized racism in this country. When Douglas did so in a lecture before a churchwomen's group, she recalled that a hush fell over the room, but she persisted. "This was straight-out apartheid."[9]

To be certain, apartheid structures in South Africa and the United States were not one and the same. White political leaders in South Africa erected *grand apartheid*—arguably the most centralized and elaborate form of state racism in world history—via public policy measures such as the Population Registration Act and the Group Areas Act, which gave the country's White minority possession of over 80 percent of the land and absolute control over its political economy. Yet, both countries have witnessed the prevalence of other white supremacist structures, including *petty apartheid*, the provision of separate and unequal facilities according to arbitrarily defined racial classifications. The existence of apartheid structures in the United States was most clearly (though by no means exclusively) manifested in the Deep South during the Jim Crow era. The effort by grassroots activists and members of established organizations to dismantle these structures in Atlanta and throughout the South led to the obliteration of petty apartheid during the 1960s. Nevertheless, the demise of a particular form of institutionalized white supremacy did not signal an end to the Black struggle for human rights. Instead, it provided activists with opportunities for confronting more entrenched forms of racial oppression, as well as contexts for posing fresh questions about the nature and direction of the human rights struggle.

The third interpretive frame seeks to reiterate in explicit terms the bedrock centrality of Black women to every phase of the broader human rights struggle. Black women activists sought to redefine and complicate their understanding of that struggle as radical Black nationalists, grassroots neighborhood organizers, and activist intellectuals. A number of scholars in the field of Black women's history have demonstrated that Black women were part and parcel of the Black freedom struggle at every level. The evidence from Atlanta simply confirms this. Black female college students worked alongside their male counterparts during the sit-in movement as they simultaneously attempted to negotiate and refashion middle-class perceptions of what their role should be. A significant number of these activists became full-time organizers with the Student Nonviolent Coordinating Committee, some becoming project directors. Gwendolyn Robinson (Zoharah Simmons), a Memphis native who came to Atlanta to attend Spelman College, directed a freedom school project in Laurel, Mississippi at the age of nineteen and later co-directed the Atlanta Project with Bill Ware. Robinson's experiences spoke directly to the ways in which a number of Black women in SNCC further gendered the drive for self-determination within the group by struggling to come to terms with what the issue of Black control of the organization meant to them as women.

Black women also sought to redefine the larger human rights struggle from both the grassroots and from positions of relative privilege. Ethel Mae Mathews, who headed the Atlanta chapter of the National Welfare Rights Organization (NWRO), embodied the spirit of organic freedom-fighting intellectuals such as Fannie Lou Hamer and Ivory Perry. Mathews had witnessed first-hand the effort by Atlanta power brokers to marginalize the Black working poor. First propelled to action by violent neighborhood protests against police authority, Mathews later offered an elaboration on the familiar slogan uttered by Black Panther activists by proclaiming "Power to the People. And Bread and Justice to all Poor People." Black women professionals in Atlanta led by Beni Ivey and Jan Douglas launched Sojourner South, a clandestine organization named for the suffragist and abolitionist Sojourner Truth. Sojourner South confronted employment discrimination in the city and helped to mobilize support for the Black freedom struggle in South Africa in the wake of the June 1976 Soweto uprising. In the spirit of the Black club women's movement in the late nineteenth century, Sojourner South represented an eclectic group of women, from socialites to intellectuals, whose principal concern was fighting for concrete change in Atlanta's political economy.

To the extent that scholarly work is also an enterprise that embraces self-determination, it should be noted that the term *Black* has been capitalized as both a noun and an adjective when referring to people of direct African descent. (The term *White* is also capitalized, except for *white supremacy* and *white skin privilege*.) Numerous authors, from Haki Madhubuti to Martha Biondi, have engaged in this practice, as have publications such as *Emerge* and *Ebony*. For all of the organizational and personal animosity between W. E. B. Du Bois and the NAACP and Marcus Garvey and the Universal Negro Improvement Association (UNIA) during the early twentieth century, one of the areas on which there was absolute agreement was that the term *Negro* be capitalized, even though most major newspapers and publishing houses refused to do so at the time. Almost a century later, some scholars now exclusively use the term *African American* precisely because it *has to be capitalized*. In the spirit of Gwendolyn Brooks, I join with other scholars who do not intend to abandon *Black* as a descriptive term, especially given its inextricable link to the Black Power phase of the movement.[10]

■ ■ ■

The first chapter of the book focuses on the initial phase of the pivotal student nonviolent direct action movement to end petty apartheid in Atlanta. It was during this period that a highly organized cadre of Black college students, together with younger professionals, sought to challenge the more moderate strategy of negotiation and legal redress championed by established activist clergy and educators. Despite underlying tensions that eventually came to the fore regarding tactics, Black activists were able to maintain a relatively united front across class and generational lines in the battle against lunch-counter segregation. The second chapter follows the second phase of the sit-in movement, which often targeted restaurant and hotel segregation as well as gross inequities in the administration of health care. In conjunction with the local Committee on Appeal for Human Rights, the national office of the Student Nonviolent Coordinating Committee began to play a greater role in organizing protest activity. It was at this point that protests often defied the middle-class notions of civility that had come to dominate earlier demonstrations.

The third chapter of the book chronicles a critical transitional period during the mid-1960s when radical Black nationalism helped to alter the trajectory of larger freedom struggles in fundamental ways. It was a period of dialectical interplay between life-changing frontline activism in the crucible of the Black freedom struggle and the influence of key external factors such as Revolutionary Action Movement activists and former Nation of Islam minister Malcolm X. As leader of the Organization of Afro-American Unity, Malcolm made direct overtures to grassroots and younger activists in the Deep South to join forces in challenging white supremacy. It was during this period that earlier disputes concerning tactics began to give way to more fundamental ideological cleavages regarding the internationalization of such struggles, the relevance of a class analysis, and a reassessment of nonviolent direct action. The experiences of several key SNCC activists outside Atlanta during this transformative period influenced their work in the city upon their return.

The fourth chapter chronicles the specific work of the controversial Atlanta Project of SNCC. The Atlanta Project is perhaps best known for contending that Whites be expelled from voting positions in the group. A reassessment of this early urban experiment in SNCC community organizing, based on archival and oral sources, reveals that the group's legacy, as well its work on the ground, was far more complicated. What has often been portrayed as an anti-White attitude on the part of Atlanta Project activists, for instance, can be better analyzed within the context of a growing critique in the movement of white skin privilege. The difference is an important one and can be best seen by drawing both parallels and differences with Steven Biko and Black Consciousness Movement activists in South Africa. This chapter also seeks to show that a different picture of the Atlanta Project emerges when the voices of its activists, particularly project co-director Gwendolyn Robinson, are taken into account. Indeed, what emerges is the significance of a radical Black activist sisterhood that often transcended Atlanta Project/SNCC national office boundaries.

The fifth chapter focuses on the violent neighborhood protests that rocked several Atlanta neighborhoods during the late sixties. These grassroots protests, like others throughout the country during this volatile period, were sparked by confrontations between poor Blacks and police. Although not as violent or protracted as the protests and uprisings in Northern cities, the protests in Summerhill-Peoplestown and Dixie Hills represented as direct a challenge to Atlanta's moderate Black leaders as they did to the Whites who wielded power in the city. These protests also gave rise to a core group of grassroots activists, most notably Ethel Mae Mathews, of the local chapter of the National Welfare Rights Organization, who uncompromisingly championed the concerns of the most voiceless group in the city: its working poor.

The sixth chapter chronicles the establishment of relatively autonomous Black intellectual institutions in Atlanta, particularly Black Studies programs and the Institute of the Black World. Led initially by activist historians Vincent Harding and William Strickland, the scholars of the IBW research staff embraced the notion of engaged scholarship in the service of the broader Black freedom struggle worldwide. Although the institute suffered from a lack of support from Atlanta University Center administrators, it commanded the respect of noted scholars throughout the global African world. Instead of impeding progress, involvement in the larger Black freedom movement served to propel the work of scholars such as sociologist Joyce Ladner, embodying a tradition of activist scholarship dating back to the groundbreaking work of Du Bois.

The seventh and final chapter seeks to demonstrate that the 1970s were as full of Black movement activity as were the early 1960s. The key, however, was that the Black struggle for human rights in the city tended to reflect movement on four distinct, yet connected, fronts. Grassroots neighborhood activists continued to press for better wages and dignity for the working poor. The largely grassroots Georgia State Chapter of the Black Panther Party sought, with mixed results, to capture the hearts and minds of younger residents in five of the city's poorest neighborhoods. On a moderate front, the 1970s witnessed gains in Black electoral political strength, most notably Maynard Jackson's 1973 mayoral victory. Black women activists already had been central to the movement of the freedom struggle. These activists demanded in explicitly Black feminist terms and in women's organizations such as the underground group Sojourner South that issues and experiences specific to Black women be confronted as part of a larger concern with embracing self-determination.

The longstanding preoccupation with constructing an image of Atlanta as a progressive city in racial terms—first by White power brokers concerned with maintaining "positive" race relations and later by Black power brokers concerned with creating a middle-class Black haven—has served to obscure its significance as a site for on-the-ground activism. Yet, an eclectic group of Black activists from the city, region, nation, and larger global African world embarked on an incredibly important series of journeys in Atlanta as they lent form and definition to the varied dimensions of the Black struggle for human rights. This study seeks to chronicle and illuminate those journeys.

ABBREVIATIONS

AAPRP	All-African Peoples Revolutionary Party
ABMU	Atlanta Baptist Ministers Union
ACARSA	Atlanta Coalition Against Repression in South Africa
ACCA	Atlanta Committee for Cooperative Action
ACLU	American Civil Liberties Union
ACPL	Atlanta Civic and Political League
ACRC	All-Citizens Registration Committee
AFSCME	American Federation of State, County and Municipal Employees
ALSC	African Liberation Support Committee
ANC	African National Congress
ANVL	Atlanta Negro Voters League
ASLC	Atlanta Summit Leadership Conference
AUC	Atlanta University Center
AUL	Atlanta Urban League
AUSLG	All-University Student Leadership Group
BCM	Black Consciousness Movement
BLF	Black Liberation Front
BPP	Black Panther Party
BPC	Black People's Convention
BSA	Black Student Alliance
BSU	Black Student Union
BUF	Black United Fund
BWC	Black Workers Congress
CAAS	Center for African and African-American Studies
CAP	Congress of African People
CBC	Congressional Black Caucus
CEP	Citizenship Education Project
CFSA	Coalition for a Free South Africa
CIC	Committee on Interracial Cooperation
COAHR	Committee on Appeal for Human Rights
CORE	Congress of Racial Equality
COTI	Amilcar Cabral Community Organizing Training Institute
ERA	Equal Rights Amendment

GABEO	Georgia Association of Black Elected Officials
IBW	Institute of the Black World
IFCO	Interreligious Foundation for Community Organization
ITC	Interdenominational Theological Center
LCFO	Lowndes County Freedom Organization
MFDP	Mississippi Freedom Democratic Party
NAACP	National Association for the Advancement of Colored People
NBAWADU	National Black Anti-War Anti-Draft Union
NBFO	National Black Feminist Organization
NBWHP	National Black Women's Health Project
NCBC	National Committee of Black Churchmen
NDWU	National Domestic Workers Union
NOI	Nation of Islam
NOW	National Organization for Women
NUSAS	National Union of South African Students
NWRO	National Welfare Rights Organization
OAAU	Organization of Afro-American Unity
PAC	Pan Africanist Congress
PCIJ	Peoples Committee to Insure Justice
RAM	Revolutionary Action Movement
SALC	Student-Adult Liaison Committee
SASO	South African Students' Organization
SCL	Summerhill Civic League
SCLC	Southern Christian Leadership Conference
SDS	Students for a Democratic Society
SNCC	Student Nonviolent Coordinating Committee
SSOC	Southern Student Organizing Committee
STOP	Committee to Stop Children's Murders
SRC	Southern Regional Council
UMBU	University Movement for Black Unity
UNIA	Universal Negro Improvement Association
WVL	Westside Voters League

NONVIOLENT DIRECT ACTION

THE COMMITTEE ON APPEAL FOR
HUMAN RIGHTS AND PHASE ONE
OF THE DIRECT ACTION CAMPAIGN

L onnie King faced an all-too-familiar dilemma following his first year of studies at Morehouse College in spring 1954: "I ran out of money." With employment options limited for Blacks in the apartheid South, the seventeen-year-old decided to enlist in the U.S. Navy because it provided a two-year "kiddy cruise" option for those under eighteen and because "I could swim instead of ducking those bullets." Accompanied by his mother, King went to the induction center. There, his mother told a recruiter her son would not be a "sea-going busboy," a steward's mate who served White officers. " 'He can wait tables here in Atlanta,' " he recalled her saying. She added that she would revoke her signature if the Navy did not comply with her wishes. "I was never asked to be a steward's mate, although every other guy in my boot camp who was Black was." Nevertheless, King "ran into a lot of discrimination" in the Navy, which "caused me to realize that something really had to be done about this mess."[1]

While stationed in Hong Kong before returning to the United States, King came to terms with his sense of mission. He told a shipmate named Everett Render that "at some point I believe we are going to end this discrimination and segregation we face in the South, and I want to be there when it happens." King's epiphany had been no different from that of thousands of Black servicemen throughout the global African world who left the racial or colonial contradictions of their place of birth to experience what appeared to be a dramatically different reality in faraway places. His overseas experience helped to complicate the politics of the Cold War, as U.S. policymakers struggled to address domestic forms of apartheid as they championed the virtues of living in a supposedly free land. For King, however, the contradiction had become clear. "By this time, we had a chance to see what freedom was like. We had been all over the world. We did not have a situation in Hong Kong, or in Korea, in Japan, or in San Francisco, where we had to go in the back door."[2]

In 1957, the same year that King returned to Morehouse, a group of Black high school students affiliated with the Oklahoma City chapter of the NAACP began a series of sit-downs to protest racial exclusion at department-store and drugstore lunch counters. Led by fifteen-year-old Barbara Posey, students often packed a given luncheonette one-hundred strong, politely requesting service. On several occasions Whites tossed soft drinks or milk on them, but they most often hurled epithets. The ten-month campaign netted several victories, as several stores agreed to serve all paying customers.[3] However, it took two years for the seeds of protest planted in Oklahoma City to take root elsewhere. Four first-year students from North Carolina Agricultural and Technical College made national headlines on 1 February 1960 when Whites refused them service at the lunch counter of the F. W. Woolworth store in Greensboro. By the end of the month, lunch-counter protests had spread throughout the South, with a steadily growing number of Black college students occupying vacant seats in eateries in eight Southern states. Notably, Georgia was not among them.[4]

■ ■ ■

In the days following the Greensboro protest, students at the affiliated schools of the Atlanta University Center (AUC) discussed the need for moving forward with their own protests. Lonnie King, Julian Bond, Joe Pierce, and Benjamin Brown held informal discussions at Milton's Drug Store, anxious to begin activities. Soon students from Spelman College joined the discussions, and regular meetings began in Sale Hall. When Benjamin Mays, president of Morehouse, got wind of the meetings, he invited King to his office. When Mays expressed the opinion that a legal strategy was preferable, King respectfully disagreed, asserting the students' position that with action in the courts alone, "we'll be doing this for another fifty years." Mays suggested that King and the other students who had been gathering at Sale Hall come to a special meeting of the AUC Council of Presidents.[5]

When the students arrived at the special meeting, they quickly realized that the AUC presidents had done some organizing of their own. The AUC educators had extended invitations to the student government presidents of each college. It became clear to King that the presidents of the affiliated schools were largely supportive of possible protest action as a matter of principle. James P. Brawley of Clark College, who argued that protest activity " 'would just embarrass' " him, was the lone exception. Led by Atlanta University President Rufus Clement, the educators contended that the students would be better served if they presented their concerns in writing before organizing lunch-counter protests. "We advised them to begin by telling everyone what [they were] crying about," Clement recalled.[6]

Responding to the challenge, members of the All-University Student Leadership Group (AUSLG) accelerated the pace of the Black freedom struggle in Atlanta without even leaving their residence halls. On 9 March 1960, AUSLG placed a full-page advertisement, "An Appeal for Human Rights," in each of the city's daily newspapers; a week later the ad appeared in the *New York Times*. Written principally by Roslyn Pope, Spelman College's student government president, the Appeal had a direct tone that forced city business and political leaders to take notice, transforming the political landscape in ways that surpassed those of the Atlanta Committee for Cooperative Action (ACCA) pamphlet that had ushered in the new decade.

The introductory section alerted readers that students at the six Atlanta University Center schools had joined their "hearts, minds, and bodies in the cause of gaining those rights which are inherently ours as members of the human race and as citizens of the United States." In pledging their "unqualified support" to students in the burgeoning sit-in movement, the members of the AUSLG also made a conscious attempt to place the issues within a moral context. The Appeal stated unequivocally that "we cannot tolerate, in a nation professing democracy and among a people professing Christianity, the discriminatory conditions under which the Negro is living today in Atlanta, Georgia—supposedly one of the most progressive cities in the South."[7]

The second section of the Appeal drew heavily from the statistical analysis and organizational framework provided by the ACCA and its *A Second Look*. Employing stronger language, however, the students decried a number of "inequalities and injustices" in education, employment, housing, voting, health, recreation, and law enforcement. Whereas the young professionals of the ACCA cautiously wrote of "problems which will not simply go away if we wink at them," the authors of the Appeal asserted that "we have understated rather than overstated the problems" facing Blacks in Atlanta.[8]

The third section of the Appeal for Human Rights extended its moral indictment of white supremacy in the United States. Pope and the manifesto's co-authors wrote that during wartime "the Negro has fought and died for his country; yet he still has not been accorded first-class citizenship." The Appeal was international in scope, asserting that "America is fast losing the respect of other nations by the poor example which she sets in the area of race relations."[9] Furthermore, the language of the Appeal revealed indirectly that military veterans were not the only ones affected by travel overseas. Spelman students Pope, Marian Wright, and Herschelle Sullivan had studied abroad through the Merrill Scholarship Program. In 1959 Wright noted that "I have become an individual—aware of personal and national shortcomings and determined to correct these in every instance afforded me." Sullivan, who was studying in France when the protests began, later recalled that "this whole notion of justice in the forefront" of the African independence movement permeated the environment in Paris.[10]

The final section of the Appeal also had a moral tone. Its authors shed responsibility on those in White Atlanta who both dared to listen and had the power to change the status quo. The students did so by making a final "call upon all people in authority . . . and all people of good will to assert themselves and abolish these injustices." The drafters of the Appeal went on to announce their role in the ensuing struggle. "We must say in all candor that we plan to use every legal and non-violent means at our disposal to secure full citizenship rights as members of this great Democracy of ours."[11]

In framing the Appeal in such broad terms, its authors were part and parcel of a larger Black activist tradition. During the eighteenth and nineteenth centuries, quasi-free Africans wrote petitions or appeals that indicted the United States for the inhumanity of slavery. David Walker's *Appeal to the Coloured Citizens of the World* (1829) stridently warned Whites that "God will deliver us from under you. And wo, wo, will be to you, if we have to obtain our freedom by fighting." In the era after World War II, the NAACP and radical Black activists circulated petitions to place the question of human rights abuses against Blacks before the United Nations. As recently as 1952, William Patterson, W. E. B. Du Bois, and Paul Robeson led the charge to file the petition, *We Charge Genocide: The Crime of Government against the Negro People.* Though they brought the petition forward "as American patriots, sufficiently anxious to save our countrymen and all mankind from the horrors of war," U.S. authorities quashed their efforts, and these activists became the victims of racist and anticommunist state repression.[12]

While the Atlanta students' Appeal did not compare in scope or stridency with such earlier efforts, it was highly significant, for it couched the discussion of supposed "civil rights" concerns within the broader rubric of human rights. The students recognized that they were about to embark on a protest campaign that not only challenged apartheid structures within the United

States, but transcended its boundaries. "We felt that 'civil rights' was too limited," recalled Lonnie King. "When you talk about 'human rights' you're talking about not just the right to go to a lunch counter. You're talking about other kinds of things. In fact, you're bordering on natural rights that should be granted to you just by virtue of your having been created and in this world."[13]

Reaction to the Appeal for Human Rights was swift. Governor Ernest Vandiver issued a press release in which he charged that the Appeal was a "left wing statement . . . calculated to breed dissatisfaction, discontent, discord and evil." Pointing to the alleged link between racism and anticommunism, the governor also suggested that European leftists, not African American college students, had written it. Mayor William Hartsfield struck a decidedly different chord, asserting that the manifesto "performs the constructive service of letting the white community know what others are thinking." In an effort to recast the situation to support the carefully crafted image of Atlanta as a progressive beacon of the New South, Hartsfield then wedded the fortunes of Black students to those of the entire city. He contended that the Appeal was "of the greatest importance" to a city "too busy with progress to tear itself apart in an atmosphere of hatred, recriminations and destructive violence."[14]

Atlanta newspapers provided commentary as well. The conservative *Atlanta Daily World* applauded the student effort, especially since it represented a departure from lunch-counter protests. The newspaper considered that the "plea was intelligent and effective," and stressed that it had been "worded in an atmosphere of non-violence and we commend this approach." Margaret Long, a White columnist with the *Atlanta Journal*, lambasted the governor's reactionary sentiments and remarked that students demonstrated "restraint."[15]

The All-University Student Leadership Group had its own agenda, however, and on 15 March it launched a meticulously organized series of sit-ins at ten segregated eating establishments throughout the city. Beginning precisely at 11:30 a.m., nearly two hundred polite but committed students descended upon eateries at five government buildings, four transportation centers, and one drugstore, realizing full well that they would be denied service. As a sign of solidarity with the students, only three of twenty-one Black employees at Sprayberry's Cafeteria cleared food away when ordered to do so. Police arrested seventy-seven people in all for violation of the state's new anti-trespassing law when protesters refused to leave each establishment.

Among those arrested at the Terminal Station was Rev. A. D. William King, the older brother of Martin Luther King Jr. "We must be forever striving for the freedom that should be ours under the Constitution," he said, careful to note that he was a "spokesman" for the group but no leader. "If we are arrested day after day it won't stop us from striving for what is rightfully ours."[16]

Others who had long since finished college came to the aid of the AUSLG contingent. Established elders Q. V. Williamson and Martin Luther King Sr. led a group that posted three-hundred-dollar property bonds in an effort to have all who had been arrested released from jail. A. T. Walden, a veteran activist lawyer, worked with attorney Donald L. Hollowell to organize a special meeting of the NAACP Legal Defense and Educational Fund to study a rash of state legislation, such as the anti-trespass law, enacted in the months surrounding the lunch-counter protests. Several younger Black professionals with links to the ACCA, including Atlanta University professor M. Carl Holman, attorney Leroy Johnson, and insurance executive Jesse Hill, spoke with student leaders. Student activists continued to take the initiative, and they reorganized shortly after the initial sit-ins as the Committee on Appeal for Human Rights (COAHR), or as its members simply stated, "the Committee."[17]

■ ■ ■

Students at Atlanta's historically Black colleges and universities who were surveyed in the wake of the Appeal revealed a stark perspective on race, class, and gender. Some Black students professed a heightened mistrust of Whites, especially those who considered themselves "moderate" or "liberal" with respect to race relations. One student contended that White moderates "are our worst enemies because they practice one thing and preach another." Curiously, though, outspoken comments about Whites often betrayed intraracial class tensions. "How can they understand us?" one Black student asked. "They might understand their cooks and their yard cleaners, but they don't understand us. They can't seem to get it through their heads that there is a class structure among Negroes just as there is among whites."[18] Given that thousands of Black families paid their children's college expenses through wages earned from cooking and cleaning for Whites, such condescending notions may not have reflected the attitude of the majority of Black college students at the time.

"In many ways this was a middle-class movement in that we wanted to get arrested for the things we wanted to be arrested for," Sullivan recalled. "So we were always properly dressed, very well behaved and if, indeed, we were arrested, it would be for trespassing. We didn't block any entrance." Cynthia Griggs Fleming, in her biography of Ruby Doris Smith Robinson, asserted that during the first wave of sit-ins these activists were "precisely what they seemed to be—patriotic, middle-class college students" who believed in civility and the inherent righteousness of their cause.[19]

For female students, the inculcation of middle-class virtue was intensified by the expectation to be ladylike. Spelman College had become well known—indeed, notorious, from the perspective of many students—for its suffocating rules. Sullivan remembered that the only place in the residence halls where Spelman women and their gentlemen callers met was in the parlor. Rules restricted dates off-campus to upper-division students, and then only with a chaperone. Within this context, therefore, female students, especially first-year students, challenged the "very restrictive environment" at Spelman precisely as they embraced middle-class notions of civility by venturing off campus for unsupervised protests downtown. Perhaps because they understood the significance of the historical moment, the parents who sought to shelter such students played a critical role by encouraging their efforts. Sullivan recalled with pride that her parents "were deeply concerned" about her involvement in the protest movement. "But they raised us to make up our own minds about things."[20]

■ ■ ■

Although they often shared a similar class perspective, established Black leaders in Atlanta drew criticism from students for their refusal to employ direct action tactics. It was precisely because Martin Luther King Jr., who had just returned to the city to become co-pastor of Ebenezer Baptist Church with his father, embraced nonviolent direct action that one college student was far more inclined to look to him as "our leader. He's shown us the way to accomplish our goals."[21] Some older members of the city's African American elite had been troubled by the sudden assertion of leadership by the college students. "We understand the impatience of youth—they are young and full of energy and ambition," the Daily World offered. "It is the duty of adults to help direct this energy of youth in wise channels." The newspaper urged students to place more emphasis on voter registration, school desegregation, and passage of civil rights legislation.[22]

Leading educators largely supported the students, even if they were not as outspoken as the president of Howard University, who said of the protesters, "if your son becomes one, get down on your knees and thank God." Atlanta University's Clement asserted that he and other administrators "haven't any control over" the students and that the protests "were carried out by adult individuals." When a White businessman told the Council of Presidents that desegregation would never come to Atlanta, Morehouse's Mays responded flatly, "Never is a long time." Horace Mann Bond, a dean at Morehouse whose son Julian was among those arrested, took exception with remarks that Vandiver made following publication of the Appeal. Vandiver had claimed that Atlanta boasted more Black professionals than "any other city on the face of the earth." Bond correctly asserted that Atlanta ranked behind a host of other cities in that regard, noting that Black professionals "tend to settle where they are trained, and where they can get ahead in politics." Atlanta students welcomed such support, given that presidents of several Black colleges actually expelled students and fired teachers for participation in sit-in protests.[23]

In what amounted to a 180-degree shift from his original position, NAACP Executive Director Roy Wilkins now wholeheartedly applauded the sit-ins. The Crisis, the organization's influential publication, argued that "those Americans who genuinely believe in democracy for all should support these young people in every way possible." The group's board of directors agreed to support sit-ins at several national stores. On 17 March, Wilkins issued a memorandum to officers of the organization's state conferences asserting that chain stores refusing to serve Blacks at lunch counters "on the same basis as other customers" should be boycotted as a matter of "racial self-defense."[24]

On the national level the sit-ins were one of two items of concern for the NAACP in March. As the month drew to a close, the NAACP also called for the United States to sever all diplomatic ties with South Africa following the 23 March massacre of ninety anti-apartheid activists at Sharpeville, eighteen miles southwest of Johannesburg. Police there arrested and imprisoned Robert Sobukwe, of the Pan-Africanist Congress, and ten other leading activists for daring to challenge the most developed and firmly entrenched apartheid apparatus in the world.[25]

Authorities in Atlanta appeared to be taking a cue from those in Pretoria when they intensified efforts to repress the activity of Black college students. In April, Fulton County Solicitor John I. Kelley charged eighty-three people, mostly college students, with conspiracy to violate three state laws. Although the original charge was in connection with the sit-in at Sprayberry's Cafeteria, Kelley argued that anyone who participated in other protests on 15 March or who signed the Appeal for Human Rights on 9 March was "guilty as a principal." Undaunted by the additional charges, several members of COAHR picketed two A&P grocery stores in Black neighborhoods. The protesters carried placards asking "Negro Money, Why Not Negro Employment?" and "Our Money Isn't Different, Why Are Our Jobs?"[26]

The resumption of direct action protests may have prompted repressive measures of a cruder sort as well. The dynamiting of a Black-owned home in a transitional neighborhood in mid-April appeared to have more to do with combating Black residential encroachment. However, organized cross-burnings toward the end of the month followed the A&P picketing. Witnesses saw several White men leaving the site of burning crosses at the home of Martin Luther King Jr., the Perry Homes housing project, and on the city's South Expressway. Yet, violence did not deter the momentum of the sit-in movement in places as far away as Savannah.[27]

The spring offensive in Atlanta continued into May. Picketing at Atlanta A&P stores brought growing criticism from the *Daily World*, which berated "adult leaders" for not instructing students to first negotiate. "We deplore the use of pressure tactics in any situation which can be settled otherwise." Almost oblivious to such criticism, students from throughout the South met in mid-May at Shaw University in North Carolina to organize a Student Nonviolent Coordinating Committee (SNCC), whose base would be Atlanta. The Southern Christian Leadership Conference (SCLC) sponsored the meeting, and the SCLC's Ella Jo Baker and Martin Luther King Jr. served as advisers to the students. Nashville student activist Marion Barry, temporary chair of the coordinating committee, said the sit-ins were a "breakthrough" that "demonstrates the rapidity [with] which mass nonviolent action can bring about change."[28]

■ ■ ■

At a statewide NAACP "Freedom Rally," COAHR co-chair Lonnie King announced plans for a student "pilgrimage" past the Georgia Capitol to Wheat Street Baptist Church to commemorate the sixth anniversary of the 1954 *Brown v. Board of Education* Supreme Court decision. King later recalled that Vandiver had "decided that 'the Negroes had to stay on their campus.'" He warned students that if they set foot on Capitol grounds "'they'd be sorry.' " In a clear act of defiance, nearly four thousand students assembled on the Atlanta University quadrangle and prepared to march. At that point, Mays summoned King for an emergency meeting. He warned the COAHR chair that state troopers with nightsticks and dogs were waiting for the contingent and that violence was a distinct possibility. "I listened very respectfully to him. And when he finished, I said, 'Dr. Mays, let me take you back to a speech you made in Chapel some years ago,' " King recalled. " 'The title of your speech was "Never Sacrifice a Principle for Peace." And what you're asking us to do is to sacrifice the principle of segregation that we're trying to fight for so that we can have peace. There will be no peace as long as there is segregation.' " The Morehouse president simply responded by saying, "See you at Wheat Street."[29]

A four-block-long column of students marching two abreast, some carrying textbooks and others Bibles, worked its way from the Atlanta University Center to within yards of the state Capitol grounds. At that point, police chief Herbert Jenkins ordered King to avoid the steps of the Capitol building for fear of violence from White spectators or state police. "I really think you're going to get hurt down there. Do you want that on your conscience?" King recalled Jenkins asking him. "We would have to stray from what we had been preaching to disobey a direct order from the chief of police." The twenty-three year-old Navy veteran diverted the better part of the student contingent onto Peachtree Street and on its way to Wheat Street Baptist Church. Eighty armed state troopers dispersed without incident a group of three hundred students trailing the main body of marchers that proceeded to the Capitol anyway. In spite of the diversion, the march had been a powerful success. *Look* magazine captured the event, and many took notice, including a Greensboro high school student named Larry Fox. The photographs from Atlanta cemented his decision to attend Morehouse.[30]

Once inside the church, the orderly group became more animated, perhaps out of a sense of relief. Students began chanting "fight, fight, fight, because we're right, all around the South." Martin Luther King Jr. addressed the crowd of over three thousand marchers: "I assure you, you have been an inspiration to all people of good will, not only of this nation, but all over the world." King produced a roar from the crowd when he asserted that "old man segregation is on his deathbed. The only thing we are uncertain of is when he will be buried." William Holmes Borders, the distinguished pastor of Wheat Street, refused to be outdone by the young King. The dean of the city's Black preachers roused the students when he told them that "nobody from the top of heaven to the top of hell can stop the march to freedom. Everybody in the world today might as well make up their minds to march with freedom, or freedom is going to march over them."[31]

Borders's powerful address illustrated that the relationship between many of the older, established soldiers and their younger counterparts was often a complicated one. While many in the old guard preferred legal challenges and negotiations over direct action, they shared many of the college students' goals and could not help but be inspired by their activism. In an effort to bridge the generation gap somewhat, older activists organized a fundraising rally at Wheat Street on the night of 23 March to bolster the defense fund for the eighty-three protesters facing charges in Fulton County. Students had already raised nearly three thousand dollars, and the successful rally netted over two thousand more.[32]

Although several speakers at the fundraising rally stressed that no leadership battles existed among Black activists, tensions were nonetheless evident. Most students spoke in an uncompromising tone. Lonnie King told the Wheat Street audience that COAHR members "want freedom now . . . today." Spelman student Ann Borders stated emphatically that "what is going on will go on until what is ours is ours." Atlanta University student John Mack drew quite a response when he warned that "a certain Negro newspaper is trying to hamper our cause. But we're here to say no single newspaper is going to stop us." The thinly veiled attack on the Daily World had been lost on no one present. Local NAACP leader Samuel Williams weighed in on behalf of the students, suggesting that those who did not support demonstrations were either "victims of brain-washing or profiting from a system." Martin Luther King Sr. offered strong words in support of the students also but was careful not to offend anyone else in the process. He stressed that students "need our support in these trials coming up. We ought to fill up the courthouse."[33]

Established activists continued their effort to build a united front when they drafted and paid for "An Endorsement In Support of Human Dignity," a full-page advertisement in local newspapers supporting the May protests. The solidarity statement applauded the students "for their courage and for the pattern of orderly, peaceful and non-violent behavior that has characterized all of their activities." The Endorsement was significant in that it offered unqualified support for the Appeal for Human Rights, the lunch-counter protests, and the picketing of the A&P stores. Furthermore, the title of the advertisement reaffirmed the students' effort to use language that espoused fundamental human rights. Borders signed the statement on behalf of practically every Black political and ministerial organization in the city. Less than a week after the appearance of the statement, established leaders and student activists formed the Student-Adult Liaison Committee (SALC). Benjamin Brown would later say that the formation of SALC "gave the old guard an opportunity to get back into the game."[34]

■ ■ ■

Those members of the Committee who remained in Atlanta for the summer organized a summer publicity effort, "The Student Movement and You," to continue the process of gaining support for direct action among Blacks. Student leaders spoke at churches and civic clubs, and persuaded two radio stations to cover their activities. The summer campaign of sit-ins began on 23 June, when protesters sought service at three small segregated restaurants inside Rich's, arguably the region's premier department store. When the COAHR contingent, which included Spelman professor Howard Zinn and a few other White supporters, entered one such eatery, White employees reminded them that Blacks could eat at the Hunter Room downstairs. When Black students proceeded to sit down, Rich's employees turned the lights out. Lonnie King told the press that established organizations supported the renewed effort, contending that the NAACP backed the students "in spirit if not bodily." Richard H. Rich, president of the popular store, stated that his company was merely "following custom."[35]

The protests drew immediate editorial fire, and from all directions. The *Atlanta Journal* argued that students "made their point earlier. The hope was that common sense would keep them from belaboring it." The *Journal* issued a subtle warning when it stated that Atlanta's "ample reservoir of good will" might evaporate if protests continued. The *Atlanta Daily World*, the influential conservative Black newspaper, expounded upon the sentiments registered in the mainstream press in a lengthy editorial. It contended that battles against segregated accommodations should take place in the courtroom, and that "when it comes to questions of employment and services by private establishments, we believe our group's best interest will be served through negotiation and the cultivation of mutual goodwill and understanding." The editorial also expressed concern that events in Atlanta might duplicate those in Savannah, where months of similar protests had led to passage of ordinances banning practically all protest activity. "We are in sympathy with the aspirations of the students," the newspaper maintained, "but we feel that their methods are unnecessarily dramatic and pressure-like."[36]

The gradualist editorial position proved costly. Students had long been "deeply incensed" by the editorials, and now even older Blacks were prepared to publicly take action. The all-Black Empire Real Estate Board briefly withdrew its advertisements from the newspaper. Board president Joseph T. Bickers explained to Daily World editor-in-chief C. A. Scott that "any organization or individual who fails to take advantage of opportunities to promote the cause sponsored by these young people is detrimental to the best interests of our people." Under the direction of Atlanta University professor M. Carl Holman and with critical involvement from students including Julian Bond, activists transformed the earlier COAHR informational pamphlet into the Atlanta Inquirer, a weekly newspaper that began publication in July 1960. The Inquirer, a necessary antidote to the Daily World, had the financial backing of the realtors.[37]

The rift between the Daily World and the Empire Real Estate Board revealed that opinion among prominent Blacks was far from unanimous. Warren Cochrane, longtime head of the Butler Street YMCA and secretary of the Atlanta Negro Voters League (ANVL), agreed with the Daily World's editorial line. Although the League had supported the "Endorsement In Support of Human Dignity" scarcely one week earlier, Cochrane considered the decision to move on Rich's to be a grave mistake. Middle-class Blacks shopped at Rich's because its policies were more liberal—Blacks could actually try on clothes there—than other establishments'. To make matters worse, Richard Rich was Jewish and was considered one of the few allies in the White business elite. With this in mind, Cochrane argued that "the race must keep all of the friends it has in the dominant white world and work unceasingly to multiply them."[38]

Students refused to be edged out of the debate. In a letter to the editor of the Atlanta Constitution on 12 July, Bond noted that much had been made of not isolating Blacks from their "proven friends" in the city. "For all the good these 'friends' have done, perhaps it would be better if they were alienated," he wrote. Bond continued by asserting that outside groups as diverse as the NAACP and the Communist Party had no control over the sit-in movement. "It is now, it always has been and will be a student movement. . . ." In that spirit, individual as well as group acts of self-determination continued. Their numbers dwindled during the summer, and individual activists often found themselves taking part in one-person protests. Ruby Doris Smith, of Spelman, launched a one-woman picket outside an A&P grocery store in a Black neighborhood in addition to taking part in kneel-ins at segregated churches.[39]

Lonnie King had one of the most frightening experiences of his life when he conducted a one-person picket at a grocery store in the segregated West End neighborhood. Several Whites approached King and someone threw an acidic substance on him. As the acid ate away at his shirt and blurred his vision King struggled to make his way down the street. Fellow Morehouse student Ronald Yancy came to his aid and escorted him to a service station. The White owner refused to help the men, however, and they slowly made their way to a second service station a block or so away. Yancy finally persuaded a reluctant worker to allow him to run water from a hose over King's head and body. Later that day, however, another crowd of angry Whites, which numbered several hundred people, approached King at the store. "They surrounded me, and I thought they were going to lynch me, to be honest with you," he later recalled. "I did not move. I just looked them in the eye and I talked about how segregation was wrong. And they were calling me all kinds of names. It was really, really ugly." Fortunately for King, insurance executive Jesse Hill happened to drive by the crowd. He called police, who dispersed the group and took the student leader to the colored section of Grady Memorial Hospital.[40]

The efforts by King and other students were felt across the intraracial class spectrum. King later found out that when word of his hospitalization reached a group of Black men at an area pool hall, they went out in force, prepared to settle the score. "At that point you realized that you were beginning to reach a class of Blacks that you normally don't reach," King noted. The stark contrast between the Atlanta University Center and adjacent neighborhoods produced an estrangement that seemed to grow with each year. Black residents who lived in public housing units directly across the street from the campuses had grown accustomed to the class condescension of some students. However, the student movement rekindled a sense of solidarity. Furthermore, King's refusal to back down from the mob stirred a particular fire within Black men whose sense of manhood had been challenged daily by their inability to find meaningful employment. When students asked for people to send in their Rich's charge cards, the response was tremendous. It appeared as if the tide had turned in Atlanta, as it had in Greensboro and Nashville and scores of other cities.[41]

Atlanta students' commitment to struggle in the face of violence was part and parcel of a larger national discourse that summer concerning the relevance of the student movement and its relationship to the centuries-old Black freedom struggle. In an essay in *Ebony* magazine, scholar-editor Lerone Bennett Jr. argued, in accordance with other Black intellectuals, that the sit-in movement brought "a call to conscience" and a critical change in the way Blacks approached activism. Roy Wilkins and the NAACP underwent a "sweeping change" in policy that resulted in a nationwide drive focusing on boycotts, marches, and sit-ins. Commentator and Georgia native Louis E. Lomax went further, however, with his contention in *Harper's* that college students had "completely reversed the power flow within the Negro community" by forcing the hand of traditional groups and leveling "a telling blow against the centralization of Negro leadership." College students had done this in part because they were better able to capture the attention of the larger African American community as "missionaries" for what he termed the "theology of desegregation." Lomax did not hold his punches, especially in his critique of the NAACP. He implied that the group was a puppet organization that "immobilized" many grassroots activists with its legal strategy.[42]

■ ■ ■

Aware of the potential political power that accompanied direct action protests, COAHR co-chairs King and Sullivan hoped that well-coordinated fall demonstrations might affect the 1960 presidential election race between Richard M. Nixon and John F. Kennedy. SNCC activists embarked on a similar course at the group's mid-October national meeting in Atlanta. SNCC chair Marion Barry Jr. announced plans for a region-wide demonstration on Election Day to pressure Congress to move forward with civil rights legislation. Another theme reiterated at the SNCC meeting was tactical arrest and confinement. James Lawson, a young minister who had been fired from a teaching position at Vanderbilt University because of his involvement in the Nashville movement, urged students to forgo bail when arrested, arguing that "suffering has a role in the nonviolent movement."[43]

Just days after the SNCC meeting, Atlanta students launched what *Atlanta Inquirer* editor M. Carl Holman termed the Fall Campaign. On 19 October 1960, students targeted sixteen venues in protests that one local reporter claimed were "as coordinated as a military maneuver on a drill field." The first group of students arrested at Rich's walked proudly past a line of fifteen Black women, four Black men, and one White man carrying placards in support of the cause. Some placards read, "1-2-3-4-Don't Shop At This Store," others

"Don't Spend Cash Where You Can't Drink Coffee." Among those arrested was Martin Luther King Jr., who had been contacted by Sullivan to help draw attention to the protests. "We decided to ask M. L. to come to jail with us, and he very willingly accepted." Those not arrested at the lunch counters began reading or talking quietly as Rich's employees suspended service for the remainder of the day. After taking it all in, a White customer responded, "I know what to do with uppity niggers."[44]

If being "uppity" meant being well organized, then members of COAHR were quite uppity indeed. Morris Brown student Fred C. Bennette, an older student who organized picketers "like a drill sergeant," served as chief executive officer for the fall campaign. The deputy chief of operations was Robert "Tex" Felder, of the Interdenominational Theological Seminary (ITC). Fellow ITC student Otis Moss was field commander of the group, and public relations for the campaign came from Clark College students Morris J. Dillard and James Felder. Clark's Benjamin Brown and Daniel Mitchell served as treasurer and senior intelligence officer, respectively. A group of female student captains headed by Lenora Tait typed and dated reports of activities in the field and placed them on bulletin boards. Communication between protesters and the captains at Rush Memorial Congregational Church, COAHR headquarters, was facilitated by the use of two-way radios. One such report from Captain Tait to le Commandante Bennette announced "lunch counters at Rich's closed. Proceeded to alternative objective. Counters at Woolworth's closed. Back to Rich's for picket duty. Ku Klux Klan circling Rich's in nightgowns and dunce caps. 'Looking good!' "[45]

The Wednesday protest was the largest sit-in demonstration yet, and police reports confirmed it. Police arrested fifty-two people for violating Georgia's anti-trespass law, but attorney Donald L. Hollowell persuaded a local judge to drop charges against sixteen of them because they had been asked to leave a dining room, not Rich's itself. Martin Luther King Jr. contended during his arraignment that segregation was a "festering sore" and the "most vital issue facing America today." He continued by stating that one advantage "of living in a democracy is that citizens have the right to protest for what they believe is right." King's participation in the protest spoke to his commitment to nonviolent direct action and redemptive suffering. "I have tried to emphasize the importance of jail-going. In order to serve as a redemptive agency for the nation and to arouse the conscience of the opponent, you go to jail and you stay."[46]

Morehouse College student and Committee on Appeal for Human Rights co-chair Lonnie King,
Spelman College student Marilyn Pryce, and Martin Luther King Jr. in front of Rich's department
store during the first phase of the sit-in campaign that challenged petty apartheid in Atlanta.
Authorities arrested Martin Luther King and fifty-one students.
Photo courtesy of Herman Mason Jr.

Lonnie King in 2004. Photo courtesy of Lonnie King.

Wave after wave of impeccably dressed students had occupied luncheon-ettes throughout the city. It came as no surprise when Whites who saw a group of Black women headed directly for the state Capitol expected the worse and alerted state troopers. The women were there for a nurses examination, not to test the law. The same did not hold true for the nineteen women and sixteen men arrested that day. Like Martin Luther King Jr., they willingly faced the possibility of spending the next six weeks behind bars if they refused bond. Bobby Schley, a Morris Brown student and Army veteran, said, "I fought three years for freedom. I'll take [counter] service or jail."[47]

But the reality of incarceration proved unsettling for college students. Sullivan and other women "sang a lot" of freedom songs to help ease their anxiety. Benjamin Brown, who had been separated from the other male protesters, remembered that "I was absolutely frightened to death." As other inmates began yelling "college boy," the first-time prisoner worried that "they were going to do something to me that night." Yet, in one of those bittersweet moments when statistics and life collide, something unexpected happened. "Finally, one guy spoke up. 'Ben, you don't remember me, do you?' " One of the boys he had grown up with in College Park had recognized Brown. "He told those guys, 'Man, you better not mess with this boy, 'cause he's working on something that's right.' " A similar situation awaited the female students when they realized they were sharing a cell with the mother of a classmate who had shot the student's father, most likely in self-defense. Sullivan was struck by the woman's concern for her appearance, noting that she applied cosmetics meticulously each morning despite being incarcerated. That simple affirmation of dignity so affected Sullivan, she said, that she has done it every day of her life ever since.[48]

Thursday, the protests continued as students either sat-in or picketed at more than sixteen restaurants downtown. Police arrested twenty-five Blacks at the Terminal Station on loafing and disturbance charges, including A. D. Williams King, Martin's older brother. Unlike the previous day, almost all the restaurant owners and managers simply decided to close lunch counters outright when protesters arrived. Picketing continued on Friday, but actual sit-ins declined, with just two students arrested for trespassing at Lane's Drug Store. Municipal Court Judge James Webb admonished the two and warned that future defiance of the segregation laws would "be dealt with as irresponsible mob action." Nevertheless, arrested Committee member Harold Andrews maintained before the judge that "I was doing something I believed in."

Undaunted by the power of the bench, the twenty-two-year-old continued, "I think this is more educational than college. If I went to college for four years, I still couldn't go in there and get a glass of water."[49]

The defiant attitude of student activists such as Andrews and the rise of Klan counter-picketing led Mayor William Hartsfield to call for a temporary end to the protests on Saturday. After a meeting in City Hall which lasted nearly three hours, sixty Black leaders agreed to a monthlong truce so that the mayor could attempt to have White business leaders approve some type of agreement. In return, Hartsfield ordered the release of twenty-two Blacks and one White student arrested in protests on city-owned land, leaving thirty-nine people jailed on county charges. William Holmes Borders termed the meeting "one of the greatest things that has ever happened in Atlanta, which will help the city and everyone in it."[50]

During the truce that followed, Rich's management met with moderate established Black leaders on two occasions at the behest of the mayor. At the second meeting, those in attendance agreed to hold a third meeting with a COAHR leader and an older, established leader allied with the students to begin actual negotiations. But when Lonnie King and Jesse Hill realized they were the only two sit-in supporters invited, they refused to attend. An agreement had not materialized by Thanksgiving Day. As a result, a young White architect named Cecil Alexander arranged a midnight meeting between the mayor, leading Black businessmen, student leaders, Martin Luther King Jr., and Richard Rich in a twelfth-hour effort to avoid further demonstrations. The end result was a continued stalemate, however, and probably meant the thirty-two-day truce would come to a close.[51]

With no agreement in sight, and steadfast in the belief that downtown merchants left them no alternative, COAHR activists embarked on the second major assault of the fall campaign. Students had not anticipated a suitable agreement, and they were well aware that organizing massive sit-in demonstrations on the Friday following Thanksgiving—traditionally the busiest shopping day of the year—could prove vexing for owners of segregated businesses. Students flooded Rich's, Woolworth's, and McCrory's with professionally made placards reading "Wear Old Clothes and New Dignity: Don't Buy Here" and "The Presence of Segregation Is the Absence of Democracy: Jim Crow Must Go." Several White students from Emory University and Agnes Scott College joined the demonstration, as did older Blacks including Martin Luther King Sr. and his son A. D. Williams King. Established Blacks such as Daddy King may have been frustrated by an apparent lack of good faith on the part of White merchants. Whatever the reason, these leaders maintained their public support of COAHR. "Right now the community wouldn't go to heaven without the students," Borders stated unequivocally.[52]

The sit-ins and picketing continued unabated through December, provoking a mixed response from local Whites. On certain occasions Black students crossed paths with Klansmen, though without incident. Because state law prohibited members of the Klan from engaging in public demonstrations with their faces covered, police estimated that the bulk of the counterprotesters were from outside Atlanta. During the course of the fall campaign Atlanta's segregated White YWCA served a handful of Black students, with the leaders of the service organization finding cause to "rejoice in this instance" because they were "able to base our practice on our principles."[53] White YMCA officials were not willing to integrate their dining facilities, however, and neither were the vast majority of White business leaders. The protests sparked a groundswell of support within Atlanta's Black neighborhoods. As the year came to an end, a "puzzled brown teen" wrote a letter to the editor of the Atlanta Journal that spoke to the growing resolve of sit-in activists to demand equality from a society unwilling to come to terms with the hypocrisy inherent in segregation. "Aren't we, as Negroes, human beings, citizens of the United States, and children of God?" the anonymous writer asked. "Doesn't the Declaration of Independence clearly state that 'all men are created equal'? Without any doubt, the answers to these questions are yes."[54]

The new year began on a sobering note. In the town of Athens, site of the University of Georgia, a mob of White students encircled the dormitory of Charlayne Hunter on the night of 11 January. She and Hamilton Holmes were the first Black students to enroll at the state university. Campus police used tear gas to dissolve the crowd after a number of students continued to throw bricks at Hunter's window. School officials temporarily suspended the Black students, who had been on the campus for all of three days.

While Hunter and Holmes struggled to desegregate the University of Georgia, students at Atlanta's historically Black colleges and universities struggled to bring business to a close at lunch counters throughout the city. On the very day that White students terrorized Hunter, Atlanta authorities bound over for trial four students led by Spelman College's Ruby Doris Smith for a 12 December protest at the Terminal Station. The arrests were the first since October. The month ended with smaller groups of students limiting sit-ins to Fridays and Saturdays in order to study for final examinations.[55]

Once the examination period ended, COAHR students returned to their protest activity on Tuesday, 7 February, prompting merchants to press for arrests on trespassing charges. Police arrested and jailed thirteen students at a sit-in at Sprayberry's Cafeteria. COAHR co-chairs King and Sullivan posted bail, but the others refused bond. The next day an additional twenty students entered jail following further protests. "It's a personal conviction on the part of every student there to remain in jail so that citizens of Atlanta and all over the world will know that injustice is prevalent in the South," COAHR treasurer Benjamin Brown explained. Brown contended that refusal to post bond also galvanized "the Negro race in the area of economic withdrawal and for support for the entire student movement program."[56]

Thursday, the third consecutive day of protests following examinations, police arrested thirty-nine students for demonstrations at several establishments downtown. With another six arrests Friday, the total number of incarcerated Committee activists had ballooned to eighty-two. The young inmates spent most of their time at the new Fulton County Jail studying, writing letters, or speaking with fellow inmates about the sit-in movement. "I might miss a semester, or even a year, but it's worth it," noted eighteen-year-old Morris Brown student Leon Greene. "It is worth anything to do this." While most students jailed shared Green's sentiments—only three opted for bail— they still felt a great deal of pressure to maintain certain academic standards. Administrators and faculty understood this much. Morehouse president Benjamin Mays instructed professors to "make allowances" for COAHR members. Nevertheless, a number of students, including Morehouse's Julian Bond, considered it necessary to leave school temporarily in order to devote all their energy to the desegregation effort.[57]

The sacrifices of the student foot soldiers were not lost on older activists, many of whom felt inspired to engage in direct action tactics. Police arrested eight clergyman, seven Black and one White, who participated in a 15 February sit-in at the Terminal Station cafeteria to express their solidarity with COAHR. Although Otis Moss Jr., the spokesman for the group, was twenty-five, the average age of those arrested was thirty-six. The solidarity protest not only provided a significant unifying charge to the larger African American community in Atlanta, but it strengthened the precarious intraracial coalition of established Black leaders, young professionals, and college students.[58]

At a mass meeting held on the day of the solidarity protest, local NAACP leader Samuel Williams proclaimed that older Blacks were "going to stay with, and even *die* with the students if necessary!" For their part, COAHR leaders requested that veteran activist A. T. Walden act as an intermediary in extracting an agreement from White merchants. Walden asked that he be provided thirty days to complete the task. Perhaps students had read Carl Holman's editorial in the *Atlanta Inquirer*. Holman, himself an ACCA activist and university professor, astutely noted that students would do well "to consider how much harsher then was the opposition to the NAACP than today's daring young sit-in pioneers are faced with."[59]

As Walden worked behind the scenes, COAHR leaders planned a march from the Atlanta University campus to the Fulton County Jail, where a solidarity rally would take place. When authorities alerted the Student-Adult Liaison Committee that White counter-demonstrators might incite violence, Black activists agreed to hold the 19 February rally at Wheat Street Baptist Church instead. Sullivan, co-chair of both COAHR and the newly formed SALC, told the largely non-student audience that the eighty-plus jailed students intended to remain incarcerated for as long as it took to desegregate the city's lunch counters. Borders offered brief remarks concerning the state anti-trespassing law, contending that the statute was "unconstitutional, undemocratic, and un-Christian."[60]

Benjamin Joseph Johnson, who at forty-nine was the oldest minister arrested the week before, warned against moving too slowly. "The time is right when people get right. I do not share the views of those who say 'wait.' I am not a student of gradualism. The time is now." The Baptist preacher continued by placing the Atlanta protests within a broader context. "The New Negro will not rest until all the indignities of the American scene are eradicated." After the upbeat rally had officially ended and a collection on behalf of the students had been taken, Martin Luther King Sr. minced no words. After admonishing those present to maintain their boycott of segregated stores, he warned local politicians who "get elected and reelected" in part because of the African American bloc vote that "from here on in, they've got to come by" the Black community and best "be careful how meanly they treat us."[61]

By early 1961 most Blacks in the city, especially younger professionals, had come to embrace the sit-in campaign wholeheartedly. The day of the Wheat Street rally, police arrested eight Black doctors attending a meeting of the Atlanta Graduate Medical Assembly at the posh Biltmore Hotel when they refused to leave one of its restaurants after being denied service. Unlike the clergyman arrested the previous week, the doctors posted bond and spent no time in jail.

Meanwhile, the prospect of meaningful negotiations had heartened the scores of students who did remain in jail. Confident that Walden might procure an agreement, the COAHR leadership made a tactical reversal and announced on 23 February that the fifty-two students in the Fulton County Jail would post bond. Walden contended that students had succeeded in expressing their opposition to segregation and in rallying older Blacks to support them. He asserted further that the students "shall henceforth walk arm [in] arm with their elders in a supplemental strategy which has been developed by the composite . . . judgment of youth and age."[62]

■ ■ ■

Walden spoke with such confidence primarily because his "supplemental strategy" actually sought to undercut the influence of student activists, not respect it. Historian William Chafe noted in his study of the Greensboro movement that even the most successful sit-in activity "revealed its limitations as an ongoing strategy. Once the demonstrations ended, control over negotiations reverted to those who exercised power in the first place. They set the rules. They determined the framework for discussion." Jesse Hill called Lonnie King on 7 March to inform him and Herschelle Sullivan of " 'the most important meeting of your lives,' " a confab downtown with White business leaders and established Black moderates later that day. The Committee co-chairs headed downtown without notifying their adviser, Holman.[63]

When the two students entered the meeting it became apparent something was in the works. They saw Walden, of course, as well as elders Martin Luther King Sr. and John Calhoun. Also present were Ivan Allen, head of the Atlanta Chamber of Commerce, and several other prominent White businessmen. "The old-line Blacks had cut a deal on our behalf with the White power structure," Lonnie King remembered. Those present simply wanted the students to sign off on an agreement that luncheon facilities throughout the city would remain segregated for now but would be opened to everyone within "a reasonable time" of the desegregation of Atlanta's public schools in the fall, and no later than 15 October. Furthermore, merchants were to rehire, "where practicable," the six hundred Black employees who had been laid off by White merchants during the protests.[64]

Thunderstruck, the student leaders engaged their elders in a passionate debate as the White businessmen observed. Calhoun made a plea to the students to accept the terms of the agreement, observing that as a personal witness to Jim Crow for seventy years, an extra "few days" would not matter much. Lonnie King responded by noting that desegregation of lunch counters and schools were separate issues, with the former affecting the entire Black population and the latter a specific segment. Besides, King and Sullivan stressed, they could not sign any agreement without first speaking to the steering committee of COAHR. It was at this point that Daddy King, who had baptized Lonnie King as a boy, shouted angrily " 'Boy, I'm tired of you! I'm tired of you!' " Lonnie King recalled. "And then he proceeded to excoriate me in front of all those people." Feeling beaten down, a reluctant Lonnie King and an even more reticent Sullivan committed themselves verbally to the agreement but stressed that they would need to explain the situation to the rest of the COAHR leadership. After they entered a car to return to campus, King turned on the car radio only to be jolted again. "Ivan Allen called the radio station and said, 'The Negroes have agreed to allow the lunch counters to be reopened tomorrow—segregated.' "[65]

News of the dubious agreement sparked a firestorm of dissension within the Black community. In a January column in the *Atlanta Inquirer*, Julian Bond had already condemned the notion of delaying the school desegregation process, noting that it was "like waiting for this year to roll around again. The accommodationists and the settle-for-lessers are willing to do just that." Following word of the accord, *Inquirer* editor and COAHR faculty adviser Holman termed the settlement "treason and heresy." Feeling pressure from all sides, King and Sullivan submitted their resignations but were quickly reelected at a heated COAHR meeting Wednesday after activists realized "how much of a double-cross had gone on." Sullivan and other students had always admired the way Lonnie King "reveled in this moment," and that made recent events more difficult. "I was only 22 years old. I felt as if the weight of this whole thing was on me," King recalled. "I would never have believed that Daddy King and company would have sold me out like that."[66]

SALC held an emergency public meeting on Thursday, 10 March at Warren Memorial Methodist Church to address community outrage. If it had not been clear to them before, it was obvious now that the students "were fighting two different battles," one against the city's apartheid apparatus and the other against shrewd elders who intended to retain their limited influence. A crowd of more than two thousand people filled the church, with several hundred more listening intently to loudspeakers placed outside. A contingent from the Nation of Islam (NOI) handed out leaflets that lambasted SALC for "selling out to the Chamber of Commerce."[67]

One by one, all fifteen members of SALC found a seat on the platform, facing the crowd. The meeting opened on an upbeat note, with the singing of freedom songs and the introduction of the "jail birds." Atlanta NAACP leader Samuel Williams explained that the agreement was not as vague as newspaper accounts had reported it to be. Walden then offered brief remarks and received polite applause. Then COAHR treasurer Brown addressed the audience, roughly a third of whom were fellow students. "We have great confidence in our leaders, Lonnie and Herschelle, and the persons who signed the agreement," Brown insisted. "We don't feel they have sold us down the river," he continued, receiving applause from the crowd. "However, I must make this clear: it is the thinking of the majority of the students that we must continue to stay out from downtown." This last sentence provoked a thunderous response and prefigured the tone of the meeting.[68]

The meeting proceeded for the most part without incident. That would change, however, with the onset of the question-and-answer period. When audience members asked those on the platform to explain in detail the various aspects of the agreement, elegance and decorum began to evaporate in the heat of the packed sanctuary. "Compromise is a part of life, none of us get all that we want from life . . . but you can't have real social progress without it," Walden responded to community members and students. "What difference does a few months make in social progress? We've been fighting for this thing for one hundred years; now we have it within our grasp. Let's have the good sense not to throw it away."[69]

The heckles that peppered Walden's talk grew as he finished. Members of the audience also heckled the chair of the meeting when he tried to prevent pastor J. A. Wilburn, of Union Baptist Church, from approaching the microphone, shouting "We want Wilburn. We want Wilburn." The chair finally relented. "I simply want to ask you if you thought those students were playing when they went to jail," Wilburn jabbed, eliciting cheers. "We don't have to please the downtown merchants; when we go downtown we aren't begging, we're buying! No self-respecting Negro can go back downtown under these conditions." Soon calls for outright repudiation of the leadership flooded the church. Brown attempted to regain control of the meeting and reach some semblance of unanimity. "This is a crucial time, this is no time to change leadership!" he yelled in an effort to be heard over the clamor of an agitated audience.[70]

By this time chaos prevailed as respected giants such as Martin Luther King Sr. and William Holmes Borders found themselves powerless to defend themselves in the face of a constituency that felt profoundly betrayed. As Daddy King spoke briefly about his thirty-year effort on behalf of Blacks in Atlanta, a woman rose from her seat in the balcony and shouted, " 'And that's been the problem!' " Bedlam reigned in the sanctuary as a humiliated Martin Luther King Sr. took his seat. Clearly, Martin Luther King Jr. had been humiliated as well. "I could see tears well up in his eyes as they derided his dad," Lonnie King remembered. Borders asked Lonnie King to speak, but Holman interceded. " 'No, hell you don't. You snook him into this mess. You created it. You solve it.' " It was at this point that the younger Martin Luther King said, "Let me speak."[71]

A hush fell over the church as he approached the rostrum from the rear. Scholars may debate the influence that the SCLC president had on the trajectory of the Black freedom movement in his native Atlanta. Yet, on that second Thursday in March, the young minister accomplished more in twenty minutes than he had done in over a year since returning from Montgomery. In a solemn speech tantamount to an impromptu sermon, King criticized the attacks on the combined leadership and argued instead for trust and unity. "We must move out now on the road of calm reasonableness. We must come to a mood of mutual trust and mutual confidence," he contended. "No greater danger exists for the Negro community than to be afflicted with the cancerous disease of disunity. Disagreements and differences there will be, but unity there must be!" King also took special care to address class issues within the community, noting that privileged Blacks "must see in this struggle that Aunt Jane, who knows not the difference between 'you duz' and 'you don't,' is just as significant as the Ph.D. in English."[72]

King ventured from the secular as he continued to mend the torn fabric of the meeting by using his authority and eloquence as a preacher. "Caleb and Joshua have been over," he offered by way of Biblical allusion. "They have come back with a minority report saying that we can possess the land in spite of the giants." The charismatic leader was at his best, however, when he resorted to self-deprecation in an attempt to defend SALC from additional criticism. "If I had been on that committee that met Monday afternoon, I wouldn't mind anybody saying, Martin Luther King, Jr., you made a mistake. I wouldn't mind anybody saying Martin Luther King, you should have thought it over a little longer." At one now with an audience that had become his congregation, King continued to make a hypothetical example of himself. "I wouldn't have minded anybody saying to me, Martin Luther King, maybe we made a tactical blunder. But I would have been terribly hurt if anybody said to me, Martin Luther King, Jr., you sold us out!"[73]

The speech touched the two co-chairs of the Committee. Although she did not have much respect for his father, Sullivan had been inspired by the oratorical power of Martin Luther King Jr. "One couldn't help but admire the way he could control a crowd," she remarked. "I have not heard anyone who had that kind of cadence and could build up to a crescendo they way he did." Lonnie King offered praise as well. "Martin made the greatest speech I have ever heard him make, including the speech at the March on Washington," he asserted without hesitation. "He carried the crowd from Aristotle down to the current [moment], all with tears in his eyes over the fact that his dad had been humiliated." The two thousand "surly" folks who came to the church may not have been satisfied with the agreement, Lonnie King said, but they had been "quelled by his oratory."[74]

The ovation that followed was as much to celebrate the survival of the movement as it was to honor the galvanizing force of Martin Luther King Jr. It was apparent to everyone at Warren Memorial that a catastrophe had been avoided. Nevertheless, deep divisions concerning strategy and tactics finally had come to the fore. An older leader remarked that students "will never get anything done on their own" because they operated "in a righteous vacuum over there." A number of students contended that the older men who engineered the agreement had behaved like "handkerchief heads" and "Uncle Toms." As political scientist Jack L. Walker has noted, however, the established leadership was not monolithic.[75] While students may have been the most visible proponents of direct action and immediate desegregation, individuals such as Wilburn, though having more in common with established leaders in terms of age, profession, and status, argued for continued demonstrations as well.

The pivotal Thursday-night meeting also revealed the extent to which SALC

—dominated from the start by non-students—had underestimated the sentiment in the larger community in favor of immediate lunch-counter desegregation. Butler Street YMCA head Warren Cochrane was one of several established leaders who expressed surprise at how poor, working-class Blacks who
lost their jobs because of the sit-ins continued to support the Committee.
Martin Luther King Jr., who had seen first-hand the power of a working-class
movement in Montgomery, noticed a change in the mood of the larger African
American community in Atlanta. "Something wonderful is happening in this
town. The low-down Negroes are getting tired. I mean the kind of folks who
just come and go like the rain," he said. "White folks never paid them any
mind, but they're tired. They just aren't going to take it like they always
have before."[76]

King's presence at the emergency meeting broadened his influence in
Atlanta. The SCLC leader helped organize a revived All-Citizens Registration
Committee (ACRC) there in the summer. The group, led by SCLC information
director Joe Wood, included three paid staff members and sixty volunteers and
would work with established groups such as the Atlanta Negro Voters League.
The establishment of the voter registration group won King points with older
activists who privileged voting over protests. Yet he continued to speak out
nationally in favor of the nonviolent direct action protests sweeping the region. In a September essay in the *New York Times Magazine*, King wrote that
the sit-in movement was no revolt against a "timid, fumbling, conservative
leadership" but rather, the fulfillment of a "revolutionary destiny of a whole
people." In noting their "extraordinary willingness to fill the jails as if they
were honors classes," King correctly asserted that Black college students
had initiated new forms of protest, among them the sit-ins and the freedom rides.[77]

That very month, Atlanta's Black college students found themselves in the
unfamiliar position of being customers, not protesters. A few weeks after
token desegregation of city high schools, and in accordance with the controversial March agreement, seventy-five stores agreed that on 28 September 1961
they would open their counters to Blacks. "Four well-dressed young Negro
women" desegregated the Magnolia Room at Rich's, where they received
service without incident. Thus, the Southern Regional Council noted, Atlanta
had become the 104th city to integrate its lunch counters since February 1960.
Even Savannah to the south, a city that witnessed some of the more violent
protests in the state, had desegregated its counters in July.[78]

In eighteen months, the men and women of Atlanta's historically Black colleges had successfully led the challenge against petty apartheid in the city by relying on the moral force and economic weight of nonviolent direct action. Although their outlook was decidedly middle class, they had earned the respect of working-class Blacks through their dedication. And these students had earned both respect and enmity from older activists who saw their own influence challenged at the grassroots. The tumult, debate, and ultimate success of desegregating lunch counters strengthened the resolve of student activists—for they realized that larger prizes had yet to be claimed.

CHAPTER TWO

PHASE TWO OF THE DIRECT ACTION
CAMPAIGN AND THE FALL OF
PETTY APARTHEID IN ATLANTA

With the desegregation of lunch counters a reality in Atlanta, proponents of nonviolent direct action continued to challenge the city's apartheid political economy. As a result, intraracial fault lines that separated activist students and young professionals from older businessmen and clergy began to deepen, in part because of the alliance between the local COAHR and the national office of SNCC. The two groups, drawing upon the organizing skills of individuals such as Ruby Doris Robinson and Larry Fox, who floated between them, launched a second phase of protests that increasingly challenged middle-class notions of civility. Direct confrontations with members of the Ku Klux Klan became the order of the day. Other locales—like Albany to the south and Birmingham to the west—had become frontline public sites of the Black struggle for human rights. Yet, in part because powerful people in Atlanta had invested so much energy in crafting an image of the city as "progressive," student activists concerned with exposing the city's contradictions remained steadfast.

■ ■ ■

Ivan Allen Jr. walked away with the 23 September 1961 Democratic mayoral primary, in effect the general election, by nearly doubling the number of votes garnered by avowed white supremacist Lester Maddox. Allen, the former Chamber of Commerce president, had aided his cause by attending virtually every election forum held in the Black community. He usually declined to say anything more than a polite greeting, astutely deferring to Black supporters such as the ubiquitous elder, A. T. Walden. "The reason we have had such a good climate in Atlanta is because you have had the good sense to join up with the people of another race who are right-minded," Walden remarked. Blacks in Atlanta still remembered that Walden and Allen played leading roles in orchestrating the unsatisfactory agreement to end sit-in protests earlier in the year. However, Blacks also realized that Allen represented a better bet than Maddox. The fifty-seven percent turnout for the December general election was significant for Blacks in the city, for it marked the first time in Atlanta history that Blacks outnumbered Whites at the polls.[1]

Black participation in the local electoral political process had not translated into substantive results, however, especially with regard to fundamental human rights concerns that had long troubled city residents, namely health care and hospital access. Throughout the summer and early fall, R. C. Bell, a Black dentist, went before the Fulton County Commission to complain about limited doctor's privileges and patient accessibility at Grady Memorial Hospital and its segregated annex built in 1952, the Hughes Spalding Pavilion. When the commission ignored him, Bell turned to the mayoral candidates, including Allen, again to no avail. The only tangible response Bell received from most Whites were phone threats and vandalism to his car. Black doctors had no privileges at Grady, not even as visiting physicians. Practically nothing had changed since Homer Nash, a graduate of Meharry Medical School, opened his private practice on Auburn Avenue in 1910. "If I went in Grady Hospital, I didn't go in as Dr. Nash, I went in as a visitor," he said. Nash explained that each Black physician "lost [his or her] patient at the front door. When the patient got there he belonged to somebody else."[2]

Black college students took to the streets once again, vowing to make good on an earlier commitment to health care in the city. Led by new COAHR chair Charles Black, over forty pickets including Bell walked back and forth along three sides of the Grady complex during a 10 November demonstration. Some protesters carried green placards reading "Grady Has 75 Per Cent Negro Patients, Zero Per Cent Negro Staff Physicians, Zero Per Cent Interns, Zero Per Cent Negro Board Members—Why?" and blue ones reading "Disease and Death Row Know No Race—Give the Other One-Third of Atlanta an Equal Chance to Live." Although COAHR announced it would not conduct any more protests at Grady in the near future, the picketing helped Bell's efforts to meet again with county commissioners. At that meeting, Bell and a mixed contingent of activists stressed the "deplorable conditions" at the Hughes Spalding annex, where Blacks often waited up to ten hours before receiving treatment.[3]

When, in response to pressure from activists, the hospital placed the name of one Black person on its list of possible interns, COAHR activists reacted by resuming picketing at the hospital on 6 February 1962. The group issued a statement criticizing the hospital's "meager attempt to pacify the discontented Atlanta community." A week later police arrested thirty-four demonstrators at the state Capitol and at Grady Memorial. SNCC workers joined COAHR members at both locations. James Forman, who had joined SNCC several months before as the group's first executive secretary, later remarked that the Atlanta protests addressed just one facet of a larger apartheid apparatus, for they "served only to expose one more nerve in the festering body of the racist United States. There were a thousand others to be exposed." Ruby Doris Robinson, the dedicated Spelman activist who had begun splitting time between COAHR and SNCC, made a bold personal statement during a protest to gain entry into the segregated hospital. When a White receptionist remarked that no protesters were physically ill, Smith vomited on the desk and asked, "Is that sick enough for you?"[4]

In large part because of student activism, the situation at Grady finally became a central focus of the city's established Black leadership. In early March, Bell led a contingent of prominent Blacks, including Martin Luther King Sr., Martin Luther King Jr., and Wyatt Tee Walker, of the SCLC, before the county commissioners to press for a definitive timetable for complete desegregation of the city hospital.[5] In the spring the Fulton DeKalb County Hospital Authority began to make token changes just as the SNCC-led desegregation drive in Albany began to capture an increasing amount of attention in Atlanta. The hospital offered appointments to two Black physicians, Asa G. Yancey and Gwendolyn Cooper Manning. This did not prevent NAACP attorneys from filing a federal lawsuit in June against Grady Memorial calling for the hospital to desegregate its patient rooms, training programs, and medical societies. The suit challenged the separate-but-equal provisions of the Hill-Burton Act, which had thus far authorized the payment of nearly two million dollars in federal funds to the Hospital Authority.[6]

■ ■ ■

Atlanta became the focus of the national NAACP when the civil rights organization held its fifty-third annual convention in the city's Municipal Auditorium in July 1962. A number of delegates protested pervasive hotel and restaurant segregation and picketed Johnny Reb's Canteen in a driving rain. Keynote speaker Bishop Stephen Gill Spottswood, chairman of the group's board of directors, noted that not much had changed since the organization's 1951 convention in Atlanta. Of the twenty-four largest cities in the

SNCC organizers (from left to right) Mary King, Judy Richardson, Mildred Forman, Roberta Yancey, and Spelman student Ruby Doris Smith share a photo opportunity with SNCC Executive Secretary James Forman during the second phase of the sit-in campaign that challenged petty apartheid in Atlanta. Photo courtesy of Herman Mason Jr.

United States, he said, only Memphis, New Orleans, and Atlanta maintained a " 'white' hotel policy.' " Executive director Roy Wilkins was quick to note that difficulties in finding accommodations for Ralph Bunche and other dignitaries would not thwart the success of the meeting. Responding to delegates who wanted to organize demonstrations, Wilkins remarked rather condescendingly that "a sit-in at a restaurant may be psychologically important" but was "not the main business of this convention."[7]

Delegates passed eighty-six resolutions including a call for a "Department of Urban Affairs with cabinet status for its head." The group called on President John F. Kennedy to issue an executive order banning discrimination in housing projects funded by the federal government. One of the most strongly worded resolutions condemned "all separatist philosophies . . . whether espoused by white supremacy groups such as the Ku Klux Klan, White Citizens Council, and the American Nazi party, or by Black Muslims and black nationalists which preach race supremacy of any kind."[8] The conflation of the NOI and the Klan in this last resolution may have spoken as much to the NAACP's concern over the burgeoning influence of the NOI under founder Elijah Muhammad and key lieutenant Malcolm X as it did to a condemnation of racial separatism.

The focal point of local Black activism in the autumn was not the NAACP, however, but the Southern Christian Leadership Conference. Area ministers joined forces with the SCLC to launch a drive for equal employment. John Middleton and Ralph D. Abernathy led the effort to target bakeries, bottling companies, department stores, grocery chains, newspapers, and utilities for a possible holiday boycott if these establishments refused to participate in good-faith negotiations. "We spend a lot of money in the city and make it possible for a lot of white collar jobs to exist," Middleton noted. "Since we do that, we would like to have some of those jobs coming our way." The effort was part of a larger program, Operation Breadbasket, initiated by Philadelphia Baptist minister Leon H. Sullivan. In publicizing a November planning meeting, the Atlanta SCLC office noted that it was "often necessary for Negro girls with one or more years of college training to work as maids. Negro men must take their college diplomas to the Post Office to work sorting mail."[9]

Operation Breadbasket produced results throughout early 1963. In February nearly five hundred civic organizations and social clubs joined local ministers in a "selective buying campaign" targeting Highland Bakeries after it refused to provide new jobs or promote current Black employees. But other bakeries did meet ministerial demands. Southern Bakeries either hired or promoted fifteen Black employees, adding nearly sixty-eight thousand dollars in purchasing power to Atlanta's African American community. The Bread-basket network also was effective in allowing individual congregations to develop consumer education programs and then spread word of compliance or boycott throughout a given neighborhood. In March, the Atlanta Baking Company hired eight Blacks and desegregated its facilities. The Krispy Kreme Doughnut Company was not as willing to comply with such demands, how-ever, and activists planned a boycott of its popular stores in April.[10]

As important as direct action strategies had become, electoral politics—that mainstay of the moderates—continued to reap rewards for the Black community, particularly for its professionals. When thirty-four-year-old at-torney Leroy Johnson entered the state Legislature as Georgia's first Black state senator since 1870, he had both the audacity and foresight to predict that within twenty years Blacks would be "fully integrated into the Democratic Party in the South." Johnson beat four White candidates in the primary elec-tion and proceeded to trounce Black Republican T. M. Alexander in the gen-eral election, thanks in large part to well-organized middle-class Blacks on Atlanta's West Side. Johnson said he did not "want to be a Negro senator. I want to be a representative of all the people."[11]

The African American bloc vote also proved crucial in an ongoing battle over passage of municipal bonds. In 1962, Blacks withheld their support for an eighty-million-dollar city-county bond referendum that did not provide resources for improving most Black neighborhoods. In spring 1963, Mayor Allen brought a revised set of bond issues before the Black community that targeted health and welfare, parks, libraries, schools, and urban renewal projects. Each bond issue passed in this instance, despite sizable White op-position. Blacks had voted almost entirely as a bloc, approving the referen-dums by an eight-to-one ratio. *Atlanta Daily World* managing editor George M. Coleman praised the bond victory, declaring that the "Negro has grown into an intelligent voter, able to see issues clearly and rationalize for both his personal gain and civilization's advancement."[12]

■ ■ ■

With the exception of the Grady Hospital protests a year before, Black college students had been relatively inactive in the city. There had been a few SNCC-led sit-ins at Jake's Fine Foods, a segregated restaurant adjacent to the

Trailways bus station. Most SNCC field workers had been dispatched to the battle in Albany. Yet those student activists who remained in Atlanta recognized there was unfinished business. On 12 March 1963 a small COAHR contingent initiated a "lie-in" in the lobby of the Henry Grady Hotel. Although lunch counters had been desegregated, the majority of Atlanta's restaurants and practically all of its hotels and motels remained segregated. Police arrested two of the four Black students on trespassing charges after they entered the hotel lobby and quietly lay down, pillows and blankets in hand. A White Spelman College student already had paid for accommodations for five people without the hotel knowing they were Blacks. Students stationed outside the hotel picketed in shifts of eight, carrying placards with slogans such as "No Room At This Inn" and "Dallas, Houston, Miami—Why Not Atlanta?"[13]

Two days after the Grady Hotel demonstration, nearly three hundred COAHR protesters marched from the Atlanta University campus to the steps of City Hall to further protest discriminatory hotel policies. They sang freedom songs and chanted "Freedom! Freedom!" before Committee chair Gwendolyn Isles handed Allen a letter listing several Southern cities that had desegregated hotels. Allen, ever gracious, read the letter and congratulated the student activists "on the manner in which they approached their city government," but, in characteristic fashion, he took no action. The renewal of protests inspired Morehouse College president Benjamin E. Mays to comment on hotel segregation in his syndicated column in the *Pittsburgh Courier*. "One would think that enlightened Atlanta, which has been dramatized as the showplace of the nation for intelligent handling of racial problems, would open its hotels without a struggle," he wrote. The SCLC national office in an April position paper supported the renewed protests and contended that student direct action had been "the most important development in the southern struggle."[14]

The hotel demonstrations helped renew the commitment by the Committee and SNCC's Atlanta office to the second phase of the direct action movement, a joint effort that often involved a small but dedicated group of local White students. On 25 March police harassed Ruby Doris Smith, now a full-time member of the SNCC staff, after she used a restroom at the Union Train Terminal reserved for Whites. COAHR activists intensified their efforts in April and May, with police arresting forty protesters during sit-ins at restaurants throughout the city. At one point nearly one hundred Black spectators watched and then applauded students who sang "We Shall Not Be Moved" as police carried them into wagons. A racially mixed group of demonstrators, ignoring a plea by Allen to halt protest activity, marched to the City Hall cafeteria, where they were denied service. With the election over, students made certain to commemorate the ninth anniversary of Brown v. Board of Education with further protest activity.[15]

The next day four Black and three White students received more than they bargained for when they entered Pickrick, the chicken restaurant owned by arch-segregationist and former mayoral candidate Lester Maddox. Maddox grabbed two of the Black students and threw them out of his restaurant. He then told his Black employees to remove the remaining protesters, telling them "to get them out or go out themselves." One employee did escort a student outside, but the others refused to follow the order. In an apparent effort to entice them, Maddox told them, "Ten dollars if you throw them out and hurt them." The employees did not budge. "We decided that rather than have the Negro men lose their jobs, we would rather leave," protester Ralph Moore explained. An already tense situation became more inflamed by a White customer who flashed a switchblade and smiled, "Lester, if you don't mind getting the blood off the floor, I'll get 'em out."[16]

In an effort to maintain momentum, another interracial group of students camped out in front of a second downtown restaurant, Leb's, two days later for over four hours. A Black protester claimed that owner Charles Lebedin had an employee throw him to the ground when he set foot inside, but a judge refused to issue a warrant for assault and battery because a police officer who had been nearby apparently saw no need to intervene. The incidents at Pickrick and Leb's so troubled the Atlanta Chamber of Commerce that its board of directors, influenced no doubt by mayor and former Chamber president Ivan Allen, voted unanimously to ask all businesses catering to the public in any way to desegregate their facilities. "The future of Atlanta is too bright and too sure," the board asserted, "to be tarnished by hatred, strife and discord."[17]

Whether for personal ideological reasons or out of a more basic concern to not alienate White customers, merchants seemed intent on ignoring the Chamber of Commerce's edict. Barely a week had passed since the restaurant protests when the U.S. Supreme Court ruled unconstitutional in Peterson v. City of Greenville any arrest of sit-in participants that took place in public facilities. The ruling, which was based on a South Carolina sit-in protest, was a decisive victory for COAHR members, who celebrated by organizing a daylong series of demonstrations on 14 June. Three days later violence erupted when police arrested another racially mixed group of protesters at Leb's. Sitting down, the activists formed a human chain on the sidewalk in front of the restaurant. White employees shoved and punched the students, then hecklers jeered as employees stomped one White student on the head. The next day a White man stabbed Benjamin Anderson, a Black high school student at a sit-in at Morrison's Restaurant. The Atlanta NAACP, "outraged at the stabbing of a 15-year-old boy," requested for the second time in two weeks that Allen dispatch police to protect demonstrators.[18]

In an effort to stem further violence, White merchants offered measures designed to bring about token desegregation. Fourteen hotels and motels agreed to open their facilities to "conventions with a limited number of Negro delegates." Allen explained that Blacks who were "identifiable by convention badge" could even eat at hotel restaurants. Some of the finer hotels in the city, including Heart of Atlanta, Henry Grady, and Peachtree on Peachtree, refused to sign the agreement. An insulted C. Miles Smith, local NAACP leader, questioned the merits of the agreement, noting that Blacks who had been privy to the negotiations understood it to mean "complete [hotel] desegregation immediately." On 20 June 1963, fifty restaurant owners reached a far more sound, albeit informal, agreement calling for complete desegregation of facilities.[19]

Even with the informal agreement and a summer without classes, COAHR activism did not grind to a halt. Committed to employing "every non-violent means at our disposal," students waged battles against deeply embedded racially discriminatory policies in Atlanta. Their unwillingness to be satisfied with earlier victories helped spur a larger struggle against petty apartheid. The Committee organized pickets against merchants in the Atlanta University Center area who had a history of mistreating their employees or customers. In June, college students participated in a march downtown in solidarity with three hundred striking Black workers at the Dobbs House airport restaurant. The march, which had been coordinated by the Hotel and Restaurant Workers Union Local 151, SNCC, and COAHR, was attended mostly by striking workers and their families. The two-month strike over wages and working conditions had been costly and violent, with several clashes between strikers and Black replacement workers.[20]

■ ■ ■

The joint solidarity march prefigured the establishment of a broader activist coalition in the fall. On 19 October 1963 representatives of nine Black organizations met to discuss the possibility of organizing a campaign to press for complete desegregation of public accommodations, employment, education, health, housing, law enforcement, and electoral politics. These were the very issues that the young professionals of the Atlanta Committee for Cooperative Action and student activists of the Committee on Appeal for Human Rights had highlighted almost four years earlier. Those who attended the "summit leadership conference" agreed that if full desegregation was not attained by 11 November, further direct action would be the response. The *Atlanta Daily World* criticized the summit group's choice of a deadline and argued that if the "unusually high degree of unity" dissipated, it would be because of the imposition of "an extremist leadership on the Negro community." The coalition of groups ranged from SNCC and COAHR on one end of the spectrum to the All-Citizens Registration Committee and Atlanta Negro Voters League on the other.[21]

COAHR activists took immediate steps to plan a demonstration for 16 November. At a speaking engagement featuring Martin Luther King Jr. they passed out leaflets announcing a possible demonstration. Some older activists were troubled by this move, considering it a violation of the spirit of the October summit in that the broader coalition of groups had not met to discuss specific protests. Most activists recognized that full desegregation was no imminent reality, however, especially after the city's Board of Aldermen voted nine-to-three against a desegregation resolution. On Thursday, 21 November, SCLC secretary-treasurer Ralph D. Abernathy and new COAHR chair Larry Fox led several hundred Atlanta University Center students in a demonstration in front of Rich's calling for increased Black employment. A. T. Walden, co-chair of what had become the Atlanta Summit Leadership Conference (ASLC), made it known he was "greatly disappointed" with the protest. Walden had entered into negotiations with Rich's on the issue of Black employment and feared the worst.[22]

If not for the assassination of President Kennedy in Dallas, protests would have continued. Instead, Abernathy and Fox agreed to "halt indefinitely" further demonstrations at Rich's out of respect for the slain president and his family. Three weeks later, the ASLC announced plans for a ten thousand-person "Pilgrimage for Democracy" in December to protest segregation in the city. Congregations from throughout Atlanta were to converge on Hurt Park downtown in a march and rally modeled after the successful March on Washington that summer. Scheduled speakers included James Forman, Fox, C. Miles Smith, and Abernathy. However, the big invitee was Martin Luther

King Jr., who had planned to be in Washington, D.C., but changed his schedule to accommodate the Pilgrimage. In what appeared to be an about-face, Walden supported the demonstration. Perhaps he had gauged the overwhelming level of support for the march and did not want to alienate other Blacks. He asserted that the Pilgrimage showed that Blacks had "come together as never before." Nevertheless, Walden warned, if the move toward desegregation did not proceed quickly, "then God help us."[23]

The best-laid plans of activists have been spoiled by inclement weather, however, and the Pilgrimage for Democracy was no exception. Bitterly cold temperatures made the march from individual churches to Hurt Park a difficult proposition for many Atlanta Blacks. Nonetheless, over three thousand people participated. Forman placed responsibility for the course of the African American human rights struggle in Atlanta and elsewhere squarely on those assembled. "No one leader, no group of leaders, can get your rights," Forman asserted. "You have to get them for yourselves." King stressed the importance of commanding the attention of those in power. "If our words fail to move them . . . then our actions must show them."[24]

■ ■ ■

The pace of protest activity accelerated toward the end of the month. Police arrested and jailed twenty-one protesters during sit-ins at the Toddle House restaurant downtown, including Lillian Gregory, the pregnant wife of activist comedian Dick Gregory. Several of those jailed maintained that police used excessive force in arresting them. In an innovative effort to have the mayor address the issue of possible police brutality toward protesters, eighteen SNCC and COAHR members braved the cold to sing Christmas carols and freedom songs in the driveway of Allen's house the following evening. When the mayor greeted the group and asked them to identify themselves, the activists responded that they were the "Freedom Choir." The next morning, Christmas Eve, Forman led a group from SNCC that conducted a "stand-in" at the mayor's office. The protesters demanded more government jobs for Blacks and passage of a public accommodations ordinance.[25]

Older established activists did not leave students in the cold. After two hours of debate, the steering committee of the Atlanta Summit Leadership Conference voted unanimously on 3 January 1964, to consider massive street demonstrations. Wyatt Tee Walker, a key SCLC activist with experience in Albany and Birmingham, presented a "battle plan" for future demonstrations at the meeting. Summit co-chair Clarence Coleman, himself head of the relatively conservative Atlanta Urban League, expressed discontent with the absence of a response from White community leaders. While organizations such as the Chamber of Commerce had passed resolutions in favor of desegregation, "no concrete results" had materialized, he said. Leroy Johnson asserted that if protests did take place, "I'm convinced that the demonstrations will be supported by the total Negro leadership in Atlanta." Others were not so certain, however, and some activists wondered privately whether the summit group would survive the coming weeks.[26]

A principal fear of older activists was that college students would continue to organize demonstrations independently. A full week had not passed when 150 Black protesters, including many students from Booker T. Washington High School, descended upon Allen's office in City Hall on 7 January and then attempted to eat at two fast-food restaurants. SNCC chair John Lewis and COAHR chair Larry Fox led the youthful contingent through downtown, the group singing freedom songs along the way. The mayor refused to see the "truants" who came to his office to protest what Lewis called "overcrowded conditions and inadequate facilities" at their school. The SNCC leader refused to apologize for those who "play hooky for freedom," and he asserted that it was "my feeling that most of the students involved will learn more in one day in a freedom school than they will in a whole year in a segregated school."[27]

Reaction to the protest was as swift as it was predictable. The Daily World remarked that the high school students who participated in "hooky for freedom" made a grave mistake when they "dodged classes" and jeered their principal. Nevertheless, the Daily World asserted, the biggest error in judgment rested with the SNCC leadership. "With the dropout rate among teenagers at an all-time high, our students can ill-afford to flout discipline in the class room and 'learn civics in the streets' or 'history at the counters.'"[28] Criticism of the Washington High protest did little to cool what would become a fiercely contested protest campaign, primarily because there was a large enough coalition in favor of direct action to carry the movement forward.

The movement's viability became clear on the night of 11 January. Police arrested the SCLC's Wyatt Tee Walker, Rush Memorial pastor Joseph Boone, SNCC organizer Prathia Hall, and several other activists in a sit-in at the Heart of Atlanta Motel. At one point an employee of the motel dragged SNCC organizer Judy Richardson several feet outside the motel lobby. Georgia Baptist Hospital refused to treat Richardson, but an ambulance worker relented.

A biracial group of female activists conducted sit-in protests at two Krystal fast-food restaurants, with police arresting eight women. Demonstrators stomped their feet and pounded on tables as they sang freedom songs. Several other Krystal locations closed for business when protesters approached. A sign on the front door of one of the franchises stated simply, "Closed because of Niggers." Subfreezing weather did not deter protesters from returning to several Krystal locations two days later, resulting in additional arrests.[29]

It was apparent that the Krystal fast-food restaurants had become a key site in the struggle to end overt segregation in the city. A group of ten robed Klansmen entered a downtown Krystal for some early evening coffee on Saturday, 19 January. Soon afterward, a handful of SNCC and COAHR pickets assembled outside, singing freedom songs and taunting the white supremacists inside. In a matter of minutes, nervous Klansmen watched the vociferous group outside mushroom in number. When police arrived to remove activists to awaiting wagons, one protester fell to the ground. Forman yelled, "Under the wheels! Under the wheels!" One group of demonstrators encircled one police wagon while another group rolled under a second one. A brief melee ensued when police endeavored again to place demonstrators inside the wagons. Three hours and scores of arrests later, the relieved Klansmen finally left the empty restaurant, robes tucked securely under their arms.[30]

After either spending the night in jail or participating in a solidarity rally in the Krystal parking lot, student activists returned to the AUC on Sunday morning to organize further demonstrations. They had no doubt been buoyed by their ability to intimidate Klansmen to the point of locking themselves in a fast-food restaurant that had long since closed for the evening. At a campus rally that afternoon, Lewis spoke of plans for demonstrations later in the week in conjunction with the visit by the United Nations Subcommission on the Prevention of Discrimination and Protection of Minorities.[31]

As students prepared for further action they also girded themselves for an unflattering portrayal of the Krystal demonstration in the press. The *Atlanta Constitution*, "while condoning peaceful demonstrations," lambasted student activists for what it termed the use of "the dangerous and utterly cynical tactic of deliberate provocation." The newspaper not only asserted that the students had descended to the level of the Klan itself, but that "this small core of demonstrators seems determined to stampede Atlanta onto a purely destructive course." The editorial turned a history of Klan-organized terrorist violence on its head. It was also revealing that the *Constitution*'s editors said they were "confident" that established Black leaders would condemn the protest. Two Morehouse professors did precisely that in a strident letter to the *Atlanta Daily World*. Arthur C. Banks and Finley C. Campbell argued that Black moral superiority in the "whole racial struggle" had been compromised. "We are not against provoking the opposition, but we want that opposition to stumble over their own feet, not ours." Finally, the professors asserted that Black students had no business becoming so agitated over entry into a fast-food restaurant. "Someone should tell the leaders of those demonstrators that, in a sense, they are fighting in the marshes, not on the front line."[32]

Their criticism was instructive in several ways. By this point, the editors of the *Atlanta Daily World*, who had come to symbolize some of the most reactionary positions on the question of student-initiated direct action protests, probably welcomed such a letter. The key for Banks and Campbell was not the principle of protest itself, however, but what they considered a violation of that principle. Unlike the lunch-counter protests during the first phase of the sit-in movement, these later demonstrations were becoming confrontational and far less concerned with upholding middle-class notions of decorum. In contending that protests at fast-food restaurants were struggles "in the marshes, not on the front line," the Morehouse professors revealed an elitist position shared by some middle-class Blacks. Few professionals sympathetic to student tactics raised eyebrows when students conducted protests at segregated upscale hotels and restaurants. Indeed, professionals were more inclined to even join such downtown protests because they spoke directly to the ways in which petty apartheid constrained their class mobility.

In the wake of the Krystal protests, students turned their attention to a world audience. Eight pickets greeted the members of the UN subcommission when they arrived at the airport at the end of January. They carried placards that read "We serve the Ku Klux Klan but not black Americans," "Open the open city," and "Atlanta's image is a fraud." Apparently, some in the delegation thought at first that they were the targets of student criticism. That afternoon, over five hundred students gathered for a rally at Morehouse, coordinated by SNCC and COAHR, which took place as Morehouse President Benjamin E. Mays and other Black educators met with the UN delegation to discuss race relations in the city and region. Following the rally, three hundred students left the campus, marching in formation and singing freedom songs, to conduct a sit-in at Leb's. Along the way, marchers passed without incident groups of Klansmen who stood in front of some of the sixteen restaurants that had been desegregated. Once they arrived at Leb's, protesters quickly sat in available seats, leaving a sizable contingent outside to lead chants and freedom songs.[33]

When Leb's owner, Charles Lebedin, arrived, he asked two Black police officers to arrest the activists, but they refused to do so without a warrant indicating just cause. The resulting stalemate lasted for several hours as the number of protesters outside dwindled to one hundred. Then twenty robed Klansmen, including Grand Dragon Calvin Craig, arrived with sympathizers. In response, the demonstrators formed two parallel lines in front of the entrance, with many protesters sitting down. Remembering the showdown at Krystal only days before, demonstrators chanted "The old K-K, she ain't what she used to be." An angry Craig fired back, "Let's show that white people can get together in Atlanta." As the Klansmen began to walk between the lines of protesters, pushing ensued, and seconds later Klansmen and protesters began throwing punches. Fifty police officers, most of them Black, were called to the scene but made no arrests. At least two Whites were visibly injured, one with a bloody nose and the other with a bruised forehead.[34]

Unapologetic about their use of force and more determined than ever, SNCC and COAHR activists followed the clash with another assault on segregated downtown merchants. Protesters rushed the front door of Leb's in waves, only to be turned away. Police began arresting activists, in this instance without warrants, for disturbing the peace. Police may have been motivated by the sight of one of their brethren lying with a concussion. Four protesters, including Washington High student Deloria Zellar, were hurt as well. The activists left Leb's and moved on the Downtown Motel, where Lebedin owned another segregated restaurant. Scores of protesters lay down in the motel lobby, prompting Black police under the command of Howard Baugh to arrest them and carry them to wagons. Certainly, onlookers must have been intrigued by the sight of Black policemen prying loose Black protesters who clutched coat racks and desks with as much strength as they could muster. Those who had not been arrested returned to Leb's, at the intersection of Forsyth and Luckie streets, and set up camp in the middle of the street, temporarily forcing police to reroute traffic. Ivan Allen remarked that local segregation laws had been repealed and that it was "regrettable that such groups seek national publicity at local expense."[35]

Yet student activists recognized that it was necessary to confront the force of custom supporting segregation with the force of protest affirming full human rights. In all, Atlanta police arrested eighty-four people that day. The combined forces of SNCC and COAHR pressed forward with an even larger series of actions the last week in January. This latest wave of demonstrations, many ending in violence, had produced tangible results. When members of the UN subcommission asserted that they had not received a full accounting from the city's White business and political leaders, arrangements were made to conduct a meeting with an eclectic group of Black activists at the Butler Street YMCA, including Forman and Dick Gregory.[36]

Many activists in COAHR and SNCC had become experienced practitioners of direct action. If they were not easily intimidated before, they were practically intractable now. SNCC activists—a number of whom had been introduced to the freedom movement through COAHR and other city-specific organizations—had become frontline soldiers in fierce struggles in Albany and elsewhere. As a result, an increasing number of fulltime activists experienced battle fatigue as particular protest experiences began to take a toll on their mental health.[37] At the same time, however, there were advantages to becoming veterans of such activity. Finding oneself in the crucible of struggle often inspired confidence, and confidence brought with it tenacity. Few Blacks could have imagined such brazen defiance of Klansmen in downtown Atlanta even a year earlier.

Prathia Hall, who had worked in the bitter southwest Georgia SNCC campaign, personified the uncompromising spirit of these younger activists. A Philadelphia native and graduate of Temple University, Hall and several other activists in Dawson were wounded by White terrorists. She went to Atlanta with an undeniable sense of mission. "Negroes must also bear the blame for the desecration of humanity that is segregation. For we have been silent much too long," Hall remarked at an Atlanta SNCC meeting in December. "We've been preoccupied with telling our city power structure not what it needs to know, but what it wants to hear. We are here today because we can no longer bear the shame of our guilt, because delay means compromising our dignity."[38]

Students took part in over eight hours of protests on Monday, 27 January. That afternoon, two hundred students marched to Leb's once again, moving single file and three feet apart, in keeping with an informal agreement reached with Atlanta authorities. Police arrested some students who attempted to enter the restaurant and others who sat down in the middle of a nearby street. At one point, authorities declared a two-hour state of emergency downtown. After nightfall a group of over one hundred protesters marched to the city jail, where they held a solidarity rally for those arrested the night before. Police cordoned off all entrances as the protesters proceeded to march around the facility several times and the incarcerated activists sang freedom songs in their cells. The main body of protesters headed back toward Leb's, but police stopped them. Unbeknownst to the police, however, a smaller group of activists arrived at the restaurant via a different route.[39]

Both protesters and paying customers had been prevented from reaching the entrance to Leb's earlier because of a police barricade. Being denied business upset Lebedin and his employees. Waitresses crafted placards of their own that read "Eat at Leb's. He is your friend and mine" and "Do you call this Freedom?" Other Whites offered a different message. Lawyer and Klan sympathizer James R. Venable warned the mayor and other politicians that if demonstrations did not end in two days, Klansmen would be deployed "to restore order." The heightened protest activity and the response that it elicited alarmed the *Atlanta Daily World*, which was careful not to condemn any particular group or individual. Nevertheless, the newspaper maintained that demonstrations "are getting out of control."[40]

The conservative *Daily World* expressed the minority view within the city's African American community. NAACP and SCLC leaders made public their support of the two student-led organizations, with the NAACP's Leon Cox lamenting that the "chaotic conditions" were the result of a "woeful lack of leadership on the part of both races." Tuesday, activists turned their attention once again to Allen. Seventy protesters marched to the steps of City Hall singing "We Shall Overcome," carrying a large banner that stated, "As a first step we want a Public Accommodations Law." E. H. Dorsey, pastor of Tabernacle Baptist Church and newly elected president of the Atlanta Baptist Ministers Union, pledged the unanimous support of the 250 clergy in his organization. SNCC organizer Prathia Hall asserted that in "the past the only difference between Atlanta and Birmingham was Atlanta's right to protest peacefully. This right has been taken away now."[41]

Once inside the building Hall made her way to Allen's office as others packed the corridor. "Despite its liberal reputation, Atlanta is still a segregated city," the Philadelphia native remarked. "We demonstrate as a means of communicating our determination that Atlanta will have its reputation a reality or will admit before the world that it is a carefully fostered fraud." Noting that students had grown accustomed to direct action tactics, Hall emphasized that students would "continue to communicate with our bodies" until segregation of restaurants and hotels was a reality. Finally, she warned that once desegregation occurred, student activists had every intention of challenging "more fundamental problems: housing, jobs, welfare services, medical facilities, and schools." The mayor listened to Hall and then, as was his custom, remarked politely, "I will pass this on to the people in Atlanta who are trying to eliminate segregation." Word of the joint SNCC-COAHR statement passed to other interested observers, including FBI agents who had begun surveillance of SNCC's Atlanta office.[42]

Authorities were more intent than ever on cracking down. William Boyd, Fulton County solicitor general, maintained Tuesday evening that he would use "all the powers" of his office to prosecute those who violated the law, and he criticized those who "would seek their day of court in the streets." Wednesday afternoon, Allen chaired a meeting with members of practically every mainstream civic and political organization, as well as the steering committee of the all-but-forgotten Adult Student Liaison Committee. In fact, the "meeting" was more of a mayoral address, with Allen declaring in his twelve-page speech that "irresponsible" demonstrations would have to end. He called for a thirty-day truce and suggested the formation of a civil rights division in his administration to ensure that Blacks enjoyed full rights "in the matter of public facilities, jobs, job training and housing."[43]

The response to the mayoral address was predictable, following what had become established fault lines among Black activists. Most members of the established Black leadership elite adopted a moderate stance and approved the mayor's speech. A. T. Walden, William Holmes Borders, and Martin Luther King Sr. applauded, aware perhaps that Allen was walking a tightrope held by White business leaders who termed his administration "coercive." Borders told the mayor that "we are going to do our best to stand by you." Other elders, especially the college and university presidents, supported the students. "Young people today are impressed with a different view of democracy," explained Clark College's James P. Brawley. "They want to see progress made now." The offer may have appeased some Black leaders, but not James Forman, whose comrade John Lewis was among those behind bars. "He is really throwing down the gauntlet," Forman said of Allen. "The tone of his speech is going to create that which he is trying to avoid." The SNCC leader made it clear that there could be no truce without the release of prisoners. Meanwhile, the

Daily World's editorial position remained consistent. After noting that Forman said, " 'If we must violate unjust laws to achieve democracy for Negroes, that's what we'll do,' " its editors replied: "There is no need to manifest this spirit of defiance in Atlanta. . . . We hope Mr. Forman will drop this attitude; it will not serve our race's best interest."[44]

The fifty-three prisoners who remained in jail took some solace from the support they received from certain established leaders. NAACP activist Leon Cox asserted that direct action challenged the "false image of Atlanta" the city's boosters had carefully crafted for decades. Cox did not limit his criticism to that of White leaders, however, contending that many established Blacks had been inclined to "talk, talk, talk" at the negotiating table while "the more militant groups decided the time for action has come." The All-Citizens Registration Committee endorsed the students also, asserting that until "they agree to a cooling-off period, there will be none." Martin Luther King Jr.—the only person in the city who commanded consistent national attention—noted that there were now "nearly one thousand cities" witnessing desegregation protests. King applauded the use of direct action tactics in general terms, but predicted that the "innovation for the year will be large-scale selective buying programs" such as those launched throughout the country by Operation Breadbasket.[45]

Meanwhile, a group of Black male trusty prisoners harassed and assaulted four women activists, three Black and one White, in a unisex holding cell. A seventeen-year-old Black student said the trusties, with alcohol on their breath, had hit and fondled the women. At one point a number of male prisoners, including Dick Gregory and Atlanta University professor Morris Eisenstein, constructed a makeshift barricade of metal cots to guard against assaults. The four activists brought charges against the trusties, but a local judge dismissed the case for lack of evidence.[46]

As January came to an end, divisions intensified among Black activists and between most Blacks and the mayor. SNCC and COAHR leaders had been frustrated by the ASLC's refusal to endorse continued demonstrations. At the same time, the moderate group headed by Walden did not receive what he so desperately wanted, namely an endorsement of the mayor's proposals by a broad coalition of Black activists. The consensus position was to establish an ASLC action committee that would review Allen's speech and draft a counterproposal. The ASLC committee wasted little time crafting its own three-page proposal, which called for release of all political prisoners, equal employment opportunities, and an end to segregation of both Grady Memorial Hospital and federally funded public housing. Allen rejected the ASLC platform on 1 February, however, asserting that the courts would settle the issue of arrest and detention. He insisted that the other issues would "receive full consideration." Jesse Hill, chair of the action committee, declared that "hope for a thirty-day cooling-off period has gone up in smoke."[47]

Most Black activists had anticipated that the ASLC proposal would be rejected. Indeed, C. Miles Smith announced plans of a downtown boycott before he received word of Allen's decision, but he noted that the larger African American community "had been asking for it" for some time. Students organized picketing of Leb's in the afternoon, as much in commemoration of the Greensboro sit-ins as in response to the mayor. Student activists handed out leaflets in front of the restaurant that contained a joint SNCC-COAHR statement. In it Lewis and Fox declared that "the City of Atlanta must realize that there are people in this city, both black and white, who are not and will not be satisfied with segregation."[48]

Almost on cue, thirteen White college students picketed Leb's the next day. They carried placards that read "Georgia Students Protest Segregation" and "Atlanta Must Be Desegregated." One of the groups represented was the Emory Committee of Georgia Students for Human Rights, whose members passed out a leaflet stating in part that "it is wrong to refuse service to a Negro. We believe a free city must be open to all its citizens and further, that it is the obligation of all Atlantans to make it free." White allies such as these often encountered violence, and Atlanta was no exception. A middle-aged White man from Augusta struck a White female SNCC activist "solidly in the face" during a demonstration at the Ship Ahoy restaurant on 8 February. A scuffle ensued when the man continued swinging at other protesters.[49]

Authorities singled out Mardon Walker, a White exchange student at Spelman College, for harsh treatment as well. Judge Durwood Pye sentenced Walker, whose father was a naval officer, to eighteen months in jail, including a year of hard labor, for her activism. She had been the first person arrested during the 13 January protest at the Krystal fast-food restaurant. No doubt, Walker's privileged Northern background served both to provoke disdain from White supremacists and chauvinistic praise from liberal Whites who made her a *cause célèbre*. Ultimately for Walker, though, being a principled activist appeared to be the paramount issue. She refused to be released on cash bond pending trial, because she realized that doing so was all but impossible for incarcerated Black student activists.[50]

■ ■ ■

The participation of White students drew national attention to the continued existence of apartheid structures in Atlanta. Walter Cronkite highlighted the events of early 1964 in a "CBS Reports" documentary. The local uproar over the documentary inspired Martin Luther King Jr. to remark that in the two years since Atlanta adopted lunch-counter desegregation and token school integration, ten other Southern cities had "vaulted past us in race relations." He cited a Southern Regional Council report saying that only thirty of 150 restaurants and sixteen of 125 hotels and motels had been opened to Blacks. Although accounting for 40 percent of the population, Blacks continued to occupy only 16 percent of the city's residential land. While less than 50 percent of Black families lived on 3,000 dollars a year, more than 50 percent of White families lived on 6,400 dollars a year. Yet, King remarked, "the power structure is screaming for a thirty-day truce" after only a few weeks of boycotts and mass demonstrations. The SCLC president did not mince words. "We must be sure that the sacrifices of Birmingham, Medgar Evers, the innocents of the 16th St. Baptist Church and our late President Kennedy are not prostituted by our being lulled to sleep and losing precious ground that has been so hard to gain."[51]

Without question, there was a certain spirit in the air. At an Atlanta University town meeting, SNCC chair John Lewis declared that "we have a mandate to destroy this painted image" of the city. When asked about recent reports tying the organization to the Communist Party, Lewis responded that the entire student-driven movement was "not a Communist effort but a cry of a common, oppressed people." The next day forty Black physicians and dentists participated in a sedate march downtown in conjunction with the Easter season store boycott. But they were marching nonetheless, asserting that "we cannot lend our moral or financial support to a city which practices injustice and which does not respect the dignity of all her citizens as children of God."[52]

For the next several months, the Atlanta movement's primary foot soldiers were Donald L. Hollowell and Howard Moore Jr., the two attorneys who led a protracted legal battle on behalf of the remaining fifty-eight defendants in the state's anti-trespass case. Most SNCC organizers would do battle now in

Mississippi. It was not until July, however, when Congress passed and President Lyndon B. Johnson signed the Civil Rights Act of 1964, that the legal war ended in victory for SNCC and COAHR activists. Likewise, it was federal legislation that finally forced the hand of White merchants. Student activists in Atlanta and elsewhere realized, though, that it was their sacrifice that had paved the way for the final legislative assault. For their part, older activists stressed making the transition to a less segregated city as smooth as possible. The ASLC urged that the "Negro community assume some of the responsibility for the peaceful transition to the kind of society for which the summit leadership and its member organizations have worked. . . ."[53]

Nevertheless, Lester Maddox and his loyal clientele had other intentions. On 3 July, three Black divinity students drove into the parking lot of his Pickrick restaurant to test the federal legislation. Maddox raised a pistol and told them to "git out and don't ever come back." A group of twenty Whites wielding shiny new ax handles began beating on the car before the students managed to get away. Less than an hour later, more than one thousand Whites, including hundreds of children, surrounded what had become a fortress of a restaurant. Meanwhile, Lebedin covered the windows of his restaurant with streamers that read "From Charlie Leb" and "To My Friends" that protested desegregation. A beaten Lebedin noted that "I lack the strength to fight the lies printed by the Atlanta newspapers. I intend to obey the laws of the United States and Georgia as I have done for fifteen years before the civil rights bill was passed."[54]

Over the next few months, the defiant Maddox lost time after time in court but won the hearts and minds of a sobering number of White Georgians. When he did not sell "Pickrick Drumsticks"—ax and pick handles with his stamped autograph on them—he campaigned for Senator Barry Goldwater. After incurring over one hundred thousand dollars in legal expenses and fines, Maddox relented on 8 February 1965, his wife and customers sobbing uncontrollably. When a lone Black man placed an order at his cafeteria the next day, Maddox closed up shop for good. He was not down for long, however, if he was down at all. His recalcitrance had paved a path that would take him directly to the governor's mansion the following autumn.[55]

The student-driven coalition of Black activists and their White allies had, in the course of four years, worked to end petty apartheid in the city of Atlanta. Yet, there were debates along the way. Disagreements particularly continued among established and increasingly vociferous older leaders and between non-students and students over the appropriate use of direct action tactics. Nevertheless, veteran elite activists shared enough common ground with students and younger professionals to maintain a fairly viable united front in what remained a middle-class-led movement in Atlanta. In the coming months and years, however, these debates would develop into more profound and fundamental ideological cleavages, as events that transcended the boundaries of Atlanta would alter the trajectory of the Black struggle for human rights in ways that most participants in the sit-ins scarcely could have imagined.

DEMANDING BLACK POWER

CHAPTER THREE

BRIDGES

The principal frontline activity of the Black freedom struggle drifted away from Atlanta following passage of the Civil Rights Act of 1964, evidenced in part by the fact that the city witnessed only minor skirmishes between protesters and defenders of white supremacy. In early July, violence erupted during an initial test of the new legislation at a restaurant in the Lakewood Park section of the city. As expected, the *Atlanta Daily World*, the longstanding conservative Black newspaper, criticized Blacks who sought service at the eatery, contending that "running through the pasture with a red flag will only serve to infuriate the bulls." However, the worst violence in Georgia occurred outside Atlanta. White terrorists murdered Lemuel A. Penn, a Washington, D.C. superintendent of schools and lieutenant colonel in the Army Reserve, as he drove his car on Highway 172 in Madison County.[1] Penn's murder served as a reminder to activists that the struggle against apartheid had taken the bloodiest toll on Blacks in little-known places in Mississippi, Alabama, and rural Georgia. Indeed, the sheer intensity of frontline experiences outside Atlanta had a particularly profound impact on a number of Student Nonviolent Coordinating Committee activists who returned to the city. Such experiences, along with pivotal external influences such as that of revolutionary Black nationalist Malcolm X, served to further radicalize women and men concerned with the Black struggle for human rights, particularly as the issue of self-determination came to the fore.

■ ■ ■

On-the-ground work provided the baseline in a dialectical process of ideological transformation for young Black activists. For SNCC frontline organizer Willie Ricks, who came to the movement as a militant teenager in Chattanooga, white supremacist violence was the inevitable response to SNCC activism in southwest Georgia during the early 1960s. "Death and extreme

Frontline SNCC organizer and radical Black nationalist Mukasa Dada (Willie Ricks) in 2003. Mukasa, who was the first SNCC activist to call for Black Power during the historic 1966 Meredith March Against Fear, has remained active in the Black struggle for human rights. Photo by the author.

brutality" permeated the environment, so much so that he and several other SNCC workers expected to die. "It took us through a lot of different kinds of changes to see the extreme savage brutality and racist behavior of not just the police, but the judge and the entire system that was oppressing and holding our people down," he said. He noted that it was in the field, then, that reassessment of the strict adherence to nonviolent direct action took place. Asserting that he and other workers "grew from the battlefield," Ricks later explained, for instance, that the departure from nonviolence did not take place theoretically. "There were times when these crackers came to attack and we had no choice but to swing back because their behavior was so vicious."[2]

As dangerous as southwest Georgia had become for freedom fighters, Mississippi remained the epicenter for state-supported racist terrorism and firmly entrenched apartheid structures. As noted historians such as John Dittmer and Charles Payne have demonstrated, local grassroots activists courageously had endured years of abuse and violence long before SNCC workers arrived in significant numbers during the mid-1960s to launch voter registration and educational initiatives. For most SNCC workers the Mississippi experience had been more bitter than sweet. In 1964 alone there had been over one thousand arrests, thirty-five shootings, and six murders of Black and White student activists. "Maybe the summer was just too much effort, too much tension," recalled Julian Bond, who witnessed firsthand the refusal of the Democratic Party to seat the Mississippi Freedom Democratic Party (MFDP) delegation at the national convention in Atlantic City. "A lot of people were burned out after it."[3]

The Mississippi experience would become indelibly imprinted in the life and mind of Gwendolyn Robinson. The Memphis native became an active member of the Committee on Appeal of Human Rights not long after beginning her studies at Spelman College. Having distinguished herself in the movement to end petty apartheid in Atlanta, Robinson was elected as an at-large representative to the SNCC steering committee. A student of Staughton Lynd, she became "very involved" in providing curriculum development for SNCC's Freedom School Project and looked forward to the challenge of being a freedom school director in the Pine Belt town of Laurel, Mississippi. Laurel was in Jones County, a notorious base for Ku Klux Klan organizing and terrorism. Understandably, then, Robinson's family objected vehemently to her decision. "I knew my folks would try to chain me to the bedpost to prevent that from happening," she recalled, noting that her grandmother had remarked that she would rather see her dead than travel to Mississippi. "But nonetheless, I was clear that I was going to do it."[4]

The stakes were high for Robinson, a gifted student who became one of an increasing number of college activists who decided to suspend their academic studies in order to devote full attention to the frontline battlefield of the Black human rights struggle. She said her grandmother had warned her all her life to stay clear of the state, recounting stories of White men, bloodhounds in tow, searching for enslaved Africans who had made their way to Memphis from Mississippi plantations. Spelman administrators notified Robinson's family of her intentions, and they traveled to Atlanta to take her back home. When SNCC wired her money to make the trip for her orientation session, her grandmother intercepted the letter and destroyed it. After Robinson arranged for the money to be wired to a friend's house, she received one final ultimatum from the elderly woman, who had undertaken the primary responsibility of raising her. "She said, 'If you leave, don't ever come back,'" she recalled, noting, "she was trying to save my life."[5]

It quickly appeared Robinson's worst fears had been confirmed. During the orientation session at Miami University, in Ohio, scholar activist Vincent Harding joined with SNCC activists James Forman and Bob Moses in announcing that SNCC workers James Chaney, Andrew Goodman, and Michael Schwerner were missing and presumed dead. Yet only three volunteers left the orientation session after hearing the somber news. Soon Robinson found herself in Hattiesburg, thirty miles from the proposed site of the freedom school, since it was simply too dangerous to reside in Laurel. Being so far from the project site posed particular problems for her because she did not drive. She learned fast, however, recalling that on "at least one occasion I had to do a hundred miles an hour outrunning a White man that was after me!"[6]

As a young Black female SNCC project director, Robinson had to wage what often amounted to a two-front war, not only confronting Mississippi terrorists, but also, the combined male and white skin privilege of the majority of her staff members. She had already ruffled the feathers of some male SNCC activists, both Black and White, when she adopted an uncompromising anti-sexual-harassment policy for the Laurel Project. The policy, termed the "Amazon Project" by Robinson, had been spurred by an incident at an earlier Ohio orientation session in which male trainees attacked her sexually and SNCC organizers refused to respond to her report of the incident. Now in Laurel, the nineteen-year-old Robinson was responsible for a staff of volunteers that was largely White and male. "They were from Yale. They were from Stanford. They were from Princeton," she later recalled. "They thought they were hot shots, understandably." The notion that "some little *Black* woman, in some cases not as old as them," had direct authority over them was an unsettling prospect indeed for some of these White male SNCC volunteers—at least "until they got scared and realized, 'Hey, you could lose your life down here.'"[7]

The violence and fear of violence that permeated the atmosphere in Mississippi began to affect Robinson ideologically. Terrorists set fire to a building that local residents had constructed to house the freedom school, and, predictably, the Laurel fire department refused to respond. When SNCC workers opened a second, "much less impressive" office in a duplex dwelling, terrorists responded by placing a bomb directly under the gas line that ran to the house. A family of five lived in one apartment and two SNCC workers lived in the other. The bomb detonated, "but as fate would have it, the bomb blew the gas line away from the house," and seven lives had been spared. Although she had grown up in segregated Memphis, "I really didn't have a hardened hatred of Whites. It developed in Mississippi. I mean, it was hell, you know. It was *hell*." For eighteen months, the former Spelman student had bypassed college and been shunned by her immediate family only to face the daily prospect of terrorist violence. "'These people hate us. They want to kill us,'" Robinson recalled remarking to herself on more than one occasion. "'They are *crazy*. I don't know what it's going to take to get their feet off our necks. These people are dangerous.' I developed that attitude while there."[8]

As important as field experiences were for activists such as Robinson and Ricks, the general reassessment of nonviolent direct action and the concomitant drive to embrace Black self-determination also was informed by external ideological influences. Direct field experiences and more indirect external influences constantly informed one another and, in turn, further radicalized activists during the mid-1960s. A significant external theoretical challenge to proponents of nonviolent direct action came from a group of Northern radical Black activists, including Max Stanford (Akbar Muhammad Ahmed) and Playthell Benjamin, who formed a "study/action group" in January 1963 that they named the Revolutionary Action Movement (RAM). RAM began publication in Cleveland of a 24-page theoretical journal entitled *Black America* and a one-page newsletter, RAM Speaks, a title no doubt influenced by the Nation of Islam's *Muhammad Speaks*. The group first made a name for itself in North Philadelphia by joining forces with the NAACP at demonstrations protesting racism in the construction industry and organizing forums for high school and college students. Soon the group broadened its base to include other northeastern cities, and exiled radical North Carolina NAACP leader Robert Williams became RAM's "chairman-in-exile."[9]

In an effort to influence the March on Washington, RAM activist Donald Freeman convoked a secret all-male Black Vanguard Conference in Cleveland. The primary outcome of the conference was the formation of a coalition group called the Black Liberation Front (BLF). Stanford later contended in his master's thesis that the exclusion of women at the conference was not surprising, "given the historical period." Yet, even he had a difficult time rationalizing this blatant contradiction given the influential work of women activists, noting that it was "somewhat surprising given that . . . women were key in RAM's formation and development." Ethel Johnson, a former comrade of Williams in North Carolina, had since moved to Philadelphia. She helped organize RAM and became a member of its central committee. Queen Mother Audley Moore, a longtime activist and member of the Universal Negro Improvement Association founded by Marcus Garvey, was an important activist mentor, too, training "RAM cadre in the philosophy of black nationalism and Marxism-Leninism." Moore acted as a leading mentor to RAM cadre in both Philadelphia in 1963 and New York City in 1964.[10]

BLF-RAM activists played an influential role at another important conference, the Afro-American Student Conference on Black Nationalism at Fisk University in Nashville in May 1964. Through their experiences in the field, a growing number of Black student activists in the South had come to embrace the possibility of launching autonomous Black political and cultural institutions. Ricks later observed that grassroots and student activists "didn't even know what nationalism was, never even heard of it. But their work, and their action, were very nationalistic, and moving in the same direction." Freeman chronicled the Fisk student conference in *Black America*. Students criticized the absence of an international analysis among established Black leaders. They also criticized the rigidity of "traditional American Marxism," a position shared by most progressive college students at that time. Unlike young White activists, however, the Fisk conferees called for "ReAfricanization," a collective cultural revolution as a "prerequisite to a *genuine* Black Revolution." Although Freeman's analysis prefigured the problematic tendency by many radical nationalists to foreground politics in a rigid cultural/political binary

relationship, it was significant in evidencing a burgeoning Black consciousness movement among young Black activists.[11]

RAM activists did not limit their involvement in the South to the Fisk
conference. They persuaded SNCC chairman John Lewis to agree to an "ex-
perimental black nationalist self-defense project" in Greenwood, Mississippi.
As a result, internal battles occurred between veteran SNCC organizers and
BLF underground members. RAM activist and cultural worker Roland Snellings (Askia Muhammad Toure) contended that SNCC "is being shaken with a
new and deadly crisis from within. This new crisis stems from the revolt of
black field workers against the white-led offices—main and field." Snellings
was particularly critical of "Beastina"—White female activists who supposedly
seduced "young leaders," Black male SNCC workers—although he conve-
niently absolved Black men of any responsibility for their own actions.[12]

A key platform for RAM's critique of Black moderation was Black America.
One issue of the journal raised the prospect of urban guerrilla warfare: "The
AfroAmerican is backed against a wall with nowhere to go but forward, and
standing in his way is White America. More and more the AfroAmerican is
being forced to think like a guerilla fighter." In "We Can Win," Stanford
wrote of the specific potential for a successful guerrilla movement in the
United States. While advocating the need for Blacks in this country to align
themselves with African and Asian nations, he stressed the goal of simultaneously making revolution "at home."[13]

Members of RAM were among the first activists in the United States to
demand an end to the war in Vietnam. A 1964 solidarity letter issued to the
South Vietnamese National Liberation Front on the Fourth of July stated in
part that RAM congratulated the NLF "for their inspiring victories against U.S.
imperialism . . . and thereby declare Our Independence from the policies of
the U.S. government abroad and at home." In the March 1965 issue of the
Crusader, Robert Williams published the text of a speech he delivered in Hanoi
at the Democratic Republic of Vietnam Solidarity Conference. He spoke "in
the name of Afroamerican freedom fighters who are waging a determined
liberation struggle against mainland American colonialism," and told those
present that the Vietnamese had been a source of inspiration to Blacks in the
United States.[14]

The connection between domestic and international issues in RAM discourse spoke to the group's developing radical Black nationalist ideology.

According to Stanford, this ideology understood "that the major contradiction in the world was between Western imperialism and the revolutionary people of color," and that class was a "secondary contradiction." One of the leading architects of this philosophy had been Nation of Islam and later Organization of Afro-American Unity (OAAU) leader Malcolm X (El-Hajj Malik El-Shabazz). Malcolm X had asserted "that colonialism or imperialism, as the slave system in the West is called, . . . creates what's known not as the American power structure or the French power structure, but an international power structure."[15]

The writings of Mao Zedong, chairman of the Chinese Communist Party, represented another key ideological influence for RAM activists. Mao contended that "the riffraff," or poor peasants of China, played a leading role in the Chinese Revolution. A reformulation of this contention would become a central tenet of later Black political groups such as the Black Panther Party. Of particular significance for RAM activists of the mid-1960s, was Mao's argument for a strategy of encirclement of the Western capitalist countries by the emerging "Third World" nations, a phrase he coined. Williams succeeded as early as 1963 in getting the Chinese leader to issue a statement in support of the African American freedom struggle in the United States. Mao called for "workers, peasants, revolutionary intellectuals, enlightened elements of the bourgeoisie and other enlightened persons of all colors in the world . . . to oppose the racial discrimination practiced by U.S. imperialism."[16]

The task at hand for RAM theoreticians was to build an ideological bridge between "Bandung" struggles and the Black freedom struggle in the United States. These activists constructed an internal colony model that argued that African America was precisely that, a captive nation within a nation. In an elaboration on the self-determination thesis of the Communist Party during the 1930s, which called for an independent Black nation within the Deep South, RAM would lead a "national democratic revolution" to liberate the states of the Black Belt South. Once liberated, the new nation would be financed in part by "a substantial payment of reparations" by the U.S. government.[17] Williams urged support for the African American struggle from those outside the United States. In a statement issued from Havana he advocated worldwide condemnation of "racist America's campaign of genocide against her citizens of African descent." The issue did not end, however, with public criticism. Williams also called on "the decent and civilized" people of the world to support the North American Black liberation struggle, both morally and financially.[18]

The influence of RAM activists on certain SNCC workers, while not extensive, was certainly tangible by 1965. Michael Simmons, a Philadelphia native who came to SNCC as a student from Temple University, had attended forums sponsored by the group while still in high school. "I thought they were gods," Simmons noted of Max Stanford and Playthell Benjamin. He remained in contact with Stanford and worked directly with him in organizing protests against the Vietnam War at Howard University. However, Simmons realized from the moment he and fellow Temple student Dwight Williams came to the Atlanta office during spring break in 1965 that "SNCC was the group that clearly had my heart."[19]

■ ■ ■

The most profound external force for the radicalization of students within the crucible of the Black struggle for human rights was Nation of Islam (NOI) minister Malcolm X. Malcolm made his first overtures to established national Black leaders in 1963. The NOI, a socio-religious group under the direction of Elijah Muhammad, had grown considerably in the three decades following its creation in Detroit in 1930.[20] The NOI claimed over forty thousand members by the early 1960s, due in large part to the activism of younger ministers such as Malcolm. The summer of 1963 witnessed heated verbal confrontations between Southern Christian Leadership Conference (SCLC) leaders and Muslims in New York City. In spite of this, Malcolm had sent telegrams offering support to SCLC president Martin Luther King Jr. in Florida and to SNCC executive secretary James Forman in Mississippi. Prior to the August 1963 Washington March for Jobs and Freedom, he sent a letter to several established leaders, including King and Roy Wilkins of the NAACP, inviting each to a Harlem rally sponsored by the NOI. Malcolm asserted that if John F. Kennedy and Nikita Khrushchev could dialogue peacefully "it is a disgrace for Negro leaders not to be able to submerge our 'minor' differences in order to seek a common solution to a common problem posed by a *Common Enemy*."[21]

The charismatic minister, whose only visit to Atlanta came in 1961 when he held secret meetings with the Ku Klux Klan leadership to discuss tentative plans for a separate Black political state, also recognized that the NOI was beginning to lose face for not engaging in direct action. Malcolm had come to believe that "wherever black people committed themselves, in the Little Rocks and the Birminghams and other places, militantly disciplined Muslims should also be there." Yet the NOI's "general non-engagement policy" continued. Furthermore, established national leaders rebuffed Malcolm, however; King consistently characterized the Nation of Islam as one of several "extreme nationalist sects advocating black supremacy."[22] As a result, Malcolm realized that most Blacks saw the NOI as "separated from the Negro's frontline struggle."

Of course, King was aware of activist critics of nonviolence in the South as well, the most prominent being Robert F. Williams, the exiled former head of the Union County, North Carolina branch of the NAACP. Williams argued for armed self-defense in the face of racist terrorism in the apartheid South. He found himself on the run shortly after a mob of Whites met with an armed Black challenge in late August 1961. Local police charged the NAACP leader with the kidnapping of a White couple during the riot, despite the fact that his offer of refuge kept them safe from possible retaliatory violence. With the Justice Department in pursuit, Williams fled the United States, first to Canada, and later to Cuba and to China. He continued to advocate armed self-defense while in exile in broadcasts of "Radio Free Dixie" from Havana and in articles in the *Crusader.*

On the one hand, Williams contended that the "principle of self-defense is an American tradition that began at Lexington and Concord." On the other, he argued that "the average Afro-American is not a pacifist." His grassroots call for armed self-defense was a bold counterpoint to the overarching nonviolent protest strategy of most established activists of the late 1950s and early 1960s. Furthermore, the harsh condemnation of White supremacy leveled by Williams and Malcolm also forced moderates such as Wilkins to at least adopt a more militant stance with respect to local desegregation activities. Malcolm was probably correct in his assessment that younger ministers in the Nation of Islam had "made many of our people dare to get loud for the first time in 400 years."[23]

The chasm separating radical nationalists and the established leadership of the Black freedom movement remained as vast as ever, then, when Malcolm X announced his official break with the NOI and the formation of the Muslim Mosque, Inc. and the Organization of Afro-American Unity (OAAU) in March 1964. The mainstream media did nothing to bridge the ideological gap between radical nationalists and established leaders. "Violence only aggravates problems and never solves them," the editorial staff of the *Atlanta Constitution* was quick to note following clashes between police and Harlem residents in July. "We in the South have seen that truth again and again. . . ." The *Atlanta Constitution* lamented that "Negro extremists" had castigated Martin Luther King Jr. for calling for an end to the violence, despite his being considered the most popular of all Black leaders in a recent poll taken in Harlem. The editorial asserted that Malcolm X, on the other hand, "knows an emotionally boiling segment of the Negro population would rather hear him say 'there are more Negroes in America than police, and the time has come for our people to fight,' than to hear calm and reasoned proposals."[24]

Malcolm, however, did offer reasoned proposals of his own, although they probably were not what the editors of the *Constitution* had in mind. In his first public appearance since his most recent visit to Africa and the Arab world, the OAAU chairman supported the suggestion of a fellow activist at a rally at the Audubon Ballroom in Harlem that Black volunteers be sent to Mississippi as well as to the Congo. In the Congo, freedom fighters sought to oust the government of U.S.-supported Moise Tshombe, the man whose forces had overthrown popular leader Patrice Lumumba in a CIA-backed coup. "When I speak of some action for the Congo," he noted, "that also means Congo, Mississippi." Three days later he appeared on the Les Crane Show. He spoke again of the need for dialogue with moderate leaders. While stressing that no one "should be above criticism," he added, "I don't think it serves any purpose for the leaders of our people to waste their time fighting each other needlessly." Nevertheless, he continued to support the arming of Blacks in the South for self-defense "where the government has proven . . . its inability or unwillingness to protect the lives and property of our people."[25]

Malcolm developed his effort to link the struggle against white supremacy in the United States with African liberation movements in another speech, published in RAM's *Black America*. He asserted that the coming months would witness "the Negro revolt evolve and merge into the world-wide black revolution that has been taking place, on this earth, since 1945." Like Williams, however, he drew a distinction between those Blacks who operated from what he termed a "civil rights perspective" and those who embraced a broader one. Those who viewed their struggle as one for human rights and who recognized they constituted a majority in a world context had the proper frame of mind. "They look upon themselves as a part of dark mankind."[26]

One of the most significant aspects of Malcolm's multidimensional analysis during this eleventh hour of his life was that he made inextricable linkages to frontline struggles in the South. He worked at a fevered pace in part because of his desire to spread the human rights agenda of the OAAU.[27] Yet, Malcolm's efforts were also part and parcel of a larger ideological epiphany on his part. In a pivotal development, he had come to appreciate fully that frontline struggles by activists in the South had concerned fundamental human rights issues all along. As a minister with the Nation of Islam, he lambasted nonviolent direct action tactics and the established leaders who utilized them. However, he had always maintained a healthy respect for the courage and dedication of younger activists, and his speeches confirm this sense of solidarity with frontline activists from 1963 onward. Malcolm's encounters with grassroots and student activists spoke directly to this solidarity and reveal the force of a dialectical relationship that helped propel the Black Power phase of the larger freedom struggle.

On 20 December the OAAU leader shared a Harlem platform with grassroots activist and Congressional candidate Fannie Lou Hamer, of the Mississippi Freedom Democratic Party, at an afternoon rally to start a drive to remove the state's Dixiecrats from Congress. Hamer had been at the center of the MFDP's failed challenge to unseat the Mississippi "regulars" at the 1964 Democratic National Convention in Atlantic City. Hamer commented on the absence of federal protection in her native state , which had helped to account for the loss of so many lives. "They can't do a thing in the South, but when a white gets killed in the Congo," she remarked, "look what happens." Later in the rally the OAAU chairman applauded the courage and tenacity of the MFDP at the Democratic Convention. "All of these crackers belong to the Democratic Party. Johnson and Humphrey could have opened their mouths and had her seated," he said, pointing to Hamer. "Northern crackers smile in your face and knife you in the back." He continued his assault on the Democratic Party by stating that if they chose to ignore the MFDP "we'll give them something else to deal with."[28]

After the rally, Malcolm X invited Hamer and the SNCC Freedom Singers to the regular Sunday evening meeting of the OAAU at the Audubon Ballroom. He introduced Hamer as "one of the best freedom fighters in America today. She's from Mississippi, and you've got to be a freedom fighter to even live in Mississippi." He then reiterated that his organization was "solidly behind any struggle of our people for freedom." Hamer then delivered what two reporters from the *Militant*, the radical national publication of the Socialist Workers

Party, termed a "rousing, militant speech" in which she talked about her experiences during a SNCC-led visit to several African countries. "Yes, I love my African brothers and sisters," she told the audience. "I'm not only concerned about the black people of Mississippi, but about the black people of Harlem, too." After Hamer spoke, Malcolm made a point of explicitly addressing the men in the audience. Now more grounded in his recognition of women's pivotal contributions to African liberation struggles, he made an effort to gender the necessary linkages. "I hope that our brothers, especially our brothers here in Harlem, listened very well, very closely. You don't have to be a man to fight for freedom. All you have to do is be an intelligent human being."[29]

On 31 December, Malcolm addressed a delegation of thirty-seven teenagers from McComb, Mississippi whom SNCC had flown to New York City in recognition of their work as grassroots activists. The OAAU chair spoke to the young people at the Hotel Theresa for a lengthy period of time. "This generation, especially of our people, has a burden, more so than [at] any other time in history. The most important thing that we can learn to do today is think for ourselves," he told them. "How do you think I feel—and I belong to a generation ahead of you—how do you think I feel to have to tell you, 'We, my generation, sat around like a knot on a wall while the whole world was fighting for its human rights—and you've got to be born into a society where you still have that same fight.' " After pledging his continued support to the high school students, he said, "I hope you've gotten a better understanding about me. I put it to you just as plain as I know how to put it; there's no interpretation necessary."[30]

On 7 January, in a speech at the Militant Labor Forum in New York City, the OAAU chairman continued to link the struggles of Blacks in the United States with those of African freedom fighters. He condemned U.S. military activity in the Congo and in Vietnam. "What she's doing in South Vietnam is criminal," he told his largely White audience. "She's causing American soldiers to be murdered every day, killed every day . . . for no reason at all." He then shifted the focus of his remarks to domestic politics. He argued that the Civil Rights Act of 1964 was "designed to lessen the explosion" following violent protest demonstrations in Harlem, Rochester, and Philadelphia. "In 1965, even more blood will flow. More than you ever dreamed," he asserted, adding that it "will flow downtown as well as uptown. Why? Why will it flow? Have the causes that forced it to flow in '64 been removed?" Noting that the answer to that question was an obvious one, Malcolm ended his speech by asserting that the OAAU could enter into principled coalitions with Whites only if they were "willing to do as old John Brown did."[31]

In a 28 January radio interview on New York City's WBAI-FM, the OAAU leader discussed his plans to bring the oppression of U.S. Blacks before the General Assembly of the United Nations. He elaborated on the perceived distinction between civil rights and human rights in international law and politics. "Human rights are international," he asserted. "Human rights are something that a man has by dint of being born." He contended that most leaders of African and Asian governments had adopted a hands-off approach toward the African American freedom struggle because they considered it a "domestic" issue. As had become the case increasingly, Malcolm also stressed that the OAAU would "support fully and without compromise" a progressive intraracial coalition among various political organizations. "I'm for anything that they're involved in that gets meaningful results for the masses of our people—but not for the benefit of a few hand-picked Negroes at the top who get prestige and credit, and all the while the masses' problems remain unsolved."[32]

Less than a week later, Malcolm left for Alabama, where students at Tuskegee Institute had invited him to give a lecture. SNCC workers, who had been actively engaged along with SCLC forces in the voting rights campaign in nearby Selma, looked forward to the OAAU leader's arrival. Malcolm had been fond of saying that SNCC was his "favorite Civil Rights organization," and he had enjoyed spending time with Hamer and the SNCC Freedom Singers in December. Activist intellectual James Baldwin, who on one occasion moderated a radio program with Malcolm and a student activist, noted that he "talked to him as though he were talking to a younger brother, and with that same watchful attention."[33]

■ ■ ■

Malcolm X had met briefly with Black student organizers a few months earlier in Africa. In keeping with the spirit of the 1964 Fisk conference on Black nationalism, a delegation of ten veteran SNCC organizers traveled to Africa along with MFDP stalwart Fannie Lou Hamer in September to chart the progress of anti-colonial liberation struggles taking place there. The group spent a great deal of time in the newly independent country of Guinea as guests of its president, Sekou Toure. SNCC executive secretary James Forman recalled that in "the United States we were strangers in a foreign land. We were separated from our people. We belonged here in Mother Africa, helping to build the continent of our brothers and sisters." The time in Guinea, which had adopted socialism but remained a part of the growing nonaligned bloc of African countries, led Forman to assert that the West African nation was "the antithesis of everything to which we had been exposed in the United States."[34]

During their visit, SNCC chair John Lewis and staff member Donald Harris had a chance meeting with Malcolm X at the airport in Nairobi. The OAAU, which took its name from the Organization of African Unity, formed in 1963, seemed to have made an impression on the Africans. Apparently, a number of people had inquired about "SNCC's relationship with the Organization of Afro-American Unity," and not vice versa. According to a report the two SNCC workers wrote documenting their travels, the OAAU leader "felt that the presence of SNCC in Africa was very important and that this was a significant and crucial aspect of the 'human rights struggle' that the American civil rights groups had too long neglected."[35]

Arguably, the most substantive contact between SNCC organizers and Malcolm X took place in February 1965—the month of his assassination—during the voting rights struggle in Selma, Alabama. Thousands of activists, including SCLC president Martin Luther King Jr. and former COAHR leader Larry Fox, were behind bars in what would become the last high-profile protest battle prior to the formal demise of disfranchisement, a key component of apartheid in the United States. Tensions were high between SNCC and SCLC staffers, however, as a growing number of younger activists questioned high-visibility protest demonstrations in lieu of grassroots organizing. Silas Norman, SNCC project director in Selma, later noted that SNCC activists were "becoming more radicalized through our experiences" in the field. Norman had visited several African consulates in New York City as part of his own search for answers. "We were looking to Africa," he noted. "We were looking to other voices in the Black community to give us some support for the direction in which we thought we needed to move."[36]

At an informal meeting, SNCC organizers decided that Norman and relative newcomer Fay Bellamy would travel to Tuskegee to invite Malcolm X to return with them to speak to young activists. On Thursday, 3 February, they arrived on the Tuskegee Institute campus just as the OAAU chairman had begun speaking. "If they had had rafters, people would have been hanging from them," Bellamy recalled of the crowd of several thousand students who jammed a campus auditorium. Malcolm spoke again of the ongoing Congo crisis and asserted that Moise Tshombe would not remain in power long without outside assistance. "When he doesn't get support from white racist mercenaries, the United States has to increase the number of its own soldiers." Bellamy was particularly impressed by Malcolm's patience in fielding questions for nearly three hours following his speech. "One of the things that was wonderful about Malcolm," she noted, "was that he took his time. He answered questions. He was thoughtful and thought-provoking."[37]

Following the question-and-answer session Malcolm agreed to head back to Selma with the two SNCC workers the next morning. "He was a very imposing, calm, and persuasive individual," Norman remembered. "Really, it was awesome to be in his presence." As they talked informally, Bellamy, who had spent some time in New York City after leaving her native state of Pennsylvania, asked him about a mutual acquaintance of hers and Betty Shabazz, Malcolm's wife. " 'She's doing fine, but she'd be doing better if she were down here doing what you're doing,' " she recalled him saying. His words were uplifting because "we had heard so many times that people in the Nation of Islam, or people who were in the Black nationalist movement, thought we were wasting our time, or being stupid," Bellamy said. "So when this brother whom I admired so much said this of someone I knew he loved as a friend, it meant a lot to me." In all, the OAAU leader spoke to Norman and Bellamy for nearly an hour that night at the Tuskegee Guest House. Bellamy recalled that "little doors were clicking in my head—just opening up. This man has so much sense. And when he was talking to you it would just create thought. I've since talked to several people who say they felt a similar kind of thing when talking with Malcolm."[38]

On Friday, SNCC organizers did what they could to shield Malcolm from journalists before his speaking engagement at Brown's Chapel A.M.E. Church. With three thousand arrests and Martin Luther King Jr. still in jail, the Selma area had been deluged by reporters from around the world. When journalists finally spotted the OAAU leader, Bellamy and Norman arranged for a brief press conference. Malcolm stated that he needed to get a "good, closer look" at the situation in the South in order to more effectively "represent the plight of the Black man" at a conference of African organizations in London that weekend. When asked about his relationship with King, he asserted that those in power "would do well to listen to Dr. Martin Luther King and give him what he's asking for, and give it to him fast, before some other factions come along and try to do it another way." He made it clear that there was no disagreement regarding the specific objectives of the voting rights campaign in Alabama. "What he's asking for is right. That's the ballot," Malcolm noted. "And if he can't get it the way he's trying to get it, then it's going to be gotten, one way or the other."[39]

Journalists refused to leave the matter alone, however, and they pressed him for clarification, especially with regard to his position on nonviolent direct action. "I don't believe in any kind of nonviolence," he responded initially. "I believe that it's right to be nonviolent with people who are nonviolent. But when you're dealing with an enemy who doesn't know what nonviolence is, as far as I'm concerned you're wasting your time." As SNCC workers rushed to get the OAAU chairman away from the journalists he offered words of solidarity for those who had placed their lives on the line in Selma and refused to condemn outright the tactical use of nonviolence. He asserted that "Dr. King and his followers are very intelligently" attempting to realize their aims. Yet, as was often his fashion, Malcolm X also stated that if Whites were not "intelligent enough" to respond favorably, "then I think the intelligence of the Black people in this area will compel them to devise another method that will get results."[40]

Once inside the church, SCLC organizers quizzed Malcolm about his upcoming speech, obviously concerned about what he might tell the teenagers in attendance. Bellamy recalled that Andrew Young and James Bevel "got flustered" when they first received word that Malcolm had agreed to come to Selma, and they questioned him as though "he'd came to start a revolution overnight." Young made certain to place Malcolm between Bevel and Fred Shuttlesworth on the program, but SNCC activists won a key victory by introducing him. In his speech, Malcolm focused on the need to contextualize the Southern struggle internationally, once again raising the issue of the Congo crisis. As he neared the conclusion of his speech he noted with a smile that "I hope I haven't put anybody on the spot. I'm not intending to try and stir you up and make you do something that you wouldn't have done anyway." When the laughter and applause that filled the sanctuary subsided, he continued. "I pray that God will bless you in everything you do. I pray that you will grow intellectually, so that you can understand the problems of the world and where you fit into . . . that world picture." Finally, he applauded the students for their courage in the face of White terrorists who chose in cowardice to conceal their identities. "The time will come when that sheet will be ripped off," he stated. "If the federal government doesn't take it off, we'll take it off."[41]

Coretta Scott King arrived at Brown's Chapel to speak shortly after Malcolm had finished his well-received speech. The OAAU leader reassured her that he had not intended to make her husband's work there more difficult than it already had been. "I really did come thinking that I could make it easier," he told her. "If the white people realize what the alternative is, perhaps they will be more willing to hear Dr. King." She had been impressed by his "obvious intelligence" and noted that "he seemed quite gentle" as he spoke to her. Norman and Bellamy talked informally with Malcolm a final time as they drove him to the airport in Montgomery, the only other cars on the cordoned-off highway being state police cruisers. Bellamy recalled that he told them, " 'I want to come South. We're thinking about coming South to help you-all do this work. Would SNCC work with us?' " Bellamy's response was swift indeed. "Are you kidding? I know they'll work with you." Norman agreed. "Certainly, we felt that we had a lot of support from him, even if he disagreed with some of the tactics that we had used up to that point," he recalled. "We had every feeling that there was a sense of solidarity within the movement."[42]

Malcolm X did not return to the South. Several gunmen who claimed an affiliation with the Nation of Islam assassinated the OAAU chairman as he spoke at a meeting at the Audubon Ballroom on 21 February. The *Atlanta Daily World* published two editorials after the assassination. In "Violence Begets Violence," the publication asserted that while "we unequivocally disagreed" with Malcolm X's nationalism and advocacy of armed self-defense, "we deplore his ruthless killing and hope those responsible will be brought to justice." In a rather curious statement, the Black newspaper also contended that assassinating "persons because of their opinions is not the American way." In a second editorial, the *Daily World* reiterated its opposition to "Malcolm X's philosophy of racism to the extreme point" but suggested that other more moderate Black leaders might be in danger as well.[43]

Henry Lee Moon, public relations director of the NAACP, was even less charitable in his assessment of the slain Muslim minister in the *Crisis*. Moon asserted that Malcolm X was no original thinker. "His militant call for armed self-defense but echoed [David] Walker's stirring 'Appeal' of 1829. His advocacy of Pan-Africanism followed W. E. B. DuBois by a half century." Although the OAAU chairman had not been a minister under Elijah Muhammad for nearly one year, the NAACP public relations director also cited several polls taken by mainstream publications such as the *New York Times* and *Newsweek* indicating disapproval of the Nation of Islam in the African American community as proof of Malcolm's limited influence. Moon correctly noted that the mainstream media, "while deploring him editorially," promoted him in news stories because he was "good copy." He contended that White reporters, specifically, clung to the OAAU leader's every word and even "experienced a masochistic orgy" in the process. Finally, Moon argued that while Malcolm X voiced Black frustrations, "he failed utterly to comprehend or voice the Negro's aspirations. He did not seem to understand what the Negro in America really wants."[44]

Others who had been placed squarely in opposition to the slain OAAU leader offered kinder words. Perhaps it was because, as Coretta Scott King later noted, Martin Luther King Jr. and Malcolm X "had talked together on occasion and had discussed their philosophies in a friendly way," that the SCLC president sent an immediate telegram to Betty Shabazz to express his condolences. Perhaps it was because the thirty-six-year-old King, himself only three years younger than the slain OAAU leader, had to come to terms once again with the possibility of his own assassination. Whatever the case, he wrote Shabazz. "While we did not always see eye to eye on methods to solve the race problem, I always had a deep affection for Malcolm and felt that he had a great ability to put his finger on the existence and root of the problem." Coretta Scott King would later note that the assassination of the OAAU leader "affected me personally. Perhaps it was because I had begun to understand him better."[45]

■ ■ ■

As was the case for a significant number of Blacks, freedom school project director Gwendolyn Robinson did not become familiar with Malcolm X until after his assassination. Not long after White terrorists firebombed the Laurel, Mississippi duplex that SNCC organizers shared with a local Black family, Robinson received a record of a Malcolm X speech from a friend. "I had never heard him before in my life. I didn't even know anything about the Nation of Islam growing up in Memphis. I was totally unaware of them," she recalled. "And when I heard Malcolm—in Mississippi, on a little record player—I was like, 'Oh my God! Oh God! Oh God!' There was a man saying stuff that just electrified me. I said, 'This is the truth, the unadulterated truth.' " Robinson left Mississippi in November 1965, "disheartened and angry" on the one hand, and yet buoyed and hopeful on the other.[46] Like a number of frontline SNCC organizers, she found herself undergoing a key ideological transformation within the crucible of the Black human rights struggle. At the heart of this process was an effort to come to terms with the principle of self-determination and what that meant for Blacks locally, nationally and globally. For Robinson and several other SNCC organizers, the most intriguing site for the realization of this process would be the rigidly segregated and economically starved Black neighborhoods of Atlanta.

CHAPTER FOUR

THE ATLANTA PROJECT OF
THE STUDENT NONVIOLENT
COORDINATING COMMITTEE

During the winter holidays of December 1965, veteran SNCC workers Charles Cobb and Gwendolyn Robinson returned to the Atlanta national office from work in the field, as did relative newcomer Michael Simmons. Indeed, Atlanta represented a way station for most SNCC organizers. "Regardless of how bad things may have been in Atlanta, you always felt safe when you got there," Simmons said, "because I was scared out there in the field." Robinson's eighteen-month stint as project director of the Laurel, Mississippi freedom school had been traumatic. "I was in really bad shape," she recalled of the psychological toll that the threat and reality of terrorist violence had taken on her. SNCC executive secretary James Forman suggested that she spend some time in the group's New York City office to relieve some stress while maximizing fundraising skills she had honed in Mississippi. "I might have become a mental vegetable if he hadn't got me out of there," Robinson noted. "I was in such bad shape." After less than a month in New York, however, Robinson found herself in Atlanta for a holiday staff meeting with several members of the organization's executive committee, including John Lewis, Forman, and Ruby Doris Robinson.[1]

Everyone at the Atlanta staff meeting debated the idea of drafting a statement critiquing U.S foreign policy in general and military involvement in Vietnam and the Dominican Republic specifically. SNCC workers had raised the issue of Vietnam in 1964 in McComb, Mississippi, but had yet to do so in a national statement. Some objected to the idea, but for strategic reasons— namely, that drafting such a statement was likely to alienate the group from potential funding sources. Nevertheless, those present in Atlanta decided to move forward with an antiwar statement. On 6 January 1966, SNCC chair John Lewis, who had been classified as a conscientious objector, held a press conference in which he read the statement aloud. "The Student Nonviolent Coordinating Committee has a right and a responsibility to dissent with United

States foreign policy on any issue when it sees fit," Lewis pronounced. He stated that SNCC was "in sympathy" with those men who refused "to contribute their lives to United States aggression in Viet Nam in the name of the 'freedom' we find so false in this country."[2]

SNCC contended that the federal government had deceived the public regarding the situation in Vietnam while it refused to guarantee freedom for oppressed people in this country. "We take note of the fact that sixteen percent of the draftees from this country are Negroes called on to stifle the liberation of Viet Nam, to preserve a 'democracy' which does not exist for them at home." Lewis continued, asking, "Where is the draft for the freedom fight in the United States?" The statement contended that participation in the Vietnam War was in violation of international law, that the United States was "no respector [sic] of persons or law when such persons or laws run counter to its needs and desires." Clearly, the recent cold-blooded killing of a SNCC organizer who attempted to use a segregated restroom by a White gas station attendant had affected the organization in a profound way. "The murder of Samuel Young in Tuskegee, Alabama is no different than the murder of peasants in Viet Nam," Lewis read to an uneasy press contingent, "for both Young and the Vietnamese sought, and are seeking, to secure the rights guaranteed them by law."[3]

Word of the SNCC antiwar statement spread like an awful rumor throughout Atlanta. "It was like we had burned something down," Simmons remembered. When SNCC information director Julian Bond—who also happened to be the representative-elect for the 136th District of the Georgia Legislature—arrived at the airport from a trip out of town, a throng of reporters bombarded him with questions concerning the statement and his relationship to it. Bond, who had yet to read the statement, responded as a matter of principle that he agreed "fully" with it. He added that while he would not destroy his own, he "would admire the courage of anyone who burns his draft card."[4]

The next few days were frenzied for the twenty-five-year-old Bond, SNCC organizers and attorneys, and White state legislators who intended to do whatever was necessary to deny the young representative-elect his seat in the Statehouse. State legislator Jones Lane led the charge, arguing that "anyone who gives aid or comfort to enemies of the United States or to the enemies of Georgia" was "guilty of treason." Some SNCC workers were afraid for Bond's safety on Monday, 10 January, the day that the state's elected officials took their oaths. State law allowed for legislators to bring weapons inside the Capitol, and the response from politicians like Lane had been vitriolic. "Julian was scared to death and I don't blame him," Simmons recalled. Bond remained seated during the morning session as one by one, every other legislator took his or her oath of office. Fortunately, the only weapons White legislators brandished that day were five petitions calling for Bond's ouster. Black state representatives J. C. Daugherty, William H. Alexander, and former COAHR activist Benjamin Brown spoke on Bond's behalf at a special committee hearing, as did Black state senators Leroy Johnson and Horace Ward. House Speaker George T. Smith claimed that Daugherty "made one of the finest pleas for a lost cause I've ever heard." The eleventh-hour effort was to no avail, however, as the committee voted twenty-three to three not to seat Bond.[5]

Smith then called for a full vote on the matter. The Georgia House voted 184–12 not to seat Bond. Black legislators, including former Urban League stalwart Grace Towns Hamilton, supported Bond, as did several White colleagues from the Fulton and DeKalb county delegations. SNCC attorney Howard Moore declared that the issue at hand was Bond's "right to make a statement, his right to dissent." Moore added that the SNCC information director "has no unAmerican attitudes" and "has not engaged in any treasonable activities." Bond, who appeared composed yet weary, read a prepared statement. "I hesitate to offer explanations for my actions or deeds, for no charge has been levied other than the charge that I have chosen to speak my mind, and no explanation is called for, for no member of the House has ever, to my knowledge, been called upon to explain his public statements or public postures as a prerequisite to admission to that body."[6]

Thus, Bond was denied a seat inside the state Capitol for the second time. On the first occasion, in 1962, state police had removed him and fellow activists from the Committee on Appeal for Human Rights after they had tried unsuccessfully to desegregate the gallery inside the building. Now he could enter the Capitol, but even as a newly elected state representative his politics continued to prevent him from taking his rightful seat. Activists from SNCC and SCLC joined forces to prepare for a march and rally on Thursday to galvanize support for Bond. That was a promising sign, given tensions between leaders of the two groups concerning tactics during the voter registration campaign in Selma. The issue of Bond's ouster was fairly clear-cut, however, even if most SCLC officials did not agree, at least publicly, with his position on the Vietnam War.

The 14 January demonstration at the state Capitol began, as had so many earlier protests in the city, with a convergence of marches from other points in Atlanta. Horace Mann Bond, dean of education at Atlanta University and Julian's father, led one contingent from Ebenezer Baptist Church on Auburn Avenue. The other contingent, headed by student activists, approached downtown from the Atlanta University Center. By the time Martin Luther King Jr. began speaking, over fifteen hundred people had assembled on the Capitol lawn. King delivered what Simmons termed "a masterful speech," replete with metaphors regarding "the foxholes of Mississippi and trenches of Alabama." And he praised the front-line activists of SNCC, asserting that its "workers have moved in a meaningful orbit." He noted that "they have worked all over the Southland and all over the nation . . . by standing up for what is best in the American Dream." The Ebenezer co-pastor ended his remarks by leading the exuberant crowd in a chant, "We want Julian Bond. We want Julian Bond."[7]

Not long after King's speech and the apparent end of the rally, a group of SNCC workers began marching around the Capitol. As the breakaway contingent completed its third trip around the building, Willie Ricks (Mukasa Dada), a key organizer in the SNCC campaign in Americus, Georgia the previous summer, led a surprise charge of over one dozen pickets up the steps of the south entrance of the Capitol. Protesters used umbrellas and signs as they exchanged blows with state troopers in a melee that left two policemen and one demonstrator injured. When police jostled a female demonstrator during the course of the scuffle, she used her purse to club two officers, including state Director of Public Safety Lowell Conner. Not long after the initial rush, state police were able to get the upper hand, pushing the protesters backward and sending several tumbling down the steps. After SNCC workers regained their equilibrium, they ran directly across the street and entered the City Hall lobby, where they sang "We Shall Overcome" and "You Can Do It, Julian Bond, You Can Do It."[8]

The SNCC assault had taken more than a few folks off-guard, including Martin Luther King. The SCLC president, who had already left the scene, noted that he was "hurt and shocked" by word that the demonstration had "degenerated into violence." Although police made no arrests, many SCLC activists contended that more than enough damage had been done. For obvious reasons, King "wanted it to be orderly. But SNCC had to do something like this," a highly agitated SCLC aide declared. "This is it—as far as Dr. King is concerned. There wouldn't have been much of a march if Dr. King had not decided to get into this controversy."[9] The man at the center of that controversy, Julian Bond, had not been present at any of the day's activities.

SNCC workers Judy Richardson and Ivanhoe Donaldson had organized Bond's successful grassroots electoral campaign during the spring, but had since left Atlanta for other projects. That left Bond with no campaign apparatus for a late February special election to fill his empty seat. Although Bond, Moore, and American Civil Liberties Union (ACLU) regional director Charles Morgan Jr. all anticipated an eventual victory in the federal courts, they also realized that no court would decide the matter in such a short period of time. Given the vacuum left by the departure of Richardson and Donaldson, several SNCC workers—including those involved in drafting the antiwar statement—took it upon themselves to organize a second campaign for Bond.[10]

Even though Bond's competitors in the earlier campaign had agreed not to run against him in the special election, Moore still stressed the need for a large turnout at the polls. With that in mind, Dwight Williams designed a number of leaflets calling attention to the issues in what had become a one-man race. SNCC organizers were out at bus stops and coffee shops at five each morning armed with leaflets and other literature. Simmons recalled, however, that Bond did not take part in this aspect of the process. "Julian didn't know any of us," he noted. "Julian never participated with us in this campaign."[11] Nevertheless, the constituents of the solidly Black 136th District came to the polls in impressive fashion, with over 80 percent of registered voters casting their ballots for Bond.

Throughout the reelection campaign, several SNCC activists had discussed the possibility of launching an urban project that would extend beyond the special election. Near the end of February 1966, SNCC formally launched the Vine City Project, although it quickly came to be called the Atlanta Project. The co-directors of the Atlanta Project were seasoned SNCC activists Gwendolyn Robinson and Bill Ware. Roughly ten years older than most SNCC activists, Ware had been born and raised in rural Mississippi. In Atlanta while en route to a freedom school headed by South Carolina activist Septima Clark, Ware also had agreed to help coordinate Bond's reelection campaign. Robinson, a Memphis native and former director of the freedom school project in Laurel, Mississippi, had notified James Forman that she wanted to return to the South from New York. Aware of her strength as a fundraiser, Forman tried to talk her out of it. "But I was clear that I wanted to return to the 'Southern Theater,' as it were," Robinson later recalled. "And the idea of being in Atlanta, where it was a different kind of work, was very appealing to me."[12]

■ ■ ■

The Atlanta Project has been one of the most undervalued groups in the scholarly discussion of the Black freedom movement.[13] There are several explanations for this oversight. One, the Project's brash activists became embroiled early on in a heated organizational struggle with members of the SNCC executive committee that lasted throughout the urban field project's one-year existence. Two, members of the Project were among the most strident proponents of the exclusion of Whites from the organization, a controversial political line that has caused some scholars, if only implicitly, to dismiss the group out of hand. Three, because of the early demise of the Project, its activists did not receive the media—and as a consequence, scholarly—attention that subsequently engulfed charismatic male members of the SNCC executive committee, as well as Black Power groups such as the Black Panther Party and the US Organization. A reexamination of the evidence confirms, however, that the Atlanta Project was highly significant in that city and beyond. Project activists helped provide a framework for the burgeoning Black Power movement. As significant, Project activists sought, largely through activism on the ground, to come to terms with fundamental questions of Black self-determination at the local, national, and international level, further enriching the meaning of the global Black struggle for human rights.

Atlanta Project activists argued for a redefinition of the Black freedom struggle that focused on the possibilities of grassroots urban organizing. They drafted a prospectus for future work during the reelection campaign. The prospectus asserted that the refusal to seat Bond "dramatized the urgent importance" of organizing urban Southern Blacks around a multitude of issues. Focusing on voter registration exclusively, especially in a city such as Atlanta, where the majority of eligible Blacks were already registered, was not enough. Instead, the authors of the prospectus argued that "a program of political organization and education" was necessary to convince "even the poorest person in the Negro community that politics holds out the possibility of achieving human dignity and economic justice."[14] If Project activists were shortsighted in diminishing the significance of voter registration efforts—for SNCC organizers worked in certain South Atlanta neighborhoods precisely for that purpose as early as 1963—they were astute in highlighting the continued political marginalization of the Black working poor. Project activists also recognized that political work in urban areas posed new questions for activists in the post-petty-apartheid South. After establishing their base of operations at "Freedom House," a two-bedroom apartment on 69 Electric Avenue in Vine City, a rigidly segregated poor and working-class Black neighborhood, Project activists held a number of meetings in which they discussed the best ways to confront the challenges of urban organizing. "We lived together. We worked together," Robinson recalled. "We were constantly chewing these issues over."[15] After a great deal of discussion, Project organizers turned their attention to the issue of basic living conditions for poor Black families in Vine City.

SNCC activists took affidavits from tenants who lived in dilapidated buildings owned by a White landlord in the Markham Street area of the neighborhood. Elotse Daniel, a thirteen-year-old girl who lived with her family in the Markham Street Hotel, remarked that health department officials insisted that "our place wasn't decent enough for a rat to live in even though they do. It's their house. The rats are almost bigger than my doll." Rat infestation had become such a problem that Elotse recalled being bitten by one during the night. "We don't have an icebox to put food in and we put it under the metal tub, but there is some kind of way the rats get it and rip it open." Another area resident, seventeen-year-old Jacqueline Louise Dewberry, asserted that her infant son died of pneumonia because of the abysmal living conditions. "I feel he got sick because of the house. There are holes in the floor, cracks up under the building, and all," she said. "You couldn't keep too much heat in." Robert Lee Edwards, a twenty-three-year-old laborer who lived in a two-room apartment with the other seven members of his family, told SNCC workers that "we have to wear coats" inside during the winter. "The door is torn halfway so it doesn't shut right. One day, I had to kill a snake in there," he remarked. "The floor has holes and it is partly rotten. I'm afraid it will fall in."[16]

Landlord Joe Shafer owned numerous properties in the area. SNCC activists charged that he had established "a plantation-like system" akin to the sharecropping culture of the rural South, and that he served "as landlord, employer, grocer, creditor, sheriff, judge, and jury." Residents noted that he often cashed their welfare checks for them, extended credit at 50 percent interest, and offered low-wage temporary employment that could just as easily be taken away. A number of residents complained that Shafer had warned them not to speak with SNCC workers or activists from the Vine City Council unless they intended to be evicted. The affidavit contended that a number of Markham Street families had been "living in fear" of the reputed slumlord. "They have never known any legal relief from his rule; they have never known that his power could be restrained." During the bitter winter, area residents began holding meetings and agreed to launch a rent strike. SNCC workers and other community activists organized support for the tenants, including providing food, blankets, and alternative housing for those who faced eviction.[17]

The crisis soon captured the attention of Vine City's most celebrated resident, Martin Luther King Jr. The neighborhood had been home to Martin Luther and Coretta Scott King and their young children since they left Montgomery in 1960. When the Southern Christian Leadership Conference (SCLC) president toured some of the most impoverished areas of the segregated neighborhood, he admitted that the conditions were worse than those in the tenements of Chicago, where he and other SCLC activists had begun a bitter campaign against segregated housing the previous summer. King visited the Markham Hotel and quickly came to understand why residents such as young Elotse Daniel had dubbed it "Heartbreak Hotel." Realizing the need for action, but unaware perhaps of the grassroots organizing already taking place, King also suggested that the families organize a rent strike. "This is appalling," he observed. "I had no idea people were living in Atlanta, Georgia in such conditions. This is a shame on the community."[18]

Yet, as Project activists gathered evidence against the slumlord and helped spark a grassroots rent strike movement, they also angered many Vine City residents by targeting a White tenants' rights activist. Hector Black, a charismatic White priest with a degree from Harvard who had obtained federal anti-poverty funding to work in the downtown neighborhood, quickly began to raise the ire of several Black SNCC organizers. The young Quaker activist had earned the respect of a number of Blacks in the neighborhood, including the members of the Vine City Improvement Association. Indeed, most residents who submitted affidavits to the Atlanta Project mentioned Hector Black by name. In their newspaper, Nitty Gritty, Atlanta Project activists contemptuously called Black a "white Jesus" and made it known that they wanted him to work in a working-class White neighborhood. Hector Black did leave the neighborhood eventually, and Project members remained. Simmons suggested that part of the problem was that they "were in competition" with the

White activist. Yet, there was more to the lambasting of Hector Black than turf rivalry. Simmons asserted that SNCC activists had been bothered by what they perceived to be a condescending attitude on the part of Black, that he was "an obscene white liberal" who "gloried in the adulation of Black folks who were so grateful to have his white largess."[19]

■ ■ ■

The controversy surrounding Hector Black prefigured an initiative by Black activists to attack white skin privilege both within the Black freedom movement generally and in SNCC specifically. A growing number of Black SNCC workers began reassessing the relationships of Black and White activists to the larger African American struggle for human rights. When Fay Bellamy went to the SNCC office in New York City in 1964 she received an application from a courteous White worker. "I thought about it and threw it in the waste basket," although she had no problem with the woman personally. "I was very upset because she was White and she was giving me an application to a Black movement." Robinson had a similar experience in New York following her work in Mississippi. She had not anticipated that the Manhattan office would be overwhelmingly White. "When I saw that, it shocked me. I said, 'Oh, my God!' "[20]

One of the most vexing issues for Black organizers, particularly those in the rural South, concerned racial deference patterns that illustrated the pervasiveness of white skin privilege. Robinson had to confront the issue on a daily basis as a SNCC project director when local Blacks came to the project office. "If they were to come into the office and didn't know anybody, they would always go to the White person and say, "Can you help me? Do you know about this?" " She stressed that such a pattern might not be "a big deal to our understanding now, but back then it was often *painful*." While doing work in another Mississippi location, Simmons also had been deeply troubled "by how deferential Black folks were to Whites in the project." Like most Black organizers, he understood that Blacks in besieged communities were grateful to see young Whites risking their lives. Nevertheless, Simmons asserted that White SNCC workers had operated from a "more protected context" and had more resources at their disposal than did Blacks who were risking their lives as well. "It disturbed me to see that these Black folks didn't realize that they were both my teacher as well as the White folks' teacher," Simmons recalled, "and they were acting like the White folks were their teachers."[21]

The attitudes of a significant number of White SNCC activists contributed to the problem. Robinson had become increasingly frustrated with the need for "ongoing sensitivity training" for White activists who wanted to work with local Blacks. "You don't call them by their first names when they're older than your parents. You don't treat them like this." Now, back in Atlanta, Robinson also had to contend with certain White organizers who "saw themselves as a brain trust" within the national office. "In several instances I can remember being personally pushed around by Whites who were in leadership positions," Robinson said. "I was there thinking, 'This is my organization, and you're taking it over.'" Atlanta Project activists began to openly question the soundness of continuing to place White workers in projects that served the needs of Black communities throughout the South when practically no substantive work was being done in White communities. "When someone gets shot, someone chases the killer and someone heals the wounded," Simmons noted. "If everyone is just healing the wounded, then the people are going to go on shooting."[22]

The debate over white skin privilege was inextricably bound to the larger attempt by Project staff members to forge a Black consciousness movement within SNCC. Several Project workers already had engaged in consciousness-raising activities at freedom schools and other venues in Mississippi. Robinson and Bill Ware led a number of taped discussions that revolved around "our trying to understand, 'Where do we go from here? How do we run a movement when people have been brainwashed?'" Project activists met regularly at Freedom House, studied transcripts, and read a range of political education materials. Robinson noted that this "long and arduous process" led to the conclusion "that Whites needed to work in the White community, which is where the problems lie." Project activists considered parallel organizing for Blacks and Whites as just one component of an agenda for organizational self-determination. Robinson noted that Black SNCC organizers increasingly confronted White activists, asserting that "'you people cannot tell us how to run our movement, or what we should desire'" precisely because "'we need to be in charge of our own destiny.'"[23]

After receiving input from other Project organizers, Ware, Donald Stone, and RAM activist Roland Snellings (Askia Muhammad Toure) presented position papers at a volatile March 1966 SNCC staff meeting in which they raised the specific issue of Black self-determination.[24] Although Project workers had also drafted position papers on propaganda and organizing in urban areas, the Black consciousness papers generated all the heat. The principal paper (I), which focused more on the dynamics of the Project itself, argued that Whites should leave because a "climate has to be created whereby Blacks can express themselves." The paper acknowledged past contributions that Whites had made in frontline activism, especially in Mississippi. However, it asserted that the "efforts one is trying to achieve cannot succeed because whites have an intimidating effect." This level of intimidation was "in direct proportion to the amount of degradation that Black people have suffered at the hands of white people." The paper also contended that many grassroots Blacks considered Whites "the 'brains' behind the Movement."[25]

Instead of working in African American communities, the authors of the Black consciousness papers argued, White activists belonged where racism "is most manifest." Progressive Whites would have to focus their energy in White communities, the places where power and privilege had been utilized "for the express purpose of denying Blacks human dignity and self-determination." One of two supporting papers (II and III) contended that the "sensitive white intellectual and radical" could no longer seek "to escape the horrible reality of America by going into Black communities and attempting to organize Black people while neglecting the organization of their own people's racist communities." The issue had become a fundamental one. "How can one clean up someone else's yard when one's own yard is untidy?" The principal position paper further contended that the entire notion of interracial coalition building to effect larger societal changes was "meaningless . . . because of the lack of organization in the white communities."[26]

The Atlanta Project activists saw the driving force behind the position papers as a move "towards self-determination." In framing their argument they continued to develop an international perspective, linking domestic struggle with liberation movements in Africa. Position Paper III asked, "what part did the white colonizers play in the liberation of independent African nations; who were the agitators for African independence?" Explorations of those questions "compel us to believe that our struggle for liberation and self-determination can only be carried out effectively by Black people." The effort to link global African struggles required a reassessment of identity. The SNCC workers condemned "the systematic destruction of our links to Africa" and contended that Blacks were no longer "willing to align themselves with a western culture that daily emasculates our beauty, our pride and our manhood." (The explicit focus on manhood revealed that the call for a cultural break with the dominant society often included a concern for restoring Black men's place in that society's patriarchy.)[27]

According to Atlanta Project workers, the most tangible means of realizing organizational self-determination and contributing to the worldwide movements of African people involved complete Black control of SNCC. "In contrast, SCLC has a staff that at least maintains a Black facade," the primary paper noted. "The front office is virtually all-Black, but nobody accuses SCLC of being 'racist.'" Whites never played much of a role in the SCLC, which drew its strength from the resources of the autonomous Black Christian churches. The key issue for the radical nationalists in SNCC was "true liberation," which for them meant that Blacks would have to "form our own institutions, credit unions, co-ops, political parties, write our own histories." Black consciousness paper number I did assert, however, that Whites could "participate on a voluntary basis. We can contract work out to them, but in no way can they participate on a policy-making level."[28]

■ ■ ■

The debate over the Black consciousness papers has served to obscure other thoughtful Atlanta Project position papers. One essay, "The Necessity for Southern Urban Organizing," argued that doing organizing work in southwest Georgia without focusing on the state capital—"the largest and most important city in the state"—was a critical mistake because those in power escaped a serious challenge from "radical opposition." Organizing in Atlanta would expose fundamental contradictions in the city's political economy, just as the earlier sit-in protests had done. "We don't want to suggest that any city in this country has great race relations, but certainly Atlanta's aren't so 'great,' when you have Negroes, whose median income is about $3,000 a year, living in wooden shacks way up in the air on four wobbly legs, while whites have a median income of $6,000."[29]

Another important position paper written by Project workers grew out of their work with beleaguered Vine City residents. In that essay, SNCC activists called for the creation of a "Poor People's Housing Community." The activists contended that organizing protests against slumlords "is not enough," noting that several organizations had challenged horrid living conditions in places like the Markham Hotel "only to have the city jump in, condemn the buildings, and move all of the tenants to public housing projects." Project organizers proposed a leafleting campaign raising basic questions about the state's relationship to private housing. Project activists intended to ask why the only option facing most poor residents who wanted better living conditions was "some cheerless, box-like housing project," and why the government encouraged the building of expensive private homes but discouraged quality low-income private housing, noting that building contractors "are given better loans and tax allowances" on the former. A key problem for the SNCC workers was that city officials planned the "indiscriminate destruction" of certain neighborhoods as a solution to the housing crisis, thus destroying "all of the ties that have developed over the years among families in the neighborhood."[30]

Project activists also wrote a position paper about Nitty Gritty, their eight-page newspaper. "We intend to tell it like it is," they declared, "we intend to speak to 22 million forgotten children; we intend to deliver a message of hope and inspiration." The three-person staff of Nitty Gritty intended to develop the newspaper into a vehicle of "protest and dissent that will rival any street demonstration." They also envisioned a practical side to the newspaper, allowing Atlanta Blacks to develop writing and publishing skills. In addition to carrying news articles chronicling the struggles of Blacks from throughout the global African world, the staff intended to run weekly educational feature stories that would not only serve to "inspire our people with the strength and beauty of their past," but would point to "real possibilities in the future—if they themselves will act!"[31]

These other essays did not receive the attention they deserved precisely because "all hell broke loose" at the meeting following the presentation of the Black consciousness essays. Members of the SNCC national office, including executive secretary James Forman and field secretary Stokely Carmichael, opposed the call for a wholesale dismissal of Whites, even if they were themselves influenced by the budding nationalist sentiment. The argument that Whites should work in White communities was raised at a national SNCC meeting less than two months later near Nashville. Although Atlanta Project activists did not attend the turbulent 8 May meeting at Kingston Springs, it had become fairly clear that the arguments raised in the earlier staff meeting reflected a near-consensus among Black SNCC workers. The impact of nationalism on SNCC would be felt nationwide when Willie Ricks and Carmichael raised the "Black Power" cry during the March Against Fear in Mississippi later in the summer. The irony was not lost on Michael Simmons and other Atlanta Project workers, for they had been criticized only months beforehand for making an explicit argument for the expression of Black self-determination. "This is wild," Simmons noted. "Why you-all fighting with us and then doing this?"[32]

In the midst of the tumult generated both by the Black consciousness papers and the later call for Black Power, White activists outside of SNCC attempted to establish direct contact with the Project staff. Jim Van Etten, president of the Marquette University chapter of Students for a Democratic Society (SDS), contacted Bill Ware to obtain permission to reprint the principal position paper in a campus literary magazine, asserting that it was "very interesting and well-written." Van Etten contended that reprinting the paper would "educate the people here at SDS and the general student body concerning Black Power" and "pave the way" for a NAACP youth group in Milwaukee challenging the organization's national leadership. Dennis Hale, an editor for the *Activist*, a progressive magazine, contacted Ware to reprint the position paper in an upcoming anthology, *The New Student Left*. "We'd like very much to update our articles from the civil rights movement with your paper and Stokely Carmichael's article in the *New York Review of Books*."[33]

Some White activists, even if well-meaning, betrayed a condescending attitude in their letters. Miriam Wasserman, a progressive White activist in Atlanta who was writing an essay on Black Power, wrote Ware after a failed initial attempt to elicit his views on the subject. Wasserman noted that the term "Black Power" had particular meanings for those who uttered it. Yet, she asserted that it "also has meaning for the people who *hear* the term," and suggested that "the practical outcomes of 'black power' will be determined by all its meanings—yours, Stokely Carmichael's, John Lewis's, Hector Black's, Ralph McGill's, and *Time* magazine's." Anticipating that Ware would continue to ignore her, Wasserman became patronizing when she further asserted that he might not "give a damn" about what Whites thought about Black Power, a move that "would be emotionally understandable but not a politically serious response—and I have to assume that you are politically serious. Among other things, analyses made from the outside may help you better to understand your own position and power relations."[34]

The response by White SNCC activists to the explicit call for Black Power within the organization was not uniform. Atlanta Project co-director Gwendolyn Robinson and SNCC head of research Jack Minnis—the only White person in a policymaking position—maintained a "very antagonistic" relationship. Robinson noted in retrospect that Minnis "just thought it was absolutely stupid to be raising the race question in the context in which we were raising it." Heated exchanges between the two SNCC activists had a deep impact on Robinson. "I thought, 'You must be totally insensitive if you don't understand what racism, White nationalism, has done to Black people in this country.'" However, other White SNCC activists approached the issue differently. Atlanta Project activists had been encouraged by the efforts of several Whites, including Sue Thrasher and Gene Guerrero, who "took up the challenge" of doing organizing work in White communities. These White activists formed the Southern Student Organizing Committee (SSOC), a group that Robinson and other Black SNCC workers affectionately called the White Folks' Project. Robinson noted that the positive working relationship between Atlanta Project and SSOC activists was ample evidence that "some of the Southern Whites had more of an understanding of what we were talking about than the Northern liberals."[35]

■ ■ ■

The debate generated by the Atlanta Project Black consciousness papers represented the initial phase of what became a broader cultural thrust launched by Black activists throughout the global African world. Stephen Bantu Biko, one of the leading architects of the Black Consciousness Movement (BCM) in South Africa, in his early 1970s essays offered a blistering critique of the refusal by White activists to confront their white skin privilege. Biko had been an active member of the National Union of South African Students (NUSAS), a predominantly White organization with a rich history of challenging apartheid structures in the country. However, he and other Black NUSAS members bolted from the organization to form their own group, the South African Students Organization (SASO), in 1968. He went on to help found the Black People's Convention, "the political wing of Black Consciousness," shortly before the Pretoria regime banned him and several other SASO activists in 1973. Biko continued to organize around core principles of Black solidarity and cultural self-determination—despite banning after banning and several forced detentions—until South African authorities essentially assassinated him via torture in September 1977. The BCM had been inextricably linked to the 1976 Soweto uprising, in which thousands of Black school children boycotted classes rather than be subjected to learning Afrikaans, the language of the ruling White minority.[36]

As fellow BCM activists Malusi and Thoko Mpumlwana have since observed, Biko saw racism as a fundamental and systemic problem in South Africa. He contended that while not guilty of practicing conscious acts of racism, progressive Whites were egregious offenders when it came to committing unconscious acts. Therefore, the BCM was a necessary antidote, for it "freed black people to become themselves." Biko did not question the goal of having a "truly integrated, non-racial National Consciousness." The key for him was that such a goal could be realized only once the BCM helped to undercut all "complexes of superiority and inferiority," eradicated notions of "emptiness of the native's past," and obliterated the dependency of Blacks on Whites. Accomplishing these tasks would signal the defeat of racism.[37]

Biko made it abundantly clear, however, that even the most progressive Whites would have to play an active, honest role in defeating institutionalized white supremacy by reexamining important assumptions. He did not mince words with his former colleagues in NUSAS, or with other White activists, insisting that they had to confront their white skin privilege. Utilizing the SASO Newsletter as a launching pad for his incisive critique, he lambasted White activists in a series of 1970 essays signed "Frank Talk." He argued that progressive Whites in South Africa could "make themselves forget about the problem" of racism in the country when they saw fit to do so. "On the other hand, in oppression the blacks are experiencing a situation from which they are unable to escape at any given moment. Theirs is a struggle to get out of the situation and not merely to solve a peripheral problem as is the case of the liberals."[38]

Biko elaborated on the significance of confronting racism in the anti-apartheid movement by focusing his attention squarely on the relationship between Black and White activists. "Instead of involving themselves in an all-out attempt to stamp out racism from their white society, liberals waste lots of time trying to prove to as many blacks as they can find that they are liberal," he asserted. "This arises out of the false belief that we are faced with a black problem. There is nothing the matter with the blacks. The problem is WHITE RACISM and it rests squarely on the laps of the white society." Biko's uncompromising critique of White activists was significant because it reiterated the point that White activists in institutionally racist societies such as South Africa and the United States tended to approach the social construction of race and the reality of racism with a degree of flexibility that their white skin privilege afforded them. These activists wanted "to remain in good books with both the black and white worlds," Biko asserted, by refusing to embrace "all forms of 'extremisms,' condemning 'white supremacy' as being just as bad as 'Black Power!' They vacillate between the two worlds, verbalising all the complaints of the blacks beautifully while skillfully extracting what suits them from the exclusive pool of white privileges."[39]

Black political thought and action have never been monolithic, and South Africa was certainly no exception. Just as Atlanta Project activists became embroiled in an internal debate with other SNCC workers concerning the Black consciousness papers, BCM activists were part of an intensely contested Black political landscape in apartheid South Africa. Nelson Mandela noted in his autobiography that angry young BCM activists who came to the Robben Island prison during the late 1970s reminded him of himself as an African National Congress (ANC) Youth League member. Noting that he had "outgrown our Youth League outlook," however, Mandela criticized what he perceived to be the limiting nature of key aspects of the BCM. "While I was encouraged by their militancy, I thought that their philosophy, in its concentration on blackness, was exclusionary, and represented an intermediate view that was not fully mature," he recalled. "I saw my role as an elder statesman who might help them move on to the more inclusive ideas of the Congress Movement."[40]

Winnie Mandela, who witnessed firsthand the Soweto Black student uprising in June 1976, often spoke of how significant the BCM had been in filling the void left by the banned ANC and PAC (Pan Africanist Congress). She asserted that BCM activists, in time also banned by the Pretoria regime, realized the "historical necessity to conscientize the people." Winnie Mandela offered particular praise for Biko, situating him within a broader political context. "Steve Biko, for whom I have the greatest admiration and who was our national idol, is not so much the Father of Black Consciousness as one of our greatest African Nationalists. That is what he understood himself to be," she asserted in her autobiography, for he "merely expounded and exemplified ideologies that existed before." Winnie Mandela—who had been banished and put under house arrest after the Soweto uprisings—had few qualms about the BCM and its relationship to the larger freedom struggle in South Africa. "The leaders of the Black Consciousness Movement knew the direction," she asserted. "They were part and parcel of the struggle. They know who the enemy is: the government of this country."[41]

Intriguingly, one of the most striking differences between the Atlanta Project Black consciousness essays and those of Steve Biko was the persistence with which the latter used male-centered language to advance core principles. Biko remarked, for instance, that the "type of black man we have today has lost his manhood" and had been "reduced to an obliging shell." He contended that Black Consciousness represented an introspective process whereby an individual male struggled "to pump back life into his empty shell; to infuse him with pride and dignity, to remind himself of his complicity in the crime of allowing himself to be misused" by the forces of apartheid.[42] To be sure, male-specific language and various manifestations of sexism would become a steady and often troubling staple of the Black Power phase of the larger human rights struggle in the United States. However, the male SNCC activists who served as the principal authors of the three Black consciousness position papers largely avoided this written contradiction, perhaps in part because of the influence of Project co-director Gwendolyn Robinson.

■ ■ ■

Tensions between Atlanta Project workers and the SNCC national staff subsided, flared up, then subsided again during the spring and summer of 1966. In large part because of better coordination with a national office whose members had become more willing to embrace nationalism, things appeared to have improved. A key cog in the SNCC organizational apparatus was Fay Bellamy, who came to the national office in the summer of 1965 following frontline work in Selma and Green County, Alabama. She played more of a secretarial role in her first months in the office. "Forman wanted me to be his secretary, so I tried that. Stokely wanted me to be his secretary, and I tried that. When Rap [H. Rap Brown] got elected chair, I said, 'I ain't gonna be none of you-all's secretary,' " Bellamy laughed. Her combination of organizing and administrative skills saw her quickly rise, and she was elected to the SNCC executive committee in 1966. She spearheaded the effort of taping and transcribing meetings as a means of enriching the archival repository of the group. Bellamy also launched the publication of AfricanAmerican, a SNCC internal organ designed to strengthen the relationship among various projects and between projects and the national office.[43]

It was during this period that the national office drew increasing criticism from the mainstream press. The Atlanta Constitution lambasted SNCC for its decision to boycott the White House Conference on Civil Rights held the first week in June. The newspaper declared that with "new and more militant leadership, SNCC has turned toward black supremacy." The Constitution further contended that the group had "finally done for itself what the White

Citizens Councils tried and failed to do. It has isolated itself and has abandoned the civil rights movement. It has turned its back on the people it professes to serve." Indeed, SNCC had undergone several significant changes since 1964. Only one White worker, Minnis, remained in a policy-making position. The geographical base of the executive committee had shifted slightly northward. A "Washington D.C. clique" led by Carmichael and Ivanhoe Donaldson had supplanted the previous Nashville and Atlanta leadership circles. And funding for the group, which reached seven hundred thousand dollars during the 1964 Freedom Summer campaign, barely reached fifty thousand dollars for 1966.[44]

The stark drop in external funding that resulted from the radicalization of SNCC over the course of two years served to further exacerbate tensions. When a check for three thousand dollars arrived at the national office, several Atlanta Project members "decided to hold onto the check as a way of leveraging a meeting" with the national staff to discuss the possibility of Project autonomy. In turn, the executive committee accused the Project staff of embezzlement and insubordination.

With the lone, painful exception of a smoldering feud between Bill Ware and James Forman, the SNCC national office and Atlanta Project workers managed to settle their differences, at least until the end of the year. "Even through all of that there was still a bond of family," Simmons asserted. "It was more of a family falling-out." In addition to coordinating a successful second election bid for Julian Bond, who finally gained his state legislative seat after a Supreme Court decision, they continued to organize around issues such as abolishing the death penalty and providing a two-dollar minimum wage. They also helped workers at a dry cleaners downtown organize to fight for better conditions. Police arrested several Project workers when they attempted to block evictions in Vine City in support of the struggling tenants' movement there.

■ ■ ■

Providing grassroots educational opportunities became an important priority for Project workers, who earlier had written a position paper calling for "community freedom-schools" for teenagers as well as for an "extensive Negro History and African Culture campaign" for teens and adults. Buoyed by the success of SNCC's freedom schools in Alabama and Mississippi, the Atlanta activists wanted to tap students from the affiliated schools of the Atlanta University Center to work as teachers. Project activists did not take up the issue of summer freedom schools until the end of April, however, in part because of continued fallout from the March staff meeting. This April meeting was instructive because it demonstrated the ways in which Project activists, several of whom were movement veterans with experience in rural settings, struggled to come to terms with the specific challenges of urban initiatives.

Ware opened the meeting by providing a rationale for freedom schools. Asserting that it was the responsibility of Blacks to "unbrainwash themselves," Ware argued in part that the schools could help students develop critical thinking skills. The adoption of a "critical attitude" would allow students to "think, to question and to begin to re-evaluate themselves, the country, and the world." Prefiguring a key argument of the Black Studies movement that later took root at college campuses across the country, Ware insisted that one of the most important aspects of embracing such thinking was that it challenged notions of pedagogy that refused to confront the status quo. "We know that Negroes in this country are not supposed to speak out against the war in Vietnam or against the slavery in South Africa," he remarked. "We have a traumatic example of not being able to discuss the war in the case of the expulsion of Julian Bond from the Georgia Statehouse."[45]

As the meeting progressed Project activists struggled to balance theoretical concerns and on-the-ground logistical issues. Gwendolyn Robinson, who had directed a freedom school project in Mississippi, asked the group to consider whether launching schools in conjunction with the SCLC was a wise idea. She contended that the Project should "aggressively pursue" such a joint effort to help address "the whole respectability problem." Noting that "some people of the higher economic bracket are afraid of us," she stressed that embarking on a project with "trusted civic groups will help allay a lot of fears." Dwight Williams argued that the freedom schools should be utilized as an organizing tool. "To me a [freedom school] is merely a vehicle to be used to establish expandable contact with people in various communities in the city." However, as significant as the schools might be in organizing, Williams did not believe the Project should focus entirely on maintaining them. "I do not feel that we should tie the majority of the staff down," he contended. "I hope that we can encourage local groups and citizens to sponsor individual centers . . . and thereby extend our base of operations."[46]

Although several activists at the meeting maintained that Project workers should not impose particular ideological positions on freedom school students, some contradicted themselves. Early in the meeting Ware criticized the public school system for not allowing students "to really make [their] own conclusions." Later in the meeting, however, he argued that student work should be related to specific Project activities. "In relation to police brutality, for example, a part of their assignment should be that they would have to attend the police review board meeting." He continued, asserting that students could then "give reports and draw up a creative weekly leaflet villifying [sic] the police department. Over a long period of time, the police department would grow sensitive to this and would see that it is not an emotional thing but a cold and calculated thing."[47]

The issue was complicated. Ware's suggestion that students attend review board hearings was fine on the face of it. The public school system did not provide resources for or otherwise encourage such opportunities for learning outside the classroom—especially learning that exposed state contradictions—even if individual teachers had been so inclined. More important, Black teenagers in Atlanta's poorest neighborhoods did not have to attend review board hearings to have a heightened understanding of police brutality, for many either had witnessed or experienced it firsthand. The problem arose when activists began viewing students, even if only implicitly, as political instruments to be manipulated in a larger activist-driven struggle against the state. Political scientist Adolph Reed has noted that this "custodial approach" on the part of radical Black activists was part and parcel of a larger tendency to categorize the undifferentiated "masses."[48]

Other activists at the meeting made a point of envisioning the freedom schools from a perspective that respected students' volition and their needs. Donald Stone argued that students who took part in the freedom schools might find themselves "radicalizing their own school's curriculum" when they returned in the fall. Stone also stressed the need for students to be exposed to as many "Afro-American cultural things" as possible. "As we all know, there is a great void in this area in the American school system. Jazz, Afro art, all these kinds of things." John Bell, one of several local residents who were Project organizers, noted that the freedom schools should also provide information on consumer buying strategies, voter registration, and improving adult literacy. "I really believe that if we get people information that they themselves will begin to suggest ways that they can do some things to help their situation," Bell asserted. "I've got to get out in the community and see how the people feel."[49]

The issue of how best to train teachers vexed almost everyone at the meeting. Project workers went to some lengths to draw lessons from the successful

SNCC Atlanta Project co-director Gwendolyn Zoharah Simmons (Gwendolyn Robinson) in the late 1990s. Simmons was active in the Committee on Appeal for Human Rights, then served as project director of a SNCC freedom school in Laurel, Mississippi, prior to returning to Atlanta in 1965 to direct the Atlanta Project with Bill Ware. Photo courtesy of Gwendolyn Zoharah Simmons.

SNCC freedom school initiatives in Alabama, Mississippi, and Arkansas. Robinson suggested that the Project contact Bob Moses to see what resource materials his group had at their disposal, and she urged someone in the Atlanta group to travel to Selma to investigate the schools there. Several Project activists agreed that a two-week orientation session would suffice for preparing the prospective teachers, who were likely to be area college students. Robinson urged caution, however. "We want to shake these kids," she implored. "We want to get over to these kids that they live in a depraved society, a depraved country, a depraved society that lies, lies, lies and then lies some more." The reason why students and their prospective teachers were unaware of key aspects of both their historical and contemporary understanding of the world, she said, "is because the society doesn't want them to know. It has kept your history from you purposefully. All I am saying is that you can't get that over in a two-week period of orientation."[50]

Pressed for time, the Project moved the freedom school initiative forward, with college students and Project activists such as Donald Stone serving as teachers. In an effort to obtain books at no cost, Michael Simmons wrote several Black publishers for complimentary titles. He stressed that the schools had a "two-fold purpose" in that they supplemented course work from existing schools while also "helping to rebuild pride and dignity in a people through the teaching of their history and an analysis of their present." A fairly exhaustive list of over one hundred books accompanied the letter, but Simmons informed the publishers not to "feel that this list is intended to limit you." SNCC activists also made good on their intention to collaborate with SCLC activists. Annell Ponder, of the SCLC Citizenship Education Project (CEP), coordinated several meetings between Project workers and Robert Green, the SCLC's education director. Although the two groups did not see eye to eye on a number of issues, including the merits of pushing for school desegregation, Ponder noted that there was consensus on fundamentals. "We all agreed unreservedly that we need to work to improve the conditions and the curriculum at the Negro schools." The two groups agreed to work together on a CEP retreat in August to train student leaders.[51]

■ ■ ■

As active as Atlanta Project organizers had been on several fronts, it was their dedicated and imaginative effort to link the Black freedom struggle and the Vietnam War that truly distinguished them as grassroots organizers.

Project workers traveled across the country, waged an important leafleting campaign in downtown Atlanta, and targeted a key induction center, all in a matter of months. It came as no surprise, then, that Atlanta authorities moved swiftly to incarcerate Project activists, sometimes placing them in solitary confinement. Project workers led the way in further cementing SNCC's antiwar legacy.

Not long after SNCC released its January 1966 antiwar statement, Project workers Larry Fox and Michael Simmons began an effort to coordinate the growing number of Black antiwar protests led by grassroots and student organizations nationwide. They organized several conferences, particularly in the Northeast, and attempted to transform a largely informal Black antiwar network into a national group. A letter sent to Black activists nationwide noted that individuals "in and around SNCC are alarmingly aware of the need for a Black Anti-Draft Program." The authors of the letter made the necessary connection between violence abroad and the impact it would continue to have in the United States. The letter asserted that the United States "has devised a way of killing two birds with one stone, i.e. brutalizing and murdering people of color around the world and exterminating Black men of this country in the process."[52]

Given the "urgency of this matter," Project activists called for a national meeting, to be held no later than Labor Day weekend, in preparation for an October draft call that would enlist more than forty thousand men nationwide. "If the country is able to get away with busting up SNCC by drafting its young members and also by drafting young Black people in general, the pattern will be clearly set for our destruction," the letter contended. In language that foreshadowed the disproportionate casualty rate for Blacks and Latinos in Vietnam just as it privileged male contributions to the human rights struggle, Project activists also asserted that these soldiers "will become the mercenaries of the future. We will be the ones who will fight all foreign wars. There will be no one here to carry on effective protest and we will be slaughtered both home and abroad."[53]

Project workers offered several possible actions on which a national antidraft organization could embark. In each instance, however, the SNCC activists warned others that any action undertaken should avoid "opposing the country directly, wherein we could be charged legitimately with treason" or being "un-American." The first suggestion called for the adoption of the "Freedom of Choice Plan." This plan allowed for Blacks to submit petitions to Congress indicating whether they intended to fight for their freedom abroad or in the United States. Project activists also suggested a cross-country march that would place pressure on Congress "to exempt Negroes" from the draft. Fully aware of what had happened to James Meredith when he attempted to march across Mississippi only weeks before, SNCC activists reasoned that such a protest "would be so dangerous that the fellows would prefer to die on the highways of their own country" than in overseas combat.[54]

A flurry of local activity accompanied the national antiwar drive, as Dwight Williams led the effort to launch a sophisticated propaganda campaign in the streets of Atlanta. Project activists designed leaflets for distribution at bus stations, corner stores, barbershops, and hair salons that targeted working-class and poor Blacks. One of the four-panel single-sheet leaflets displayed a photograph of a Black man deep in thought, with a caption that asked, "What Would You Do with $40 Million Dollars Each Day?" Once someone opened the leaflet they found the following text on the left-hand panel, just above a photograph of Vietnamese prisoners of war:

> DID YOU KNOW that the U.S. Government spends over $40
> MILLION DOLLARS everyday in VIETNAM.
> DID YOU KNOW that for each Vietnamese we murder, we
> spend $4 MILLION in supplies.
> DID YOU KNOW that we spend more in one day to kill TEN
> VIETNAMESE, than TEN MILLION VIETNAMESE spend in
> one week to eat![55]

The information on the right-hand panel of the leaflet brought matters close to home. The leaflet asked what Atlanta's Blacks could receive if President Lyndon Johnson provided them with forty million dollars each day, and it provided answers. Each Black person in Atlanta would have "enough money to buy an air conditioned Mustang and enough gas to travel across the country six times in style." For those Blacks who did not care about sports cars, there was an alternative. "EVERY FOUR MONTHS you could pay cash for a new house on Collier Drive." Project activists used the back panel of the leaflet to bring issues full circle. Featuring a photograph of hopeful Black school-children, it proclaimed:

> OF COURSE we didn't expect Atlanta's Negroes to get $40
> MILLION DOLLARS per day, but WE ALSO . . .
> DIDN'T EXPECT PRESIDENT JOHNSON TO CUT OFF $19
> MILLION DOLLARS FROM THE SCHOOL LUNCH PROGRAM.

A program that feeds thousands of Atlanta's Black children
every school day.
AND WE DIDN'T EXPECT HIM TO CUT OFF $175 MILLION
DOLLARS FROM THE COLLEGE STUDENT LOAN PROGRAM.
We are not sure how many millions of dollars he has CUT OFF
from the Welfare Program, the Health and Hospital Aid
Programs.
WE JUST WONDER, HOW WOULD YOU SPEND $40,000,000
DOLLARS PER DAY?[56]

Project workers inundated downtown bus stations during the evening rush
hour as thousands of Blacks, particularly domestic workers, transferred to
buses that would take them home to their segregated neighborhoods. Activists handed out another leaflet, this one featuring a graphic photograph of a
Vietnamese toddler and infant who had been napalmed, that asked pointedly,
"Did Your SON Do This?" The inside panels of the leaflet discussed the
tradition of Black participation in the military, even in the face of slavery and
post-Reconstruction apartheid. "Now, however, many young black men feel
they can serve their race and country better by learning to heal, to build, and to
create here in America," the Project asserted. "These young black men believe
they have the right to choose which war they fight in. These young black men
believe that their first duty is to work for and with their own people here in
this country."[57]

SNCC activists eventually decided to shift the focus of their antiwar protests
in an even more confrontational direction. Project workers, as well as a few
SNCC workers from other projects who happened to be in town, descended
upon the induction center at 12th Army Corps Headquarters on Tuesday,
16 August 1966, at about seven in the morning. Once there they began handing out an assortment of leaflets to inductees, several of whom were Black, as
they went inside. The twenty SNCC organizers quietly entered the building on
Ponce de Leon Avenue alongside a number of recruits after someone inside
spat upon a female activist from a second-story window. White bystanders
taunted the demonstrators, shouting "niggers back to Africa" and "send
all niggers to Vietnam!" Once inside, the protesters began chanting as they
continued to hand out leaflets, one of which repeated Muhammad Ali's statement, "The Viet Cong Never Called Me Nigger." SNCC workers also distributed a leaflet that expressed solidarity with freedom movements throughout
the Third World. "We are in complete sympathy with the aims and aspirations

of the liberation struggles in Viet Nam, South Africa, The Congo and the whole of Latin America and Asia."[58]

The following morning Project activists returned to the induction center to distribute leaflets inside and at the entrance. The bulk of SNCC protest literature focused on domestic issues relating to the war, such as crimes that Southern Whites had committed against Black soldiers. Most unrelenting, perhaps, was the condemnation of those in power. "We are tired of white and black leaders telling us how proud we should be to die for white people," one leaflet asserted. "We are tired of seeing our black brothers spill their blood on foreign soil so white men can continue the quest for white power over colored peoples of the world." A Black military veteran who joined the protest carried a placard that read, "I FOUGHT IN KOREA, I'M NOT FREE." At one point someone "thoroughly doused" Gwendolyn Robinson with a clear substance dumped from a second-floor window. As confused inductees looked on, soldiers began picking up chairs with SNCC activists in them and dumping people onto the sidewalk outside. "If you hurt one of our sisters I'll kill you," Simmons told one Army officer. The verbal assault waged by SNCC workers seemed to have had an effect, however, as the remaining Project organizers left without further incident.[59]

The protests at the induction center, like earlier protests against petty apartheid in Atlanta, revealed the extent to which personal experience became bound up with political action. Most male SNCC activists faced the possibility of being drafted, or knew a friend or relative who had already been through the process. Furthermore, the very site of the induction center, on Ponce de Leon Avenue, served as a symbolic cavalry post at the boundary between the Black neighborhoods of Bedford Pine and Old Fourth Ward and the White neighborhoods of Midtown, Virginia Highlands, and Druid Hills. Atlanta Project activists had every intention, then, of returning to the induction center the following morning. The day would have special meaning for Simmons because he, too, had been scheduled to report for induction. He hoped, perhaps naively, that if police arrested him but did not follow proper procedure, his case would be dismissed. As a result, he would be given a lease on life away from the armed forces of the United States. Without question, he said, "my plan was to go to jail that day."[60]

Thursday morning, a group of thirty SNCC and community activists led by Robinson, Fox, Simmons, and Stone returned to the induction center at six-thirty. They rushed the entrance as soldiers braced themselves on the opposite side of the doors. While soldiers inside the center waited for police to arrive,

SNCC activists made every effort to keep two Black inductees, luggage in tow, from entering the building. At about seven-thirty, police moved on SNCC workers after members of the group made it known that no one had any intention of leaving. The melee that ensued intensified when members of the Nation of Islam, who had conducted leafleting of their own in solidarity with SNCC activists, joined in. Police and both male and female protesters exchanged sporadic blows for more than thirty minutes as stunned motorists stopped their cars to watch. At one point, when police placed a female activist in a headlock, male protesters who had been put in a police wagon without being handcuffed rushed out to rejoin the fray. An activist ripped the shirt off one police officer and the badge off another. Simmons noted that police may have mistakenly thought that some women who wore short afros were men. Whatever the case, female activists fought as tenaciously as the males and would have it no other way. "Fay [Bellamy] knocked somebody upside the head."[61]

Police arrested twelve SNCC workers. Authorities bound Johnny C. Wilson over on an 1870 insurrection law that carried the death penalty. Others faced charges of resisting arrest and assault and battery. The presiding judge at the arraignment, whose son was on active duty in Vietnam, saw no need to be lenient. Starved for funds, SNCC activists spent two to three months in jail before obtaining bond, the longest period of political incarceration for activists in Atlanta since the direct action campaign began in 1960. In a telling moment that revealed a great deal about the true meaning of autonomy, however, Fox recalled that the national captain of the Nation of Islam brought five hundred thousand dollars in cash to the courthouse to post bond for NOI members. SNCC activists charged with assaulting a police officer served their time at the Fulton County stockade, where sheriffs made certain to separate the political prisoners from the general inmate population. The other SNCC activists spent their time in the city jail. Fox, who had begun his activist work as a Morehouse student in the Committee on Appeal for Human Rights, later remarked that the induction center melee "was the only physical confrontation I had with police forces, or anyone else, the whole time I was working for SNCC."[62]

■ ■ ■

Incarceration affected the Atlanta Project workers in different ways. Fox recalled that the decision by those jailed in the county stockade to go on a two-week hunger strike reaped dividends. "It gave me instant credibility with the other prisoners, because none of them thought I'd last for more than a day," he laughed. "So after four or five days they were starting to respect me." A few days after the fast ended, prisoners received food that had spoiled rotten. When prisoners organized a protest, they chose Fox to be their spokesman, but to no avail, since stockade authorities "refused to talk to me." After SNCC raised enough money to post bond, authorities eventually transferred Fox and the other county prisoners to the farm operated by the city jail. The farm posed its own challenges. Raised in the North Carolina countryside, Fox had no problem facing the prospect of killing hogs. But shucking corn was another story. The dust became so thick in the corn barn, the stench so unbearable, that he and another prisoner assigned to that detail refused to enter the barn. As a consequence, he said, "they put us in the hole for five days." Fox finally received some relief when he finished his second stint in solitary confinement, studying whenever possible theoreticians outside the United States. "I read a lot of Che Guevara."[63]

Other incarcerated Project activists had a far more difficult time. SNCC attorney Howard Moore listened in shock as two police officers severely beat Dwight Williams as they transferred him from a booking room to his jail cell. For other activists, the agony was more emotional, as time behind bars led to increased feelings of isolation. Robinson and Ware received a heartfelt appeal from Donald Howard, who wrote a brief letter in which he acknowledged that "I would appreciate it if you would get the money for my bond and get me out of here. I was informed Sunday that my fiancée was placed in a mental ward due to my being arrested." Clearly embarrassed at having made such a personal request, Howard explained that "I've never had anyone that close to me before, not even my mother." He no doubt realized that the funds were not there, but he reached out nonetheless. "I am asking for a favor. [I]f you love someone like I love her you'll understand." Howard ended his letter, "Yours in Black Power."[64]

In early October, SNCC workers managed to obtain enough bond money to free Howard, but when a prison guard claimed that he had shirked his work detail, he found himself in solitary confinement instead. Simmons wrote Project workers the same week and noted jokingly that "things are looking rather white (bad)." He said a new leaflet should be updated to "include the fact that attempts to discuss the situation with the warden and CO have been futile" in winning Howard's release. The entire experience had affected Simmons in ways he had not imagined. "It's amazing what being in prison has done to some of us—especially me. While one was dedicated before, being in here makes our ultimate mission a must. To see our Black Brothers get railroaded by racist cops and judges to supply free labor for this hell hole is merely a minute example of our oppression."[65]

The protest, arrest, and imprisonment of Atlanta Project workers galvanized all SNCC activists in Atlanta. Simmons recalled that Stokely Carmichael made frequent visits to see his jailed comrades and that the "entire SNCC family closed ranks around us." The most poignant demonstration of solidarity, however, took place in front of the induction center and later at the downtown bus station. Occasionally joined by other Black women from SNCC and the Atlanta community, women of the Atlanta Project—fully clad in long black dresses, veils, and head coverings—conducted silent picketing each weekday for nearly four months, until the last incarcerated Project organizers won their release from jail. Since Project activists had to wait for regular SNCC business to be finished at their print shop, they "would be up all night creating the new flier for the next day," Robinson said. SNCC activists often went directly from the print shop to the bus station at five-thirty in the morning to hand out a minimum of twenty-five thousand leaflets daily. Female activists solemnly paced back and forth, refusing to utter a word, as male activists answered questions posed by residents and news reporters. "We were shrouded," Robinson stressed. "I mean, we had heavy black veils."[66]

The silent vigil demonstrated the ways in which a sisterhood had developed that transcended Project-national office SNCC divisions and class divisions between SNCC organizers and Black working women. Even during the most volatile intra-organizational strife, Bellamy, Gwendolyn Robinson, and Ruby Doris Smith Robinson maintained a fundamental respect for one another as SNCC organizers.[67] This sense of respect was embraced by other Project activists such as Cissy Breland, Connie Henderson, and Margaret Mills.

The protests downtown were also significant for building bridges across intraracial class lines. Project activists provided thousands of city residents—an overwhelming number of whom were female Black domestic workers en route to White suburban neighborhoods—with new information and a fresh perspective on the Vietnam War. Traffic slowed to a crawl as women ran across busy streets to approach SNCC activists for the current day's material, some asking for several fliers so that they could distribute them to their husbands or other male relatives. These economically marginalized women had sons and grandsons who had few opportunities for steady employment at home and were now faced with the prospect of being sent overseas to kill or be killed. As important, a significant number of the women who waited for buses each morning had male relatives who had been incarcerated or who were on parole. As a result, informal bonds grew between SNCC workers and Atlanta residents, even if actual words were seldom exchanged. "It would get so that if we were late people would miss their bus waiting on us," Robinson recalled. "And we'd get there and they'd say, 'You are late! I don't know what I'm going to tell my White woman when I get there. Give me my flier!' It was incredible."[68]

■ ■ ■

Thoroughly exhausted, and concerned about the outcome of a judicial hearing that could determine their ultimate legal fate as a result of the induction center protests, members of the Atlanta Project were among the SNCC workers who attended the infamous early December retreat at the upstate New York estate of Black comedian Peg Leg Bates. In what has come to be the dominant narrative of the retreat, scholars have described the meeting as one that "must truly have been painful to endure" and as "a crisis that clearly meant the beginning of the end for SNCC."[69] As is often the case, however, the meeting and its aftermath were actually more complicated, revealing key ways in which gender, race, and changes in SNCC organizational culture combined to complicate the question of Black self-determination.

Carmichael, chair of SNCC, opened the meeting with a statement that included a call for SNCC to maintain its position that Whites should remain in the organization but confine their work to White communities. Perhaps sensing a serious floor fight, he stressed that there was some flexibility in the agenda, "depending on weather conditions and unexpected circumstances." Nevertheless, he asserted that it "was imperative that the time schedule be absolutely adhered to if we are not to waste our time, waste our money, and create ill will in this section of New York." The first session, which was to deal with the status of the organization and program reports, had been allotted two hours. It was during this first session that the SNCC Central Committee planned for "other staff people who have comments and reflections and criticisms" to share their views. "People are asked to keep in mind that this is a long staff meeting and there will be time for much discussion. But the Central Committee felt it important that how some people saw us and themselves should be stated early in the meeting."[70]

During this first session, Ware, the Atlanta Project's co-director, read from a two-page prepared statement. He had been slated to speak with White activist Bob Zellner on the "Role of Whites in the Movement" during the tenth and final agenda item of the afternoon session preceding dinner. Ware may have been concerned that the session with Zellner would be bumped off the agenda if the meeting ran behind schedule. Quirky and combative, Ware may have simply been spoiling for a floor flight. In any event, he began by asserting that "I am profoundly convinced that Black People and the SNCC do not understand the concept of Black Power. If they understood it, there would be no white people in the organization at this time." He then argued, sometimes in rambling fashion, that Whites should leave SNCC because doing so ensured that "the cats on the corner" would relate to the organization. Besides, Ware argued, it boiled down to "a matter of common sense. It is clear that we are not going to get any more support from white America." Therefore, "since we are not going to get any support from white America, . . . we must consciously, radically, drastically turn toward Black America."[71]

The subsequent debate over the issue of White involvement in SNCC dogged the remainder of the meeting. Carmichael asserted in his autobiography that "an organized faction" came to the meeting "to make the question of the role of whites an *ideological* one. That was not just silly. It was diversionary and destructive because it was unnecessary" since only one White staff member remained in a policy-making position. James Forman expressed frustration with the expulsion debate as well, especially since some strident nationalists remarked that Fannie Lou Hamer and other grassroots activists at the meeting were "no longer relevant" when they defended the current SNCC position. After days of debate, nineteen SNCC activists voted for expulsion, eighteen voted against it, and twenty-four abstained, including those Whites present at the meeting.[72]

It is not difficult to understand why the retreat provoked such a firestorm within SNCC. Carmichael had come to know Bob and Dottie Zellner very well and deeply respected the fact that Bob "would be arrested as many times as me or more, and the Klan would put a price on his head." Forman agreed, noting that "you do not expel people with whom you have worked, merely on the basis of their skin color." Robinson recalled the meeting "being very tense," noting that at one point during the expulsion debate "there were actually guns displayed and threats issued." She also could appreciate the particular bind in which seasoned White activists, particularly the Zellners, found themselves during the meeting. "In retrospect, I really do understand that they had put their bodies on the line," she asserted. "They had cut their ties with the White community and they were not some of the more arrogant people pushing Blacks around."[73]

The most difficult aspect of the expulsion vote for Robinson concerned her organizational relationship with Forman. Since her entry into the Black freedom movement as a Spelman student, Robinson had developed a profound respect for Forman. It was Forman who "saved my life by making me come out of Mississippi" and who had supported a number of her initiatives as Atlanta Project co-director. "He was really my hero. So for me to have to go against him was personally very, very difficult." Yet, Robinson and other Black SNCC activists both inside and outside the Atlanta Project pressed the issue, from the perspective of arguing unequivocally for organizational self-determination. "No one emphasizes that we were not talking about kicking White people to the curb," Robinson later stressed. "We were saying, 'Let's have parallel movements that we will then unite in a common struggle against the institutions that support racism and classism, and all of that.' No one ever mentions that."[74]

Often viewed in exclusively racial terms, the discussion of Black organizational self-determination was also gendered in that it revealed a critical response by Black women to interracial relationships involving Black men and White women, as well as an attempt to come to terms with firmly entrenched perceptions of self. According to Robinson, women in the Atlanta Project discussed the "whole Black man-White woman thing" among themselves and with other Black women in SNCC, especially members of the Selma Project. "That was a tension in SNCC that ran from the earliest time. Way before I went to Mississippi, I was aware of the resentment of many of the SNCC women that many of the SNCC brothers were involved in relationships with White women," she said. Black women had thrived as SNCC organizers both prior to and following the influx of White activists in 1964. Yet, the growing number of interracial sexual relationships, which tended not to involve Black women, became a personal insult because "we saw it as a rejection of us as women."[75]

Within this context the argument for Black self-determination in SNCC could also be read as an attempt on the part of Black women to take control of their lives in a society that marginalized them on a number of levels, including as sexual beings. As Cynthia Griggs Fleming has noted in her biography of Ruby Doris Smith Robinson, the fundamental issue did not involve a "general and pervasive black female resentment of white women." Instead, the central issue concerned the ways in which Black women activists viewed themselves and one another. Like many Black women, Gwendolyn Robinson encountered resistance from other Black women after she cut her straightened hair. A Spelman administrator asked her "had I lost my mind? 'What have you done to your hair?'—and I said, 'I cut it and I washed it.' And she was like, 'Don't get smart with me.'" Discussions about interracial relationships served to remind Robinson of the confrontation with the college administrator precisely because they pointed to key self-perceptions. "When you are dealing with the internalized self-hatred of skin color, hair texture, shape of nose, shape of butt, these things are issues we're still grappling with," she noted. "Thank God Black Power did burst on the scene."[76]

To a certain extent, problems at the retreat were exacerbated by an important change in SNCC organizational culture —namely the abandonment, over time, of consensus decision-making. From the 1964 Freedom Summer campaign onward, the sheer size of the group had called for straight majority votes on key issues. Prior to that time, SNCC workers embraced the notion of meeting for hours in an effort to grapple with vexing matters. Carmichael recalled a conversation with SNCC adviser Ella Baker in which he expressed impatience with the tedious process of reaching consensus. " 'Of course it's important that we all *agree*,' " Baker noted. " 'But it's just as important that we all *understand*, however long that takes.' " Gwendolyn Robinson noted that "we SNCC folk always had raucous meetings. And we always would go on. I tell students how I can remember meetings that went nonstop for thirty-six hours," she laughed. "And you just took a nap in your chair and you told somebody, 'Wake me up now, if any voting takes place.' "[77]

■ ■ ■

The stormy retreat did not signal the demise of SNCC. Forman's proposal for the establishment of nationwide "freedom organizations" was ratified at the meeting. The proposal was significant because it sought to create grassroots organizations that addressed the "day-to-day needs of the people we hope to organize." Baker, despite being deeply troubled by the expulsion vote, refused to abandon SNCC, including its Atlanta Project workers. Yet Project activists and the national leaders abandoned one another. Tensions that simply simmered during the weeks following the induction protests now boiled over when Project activists refused to return a car to the national office in

January 1967. (The feud erupted again when Carmichael and Cleveland Sellers filed charges with the Atlanta police after Simmons refused to return a car that had been used for Atlanta Project activities.) This problem had occurred before in SNCC. Ironically, Robinson had pulled a gun on Sellers to get a SNCC vehicle back when she was a project director in Mississippi. Bellamy asserted that since there were rural counties "where people didn't *have* cars," the national office had a responsibility to move quickly. Nevertheless, she also recognized that Atlanta Project workers, "in their level of intelligence, saw some things that needed to be done then, there, and they wanted that level of support, and I don't think the organization was able to switch up and provide it."[78] Ware responded with a telegram saying Carmichael had "descended to the level of calling a racist henchman cop" in order to settle the dispute. In retaliation the national office suspended Project activists with the exception of Donald Stone. No longer in SNCC but still wedded to the Black freedom struggle, Larry Fox traveled to New York City to continue his activist work. He stayed briefly at Baker's apartment in Harlem, thankful to be in the company of his North Carolina mentor.[79]

The Atlanta Project of SNCC, though in existence for only one year, made important strides in grassroots community organizing, launched the Black consciousness movement within the organization, and developed a sophisticated and audacious critique of the Vietnam War that provided the groundwork for the establishment of the National Black Anti-War Anti-Draft Union (NBAWADU). Ironically, however, its most enduring contribution has been in the role of the foil. As a consequence of their call for SNCC to be an all-Black organization and their oppositional relationship to the leading national personalities of SNCC, Atlanta Project activists have received practically none of the attention accorded their SNCC contemporaries, despite the fact that many had deep roots in the organization. Ultimately, the problem may have been a cruel act of historical timing, for the Project's activists would have been quite at home in upcoming struggles in Atlanta and elsewhere. The hard-line nationalist stand and uncompromising protest activism of Atlanta Project workers served to provide the most prominent activists in SNCC's national leadership with both the impetus and the space with which to proceed to center stage in Atlanta. As events in the city dictated, however, that stage would have to be shared with a growing number of grassroots Black activists.

CHAPTER FIVE

NEIGHBORHOOD PROTEST
AND THE VOICES OF THE BLACK
WORKING POOR

Although petty apartheid had been all but obliterated by 1965, the lives of most Blacks in Atlanta continued to be constrained by segregation and institutionalized white supremacy, signaling the resilience of other, more entrenched apartheid structures. The city's political leaders boasted that nearly 30 percent of the municipal work force was Black, and they described Atlanta as home to an ever-expanding African American middle class. However, the people of neighborhoods such as Vine City, Summerhill, Peoplestown, and Dixie Hills were familiar with more sobering statistics that revealed the inextricable connection between racism and class exploitation. The majority of Blacks in the city had no formal education above the eighth grade; half of the employed men worked in unskilled jobs. Over 40 percent of the women raised and provided for their children alone. The city's Black neighborhoods accounted for only 20 percent of Atlanta's residential land area, yet they contained nearly 45 percent of its population. Poor Blacks had been boxed in economically by poverty and geographically by zoning ordinances and the new expressways. A National Education Association study concluded that at the beginning of the decade Atlanta was the third-most segregated city in the United States.[1]

The adjacent mixed-income neighborhoods of Summerhill and Peoplestown had been disfigured by urban renewal condemnations that mandated construction of new freeways through the heart of the city. Summerhill was one of the oldest neighborhoods in Atlanta, and one of a select few that had been both ethnically and economically diverse. However, a steady stream of solidly middle-class Black families left the neighborhood in the 1950s and early 1960s to occupy new homes in more affluent segregated areas on the West Side. While these Blacks had to contend with obstacles of their own, their less fortunate former neighbors, mostly renters, battled or endured deteriorating housing conditions that sometimes included rodent infestation and an absence of indoor plumbing. "We get $85 a month to live on from welfare and Social Security," an elderly Black couple in Summerhill explained in 1963. "When we pay $45 for rent, there is not much left for food, clothes, and other things." A middle-aged divorced mother of three complained that her landlord "will not even paint this house. I have lived here for twenty-nine years."[2]

The telling blow to the Summerhill and Peoplestown neighborhoods came with the construction of the eighteen-million-dollar Atlanta Stadium in 1965. Ethel Mae Mathews, a single working mother, was one of the first renters evicted. Without notice, her landlord provided "an ultimatum to get out or be bulldozed down right immediately at that time." The bulldozer was already in the yard. "I went to crying because I didn't know what to do," she recalled. She and her four children found temporary housing with a nearby relative, "and we had to sleep on the floor." The neighborhood's middle-class home owners "scattered like flies" as government officials eventually promised Mathews and other displaced renters homes through the Model Cities Program. Actual houses never materialized during the course of the mismanaged multimillion-dollar program—only temporary mobile homes. "Twelve little old trailers, that's what they left behind."[3]

The prevailing fear among most Black and White established leaders was that violence would erupt in the neighborhood of Vine City, not in Summerhill or Peoplestown. Deteriorating living conditions and ongoing tensions with the police had plagued Vine City residents. By September 1966, the SCLC staff had become thoroughly engaged in the struggle against segregated housing in the fiercely White Chicago suburb of Cicero. The same did not hold true for the Student Nonviolent Coordinating Committee, which held a community rally on 3 September 1966 in Vine City to address community concerns. One hundred residents attended the demonstration, which featured SNCC national leaders Stokely Carmichael and James Forman. Activists from the group's Atlanta Project, which had been a fixture in the neighborhood throughout the year, did not play as prominent a role in the demonstration, since most remained incarcerated after the antiwar protests the previous month. A columnist for the *Atlanta Journal* with an eye to events in the neighborhood indicated that "if we don't do something about the Vine City area, it's going to blow, like Watts."[4] As historian Alton Hornsby Jr. has noted, Summerhill and Peoplestown, like Vine City, became two "of those poor black neighborhoods in Atlanta that most whites rarely saw and one that middle class blacks

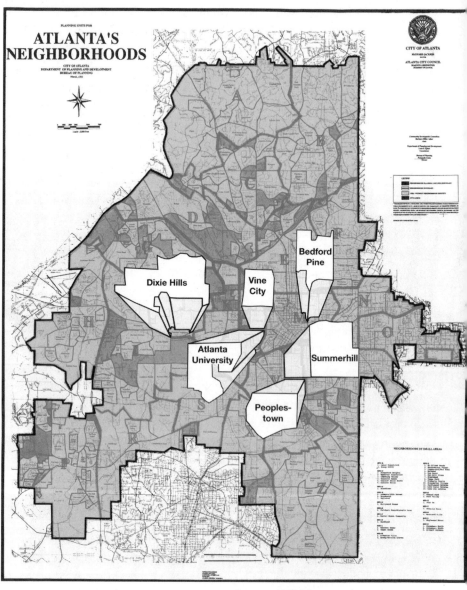

Grassroots protests rocked several Black neighborhoods in Atlanta during the late 1960s. As was often the case nationally, violent confrontations between police and neighborhood residents fueled the protests. Map courtesy of the City of Atlanta and Industrial Color Labs.

ignored."[5] Pastor Roy Williams, the vice president of the Summerhill Civic League (SCL), was aware of the unemployment, inadequate housing, and dearth of municipal services that plagued the neighborhood's residents. "I have told our city politicians we were sitting on a powder keg," he said. "The conditions here are some of the worst in Atlanta."[6]

■ ■ ■

The fuse ignited shortly after 1:00 PM on Tuesday, 6 September, in Summerhill, three days after violence had been predicted for Vine City. Atlanta police detective R. H. Kerr and patrolman Lamar Harris spotted Harold Louis Prather driving a car near the intersection of Ormond and Capitol. A man with a history of arrests for automobile theft, Prather had been suspected in yet another car theft. The police officers called out Prather's name, but he refused to follow their instructions. Instead, he leapt from the car and started running toward the home of his mother, Marjorie Prather. The patrolman called for him to stop, but Prather continued to run. Harris then fired three shots, two of which struck Prather in his right hip and side, as his mother yelled for the policeman to put his gun away. The wounded Prather stumbled, then crawled to the porch of his mother's home, but went no further. An ambulance arrived as a crowd gathered at the scene. "You ain't going to hurt him no more," Marjorie Prather shouted, her son lying in a pool of blood. "There used to be days in slavery times when they killed people like dogs, but this is another day. If you live, and he lives, you'll pay for this."[7]

In the hours that followed Prather's shooting, the crowd grew by the hundreds. As the group grew in size so did its agitation. Apparently, word spread quickly that Harold Prather had been shot for the crime of borrowing a friend's car. Bill Ware and Bobby Walton, activists from the Atlanta Project, addressed the militant crowd from a soundtruck, then provided residents an opportunity to speak about police brutality in their neighborhoods. Soon several other SNCC workers arrived from a national planning meeting less than fifteen minutes away. Roughly three hours after the initial incident, the residents of Summerhill and Peoplestown confronted police in riot gear in what had become a full-scale demonstration at the intersection of Capitol Avenue and Ormond Street.[8]

Atlanta Mayor Ivan Allen went directly to the site of the confrontation in an effort to mollify Summerhill residents. At about the same time, police reinforcements brought shotguns onto the scene. "Why the shotguns? Why the shotguns?" Black residents shouted. "They're not going to use them," Allen responded, adding, "They're here to protect you." A number of young Blacks vehemently disagreed with the mayor's take on the situation, shouting back, "Kill the white bastards, kill the white cops." Demonstrators overturned a police car and a civilian car. Allen, himself atop a police car, continued his effort at pacification, to no avail. Protesters drowned out his words with chants of "white devil, white devil" and "black power, black power."[9]

Allen found himself on solid ground again after protesters rocked his one-ton soapbox back and forth, causing him to stumble. An unidentified SNCC worker then mounted the roof of the police cruiser and urged the protesters onward. "Let's clean up the street: The only way is to start like we did to-day. . . . Atlanta is just a cracker town." Protesters pelted police and their vehicles with bricks and empty soft drink bottles. Police responded by firing two dozen warning shots into the air. Soon afterward they tear-gassed the crowd of nearly a thousand. The stunned mayor did not object, wiping his eyes and ordering police to "clear it up. Move them out of here."[10] The significance of this moment was not lost on anyone. Since his days as Chamber of Commerce president, Allen had cultivated the image of himself as an enlightened New South business and civic leader, a man who stood in contrast to white supremacists such as Lester Maddox. Yet, the mayor could also be condescending, especially in his approach to Black activists outside the elite circle of established moderates and conservatives. Like a paternalistic plantation owner who suddenly found himself in the midst of an uprising by field workers, Allen was snapped into an awareness of both the magnitude and limits of his authority.

Mayor Allen's decision to order the use of teargas struck a chord with neighborhood residents. The gassing of the crowd was particularly frightening for a sixth-grader named Columbus Ward. "I thought they were shooting bullets at first," he remembered. Ward had ignored the warnings by his school principal to avoid the protest. Particularly captivated by the constant chants of "Black Power, Black Power," the boy continued to work his way through the crowd, becoming an active participant in the demonstration for nearly four hours. Far more reluctant was Ethel Mathews, who chose at first to watch the events from the relative security of her porch. Drawn to the protest by the chants and the sight of Allen falling from grace from atop the police cruiser, she eventually joined in, although she "didn't believe in the burning." The cultural significance of the protest also intrigued Summerhill and Peoplestown residents. Several SNCC workers sported beards and African attire, something Ward described as "unique and different." Such cultural symbols were inextricably bound up with the political activity of the Black Power movement, and were particularly dramatic in the more socially conservative Deep South.[11]

Not long after Ward finally headed home, Atlanta police cordoned off a forty-eight-square-block area along Capitol Avenue from Glen Street northward to Vanira Avenue. They arrested a number of young Black men after the first major volley of rocks and bottles. Police arrested two Black women who had "shouted obscenities" at them and later hurled chunks of concrete block through the windshield and windows of a patrol car. Protesters also shattered the windshields of two cars driven by Whites through the area of the demonstration. Although protesters shattered plate glass windows at two White-owned markets, Buehler's Market and the Sol Shafer Grocery, they looted neither store. The only reported incident of looting occurred when dozens of residents helped themselves to the contents of an abandoned soft drink truck.[12]

As both organized and unorganized chaos ensued, members of Atlanta's Black clergy attempted to calm and reassure participants on both sides of the barricades. Pastors William Holmes Borders and Robert Hunter spoke to frustrated Summerhill residents. Borders, a veteran of past struggles against racism and segregation in the city, told one young resident that "we want to get what you want, but you'll have to tell us what it is." The youngster, Bobby Upshaw, told the ministers that he sought the release of relatives and friends arrested by the police. Meanwhile, Ralph D. Abernathy suggested that protesters be taken to nearby Atlanta Stadium to have their complaints heard. If Allen had responded favorably to this suggestion, demonstrators would have come face-to-face with over three hundred state troopers in full riot gear deployed at the stadium waiting for orders. Another group of Black moderates, including ministers J. T. Bickers and Clyde Williams and state representatives John Hood and J. D. Grier, huddled around Allen in an effort to convince him that the police should leave the area. Williams noted that many of "these people own their own houses and businesses here. They're not going to burn them down." Police and the mayor disagreed. One police officer remarked that "there wouldn't be a plate glass window left if we pulled out."[13]

As the evening wore on, an understaffed Atlanta fire department had to contend with a sudden "outbreak of fire alarms" in the Summerhill area.

Their numbers depleted by an ongoing strike, firefighters battled two fires set off by Molotov cocktails, including one in which protesters hurled a gasoline-filled bottle through a window of the Sexton Brothers Tire Company, gutting the entire office and warehouse. The fire-bombing caused hundreds of thousands of dollars in damage. Five other suspicious fires blazed that night, and residents reported a number of false alarms. In at least one instance a home caught fire. Witnesses watched as Black men rushed to save those trapped inside. One man entered the burning house through the roof and came out with a baby in his arms. Three older children and an elderly woman followed him out.[14]

Late that evening, three hundred Blacks met several blocks away from the most intense activity at a church on McDaniel Street. Local ministers and staff members of the SCLC contended with shouts of "Black Power." Some younger Black activists handed out leaflets while others thrust into the air posters sporting a black panther and the words "Who is afraid of black power?" SCLC official Hosea Williams argued for renewed calm and a nonviolent approach. "This is what the segregationist wants you to do." He urged those present at the meeting to "go home and cool off." But the SNCC worker who followed Williams seemed to carry the sentiment of the evening. "We're not going home to cool off. We're going home to heat up." The unidentified SNCC activist continued in a familiar adaptation of the Black call-and-response tradition:

"What do you want?"

"Freedom."

"When do you want it?"

"Now."

"Then it's black power, brothers and sisters—black power."[15]

■ ■ ■

The volatile night meeting provided further evidence of tensions among older activists, younger activists, and community members regarding appropriate protest strategies, an issue that first came to the fore during the sit-in movement of the early 1960s. Yet, there was also an increasing distance between established older activists and younger activists that revealed different perspectives in defining the very terms of the freedom struggle. In the days following the Summerhill uprising, Atlanta's mainstream media, politicians, police, and several prominent moderate Black representatives did just about

Downtown skyscrapers provided a reminder to residents of Atlanta's poor Black neighborhoods of the resilience of entrenched apartheid structures following the demise of petty apartheid during the early 1960s. Photo courtesy of Julius Lester. Copyright Julius Lester.

Mayor Ivan Allen attempts to calm residents of the Summerhill and Peoplestown neighborhoods after police wounded Harold Prather, an unarmed car theft suspect, in September 1966. Photo courtesy of Julius Lester. Copyright Julius Lester.

An unidentified activist exhorts residents just before Mayor Allen falls from atop a police car rocked by members of the crowd in Summerhill. Photo courtesy of Julius Lester. Copyright Julius Lester.

Residents targeted police cruisers during the violent protests that rocked several Black neighborhoods during the late 1960s. Photo courtesy of Julius Lester. Copyright Julius Lester.

everything possible to connect the violent protest with SNCC's national office. Given the transformation within SNCC, leaders of the Atlanta establishment did have cause for concern. The organization had become thoroughly radicalized in the course of three years, the direct result of individual life-changing experiences in the field as well as exposure to Malcolm X and other radical Black nationalists. *Atlanta Constitution* editor Ralph McGill argued from his front-page column that "SNCC is no longer a student movement. It is not now a civil rights organization. It is openly, officially committed to a destruction of existing society."[16]

The acclaimed liberal White newspaper editor had supported earlier student sit-ins that targeted petty apartheid, but McGill, like a number of older established Black activists and politicians, could not come to terms with the changing character of the Black struggle for human rights. Instead, McGill, a Cold War hard-liner, even suggested that the government of Cuba might be funding SNCC activities. Not to be outdone, the *Atlanta Journal* published a series of editorials entitled "Who Runs This City?" The editorials answered with praise for Allen and contempt for radical Black activists and neighborhood protesters. "All the mayor had to do was look the other way, and we'd be just another in the long list of cities desecrated by this tribe of revolutionary hoodlums." Instead, "the mayor faced the mob and with the help of the police outfaced it."[17]

White politicians just weeks away from the Democratic primary in Georgia's gubernatorial race weighed in against SNCC as well. Each candidate worked to "out-Lester Maddox" the segregationist governor. Former governor Ellis Arnall met with Allen, and then asserted that the Klan, SNCC, and the John Birch Society were all "brothers under the skin." In lumping SNCC in with these white supremacist and terrorist organizations, Arnall made the all-too-familiar mistake of coupling those who sought to change the status quo with those who employed racist terror to maintain it. Garland Byrd, former lieutenant governor, offered up more bravado. He maintained that the "state would not be big enough for him and Stokely Carmichael." State Senator Jimmy Carter chose not to mince his words either in a speech before the DeKalb Life Underwriters. Carter argued that Georgians "want the streets kept safe from thugs, hoodlums, and looters."[18]

The mayor and police chief were just as unrelenting in their condemnation. "Mr. Carmichael will be met wherever he comes, under whatever conditions he seeks to impose," Allen said. He argued that the Summerhill protest was "the result of a deliberate attempt by certain members of SNCC to create an incident of this very nature." Chief of police Herbert Jenkins, who had been highly agitated, claimed that SNCC had been run by "irresponsible and hoodlum leaders" and that its membership was made up of "criminals, hoodlums, and outlaws of all types." Police charged Atlanta Project co-director Ware with inciting a riot and bound Carmichael over to the Fulton County grand jury to determine if he would stand trial for the possible state charge of insurrection, a capital offense in Georgia. SNCC activists handed out copies of a statement by Carmichael to Blacks downtown in which he termed the Summerhill protest "a revolt . . . against the bestiality of a racist mayor and his corrupt police department."[19]

SNCC worker Fay Bellamy, a member of the group's executive committee and a veteran of the Selma campaign, decided to confront local authorities physically. Police arrested her after she began running alongside an officer with his service revolver drawn who had been following a Black child. The day following her arrest she exchanged blows with a White male deputy sheriff who had grabbed her tightly around the arm. "I hit him, and I hit him in the face," she recalled. Bellamy realized that being a SNCC organizer afforded her a degree of privilege that allowed her to enter into such a confrontation. With the aid of attorneys Len Holt and Howard Moore, she was able to post bond the day of the scuffle. "That's the difference between being from the community and being in an organization where you have support systems and you are not all by yourself."[20] The fate of dozens of Summerhill and Peoplestown residents arrested during the protests indicated they were not nearly as fortunate as most SNCC workers. Police were "running around grabbing people like rabbits," a frustrated resident argued before Municipal Court Judge T. C. Little. "I agree that some of them needed to be arrested," the unidentified resident conceded to the judge. "But the majority didn't. Most of those arrested were put into jail just for making smart remarks to police. It was not a riot. It was just a show."[21]

A number of established Black leaders who often had found themselves pitted against the City of Atlanta in earlier struggles against petty apartheid now sided with municipal officials in lambasting radical Black activists and those who participated in the violent demonstration. Yet, they also did some organizing of their own. Roy Williams, of the Summerhill Civic League, asserted that "before SNCC arrived we had them [local residents] under control. But they [SNCC] whipped them up with hate." A number of Black moderates formed the Good Neighbor Association the day after the protest to calm residents, criticize SNCC, and curb police "discourtesy." A local entertainer, Robert McDaniel, chaired the group. Residents earned a place in the Association if they made the Good Neighbor membership pledge, disavowing violence and refusing to "house anyone who does."[22]

Members of the Atlanta Summit Leadership Conference (ASLC), now dominated by moderates and conservatives, held a meeting following the protest. The group agreed to form a committee headed by minister James Williams to canvass "slum areas." The primary focus of the meeting, however, was SNCC and its chair, Stokely Carmichael. ASLC member O. W. Davis, a physician active in pushing for full integration of local hospitals, called Carmichael "an albatross around our necks—a parasite on the community." Otis Smith argued that the SNCC chairman "is our major concern. Whether we have a riot or not depends on him." The distinguished Wheat Street pastor William Holmes Borders was even more to the point. "We've got to stop him . . . or he's going to stop us." A vocal minority at the meeting was critical of the anti-Carmichael approach. "We should also give the majority white community a call for nonviolence," minister Robert Hunter responded. "After all, this is violence in reaction to violence." Militant SCLC organizer Hosea Williams echoed Hunter's sentiments, and added that the comments of many previous speakers made them "sort of sound like white men." Williams warned that further grassroots action might take place if the city did not address the concerns of Summerhill and Peoplestown residents, and criticized the aloofness of many Summit members. "You're talking about these people [those in the slum neighborhoods] like they were in outer space."[23]

McDaniel's Good Neighbor Association canvassed Summerhill, Peoplestown, and nearby Mechanicsville in order to present a list of community concerns to city officials. Those surveyed requested that the city build recreation centers, improve vital services, and reduce overcrowding in schools. However, frustration over the nature of the police presence in these urban Black neighborhoods topped the list of concerns. Community residents wanted the city to end "police discourtesy" and include at least one Black officer on two-person police teams. Asserting that he "had a feeling that police weren't any good anyway," Columbus Ward recalled that his older brothers had encountered police harassment involving "petty crimes." On one occasion police warned Ward's mother that an older brother " 'would be a dead nigger' " if he did not cooperate with authorities. "I have had things happen to me personally,"

McDaniel acknowledged. "About last January an officer came up to me and said 'Come here nigger,' and frisked me for nothing."[24]

In October, SCLC president Martin Luther King Jr. issued a statement criticizing the violent protests that had come to be associated with the Black Power movement. He argued that "connotations of violence and separatism attached to the black power slogan must be resolutely opposed" by the SCLC. In a clear overstatement he further noted that the "nonviolent arsenal" of his group had helped to usher in concrete gains in open housing in Chicago and would aid in the "political reformation of the South." Although the SCLC president tended to side with critics who incorrectly reduced the term "Black Power" to a slogan, he nevertheless pointed out that the term had been "exploited by the decision-makers to justify resistance to change."[25]

Of course, King's position on Black Power evolved considerably during the course of 1967, though his overall assessment of the malleable term was largely a negative one. In January, during a stay in Jamaica, he wrote a thoughtful essay on the meaning of Black Power. He spoke of the "broad and positive meaning" of the term with respect to the drive for economic and political power and as a "psychological call to manhood." King asserted from the male-centered perspective that served to frame much of the discourse and politics of the movement that the "Negro must be grasped by a new realization of his dignity and worth. He must stand up amid a system that still oppresses him and develop an unassailable and majestic sense of his own value" and "no longer be ashamed of being black." Nevertheless, King's final judgment remained condemnatory. He argued that beyond the "satisfaction of a gratifying slogan," Black Power represented "a nihilistic philosophy born out of the conviction that the Negro can't win."[26]

Stokely Carmichael moved to the forefront of the discussion, both locally and nationally. In Atlanta the heated debate over the relative merits of a Black Power philosophy took center stage at a February town hall meeting at Clark College. Pastor and longtime NAACP activist Samuel Williams engaged Carmichael in a respectful but highly charged debate on "Black Power and the Future of Negro Americans." Carmichael scored points with the largely student audience with his analysis of both individual and institutional racism. Like Martin Luther King Jr., Carmichael later expounded upon his thoughts on Black Power in writing, although from a decidedly different perspective. Along with Black political scientist Charles V. Hamilton, later that year he wrote *Black Power: The Politics of Liberation in America*. The two authors sought to provide a "framework . . . for broad experimentation in accordance with the concept of Black Power." Furthermore, they sought to "define and encourage a new consciousness among black people," a broader notion of nationhood and "communal responsibility" that linked the Black struggle for human rights and self-determination with liberation movements throughout Africa.[27]

As significant as the debate regarding Black Power was to Martin Luther King Jr., however, the issue that had come to concern him most was the Vietnam War. Coretta Scott King had spoken out uncompromisingly against the war as early as 1965 as a member of the Women's International League for Peace and Freedom. "I was, and still am, convinced," she later wrote, "that the women of the world, united without any regard for national or racial divisions, can become a most powerful force for international peace and brotherhood." However, with the exception of tepid criticism of the war offered on a 1965 television news program, her husband had been silent on the matter until spring 1967. In several sermons and speeches, the most famous of which was his April "Beyond Vietnam" address before Clergy and Laymen Concerned About Vietnam at New York City's Riverside Church, he offered a condemnation of U.S. foreign policy and its relationship to domestic poverty and racism. At a subsequent sermon at Ebenezer Baptist Church he noted that he finally had to condemn an "unjust, evil, and futile war." He asserted that the war was an "enemy of the poor," noting that "we spend 500,000 dollars to kill each enemy soldier while we spend only fifty-three dollars for each person classified as poor."[28]

King said informal discussions with young Blacks in Chicago had fueled his antiwar thinking. He found it increasingly difficult to argue against the use of violence in the streets of the inner city while continuing to remain silent on the Vietnam War. "I could never again raise my voice against the violence of the oppressed in the ghettoes without having first spoken clearly to the greatest purveyor of violence today, my own government." King's uncompromising stand drew criticism from moderate Blacks such as journalist Carl Rowan, who correctly surmised that the SCLC leader had antagonized President Lyndon B. Johnson. Curiously, though, Black radicals criticized King from another vantage point. Daniel H. Watts, editor of the Harlem-based magazine Liberator, argued that King sought "guilt money" from the peace movement and noted that the prominent leader had said next to nothing regarding the Congo Crisis. "If Rev. King is sincere in his efforts for peace," Watts contended, "he will desert his so-called white liberal friends, stop the first Soul Brother he meets, and ask for directions on how he can get to Harlem."[29]

The editor of the *Liberator* overstated King's concern for and relationship with progressive Whites, especially at this stage of the SCLC leader's involvement in the Black freedom struggle. Drawing on the earlier critique of the war developed by SNCC Atlanta Project activists, King linked domestic racism, class exploitation, and U.S. imperialism. However, Watts correctly intimated that the epicenter of Black political sentiment had shifted to the often-marginalized neighborhoods of the country's inner cities. The wellspring of protest activity during the Black Power phase of the freedom struggle rested with the urban grassroots. What Watts and other commentators overlooked, perhaps, were the ways in which Blacks of the urban South asserted their voice during this highly contested period.

■ ■ ■

The animosity between police and poor Blacks that sparked the 1966 Summerhill protest flared up again the following summer at a community shopping center in the isolated West Atlanta neighborhood of Dixie Hills. Youths and a Black security guard became embroiled in a scuffle at the Flamingo Grill on Saturday night, 17 June. A crowd of nearly three hundred watched as the police arrived and arrested three Black teens. The next evening a larger crowd assembled at the shopping center to discuss a number of basic, yet overlooked, community concerns, among them continuing problems with inadequate sanitation services and the city's refusal to build playgrounds on several empty lots to which residents had purchased titles. Dixie Hills residents agreed to hold a protest rally the next evening.[30]

The day started ominously when police wounded a young Black man who had attempted to disable a burglar alarm. Word of the shooting spread quickly, and the incident was the top item on the agenda of the Monday evening protest meeting at Saint Joseph Baptist Church. Several established Black leaders, including Alderman Q. V. Williamson and state Senator Leroy Johnson, urged the crowd of over two hundred to draft a petition listing their grievances. "Some of us may differ about procedure, but all of us are serious about obtaining first-class citizens rights for Negroes in Atlanta," Johnson argued. "If we have to march, then march we must, but within the confines of the law." Some in the sanctuary greeted the senator with chants and heckles, several shouting "Hooray for Stokely, hooray for Stokely." At one point someone told Johnson he was "wearing a white man's shirt."[31]

SNCC was represented by Carmichael, Donald Stone, and Ernest Stephens, all activists who lived in Dixie Hills. The crowd listened intently when Carmichael, wearing a Malcolm X sweatshirt, spoke about the percolating tensions in their neighborhood. He urged residents "to take to the streets and force the police department to work until they fall in their tracks." The crowd roared with laughter and applause. Carmichael's underlying message, however, was a serious one, as he condemned Black police detective J. W. Bailey for arresting the teenagers that Saturday night. "We don't want a hunkie lover like Detective Bailey in our community," Carmichael exhorted. "If that Negro comes into our community he's going to get shot."[32]

When residents at the church applauded, he quickly motioned for them to stop. He explained that "when you clap you let off steam and that's our trouble, we've been letting off steam when we should have slapped some heads." On one level, the rhetoric of the SNCC leader spoke to the often violent relationship between police and the Black working poor. On another level, it revealed the more complicated issue of the role of Black police officers and the perception on the part of a number of radical Black activists that they were no better than state collaborators in what amounted to a colonial struggle. "It's not a question of law and order. We are not concerned with peace," Carmichael stressed. "We are concerned with the liberation of black people. We have to build a revolution."[33]

SNCC activists and Dixie Hills residents joined the meeting, and soon there were over one thousand people gathered outside. The nine police officers at the scene fired warning shots in a futile effort to disperse the crowd as "fist-sized rocks" and bottles began to descend upon them from nearby rooftops. Between sixty and seventy heavily armed police reinforcements reestablished control of the crowd, but only after a great deal of damage had been done to several patrol cars. Of the ten people arrested that night, six were twenty-one or younger. Police arrested Carmichael and the other SNCC workers for threatening "to incite a riot" after they refused to vacate the area as ordered. They arrested resident Georgia Wilkins for striking officers with her purse.[34]

The city provided a swift double-barreled response to the grassroots movement in Dixie Hills the next morning. Equipment was rolled into the neighborhood to break new ground for the construction of several playgrounds. Allen also announced the formation of a Negro Youth Patrol, a volunteer group that would monitor the activities of the neighborhood's young people throughout the remainder of the summer. SNCC organizers wasted little time castigating the Negro Youth Patrol as "Black Traitors." Authorities realized full well, however, that the political initiative would have to be accompanied by a paramilitary one if the City of Atlanta was to regain control of the situation in Dixie Hills. Thus, police chief Herbert Jenkins deployed hundreds of uniformed officers, most armed for full urban combat, throughout the neighborhood.[35]

The increased police presence led to further action Tuesday on the part of residents, as well as by both moderate and radical Black activists. Leroy Johnson introduced members of the newly formed Youth Patrol to residents, asserting that the group of Black men from eighteen to twenty-seven years of age were "leaders in the community" who commanded the respect of others. Notably, the teenager shot in the hip the previous day agreed to join the patrol. A group of SNCC organizers interrupted the meeting, however, to condemn the Youth Patrol. Earlier in the day SNCC program director Ralph Featherstone contended "that the man is trying to set these Uncle Tom groups up all over the country." Now newly elected SNCC chair H. Rap Brown and field secretary Willie Ricks led the charge. "We're going to make Vietnam look like a holiday," Ricks declared, adding that "no more cops and no more white folks" would be allowed entry into the neighborhood. Brown, who had just arrived from Houston, predicted that the events in Dixie Hills were "just a prelude to what America is in for."[36]

In this instance, however, more than three hundred police confronted fewer than two hundred protesters, a sobering reminder of the contrast between the Black Power rhetoric and the reality of state police power. As two police officers chased a group of rowdy boys down a neighborhood street, an incendiary device—either a Molotov cocktail or a less destructive cherry bomb—exploded nearby. In the confusion that followed, officers responded with gunfire, killing Willie B. Ross, a forty-eight-year-old man sitting on a front porch at the corner of Verbena Street and Shirley Place, and wounding three others, including nine-year-old Reginald Rivers. "Lord have mercy, Lord have mercy," pleaded the sister of one of the victims, as an ambulance drove the wounded to a hospital. "Lord, we don't bother anybody," she said. "We were just talking about this stuff this afternoon. I don't think we'll ever get over it."[37]

That there was no further escalation of violence was due in part to the efforts of neighborhood activists who had been on the scene. More significant, of course, was the daunting police presence in Dixie Hills that had increased steadily over the past three days. Mayor Allen ordered a twelve-hour dusk-to-dawn curfew for those under eighteen and a nine-hour curfew for adults. "I don't know who the Negro leaders are out here," a befuddled Allen complained, "and I don't believe anybody else does." Reminding residents of the events in Summerhill the previous summer, Johnson and other Black moderates drafted a petition demanding that Carmichael, Ricks, and other SNCC activists leave the area. More than one thousand people signed the petition.[38]

The Dixie Hills petition revealed the limits of SNCC's influence in Atlanta's depressed African American communities. Indeed, after the Summerhill protest, a group of residents of the Vine City neighborhood gathered Project literature, bulletin boards, and other materials, piled them up, and set them on fire. Although most community members agreed with the purpose of SNCC activities, the events of the past few days had a sobering effect on them, revealing a great deal as well about the impact of state repression. "There ain't been nothing but trouble since they have been here," one resident complained. Agreed another, "I thought 'black power' meant something. It does. It means trouble. We don't want shotguns and tear gas here."[39]

Yet, in the aftermath of the deadly demonstrations Dixie Hills Black moderates could scarcely claim a triumph. At an emergency meeting Wednesday evening at Leroy Johnson's home, the Atlanta Committee for Cooperative Action (ACCA) activists—self-described "Young Turks" at the dawn of the decade—spoke of the best ways to press for moderation. "We must have some victories. Then we'll have the ammunition to fight the forces which come and tear up our communities," the senator argued. Johnson stressed that those in power should exercise "good judgment" and release residents arrested in the week of protests, if for no other reason than to "give nonviolent leaders a victory." Albert Davis, leader of the Atlanta NAACP, wasted no time in reaching the heart of the matter. "In a period of twelve hours, outsiders came in and developed a program of riotous activity, and the city reacted immediately," he asserted. Davis overstated the extent to which certain SNCC workers were not part of the neighborhood while ignoring the autonomous and often violent activism of young Dixie Hills demonstrators. Nevertheless, the local NAACP leader could not help but acknowledge who had captured the moment in the eyes of residents. "If you lived in Dixie Hills, would you not assume that Stokely Carmichael has a better program than we have?"[40]

The frank assessment underscored the political nature of the confrontations that had gripped the city over the past two years. Overwhelmingly poor and young, the participants in both demonstrations found collective voice in their clashes with the most visible symbols of governmental authority—the police and their tools. The connection to protests outside the South was not lost on those in Atlanta, especially SNCC organizers. "The riots in Watts made people listen to their problems," an unidentified activist had proclaimed at the height of the Summerhill demonstration. "Atlanta needs to be treated the same way . . . It's no different from Watts. The mayor walks around on plush carpets and wears $500 suits and eats big steaks, while we eat pig foots and chitlins."[41]

Atlanta activists certainly understood the larger national context in which such neighborhood protests occurred. Although the drive to establish independent Black economic and political institutions and to raise the collective African American consciousness—not to mention the use of the term "Black Power" itself—had organic roots in the Black Belt, its actual development appeared at a cursory glance to be strictly outside the South. In mid-1960s Atlanta, however, community protests were as significant as those in Harlem and Detroit. The Summerhill and Dixie Hills protests challenged the hegemony of the biracial Atlanta regime in ways that no previous occurrence had, including the student-led sit-in movement of the early 1960s and the induction center protests conducted by Atlanta Project activists. As historian Alton Hornsby Jr. has noted, the grassroots character of these demonstrations forced the established moderate Black leadership and its liberal White allies to confront the realities facing the city's poor Black majority. The Black Power protests not only provided a platform for established radical activists of the freedom movement, but also had a profoundly empowering effect on participants from the grassroots. "It was the beginning of my awakening in terms of protesting," Columbus Ward recalled. "I've been liking protest ever since then. If there was some injustice going on, I've had no problem protesting that injustice."[42]

The process of radicalization within SNCC that began most explicitly with the Black consciousness movement launched by the Atlanta Project activists was reflected in two documents drafted that summer. At its 1967 national staff meeting, SNCC issued a major policy statement in which it affirmed that it was "a human rights organization, interested not only in human rights in the United States, but throughout the world." Indeed, international themes permeated the statement, which had been drafted only weeks before the Dixie Hills shooting. "We see our struggle here in America as an integral part of the worldwide movement of all oppressed people, such as those in Vietnam, Mozambique, South Africa, Zimbabwe, and Latin America," SNCC activists asserted. "Furthermore, we support the efforts of our brothers [and sisters] in Puerto Rico who are presently engaged in a fight for independence and liberation there." The statement argued in unambiguous terms that Blacks should control the political economy of their communities in a way that did not privilege an elite few. As significantly, the statement called for the development of a cultural consciousness that recognized "the beauty of our thick lips, broad noses, kinky hair and soul."[43]

SNCC's national office also published We Want Black Power not long after the Dixie Hills protests. The nationally distributed pamphlet declared that "the black men of America are a captive people," a male-centered perspective that permeated the manifesto. The pamphlet contended that the oppressed status of urban Blacks placed them in the unique position of playing a vanguard role in the developing Black Power movement. Part and parcel of the argument in We Want Black Power that "the man in the ghetto" would lead the movement was an explicit critique of middle-class Blacks. Drawing a parallel between middle-class Blacks and liberal Whites, the manifesto asserted that even if "cured," more privileged Blacks could no more lead the Black Power movement than Whites could direct the Black human rights struggle.[44]

Nevertheless, the critique of middle-class Blacks was not the central concern of the manifesto. The fundamental issue, according to SNCC leaders, was in beginning "to think black and remove white things from our minds," to raise the collective African American cultural consciousness in the process of waging a national liberation struggle. "The white man has so poisoned our minds," the document argued, "that if a Brother told you he practiced Voodoo you would roll around on the floor laughing at how stupid and superstitious he was." Instead, the opposite should hold true. Blacks needed to aim their laughter at "the black man who says he worships a white Jesus. He is truly sick." We Want Black Power argued that embracing a Black world view was inextricably bound to a larger societal revolution that should be seen within the context of "poor people's movements" throughout the Third World. Expressing the sentiments of past revolutionary nationalists such as Carlos Cooks, a disciple of Marcus Garvey, and Malcolm X, the manifesto asserted that the Black freedom struggle in the United States was for human rights and not civil rights, that "we belong to the 90 percent majority . . . that the white man oppresses."[45]

Much of the rhetoric of the short manifesto, like that of Robert Williams, RAM activists, and earlier Atlanta Project workers, reflected a conscious attempt to link domestic activism with anti-colonial liberation struggles overseas. With regard to those considered "traitors," for instance, the SNCC document asserted that every effort should be made to "ostracize them and if necessary exterminate them." The manifesto offered an analysis of the politics of the Cold War, insisting that the ideological confrontation between the Soviet axis and the United States and its allies was the "biggest lie in the world." Instead, the SNCC activists asserted that the dominant contradiction in the world's political economy was between the industrial North and the "poor people's movements" throughout the Third World. The authors of We Want Black Power also asserted the need to avoid "a ready-made doctrine that will solve all our problems."[46]

■ ■ ■

The organizers of the SCLC had been spurred onward as well, but they continued to proceed down the path of nonviolent direct action. At a December 1967 press conference in Atlanta, SCLC president Martin Luther King Jr. announced plans for a national Poor People's Campaign in the spring and summer of the following year for a "guaranteed annual income." The ambitious campaign called for a "militantly demanding, not begging" march on Washington, D.C., of the poor, irrespective of ethnicity. King stated that the SCLC intended to train a core group of demonstration leaders who would operate from fifteen points of departure from across the country. As winter turned to spring, the scope of the campaign continued to grow as the connection between the national demonstration for what one SCLC aide termed an "Economic Bill of Rights" and King's antiwar activism became even more apparent, provoking criticism from the mainstream press.[47]

Harboring a mixture of disdain and respect for King, younger activists of the Black United Front (BUF), an offshoot of SNCC, agreed to endorse the campaign. Although SNCC activists had often referred to the SCLC president as "de Lawd," almost to a person they maintained a fundamental respect for King, even in the years following the highly contested March Against Fear in Mississippi during the summer of 1966. Whether it was for his principled antiwar activism or for what Julian Bond later termed his ability to "always keep his equilibrium when a lot of people were pushing and pulling on him," those who argued most vociferously with Martin Luther King Jr. admired him as well. SNCC Atlanta Project activist Michael Simmons asserted in hindsight that most radical Black activists failed to appreciate the significance of the Poor People's Campaign until after King's death.[48]

Yet grassroots community activists, such as the welfare organizer Ethel Mae Mathews, recognized the significance of the Poor People's Campaign from the start, since it directly affected their lives. She arrived in Atlanta in 1950, a recently divorced teen-age mother straight out of the Alabama Black Belt. Her parents, lifelong sharecroppers, had arranged for her to marry the father of a child conceived out of wedlock. The marriage lasted two years, and she soon found herself living with an aunt in Atlanta. Mathews worked a number of different jobs over the years, from shucking vegetables at the State Farmers Market to doing domestic work for various families in Buckhead, Atlanta's wealthy White enclave. Yet, because wages in domestic service were so low, she still needed welfare assistance to feed and clothe her children. She was responsible for having each new employer send a letter to the state welfare department indicating the amount of her wages. In the summer of 1968 she heard from neighbors of an upcoming visit from a Washington, D.C., activist named Etta Horne, a leading member of the National Welfare Rights Organization (NWRO). When Mathews told her children that she intended to go to the meeting, they begged her not to do so for fear that she might lose her benefits. She went anyway.[49]

The NWRO had grown out of the Poverty/Rights Action Center, a group launched in 1966 by Black social activist George Wiley to coordinate economic reform efforts by local antipoverty organizations. Wiley had eschewed life as a tenured chemistry professor at Syracuse University, deciding instead to focus on issues of economic justice. In 1967 he joined forces with Beulah Sanders, Johnny Tillman, and other Washington, D.C., welfare mothers in founding the NWRO, which claimed 75,000 "dues-paying members and sympathizers" by 1969. The group primarily comprised Black women and other women of color, with some White members and supporters as well. The NWRO sought to obtain the most from the welfare system and ensure that eligible women utilized its scarce resources. Because of the stigma associated with the welfare system, many Black political groups criticized the mobilization by welfare mothers. Yet, while intellectuals and organizations termed the welfare system "welfare colonialism," they did very little in the way of offering a concrete solution, progressive or otherwise.[50]

Mathews was one of four women who came to hear Horne at the 15 July meeting at Emmaus House, a community social service center run by the Episcopal Church. When Horne stressed that welfare mothers had certain basic rights, Mathews responded by saying, under her breath, "Poor people ain't got no rights." Horne heard her. "Oh yes, darling, you got a right. But you've got to learn how to exercise your right." At first Mathews told her she did not want to join the NWRO, because she could not afford to pay the two dollars in dues. But Emmaus House director Austin Ford gave her the money, and she became the fifth member of the group's Atlanta chapter. By the end of the year, an additional 150 women joined the group in Atlanta.[51]

Members of the Atlanta Welfare Rights Organization elected Mathews president not long after she joined the group, in large part because of her work as a tenacious organizer for housing rights and with the prison ministry of her Baptist church. "I've been spreading the word, educating people that they have a right, regardless if they're a welfare recipient, a Social Security recipient, a food stamp recipient, a poor person working for them 'under-wages.' . . . That's my mission. That's what God gave me to do." Mathews was unflinching in confronting those in power. She was one of several poor Black women who spoke at public hearings before the Georgia House of Representatives in July 1969 on hunger and malnutrition, launching a long and highly contested relationship with local and state elected officials.[52]

In her efforts, Mathews confronted the fact that there were a growing number of local Black elected officials. Operating from well-organized Black districts, former Committee on Appeal of Human Rights stalwarts Benjamin Brown and Julian Bond organized successful campaigns for the state Legislature in 1965, although Bond would have to wait a year to be seated because of his antiwar activism. The ranks of Black state legislators continued to grow with the successful 1969 campaign of Henrietta Canty, the first Black woman licensed to sell securities in the South. Of the city's Black elected officials, Bond was the first to enter the national political stage with his eloquent speech at the turbulent 1968 Democratic national convention. "Almost anything can happen to us in America, but black people can, through the political process, get some of the things we need," Bond asserted in 1969.[53]

Bond and other local Black elected officials would be forced to confront two pivotal issues as the year came to a close: tenants rights and police brutality. Cora Towns led the effort by tenants at the Bolton Garden Apartments to demand basic and long overdue improvements in housing. In November, Bolton tenants had agreed not to pay rent, opting instead to pay for improvements. The Bolton rent strike received concrete support from both the Atlanta Legal Aid Society and the local NAACP. A city-wide effort to organize renters into a tenants union did not materialize, however, in part because a local judge ruled against Towns and the other tenants in January, ordering them to pay over eleven thousand dollars in overdue rent. As important, though, the Bolton tenants movement also suffered from a failure on the part of most local Black elected officials to publicly endorse the rent strike.[54]

Black politicians and other established activists continued to confront police brutality and harassment in the city, perhaps because the issue affected Blacks across intraracial class lines. Benjamin Brown denounced a Fulton County grand jury report contending that incidents of police brutality and harassment in Black communities were isolated and not part of a larger pattern of institutionalized racism. Lonnie King, the former sit-in organizer who now headed the local NAACP, was not surprised. He asserted that the grand jury report "lived down" to his lowest expectations. Joseph Boone, minister and executive director of the Metropolitan Summit Leadership Congress, did not mince his words either. "It's a damn disgrace, it's a whitewash." Only a week after the report's release, a Black woman arrested for drunkenness charged the police with brutality. Wanda Jean Brooks asserted—and witnesses confirmed—that after she left a party at a downtown hotel police threw her into a police van, beat her, then assaulted her again while handcuffed to a bed at Grady Memorial Hospital. "He threw me into the wheelchair, banging my head up against the chair," Brooks recalled of one officer, "and as he did it he yelled 'shut up, dirty black bitch.' "[55]

Ethel Mathews took it upon herself as part of her grassroots mission to run for the Atlanta City Council in 1969. The local NWRO leader understood the limits of electoral politics well enough, yet believed that there were so few principled people in government that an honest representative of the voiceless might effect fundamental change. During the course of the campaign she was offered "a pillowcase of money" from an anonymous person who suggested that she drop out of the race. She refused to accept the "package," viewing the election as another avenue "to bring my people out of bondage, not just Black poor people, but all poor people." Mathews lost the election, but not her core community supporters, many of whom registered to vote for the first time.[56]

The principled activism of neighborhood organizers such as Mathews and Towns situated itself within a larger world view shared by many grassroots Black activists of the South. As historian Rhonda Williams has shown, these organizers did not embrace a specific ideology in the narrow doctrinal sense of the term; for instance, they tended not to speak of themselves as "nationalists" or "radicals." But they often worked with those who embraced such political designations.[57] The relationship between grassroots and established activists was often complicated. Some radical Black activists criticized individuals such as Mathews and Ward because of their affiliation with Emmaus House and its director, progressive White minister Austin Ford. Grassroots activists often ignored such criticism, however, cherishing instead their role on the frontline, and the selflessness that community struggles embodied. Furthermore, they were aware of their class position, both in intraracial and societal terms, to a degree that often made their middle-class Black counterparts bristle.

Unlike a growing number of radical Black organizers and intellectuals of the period, these neighborhood activists were also devoutly religious. Like countless African American activist women before her, Mathews saw no contradiction between challenging "the power structure" and being "a strong believer in God." Robin Kelley has demonstrated the significance of spirituality for the Alabama sharecroppers who joined the Depression-era Communist Party. In much the same way, contemporary neighborhood activists often placed both individual and collective work and worship at the center of their world view.[58]

Mathews also asserted that being principled meant being uncompromising. In the tradition of Fannie Lou Hamer and Malcolm X, she felt that people who lacked integrity would sell their souls, if pressured to do so. "The power structure, the businessmen, and politicians, they thought they had somebody they could buy," she recalled. "Ask Hosea Williams about Ms. Mathews. He will tell you, 'Ms. Mathews was the only one they couldn't buy.'" In a time period when federal anti-poverty dollars began to fill the pockets of opportunists, "uneducated" neighborhood activists like Ethel Mathews had a great deal of wisdom to impart. "In my work I have learned that . . . your life don't belong to you when you go to taking Mr. Chahlie's money. It belongs to Mr.

Chahlie. And when he plays a tune you gotta jump and dance, whether you want to or not."[59]

The early period of the Black Power phase of the Black struggle for human rights was characterized and propelled by urban protest and neighborhood activism. The uncompromising spirit of grassroots neighborhood activists would be tested time and again as groups as diverse as the National Domestic Workers Union and the Black Panther Party fought for the hearts and minds of poor and working-class Blacks in Atlanta. The viability of a progressive Black political front was at stake. In the more privileged sections of town, however, the energy of demonstrations such as those in Dixie Hills and Summerhill began to manifest itself in the drive for independent and activist-oriented Black intellectual institutions.

THE QUEST FOR SELF-DETERMINATION

BLACK STUDIES AND THE
BIRTH OF THE INSTITUTE
OF THE BLACK WORLD

n the wake of the April 1968 assassination of Martin Luther King Jr., college students in Atlanta began pressing for the establishment of Black Studies programs as a fitting first step toward commemorating his life's work. Best known as an apostle of nonviolent direct action in challenging petty apartheid, King also had struggled to bring bedrock issues of social and economic justice to the fore through his critique of the Vietnam War and support of the Memphis sanitation workers' strike. A number of important intellectuals in Atlanta, including Spelman College history chair Vincent Harding, had been affected in a similar way by the King assassination. "None of us was the same after that," Harding asserted in a 1970 essay, "especially as we watched a momentarily frightened power structure turn our brother Martin into a false symbol of whitened docility and ersatz unity, manipulating his image before his body was cold."[1] Nevertheless, the tragic death of "our most honored, peaceful warrior" galvanized Blacks and sparked serious discussion of the relationship between the African American experience and the academy.[2] At the national level, Black student groups demanded that colleges and universities establish Black Studies programs, one of the most tangible and significant manifestations of the Black Power phase of the larger human rights struggle.

From San Francisco State to Brandeis, colleges and universities began the process of implementing Black student programs following militant demonstrations by students and community activists. Students led by doctoral candidate James Turner won a decisive victory at Northwestern University in 1968. University administrators there agreed to provide Black students with separate residence halls, priority financial aid, and improvements in curriculum and admissions. Northwestern also agreed to appoint noted Black intellectuals Lerone Bennett and Margaret Walker Alexander as visiting professors. At Cornell University an armed contingent of the Student Afro-American Society occupied the school's administration building in 1969, an action that led to the establishment of the Africana Studies and Research Center, one of the few autonomous academic programs in the country, with Turner as its first director. Some institutions refused to concede to student demands, however, most notably Columbia University.[3]

Students at Atlanta's institutions of higher learning watched events elsewhere closely, as did radical Black activists in the city. Officials at the Atlanta University Center (AUC) helped to quell a January 1969 student takeover organized by students with help from SNCC workers Willie Ricks and Cleveland Sellers. Hugh M. Gloster, Morehouse College's president, informed the school's board of trustees in a memorandum that he had obtained a list of student demands. Apparently, students hostile to the planned takeover had made Gloster and other administrators privy to the campus action only hours before it had been scheduled to take place. Campus activists called for the rejection of the term *Negro* as "a tool of racist colonialism" and the consolidation of the six affiliated schools into one major university, and declared that the primary function of the Atlanta University Center should be to aid the Black freedom struggle worldwide. A demand that revealed the way in which blatant homophobia had become braided with a Black nationalist quest for self-determination called for the removal of "white racists [*sic*] homosexuals" from the faculty.[4]

As student activists in Atlanta made efforts to regroup, Black students at the University of Georgia made their move. In February some one hundred members of the Black Student Union (BSU) presented university president Fred Davison with a list of demands. As was the case at most predominantly White schools, the Georgia students called for the establishment of a Black Studies Department and a separate dormitory. In addition to demanding an increase in Black admissions, the students insisted that a Black person be appointed to the Georgia Board of Regents to replace avowed segregationist Roy Harris. Harris claimed the distinction of having managed George Wallace's presidential campaign in the state of Georgia. The Georgia BSU also demanded that all musical renditions of "Dixie" be halted immediately. The university's initial response to the student demands was lukewarm, at best.[5]

At first glance, it might appear as if Black student demands at the AUC should have caused less tension than those at the University of Georgia, especially given that Georgia had been segregated until the early sixties. Yet, that was not the case. As at most historically Black colleges and universities, administrators at the AUC schools wielded far more power than did faculty or students, and they were keenly aware that campus activism could jeopardize external funding. Largely supportive of students during the sit-ins of the early 1960s, these university presidents now contended with two related issues they had not been forced to encounter in struggles against petty apartheid in the city. First, they had to grapple with the rise in radical nationalist sentiment that had altered the course of the movement in the South from 1964 onward. Second, they had to confront Black student activism that challenged the status quo at their institutions. Gloster and other key administrators had avoided such a showdown in January, perhaps because other students exposed a planned takeover.

In April 1969, however, the confrontation finally materialized. A group of students demanded a hearing at the scheduled meeting with the Atlanta University Board of Trustees on Thursday, 17 April, but received no invitation. On the following day students representing several AUC institutions returned to the administration building on the Morehouse campus, but discovered that the meeting that day was of the Morehouse trustees. Determined to obtain a hearing, ten students moved quickly inside the meeting room, chaining the doors shut from the inside. Word quickly spread that students had confined the president of Morehouse and its board of trustees. Soon, rumors circulated that armed student activists had ransacked the room and threatened the lives of the trustees. After Gloster addressed a group of concerned students gathering outside, several of the students made an attempt to rush the doors, to no avail. Given the situation, Gloster took drastic action: "Since I cannot be a party to concessions made under duress to a group of ten individuals," he stated, "I am herewith submitting my resignation as president of Morehouse College."[6]

Twenty-nine hours and an informal agreement later, student activists unchained the doors and released their dazed hostages. During the takeover the Morehouse Student Government Association had called an emergency vote of students in which condemnation of the surprise protest carried the day. Students also voted overwhelmingly to ignore both Gloster's resignation letter and the agreement reached during the building occupation. Less than a week later, the campus reading center was the target of a latenight firebombing that resulted in no injuries. Morehouse student president Nelson Taylor offered a sharp denunciation of those students responsible for the events of the past week. "We will oppose you," a frustrated Taylor warned. "We will oppose you and let God decide the consequences." He organized an impromptu meeting of twenty-five students to press for amnesty for student activists and consideration of merging the six affiliated schools "more completely." While he acknowledged that many activists were sincere in their convictions, he insisted that there were others "whose primary purpose is destruction and the building of confusion." It was members of this second group, according to Taylor, "who are attempting arson on our campus."[7]

Black students at Emory University, meanwhile, embarked at first on a less turbulent route toward Black student power. In 1968, Emory students led by Henry Ambrose established the Black Student Alliance (BSA), six years after the university admitted its first two Black students. On 12 March 1969 the BSA presented university president Sanford S. Atwood with the Emory Manifesto, an eight-point document voicing student concerns and proposals for future university action. The manifesto called for the administration to issue a statement concerning the current admission of Black students as well as provide a broader framework for accepting a larger number of Black students. Emory students also proposed that the school construct a Black residential center, hire a Black administrator and psychiatrist, and establish an "Afro-American Reading Room" within the existing library that would be staffed by a Black librarian. Finally, the manifesto called for the establishment of a Black Studies program in conjunction with the Atlanta University Center.[8]

Atwood responded officially to the Emory Manifesto on 25 March, indicating that the Methodist institution would give each item careful consideration. Frustrated Black students did not take matters into their own hands for two full months—a virtual eternity for activists faced with the end of another academic year. On 25 May 1969 James Brown and Ambrose led a contingent of Black students that disrupted Sunday worship service at Emory's Durham Chapel. Students read the manifesto aloud as a surprised pastor and congregation listened. Following the worship service a group of thirty-five Blacks and several White supporters from Students for a Democratic Society marched to the Cox Hall cafeteria where they formed a "human blockade" to protest "economic slavery" at Emory. The Cox Hall protest was meant as an expression of solidarity with cafeteria workers, almost all Black, who had begun agitating for better wages. Monday, the Emory activists organized a rally on the campus quadrangle which drew more than five hundred students, a definite accomplishment at the normally apathetic school.[9]

Atwood moved quickly to obtain a restraining order from a DeKalb County Superior Court judge prohibiting further disruptions. However, the injunction proved to be a tactical blunder for the Emory administration when the student and faculty senates passed joint resolutions calling for an end to campus racism and nullification of the restraining order. Atwood, who had followed Black student protests across the country, announced the university's intention to implement a Black Studies program.[10] Emory students, like Blacks at many predominantly White colleges and universities, had fared better than their counterparts at the financially strapped and conservatively run institutions in Atlanta's West End neighborhood.

Meanwhile, the already turbulent atmosphere at the Atlanta University Center was about to receive yet another jolt. The Morehouse administration announced on 24 June that twenty-eight students would receive disciplinary action for their involvement in the 18 April occupation and lock-in. Five students, including two seniors, received full academic year suspensions, and five others received semester-long suspensions. Although Gloster declined to discuss the suspensions publicly, Ralph Lee, the outgoing academic dean, said that while he "sympathized" with student objectives he disapproved of their actions. George M. Coleman, associate editor of the *Atlanta Voice*, refused to be silent, lambasting the "immature actions by adults and students alike." Coleman asserted that while the takeover "was a foolish, mean, and vicious act," the decision by Morehouse to renege on the agreement and then suspend student activists was "snobbish" and "disgusting in every sense of the word." Instead, Coleman wrote, it would have better served Morehouse if Gloster and the trustees had been lenient. "Who knows, but that a future M. L. King or Ralph Bunche may have been thrown out into the streets like a criminal."[11]

Protest activity had not been confined to Morehouse College. Atlanta University President Thomas D. Jarrett sought an injunction against five radical Black activists, including former SNCC stalwarts Bill Ware and Willie Ricks, for constructing a protest camp at the corner of Beckwith and Lawshe streets. The camp began as a vigil after the assassination of Martin Luther King Jr. but had continued as an ongoing protest of the Vietnam War, racism, poverty, and "man's inhumanity to man." The trustees contended that the property belonged to Atlanta University and that the camp, which had been constructed as a microcosm of the Resurrection City shantytown of the Poor People's Campaign, posed sanitation problems for the surrounding neighborhood. Meanwhile, the volatile campus protest spread to the Interdenominational Theological Center (ITC). Led by Ike Hentrel, students there presented a manifesto that called for a committee to look into grievances concerning a range of issues, from academic standards to substandard cafeteria food. ITC President Oswald Bronson held several highly charged meetings throughout the fall semester in an effort to address the manifesto.[12]

At Emory, Atwood organized several meetings with administrators, faculty, and the leadership of the BSA. Student leader Rena M. Price wrote Atwood at one point during the summer to insist that Emory employ all "creative and legal ways" to ensure financial aid and targeted programming for Black students. Atwood had already secured a Black House for the BSA on Clifton Road, and he worked quickly to establish a faculty-student Afro-American Studies Sub-Committee. After a year of planning, the Emory College faculty approved the establishment of a Black Studies program, even if the notion of an autonomous department did not take root at the university. The program would offer cross-listed courses based in traditional departments, and it would offer a major for undergraduates.

Emory also launched a search for a coordinator of the embryonic program, eventually appointing Delores P. Aldridge in 1971. Aldridge, who had just completed her doctorate at Purdue University, became the first Black scholar to join the Emory faculty. The young sociologist was placed in the position of constructing the first Black Studies program in the South, an experience with "few or no parallels," she later recalled. Aldridge wasted no time, designing six core courses including Black Studies 204, the "practicum" field study course.[13] Aldridge realized full well that student activism had been pivotal in providing her the opportunity to take on the Black Studies challenge at Emory. "Protest is never easy. But, then, to have to be pushed to the point of protest has not been easy for the protester," she later noted. "All Black professors, no matter how great we are, have a debt we can never repay to students," Aldridge said. "Black folk have always been great, but we did not come into the academy until Black students got out there protesting that they wanted to see Black faculty."[14]

■ ■ ■

Activists at the Atlanta University Center did not operate in a completely hostile environment, thanks in large part to allies in the faculty. Vincent Harding, chair of the Spelman College history department, was one such professor. His first trip to Atlanta was in fall 1958, when he took a break from graduate work in religious history at the University of Chicago to visit the city with a small group from the interracial Mennonite Church. Following their stay in Atlanta, the group continued their five-state tour of the South by meeting Little Rock freedom fighter Daisy Bates. "It was a very important beginning of revelation for me," Harding later noted. In 1960 the native New Yorker took another break from his doctoral work to return to Atlanta in order to establish Mennonite House, a "rest and renewal" site for movement activists. Vincent and Rosemarie Harding lived in the same Vine City neighborhood as Martin and Coretta King, and the four became friends. The relationship was significant for Vincent Harding because he had been particularly struck by the SCLC president's focus on nonviolence and reconciliation.[15]

In 1964 the Hardings returned to Chicago so that he could finish his Ph.D. dissertation, "Lyman Beecher and the Transformation of American Protestantism, 1775–1863." Soon after, he received a call from Spelman College President Albert Manley requesting that he accept an appointment as chair of the school's history and sociology department. Ironically, while in Atlanta Harding had been part of a groundswell of community condemnation when Staughton Lynd and Howard Zinn lost their teaching positions because of their activism and involvement with SNCC. The notion of replacing Zinn, a respected colleague, under such dicey circumstances proved vexing for Harding. Nevertheless, Zinn insisted that the young activist scholar take the appointment. First, Zinn stressed that Black students needed him. Second, the former Spelman professor correctly noted that being chair of the department would provide Harding with a degree of power that other faculty members simply would not possess at a historically Black institution.[16]

Harding accepted the appointment, but on his own terms. Largely because he viewed himself "as essentially a social change worker," Harding told the Spelman president that while he was "no wild man from outer space" and intended to respect the spirit of the college and its students, his activism could not be compromised. "I was going to be working outside the institution, inside the institution, and around the institution," he reiterated, "in a way that would sometimes challenge the institution." After accepting the position at Spelman, the Hardings lived next door to "visionary" poet Stephen Henderson, chair of the English department at Morehouse. It would not be long before the two professors began entering into discussions about the possibility of the AUC being a focal point in the burgeoning Black Studies movement.[17]

Henderson and Harding first envisioned an "Institute for Advanced African American Studies," linked to the Atlanta University schools in a similar fashion as other university institutes across the country. However, both men quickly came to realize the extent to which the study of Blackness "was a dangerous idea" to established Blacks as well as to Whites in the city. Such conservative thinking did not bode well for the possibility of a Black research institute inextricably bound to academic institutions that had resisted students' demand for Black Studies. Indeed, several faculty members on campus had already been associated, "rightly and wrongly," with the April 1969 occupation and lock-in. Harding later noted that faculty members and students who embraced the emerging Black Studies paradigm were "handled gingerly" by administrators. This was in part "because the funding agencies upon whom the AU Center depended for its financial life were not happy about the early stages of Black Power, even though some of them, like the Ford Foundation, later got in on the act and tried to shape the act."[18]

Instead, AUC faculty members turned their attention in another direction. Coretta Scott King already had asked Harding to be founding director of what was first called the Martin Luther King, Jr. Library Documentation Center. Now he and other supporters of a Black-centered institute hoped that such a "research advocacy center" might exist under the auspices of what came to be known in 1969 as the Martin Luther King, Jr. Memorial Center. He recalled that doing so made sense because "it was appropriate and because we thought that would be one way of gaining some of the kind of financial resources that would be necessary for an institute like the one we were dreaming of to take place." Coretta King agreed, and as a result, the Institute of the Black World (IBW) came into being in early 1969, one of four components of the King Memorial Center. The other three elements of the ambitious project headed by Harding were a library documentation project on the post-1954 Black freedom movement, an institute for nonviolent social change, and a museum of African American life and culture.[19]

The Institute was to be "a community of Black scholars, artists, teachers, and organizers" buttressed by a governing board of twenty-seven people from throughout the global African world, according to its statement of purpose. The IBW was to be the site for a convergence of "Black intellectuals who are convinced that the gifts of their minds are meant to be fully used in the service of the Black community. It is, therefore, an experiment with scholarship in the context of struggle." Although the ultimate aim of the IBW was to focus scholarly attention on the entire African world, its staff conceded "an initial emphasis on the American experience."[20]

A ten-point program accompanied the statement of purpose. Four areas dealt specifically with educational issues within the Black community: defining and refining the field of Black Studies; developing a "new Consortium for Black Education"; supporting Black artists concerned with the "struggle for the minds and hearts of our people"; and developing new materials for teaching Black children. Two areas had a global African focus: providing basic research on peoples of African descent; and forming creative linkages with other concerned activists and scholars in the global African world. Two elements of the IBW program concerned more tangible programming: sponsoring seminars, workshops, and conferences both independently and with other institutions and organizations; and launching a publishing program. Arguably, the last two areas had the most profound long-term impact: developing a Black policy studies center and preparing "a new cadre of men and women who are at once precisely trained in the scholarship of the Black experience and fully committed to the struggles of the Black world."[21]

■ ■ ■

A capable research staff accepted the challenge of transforming the Institute's mission and program into a body of thought and action, joining Harding and Henderson in Atlanta. Lerone Bennett Jr., senior editor of *Ebony* magazine and author of the widely read 1962 book *Before the Mayflower*, accepted a position at the Institute, as did historian and former Chicago schoolteacher Sterling Stuckey, of Northwestern University. Stuckey's groundbreaking essay, "Through the Prism of Folklore: The Black Ethos in Slavery," which appeared in the summer 1968 *Massachusetts Review*, provided one of the earliest arguments for cultural autonomy by enslaved Africans. William Strickland, lecturer in history at Columbia University and deputy director of the 1967 Black Power Conference in Newark, played a key role on the IBW research team during Harding's five-year tenure as director. Chester Davis, of the Taskforce on Childhood Education, also joined the IBW research staff.[22]

One of the most revealing examples of the convergence between frontline activism and scholarship was provided by Joyce Ladner—the youngest and lone female member of the IBW senior research team—who had begun work on *Tomorrow's Tomorrow: The Black Woman*. Born in Palmer's Crossing, Mississippi, twins Joyce and Dorie Ladner went from high school valedictorian and salutatorian to attend Jackson State College, only to be expelled for their student activism. As an NAACP youth activist, Joyce Ladner participated in frontline struggles against apartheid, learning from activist mentors such as Medgar Evers, Vernon Damon, and Clyde Kinard—each murdered by racist terrorists. She continued to shine as a student after transferring to Tougaloo College, yet focused on "always trying to find a way to do both, to study and to be an activist." She entered the doctoral program in sociology at Washington University in St. Louis in 1964 and "was driven like a maniac" to finish in four years while simultaneously establishing a Friends of SNCC chapter and working with the Congress of Racial Equality (CORE).[23]

Joyce Ladner remained fully grounded in her doctoral studies and her activism, continually making linkages between the two. She organized a contingent of students who joined the voting rights battle in Selma, Alabama in 1965. The following summer she worked with Alvin Poussaint and the Medical Commission on Human Rights, finding herself back home in Mississippi. She participated in the March Against Fear, and "just happened to have been there when Willie Ricks hollered 'Black Power' and Stokely echoed it." Ladner began interviewing dozens of local Blacks for a paper that became her first publication, the foundational article "What Black Power Means to Negroes in Mississippi," which appeared in Transaction magazine. In it, Ladner, who since childhood had developed a "very keen awareness of Black people being poor," showed that "Black Power" had concrete economic meaning for people in the grassroots. At twenty-four she completed her dissertation, "On Becoming a Woman in the Ghetto: Modes of Adaptation."[24]

It was apparent that Joyce Ladner would be among the most sought-after young sociologists in the country. "I was the queen bee that year," she laughed. She received job offers from the University of California, Berkeley, Yale, and Harvard, where her adviser, Lee Rainwater, was now on the faculty. True to form, however, "I really disappointed him because I went over to East St. Louis to work with kids who wouldn't have been able to get into college. And we mainstreamed them in two years." The following year Rainwater arranged for Ladner to interview at the Massachusetts Institute of Technology and at Harvard for a possible joint appointment. Jonathan Parsons interviewed her, noting "what a privilege it would have been for me to have been a lecturer" there, Ladner remembered. Her response spoke volumes. "I just looked at him with no malice or anything else intended—I was just being honest—I said, 'Mr. Parsons, Harvard is not my reference group.'" Dumbfounded, he asked her to leave his office and then "smoked one cigarette after another" for thirty minutes. "He really did not have a response for me." When a friend asked her why she had the audacity to "insult" a Harvard professor, she explained that "my reference group is the movement."[25]

Born and raised in apartheid Mississippi by a mother who always "wanted to fix things," the young scholar had come to realize through years of activism that teaching at Harvard simply could not represent life achievement for her. "We lived our lives with sunshine, no deviousness," she explained. "You had to, because you had to know who to trust, because we turned our lives over to people in the movement who we trusted because they could be responsible for you living or dying." Ladner's frontline activist experiences confirmed for her that scholarship inextricably bound to the Black freedom struggle carried the fullest meaning. Within this context, the Ivy League offered little in the way of allure. More important, however, the meeting with Parsons exposed a fundamental disconnect within the field of sociology itself. "Here's a man who has written about social structure for a whole society, and yet he and those who have written about my people have never met them. They lived here in Cambridge, Massachusetts. They have wives who drive station wagons. They do not work, like our mothers who are slaving," she later elaborated. "They have 2.5 children, but they do not know our reality, mainly. And yet, how can you talk about 'the American family?' And then, when you talk about my family, you talk about 'sluts and perverts,' and we're 'deviants.' "[26]

The Institute of the Black World provided a welcome alternative, then, for scholars concerned with challenging dominant perspectives in both academic and activist thinking. Having already been interviewed by Harding for a position at Spelman prior to the launching of the IBW, Ladner turned her attention to the Black activist think tank. She saw the Institute as a "wonderful way in which I could go and be with people who were doing scholarship and activism." For Strickland, who had grown frustrated with Marxist theorists who downplayed the importance of race in the U.S. context, the IBW offered promise as well. He had been influenced by an eclectic group of leftists who included James and Grace Lee Boggs, as well as Jack O'Dell, of *Freedomways*. On the one hand, Strickland had grown increasingly critical of "identification with Africa" as the answer to the problems of Blacks in the United States. Yet, he also realized that some activists had relied on Marxist analysis "because really deep down into it they didn't believe Black people could win by themselves." Strickland looked forward to the opportunity to chart an independent course provided by the IBW. "When Vincent said, 'Let's rethink the world,' I said, 'Yeah, baby, let's do that!' "[27]

■ ■ ■

In the summer of 1969 the IBW research staff organized a workshop for college students and a conference on Black Studies. Intent on making Black Studies "more than a frightened concession of threatened campus administrators," the activist scholars of the Institute made every effort to equip students with the necessary tools to engage other students when they returned to their respective campuses in the fall. Taking advantage of contacts with activist scholars nationwide, the IBW entered into "cooperative relationships" with students and faculty at Brooklyn and Dartmouth colleges and at Cornell and Wesleyan universities. Furthermore, the Institute's scholars initiated the process of piecing together a Consortium for Research and Development on the Black Experience in conjunction with Howard and Fisk universities. In addition to working within the context of the academy, the IBW also established a local relationship with the Martin Luther King Community School.[28]

The first months of the IBW were marked by the eclectic cultural and political movement of Black Power. Lerone Bennett considered the IBW mission to be at one with the resurgence of Black pride and advocacy of independent institutions. "In white-oriented schools, we were educated away from ourselves—away from our people, away from our rhythm, away from our genius, away from our soul." Therefore, the IBW represented a significant and necessary journey of Black intellectuals back to the struggles and life-force of their home communities. And such a move acknowledged a certain responsibility. "We believe in the community of the Black dead and the Black living and the Black unborn," Bennett explained. "We believe that community has a prior claim on our time and our talents and our resources, and that we must respond when it calls."[29]

Members of the IBW research staff understood that their work was part of a larger tradition of activist social engagement on the part of Black intellectuals. Perhaps being in Atlanta made this point especially clear. W. E. B. Du Bois cemented his place as an activist scholar while at Atlanta University, helping to launch both the Niagara movement and the NAACP nationally and the early Pan-African movement during the high tide of apartheid in the United States. Lugenia Burns Hope founded the Neighborhood Union, a social service agency that assisted poor Blacks in the city. John Hope, the first Black president of Morehouse College, played a key role in condemning the treatment of Black servicemen during World War I. Central to these efforts was a fundamental concern for and belief in the humanity of Black people. "We believed back then that there was something authentic about the humanity of Black people, that Black people tended to be more humane toward each other than White people" Joyce Ladner asserted in retrospect, and "more likely to take care of our brothers and sisters when needed, than White people. We thought that this harkened back to the social genes of our ancestors."[30]

Eminent scholars from other parts of the global African world came to Atlanta in 1969. Jamaican-born Robert Hill came to the Institute as a visiting scholar. C. L. R. James, the Trinidadian author of the classic account of the Haitian Revolution, *The Black Jacobins: Toussaint L'Overture and the San Domingo Revolution*, conducted workshops as a scholar-in-residence. Another fixture at the Institute was Walter Rodney, the brilliant young Guyanese activist scholar, in Atlanta after completing *A History of the Upper Guinea Coast, 1545 to 1800*. "Deathly ill" when he arrived in the United States, Rodney had to be hospitalized. Joyce and Dorie Ladner immediately contacted Pat Rodney, who said her husband had probably contracted malaria while in Uganda. Provided with an anti-malarial, Walter Rodney recuperated before Pat arrived in the United States. The Rodneys stayed with the Ladner sisters, and the four forged a lasting friendship. "Rap Brown was on the run. Things were fragmented. And people picked up the fragments," Joyce Ladner remembered. "We couldn't go back to where we'd been. So the progression was to look more and more abroad for models on how to rebuild toward self-help."[31]

Underlining the IBW community's emphasis on activism, William Strickland insisted that this conscious link between IBW projects and Black freedom movements worldwide—being "committed to action that will bring about change"—set it apart from other think tanks in the United States. Joyce Ladner provided clear testimony of the synergy between activism and scholarship during her year at the Institute. "It was the single-most productive year of my academic career," she stressed. Ladner had written several articles, developed curricula on the socialization of Black children, and had helped to organize conferences. "I wrote more. I taught. I wrote *Tomorrow's Tomorrow* from start to finish there." She noted that "I had this incredible energy" personally, and yet "it was such a collaborative environment."[32]

Yet, being so overtly political placed the Institute in a precarious position financially, an issue that would complicate the efforts of its scholars throughout its existence. The annual IBW budget had been projected at roughly seven hundred thousand dollars, but reality set in quickly when Vincent Harding could speak only of "promises" amounting to no more than two hundred thousand dollars. The precipitous drop in external funding that accompanied the radicalization of SNCC should have served as warning enough, but naiveté held sway. Harding later acknowledged that members of the Institute staff "had these fantasies, as they turned out to be, of millions of dollars of American guilt money and conscience money pouring into the Martin Luther King Center."[33]

At Strickland's request, Harding wrote Coretta Scott King in November 1969 to enlist her support for a local political empowerment project conceptualized by the IBW's public policy section. "Your influence in Atlanta is significant," Harding wrote, "and I think there is a possibility of developing the kind of Freedom Program for the city which Bill [Strickland] mentions. It is certainly needed." Strickland and Harding realized that Coretta King's explicit support for the project could prove financially beneficial. Strickland also joined forces with Worth Long, a former SNCC worker now on Julian Bond's staff, to establish a concrete relationship with Black elected officials. They first sought the support of Mack H. Jones, the chair of the Atlanta University political science department, who then made overtures to other faculty members concerning the "possibility of making the resources of the social science faculties in the University Center available to local office-holders in a non-partisan and non-doctrinaire manner." Jones believed strongly that collaboration between politicians and academics "would redound to the benefit of each of us as individuals and to the Black community as a whole."[34]

As promising as these initiatives were, however, there also was mounting ambivalence. The King family and concerned friends had long been troubled by Black Power and its implications for the legacy of the slain SCLC president. Harding recalled that prominent Blacks continued to be reticent about a connection between the King Memorial Center and "anything that seemed to be this 'Black stuff.'" He noted that a significant number of people had sound reasons, of course, for having "read the Black Power movement, the Black consciousness movement, the Black Studies movement, as a movement toward separatism."[35]

Harding and other members of the IBW research staff engaged in a struggle with the Center's board of directors for a year. The board wanted the staff to prioritize Martin Luther King's life and legacy in its research and programming, take "an oath of nonviolence," and include interested White scholars. The Institute's scholars countered by asserting that the specific plight of peoples of African descent throughout the world meant that nonviolence was neither philosophically nor strategically the sole method of achieving liberation. Besides, Harding argued, the research staff surmised that a proper "analysis and definition of the Black struggle is the necessary and natural responsibility of Black people themselves." A stalemate ensued, resulting in a severing of organizational ties between the IBW and the King Center by early 1970. Nonetheless, Harding later recalled that, for the most part, it was a relatively friendly parting of the ways.[36]

■ ■ ■

In March 1970 the Institute of the Black World set out independently on its mission. One of the first tasks was discussion of an internal document entitled "Towards a Black Agenda." No doubt influenced by the past year's debate with the King Center Board of Directors, its author believed that the document had the potential to "become the central *corporate* task of the Institute staff for the next 2–3 years." The essay advocated that the researchers maintain their commitment to Black control over chronicling, defining, and interpreting "the Black experience." The essay focused on the need for research and writing, a contemporary political analysis, and development of the "ideas and concepts" of nation-building with regard to global African people. The essay also revealed that the staff had reached a degree of consensus in embracing a think-tank model over that of a Black university or consulting service. Nevertheless, the staff recognized that the term "think tank" was itself problematic in that it privileged theoretical work and the academy over day-to-day activism among those in the grassroots.[37]

The document pointed to eight items for such an agenda: education, economic development, political organizing and development, police control, health and welfare, cultural development and definition, historical research, and relationships and approaches to Third World political struggles. Through a process of research, reflection, and revision, IBW staff members produced two sets of documents: "Black Papers" on particular agenda topics, and less publicized research papers. The author of "Towards a Black Agenda" envisioned, then, that Institute participants would serve "essentially as catalysts for that organizing of Black intellect towards the revolutionary scholarship we have wanted to do."[38] Spurred on perhaps by the presence of the IBW on its campus, Atlanta University established a Center for African and African-American Studies (CAAS) in 1970. Richard A. Long, the distinguished Atlanta University English professor and lecturer at Harvard, designed the CAAS Summer Study Abroad program that year. The six course offerings included "African Tradition in the Caribbean" and a "Survey of Contemporary Black African Culture."[39]

Atlanta University set itself apart from the other affiliated schools in another way that spring. Atlanta University president Thomas D. Jarrett endorsed a joint statement condemning violence waged against student activists across the country. The statement represented one of the rare instances when students, faculty, and administrators were of one voice on an issue. On 31 May 1970 Jarrett called a press conference at which he charged that the deaths of students at Jackson State University, as well as the December 1969 murders of Chicago Black Panther leaders Fred Hampton and Mark Clark, were nothing short of "genocide." From the late 1940s onward, particular groups of radical Black activists had attempted to situate the treatment of Blacks in the United States within a broader human rights framework, including drafting genocide petitions for consideration at the United Nations. The issue of state political repression against Black Power activists brought this issue to the fore. Jarrett asserted that the entire university community now urged "all people to act now to end this reign of terror by white governments and individuals" which had "resorted to organized coercion to suppress the Black community."[40]

The Atlanta University statement spoke not only to the sobering significance of state repression, but to the galvanizing effect of Black activism. Work at the IBW was part and parcel of this mood on the AU campus. As fall approached the Institute prepared to host faculty and students for another academic year of seminars, workshops, and conferences. Among those arriving in Atlanta was a group of graduate students from the University of California, Berkeley, who had accompanied Black scholar Andrew Billingsley. Billingsley would be one of several scholars-in-residence at the Institute for the 1970–1971 school year. C. L. R. James and Walter Rodney would return for the year, along with newcomers St. Clair Drake and Sylvia Winters. The Berkeley contingent also included a married couple, Jualynne and Howard Dodson, doctoral students in sociology and history, respectively.[41]

The Dodsons welcomed the opportunity to leave Berkeley for a year. Jualynne Dodson recalled that they both had been driven "crazy" attempting to navigate the subtle racism of Whites there. "At Berkeley it was an arrogant kind of racism, a presumptuousness about the ability to define everybody, which is part of what the nature of U.S. racism is anyway," she noted. "The answer to everything is lodged in whatever mostly White males say and do." Time and again Dodson found herself in graduate seminars in sociology having to challenge the prevailing conceptions of Black life offered by both professors and colleagues. "And after I raised the question, have the professor look me square in the eye, with a quizzical look, and then turn and say, 'Are there any questions?' " Increasingly frustrated, she looked forward to embarking for Atlanta with her husband for a year of research funded by the state of California.[42]

Atlanta bustled with movement activity throughout the summer and fall. Amiri Baraka and Queen Mother Audley Moore of the Congress of African People (CAP), the dominant cultural nationalist organization on the Eastern seaboard, had organized a major conference in the city. And former SNCC worker Bernice Johnson Reagon had just formed the Harambe Singers, an a cappella group that would come to be known as Sweet Honey in the Rock. "It was the most fantastic entry into a new level of political consciousness that I'd ever had," Jualynne Dodson recalled. She had come to the Institute to do research on the intersection among Black churches, Black culture, and Black women. She spent most of her time at the Interdenominational Theological Center and Atlanta University libraries. Yet, only a short walk away, Dodson could not help but find some of her most enriching intellectual experiences at the Institute. The array of scholars and activists there was impressive indeed, but unlike her husband, she did her best not to become completely absorbed.[43]

Part of Jualynne Dodson's attempt to distance herself from IBW activities was connected to her feeling overwhelmed by "this plethora of giants"—the intellectuals whom Vincent Harding called "the elders of the clan." On one occasion she had the opportunity to meet Shirley Graham Du Bois, activist and widow of W. E. B. Du Bois. "I remember sitting at Vincent's house, having already said 'I ain't sitting at the feet of people.' " But the moment that Shirley Du Bois walked inside, "I was sitting on the floor, 'Tell me some more please,' " Dodson laughed. Without question, though, the person who influenced her most was sociologist St. Clair Drake, on leave from Stanford University. Drake, who had co-authored with Horace R. Clayton *Black Metropolis* in 1945, was a leading Pan-African intellectual, having taught at the University of Liberia and chaired the sociology department at the University of Ghana.[44]

Jualynne Dodson participated in an intensive one-week reflection seminar taught by Drake during the fall. It was during the course of the seminar that she began to give full consideration to what her role should be as a young scholar. She recalled that one evening, when Drake came by for dinner, he proclaimed with conviction, " 'I'm an intellectual,' " a simple statement but one "which was wrenching" for her nevertheless. Jualynne Dodson had to come to grips with the reality—as did most Black college and graduate students at the time—that there had been no formal intellectual tradition in her family. "Nobody in my family, for all the seven generations that we had been in the United States, ever did intellectual work," she said. "And all of a sudden I'm going to be an intellectual. Well, my grandmother scrubbed many toilets. I knew about scrubbing toilets. How could I be an intellectual?" St. Clair Drake agreed to sit on her dissertation committee and use his influence; Dodson would do the rest.[45]

■ ■ ■

Apart from the residencies and workshops launched at the end of the summer, IBW staff members also conducted outreach work with national organizations. Due in part to Harding's religious convictions, several of these efforts involved church organizations, including the National Committee of Black Churchmen (NCBC).

Religious groups across the country had been rocked a year before when SNCC activist James Forman delivered his famous Black Manifesto before a mostly empty sanctuary at New York City's Riverside Church in May 1969. Two years earlier Martin Luther King Jr. had delivered his famous antiwar address, "Beyond Vietnam," before a far more receptive audience at Riverside that had been organized in part by Clergy and Laymen Concerned about Vietnam. In Forman's case, however, the vast majority of the church's stunned congregation departed before he had finished. Those who remained heard him make an impassioned plea for "the racist white Christian churches and Jewish synagogues" to furnish five hundred million dollars in "reparations due us as people who have been exploited and degraded, brutalized, killed, and persecuted."[46]

Forman's message reached Atlanta two weeks later when three local activists interrupted a worship service at Atlanta's First Presbyterian Church to read the manifesto. The three men, Edward Jenkins, Bob Smith, and Babatunde Okello, were members of the Detroit-based National Black Economic Development Conference. They told parishioners in the wealthy Buckhead enclave that they expected First Presbyterian to cough up one-sixth of its accumulated finances. "We are asking America to speak now or forever hold its peace," Jenkins asserted. Church officials offered up no cash and vetoed the activists' demands.[47]

The point had been made, however, and for the next few months the country's major religious organizations began to grapple with the idea of funding Black community programs as well as Black caucuses within their respective organizations. For its part, the New York City–based NCBC had been vocal and movement-centered since 1966. Members of the NCBC who had attended the Conference on Black Economic Development in Detroit in April 1969 also had been privy to Forman's Black Manifesto weeks before he delivered it. Furthermore, the organization had drafted three controversial statements—on Black Power in July 1966, on racism and the November 1966 elections, and a "Black Declaration of Independence" in June 1970—with each one appearing as a full-page advertisement in the New York Times. The NCBC requested that Harding write an introduction for the October 1970 issue of Renewal, its national magazine.[48]

The IBW director agreed to do so, writing a thought-provoking essay that offered analysis and criticism of the three NCBC documents. Harding sought to illuminate the group's struggle "towards political maturity, radical vision, and revolutionary courage. For they now become the struggles for us all, on behalf of our people everywhere." Harding found ample room for criticism but offered it constructively. He asserted that in the NCBC documents "emotions are clear, and one senses the deep struggles of the soul, but programs, political acumen, and clarity of direction are not present in equal amounts." Indeed, the three published statements of the Black ministers reminded Harding "of the unprogrammed radicalization and alienation of sensitive, committed black leaders which has gone on—at least rhetorically—ever since the beginning of our pilgrimage here."[49]

Harding encouraged NCBC activists to move beyond the impassioned and often militant rhetoric in their statements. That meant engaging in a three-phase process that would take the group from rhetoric to analysis to program, the end result being "insistent, careful organizing for fundamental change." He also criticized the class bias inherent in the documents. The NCBC asserted in its 1966 Black Power statement: "We deplore the overt violence of riots, but we believe it is more important to focus on the real sources of these eruptions. These sources may be abetted inside the ghetto, but their basic causes lie in the silent and covert violence which white middle-class America inflicts upon the victims of the inner city." Harding noted that this Black Power statement had failed to capture adequately the extent to which violent urban protests throughout the country involved an intraracial class critique of an African American middle class that had gained more "economically and symbolically" from ongoing human rights struggles than did those at the grassroots. Less than a month after publication of Harding's *Renewal* essay, the NCBC reported that it had taken the "incisive criticisms seriously." The group agreed to form internal cadres to tackle specific analytical and programmatic tasks.[50]

The IBW had mixed success locally during its first year of independence, especially in its dealings with leaders of the Atlanta University Center. With the possible exception of Atlanta University, the affiliated schools on the city's West End continued to distance themselves from the Black think tank. Harding recalled a conversation he and Lerone Bennett had after a meeting with the AUC Council of Presidents. "Lerone said, 'Vincent, I'm glad that you're here, because I would not want to have to do this thing myself. I would not have the patience. I would not have the willingness to just go through all of this, day after day, week after week.'" Yet together, members of the research staff managed to make a name for the IBW, as popular magazines such as *Ebony* and *Jet* covered its activities. Harding later laughed that soon people just "started appearing at our door, just came to check you out."[51]

Being situated in Atlanta, a city with its own tradition of Black activism, meant Institute scholars also had to stay in tune with the pace of local events. "We had to constantly live with the tension," Harding noted, "that we were trying to be a national and international organization at the same moment people in Atlanta, understandably and justifiably, were always asking us, 'What are you doing in Atlanta? What's your program right here?'" Several of the scholars-in-residence spoke at local churches, but for the most part, activism outside the confines of the Institute was national in scope during the first two years of its existence. And as the IBW entered its third year in 1971, senior research fellow William Strickland established a working relationship with activists of Canada's National Black Coalition. Strickland corresponded regularly with Clarence S. Bayne, a Montreal professor who spearheaded the effort to establish an Institute of Research in the Black Experience in Canada.[52]

The work of the Institute of the Black World continued to attract attention from Blacks locally and statewide. "I greet you in peace and in the spirit of divine Love toward Black education and Black knowledge, with Black Unity," an inmate at the Georgia state prison in Reidsville wrote the IBW in late 1971. The anonymous prisoner wrote of the need to "remove the ignorance from our beautiful Black Brothers." He contended that only the IBW and other independent institutions located beyond the walls of the country's prisons could accomplish the task. Like many politicized Black and Latino inmates during the late 1960s and early 1970s, the Georgia prisoner also recognized the need to organize behind bars, himself establishing a "People's Political Library."[53] The IBW staff received another letter from a Florida activist requesting copies of an IBW Black Paper following the Attica prison revolt and massacre in September 1971. The Institute also received mail from Blacks in the military. In one such letter a soldier who was "working in race relations" at Ft. Benning in Georgia wrote the IBW for advice and information regarding the establishment of a "Black Culture Center."[54]

The heightened consciousness among Blacks helped fuel the activist scholars at the Institute. Yet, it appeared as though members of the overworked and underfunded IBW research staff were being pulled in several directions at once, coordinating residencies and workshops, writing position papers and correspondence, giving lectures and informal talks. "If you allow people to define your agenda you look up, Jack, and you'll be gone, see. You'll be in the ground. And the work that you feel is most important that you should have done will have gone by the board," Strickland said. "We had to keep our eye on threading this line between assisting others and being true to ourselves." The activist scholars at the IBW had to find time for collective study and individual reflection. With that in mind Strickland organized weekly study sessions in which the staff submitted brief written analyses of a given reading. Several sessions dealt with historian and cultural critic Harold Cruse's landmark 1967 study, *The Crisis of the Negro Intellectual.*[55]

Cruse argued that Harlem groups such as the Committee for the Negro in the Arts, which served as "the cultural arm of the Harlem political left-wing," had sought to integrate cultural arts in the United States. This earlier emphasis on integration was due partly to the influence of the White left, Cruse contended, and partly to the belief on the part of Black artists and intellectuals that conditions did not merit the establishment of truly independent African American cultural institutions. "There is no way that we shall get out of Harold Cruse all that there is to receive unless we grapple with his work with care and precision," Strickland acknowledged in a memorandum to other staff members, especially since Cruse offered "a battery of new ideas, some connected and others free-floating." He alerted his colleagues to the way in which Cruse blended Marxist and anti-Marxist methodologies in the book and posed questions for the group that dealt with the "general deficiency of theoretical thought" among the Black intellectuals whom Cruse critiqued.[56]

Discussions of theoretical thought aside, however, the Institute's research staff continued to cultivate relationships with other national organizations, especially those that represented potential sources of funding. As early as 1971 the IBW had sought funding from the Interreligious Foundation for Community Organization (IFCO). Under the leadership of minister Lucius Walker Jr., the IFCO was a Black-controlled funding group supported by thirteen national church agencies with offices in New York City and Washington, D.C. In March 1972, Walker announced the establishment of a largely autonomous group called IFCO-Action, to be headed by Owusu Sadaukai (Howard Fuller), president of Malcolm X Liberation University in North Carolina. IFCO-Action was designed to combat racist public and private policy decisions, including the importation of chrome from Rhodesia and economic support for the government in South Africa.[57]

After the IBW obtained funding from the IFCO in October 1972, Institute staff members and students agreed to participate in the IFCO's Amilcar Cabral Community Organizing Training Institute (COTI) in Washington. Strickland taught a course on the "Black struggle in America" and Pat Daly, the IBW's speed-reading specialist, taught a class as well. Strickland sent a memorandum to each of the COTI participants detailing the readings for the two-week course. Cabral's *Revolution in Guinea* topped the list. "Cabral is a little heavy, but there are hardly three more worthwhile essays in modern political literature," he noted. In addition to the work of the Guinean political theorist, Strickland assigned Mary Frances Berry's *Black Resistance/White Law*, Robert Allen's *Black Awakening in Capitalist America*, and Walter Rodney's *Groundings with My Brothers*, as well as selections from Malcolm X and Mao Zedong. The IBW senior research fellow also assigned *Red, White and Black*, by White colonial historian Gary Nash.[58]

In the spirit of Paulo Freire's *Pedagogy of the Oppressed*, Strickland also recognized that the most beneficial learning process was not static and one-directional but dynamic, often impinging upon not just the life of the student but also the life of the instructor. A group of visiting Cuban students had influenced Strickland during his COTI session in Washington, and he traveled to Cuba soon thereafter largely because of his experiences with the young people. Upon returning to Atlanta in February 1973, Strickland sent a "memorandum"—in reality a personal letter—to the group. "Cuba made many impressions upon me but I think the greatest was watching people reconstruct their society from the bottom up and doing so in the belief that all things are possible," he wrote. While in Cuba, he had visited an orphanage for children from Guinea-Bissau who had been disfigured by Portuguese napalm "made in America and dropped by American planes." Yet, he noticed that the youngsters sang a song called "La Luta Continua"—the struggle continues—to the same tune as the African American freedom anthem "We Shall Overcome." Strickland contended that activists had "grown so cynical in this country that we have lost the capacity to hope and dream and dare and risk, and that is the precise meaning of the Cuban revolution (and the Vietnamese and of Che's life): that the people will triumph if they once decide that they can."[59]

■ ■ ■

The IBW staff continued to develop its relationship with the IFCO beyond the COTI classes, no doubt in part to secure additional funding. New IBW staff member Jan Douglas, who joined the Institute after college teaching and activism in Ohio and New Jersey, wrote Jerry Vallery and Phil Littlejohn of the IFCO's New York City office in an effort to further illuminate the Institute's relationship to the larger Black liberation struggle. Although the IBW had sprung forth from the Black Studies movement, Douglas noted that members of the think tank did not want to become "locked" into an exclusively intellectual dialogue, working only with universities and using only costly books and other educational materials. The Institute had begun publication of a free monthly newsletter and had provided individual ministers with historical analyses to be utilized in conjunction with their sermons. Douglas attached to her letter a number of letters from high schools requesting materials from the Institute. Having provided the evidence for her case, she asserted, then, that IBW scholars "have taken seriously the call to break with such tradition and to make research and analysis both available and functional to struggling Black people."[60]

While Douglas worked to cement the Institute's relationship with the IFCO, Harding made overtures to the leadership of the United Church of Christ (UCC). In an internal staff memorandum to the Institute's planning committee, the IBW director reminded everyone that one of the demands James

Forman put forth in the Black Manifesto called for funding of a Black university. Harding met with Robert V. Moss, UCC president, and Black UCC official Charles Cobb to seek funding for the IBW to do a feasibility study for such a project. Of course, the stakes were high. Conducting the study could mean as much as seventy thousand dollars in desperately needed funding for the IBW. As was the case with the IFCO, however, the Institute usually combined requests for funding with collaboration. In this instance, members of the Institute participated in meetings of the Southern Committee Against Repression, a group with ties to the United Church of Christ. At the 19 May 1973 meeting of the group, the Atlanta University political science department, CORE, and IBW agreed to develop a journal on repression underwritten by the UCC.[61]

The Institute's quest for funding and recognition from progressive religious groups reached global proportions in late 1972. Strickland wrote to Charles Spivey, an African Methodist Episcopal minister from Chicago who was now a leading member of the World Council of Churches in Geneva. Spivey was general secretary of the WCC's Programme to Combat Racism, launched in 1969. Strickland proposed the development of an extensive bibliography on White racism worldwide, an undertaking that would require teams of researchers working on each existing and former European metropole. The implications of the project were evident to Strickland, who argued that "it should be clear that what one is really tackling in any fundamental investigation of racism is *nothing less than a new history of the West.*" Strickland pointed to his own work with IBW colleagues in completing a study of the 1971 Attica prison revolt and its relationship to the larger Black freedom struggle since the 1960 sit-ins in Greensboro. According to the study, Attica represented the "high point in the contemporary Black struggle against racism."[62]

Strickland was forced to acknowledge, however, that "the press of IBW business" stifled work on the project. And that led to the bottom line. He confessed that what was "really needed at this point is a grant to support the work and to give me time to withdraw from some of my administrative responsibilities." In order to effectively organize material and write a clean draft, Strickland suggested that ten thousand dollars would be just enough to work productively for one year. On 29 January 1973 Baldwin Sjollema, of the Programme to Combat Racism, wrote a brief letter to Harding informing the IBW of the funding group's decision. In what was quickly becoming a familiar line, Sjollema explained that the application had been denied due to the "relatively small amount available."[63] The increasing number of funding setbacks curtailed work on some of the more ambitious projects of the Institute of the Black World. Indeed, the national and international scope of the group diminished somewhat during the decade that Howard Dodson led the IBW beginning in late 1973, the result not of a sudden retreat by Institute scholars from the group's mission statement but of the fact that local and state programming was more easily funded.

Nevertheless, as the IBW Summer Research Symposium of 1974 demonstrated, whenever possible the members of the Institute continued to make linkages between scholarship and struggle within a global African context. Both familiar and new faces to Atlanta attended the symposium, called "Black People and the International Crisis: Where Do We Go From Here?" Walter Rodney returned to present a paper entitled "The Politics of the African Ruling Class." Harding, now chair of the IBW Board of Directors, presented a paper illuminating his ongoing reflections on "The Black Wedge in America: Struggle and Crisis, 1954–1974." After further revisions, Harding's paper appeared as "The Black Wedge in America: Struggle, Crisis and Hope, 1955–1975," in the December 1975 issue of Black Scholar. Strickland presented "The Future of Black People in the Post-Nixon Era" while Frank Smith presented "An Activist's Role in U.S. Politics." Individual contributions concluded with Robert Hill's paper, "The Pan-African Path in Caribbean Politics." Finally, the symposium ended with a more informal panel, "Where Do We Go From Here?" Sitting on the panel were Mary Frances Berry, Mack Jones, Harding, Rodney, and Strickland.[64]

For Harding, the symposium represented another opportunity to engage in the intellectual work that he and so many other Black activist scholars cherished during this volatile, yet hopeful, period. "I did not come into the academy as an end in itself. I came into the academy so that I could be developed, nurtured, trained, licensed, to teach," he noted candidly. "And so teaching, rather than what might be called academic scholarship, is the higher priority for me. And by teaching, I don't mean simply standing or sitting in front of a room." Instead, Harding and the other Institute scholars had embarked on an often turbulent journey "trying to clarify for one generation the issues of other generations, of their own generation, so that they can participate in the creation of a more humane society."[65]

Propelled by grassroots activism in poor and working-class Black neighborhoods in Atlanta and throughout the United States, a core group of college students and intellectuals in the city took it upon themselves to transform the academy. There were failures, most notably at the Atlanta University Center, where the intraracial ideological tension between radicalism and moderation was sobering. Amid the contention and confusion was the complicating presence of the Institute of the Black World, a movement-centered think tank located in the house that W. E. B. Du Bois had occupied decades earlier. There, and not in Harlem or Chicago, an engaged Black intellectual life and discourse began to flourish in international dimensions. However, the majority of the city's African American population continued to confront the legacy of slavery and reality of apartheid. Fortunately, the same movement forces that led to the establishment of Black Studies at Emory and the Institute of the Black World also set in motion human rights activity on several fronts that rivaled the sit-in campaigns of the early 1960s.

CHAPTER SEVEN

THE MULTI-FRONT
BLACK STRUGGLE FOR
HUMAN RIGHTS

O nly a decade removed from the direct assault on petty apartheid coordinated by Black college students in 1960, the city of Atlanta remained a key site for future Black activism. Black activist politics had become more complicated, however, as groups and individuals attempted to realize the full meaning of self-determination in four contexts: grassroots neighborhood activism, radical Black nationalism, progressive Black electoral political activism, and explicitly women-centered activism. These forms of activism were different and yet inextricably linked to one another by the force and fiber of the larger Black struggle for human rights. As debates over tactics between students and older moderates had revealed, the notion of a Black united front seldom came to fruition. Black activism during the 1970s demonstrated that the critical issue was not the development of a single front, but the existence of a dynamic multi-front Black human rights struggle that gave voice to particular constituencies.

GRASSROOTS BLACK ACTIVISM

The National Welfare Rights Organization (NWRO) remained a driving force for grassroots economic justice throughout the early 1970s. At the national level the organization pressed for increases in state welfare expenditures, as well as access to department store credit for welfare mothers, especially in Northern cities. Taking full advantage of the autonomy that the national organization provided, Ethel Mathews continued to lead the charge of the local chapter of the NWRO. In March 1970 the Atlanta Welfare Rights Organization pledged its support to embattled state welfare director Bill Burson and his effort to prevent further cuts in public assistance. Burson spoke to the local NWRO at the group's request toward the end of the month. In introducing Burson, Mathews lambasted his critics and those of the NWRO who claimed that welfare recipients were on an undeserving mission to bleed the state's coffers dry. "That money is rightfully ours. Our forefathers paid for it. If we are in need and if we're eligible then it's our right to get it," she asserted. "Besides, it ain't enough to be called a handout."[1]

As compelling as the work of the local NWRO chapter was, the economic justice issue that captured the attention of most Blacks was the possibility of a strike by the city's three thousand municipal workers. The focus on the looming strike was understandable, given that 75 percent of Atlanta municipal workers were Black. Yet, the stigma attached to supposedly "less respectable" welfare rights activism was certainly a factor as well. Mayor Sam Massell met for five hours with representatives of the American Federation of State, County and Municipal Employees (AFSCME), an affiliate of the larger AFL-CIO, in a final effort to avoid a strike. The city offered AFSCME a sparse pay increase and life insurance, but those measures simply were not enough. Led by Morton Shapiro and Jesse Epps, union officials made it known that members would accept nothing less than a one-step increase of 4.5 percent. Shapiro was AFSCME Southern areas director and Epps was assistant to the union's president. More significant, though, Epps had been the leader of the protracted Memphis sanitation workers' strike in 1968. Atlanta workers and city officials alike were aware of his reputation as a tenacious organizer and negotiator.[2]

As able as AFSCME national and regional officials were, local leaders such as Tom Evans and Marvin Bradford played the most significant role in rallying Atlanta municipal employees to strike on 17 March. Evans and Bradford peppered Joel Stokes, a Black banker and first-year alderman, with criticism in the days leading up to the strike. They charged that Stokes was a liar for claiming that the city was now operating at a deficit. And they were not alone. George Coleman, an editor of the *Atlanta Voice*, questioned how the city "suddenly" found the necessary funds to construct a stadium, civic center, and airport, yet could not meet worker demands. The editor of the progressive Black weekly newspaper even suggested that the strike may have resulted from "a power grab" fostered by anti-Massell forces in city government. Whatever the case, Atlanta residents would have to live without garbage collection, street and sewage repairs, and access to the Grant Park Zoo.[3]

As April approached and the municipal strike entered its third week, a broad grassroots coalition in support of the workers continued to grow, especially in the city's Black neighborhoods. Mathews organized an NWRO contingent that protested alongside striking sanitation workers on several occasions. During a 2 April demonstration, police ordered replacement workers to drive their garbage trucks through the picket lines. "They were Black policemen," Mathews recalled. "But we didn't give up. We went back the next day." That very week Southern Christian Leadership Conference leader Ralph David Abernathy announced his intention to "organize to help those poor people gain the rights they are entitled to." The SCLC was no union, but he declared nevertheless that "poor people, not just black people, are entitled to collective bargaining." Abernathy made it clear, however, that he was not out to make matters worse for Sam Massell, contending that others had given bad advice to "my good friend."[4]

As the stench from rotting garbage filled the air, striking municipal employees and their supporters marched downtown three-hundred-strong during the fourth week of the strike. The protesters chanted "On strike, shut it down" and "To hell with Massell" as Abernathy and Hosea Williams led the way. Speakers encouraged the upbeat crowd to "spread the misery" and boycott downtown businesses as a concrete way of demonstrating support for the month-long strike. Beneath the surface, however, frustration and uneasiness began to take hold. Abernathy, state senator Leroy Johnson, pastor and Community Relations Council chair Sam Williams, and business and civic leader Jesse Hill had met with little success in their behind-the-scenes effort to mediate the strike. Furthermore, while most workers continued to view Abernathy and other SCLC officials as allies, many felt differently about Johnson. At one union rally workers greeted him with boos and cries of "Super Tom" and "Massell ass-kisser."[5]

With tensions high on all sides and the morale of striking workers low, the union and the city reached an agreement on 22 April 1970, ending the thirty-six day strike. The City of Atlanta agreed to reinstate those workers fired during the strike and to drop pending litigation against union pickets. The city also provided a one-step pay increase for the lowest-paid tier of municipal employees. Yet, this increase—amounting to less than four dollars per week—was less than the city's initial offer. Maynard H. Jackson, the city's young Black vice mayor, suggested that a three-judge panel investigate a provision in the City Code that would allow for a more substantive increase. But no tonic could remedy the bitter taste in the mouths of the city's municipal workers.[6]

The SCLC's Hosea Williams criticized Johnson and other Black elected officials for their handling of the strike. He contended that the unappetizing agreement was the product of a conspiracy between "responsible black leaders" and City Hall that resulted in "the selling out of Atlanta's city employees." While Black elected officials were vocal regarding a range of other pertinent issues in April, including the need to rectify what state representative Benjamin Brown termed the "distortion and exclusion of black history" in Georgia schools, there had been a general reluctance to confront the Atlanta strike. Williams challenged any local Black politician to a public debate on the issue, adding that the underlying factor was not race but class, "the rich and the poor, the haves and the have-nots." As for the mayor, Williams maintained that Massell's hard-line stance throughout the strike was an attempt to curry favor with groups such as the Chamber of Commerce that did not support him during the 1969 election to "feather his political bed with the downtown power structure."[7]

One concern that reemerged for grassroots activists, particularly women responsible for families and children, were the cutbacks in state welfare funding. The state welfare department made drastic cuts in its public assistance payments to individual mothers following an increase in Social Security expenditures at the federal level. With help from Michael Radnoss and other attorneys from the Legal Aid Society, the Atlanta chapter of the NWRO had obtained a court order calling for the state agency to delay further action until a hearing could be held. The department moved forward with more meager disbursements, however, effectively ignoring the court order. This sparked the ire and passion of Mathews, who wrote in *Welfare Fighter*, the NWRO's national publication: "We will be fighting for our rights and justice. We will demand to be heard and will go to jail if that is what it takes. Power to the People. And Bread and Justice to all Poor People."[8]

Black activists at the grassroots conducted work in other parts of the city as well. Helen Howard established the Vine City Foundation, a neighborhood agency supported almost entirely by donations from White churches. The community-based agency, which had been in existence for six years, maintained a clinic, thrift shop, nursery, grocery store, craft shop, and home nursing course. Howard complained that a number of Black activists and elected officials continued to pay no more than lip service regarding financial support. In April she had been forced to close the grocery temporarily because of a lack of funding, and she noted that she and the nursery director were the only paid full-time staff members. Yet, Howard and Foundation volunteers persisted. "We handle anything from paying rent and utility bills to finding housing and clothing for a family burned out."[9]

RADICAL BLACK NATIONALISM

In another development only days after the controversial settlement of the AFSCME strike, Black activists in the city awaited the return of Stokely Carmichael (Kwame Ture), former SNCC chair and Black Panther leader. The Institute of the Black World sponsored an informal lecture by him in the Morehouse College gymnasium. Carmichael had spent the past sixteen months in Guinea under the tutelage of Kwame Nkrumah, the Pan-African socialist and former president of Ghana. Political rivals had ousted Nkrumah in a 1966 coup that many Black activists contended was supported clandestinely by the United States. Perhaps some Atlanta activists hoped that Carmichael might offer remarks concerning the municipal workers strike and other local issues. Instead, he surprised many in the audience when he stressed the need for Blacks in the United States to take up arms to liberate "Ghana away from America, Britain, France, and Israel," arguing in a forceful yet academic tone that "oppression knows no political boundaries."[10]

Nevertheless, the radical Black activist did devote a portion of his talk to a discussion of the Black Power movement at the national level. He criticized opportunists who sought to exploit the movement for financial advantage. He asserted that the use of Black Power slogans and symbols by advertisers of a range of products from afro combs to cigarettes reflected a historical process in which "revolutionary slogans are raised" and "the national bourgeoisie captures the slogans and run with it assuming that they will be able to get the favor of the oppressors we are trying to put out." He further argued that "these people are later crushed by the masses." Carmichael also addressed the intensification of state political repression against the Black liberation movement as a whole and against specific groups such as the Black Panther Party. Given the current political climate, said Carmichael, radical Black activists ran the risk of being provided with "three alternatives: death, imprisonment, or forced exile."[11]

Therefore, he said, Blacks worldwide needed to establish an independent land base from which to operate, a concept over a century old. He rejected the possibility of using U.S. or South African territory for such a purpose, arguing instead that Ghana was the proper choice.[12] Carmichael's remarks highlighted the explicit commitment on the part of Black activists to engage in the political struggles of Africa. That recommitment would come to fruition in the establishment of several organizations during the early and mid-seventies that sought to play a supportive role vis-à-vis the liberation struggles being waged throughout southern Africa. Many in the Morehouse gymnasium had been caught off-guard, however, by the global analysis, for they considered that the most pressing concerns remained at their doorstep.

■ ■ ■

During the spring of 1970 events outside Atlanta interrupted the work of Black activists in the city. The East Georgia city of Augusta—home to a long-standing African American protest tradition—exploded in violence on 11 May following the murder of a Black youth in the city jail. State and city police killed six Black men, each one shot in the back, during a night of violent protest. Governor Lester Maddox, who had entered office an unapologetic champion of petty apartheid, ordered police to shoot anyone seen looting and dispatched a National Guard unit to the city. Fires blazed through the night as police and guardsmen stood watch for sniper fire. The following day Maddox blamed the six deaths, scores of injuries, and millions of dollars in property damage on the Black Panther Party and "other militants" who had done community organizing in the city. Members of Augusta's established Black leadership asked for amnesty for those arrested during the demonstrations.[13]

On 16 February 1970 a group of Black Panthers held a fundraising rally before a majority-White audience at Georgia Institute of Technology. At the rally members of the fledgling Georgia State Chapter of the Black Panther Party (BPP) sold political programs to curious Georgia Tech students as well as to some anxious older observers throughout the crowd. One of the on-lookers was Armstrong Smith, a White politician who studied the events of the afternoon with great concern. The state senator later discussed the Panther rally during a speech before his colleagues on the floor of the Legislature. Smith warned of the arrival of the BPP on the local and state political scene. "Wake up America, wake up Georgia. Time is running out!" Although a bit ashamed to admit it, Smith acknowledged that he not only attended the rally but had bought a Panther program. "I paid my good money for it. I hope God will forgive me."[14]

In September 1971 the burgeoning Panther presence in Atlanta was solidified when BPP leader Huey P. Newton held an impromptu press conference at the main office of the Georgia State Black Panther Party, in a one-story frame house in the Kirkwood neighborhood. He surprised reporters with his announcement that Atlanta would become the site for the national headquarters of the organization, winning out over Dallas and New Orleans. Newton, himself a native of Louisiana, said it was "logical" to move the headquarters from Oakland to the South because Blacks there still represented a numerical majority in many locales and because "this is where the contradiction of slavery started."[15]

The decision to move the headquarters followed the leadership rift between the Newton and Eldridge Cleaver factions of the Party that had begun in spring 1970. Newton now argued for an emphasis on community coalition politics and the organization's "survival programs," such as free breakfasts for school children and sickle cell anemia and blood pressure screenings. Meanwhile, Cleaver, living in exile in Algeria, advocated urban guerrilla warfare. When the Federal Bureau of Investigation got wind of the growing chasm within the Party it launched a "concerted program" to further destabilize the group's leadership. Newton's announcement came, then, during the most destructive period in the Party's brief but important history, a time that signaled the beginning of the end for the BPP as a viable radical Black activist organization at the national level.[16]

Nevertheless, specific local chapters continued to be quite effective, which may have prompted those in Atlanta to respond quickly to the news of Newton's possible arrival. Andrew Young, former SCLC activist and current director of the Community Relations Commission, cautioned that the Black Panther Party leadership "will either have to conform to the style of operations that is confined to the South or be isolated." Young also suggested that Southern Blacks had a distinct advantage over their invading counterparts from the North. "I have a feeling that Northern black folks are afraid of white folks. Southern Blacks know the white man and therefore are not afraid of him." Ralph Abernathy was a bit less conditional in his response to the surprise announcement. At a church conference in San Francisco, the SCLC president made it known that "we would be delighted to have our black brothers come to Atlanta, an all-American city." Not surprisingly, however, White political leaders hid their customary hospitality under the welcome mat. "Their image as we know it leaves much to be desired," Mayor Sam Massell said of the BPP. Lester Maddox was blunt in his assessment, contending that the Party "is licensed to steal, destroy and kill and wage war upon our society."[17]

Panther activists had already made a name for themselves in several Black neighborhoods. In addition to the main Kirkwood office, the Georgia Panthers operated community centers in Vine City, Summerhill, on English Avenue, and in the Fourth Ward. What the Atlanta activists lacked in the way of political sophistication they more than made up for in their commitment to the Party's survival programs. But for reasons that remain shrouded in mystery, Newton and other members of the Panther central committee never actually relocated to Atlanta. Perhaps the lukewarm reception Newton received from those outside the Party influenced the change in plans. More likely, though, such a move would have been impractical given the pervasive climate of mistrust that had engulfed the BPP hierarchy.[18]

Whatever the case, the Panthers in Atlanta had every intention of continuing to strengthen their presence in the city's poor neighborhoods. By the time Newton visited Atlanta, several female graduate students from Atlanta University had begun volunteering their time at one of the BPP free breakfast sites. Emma Jean Martin was one of them, a first-year master's student in French who had seen leaflets on campus requesting volunteers. Although some of her friends eventually began working with the SCLC and other groups, Martin became more involved with Panther activity at the Kirkwood office. She studied the Panther ten-point platform and program and attended political education classes on the significance of socialism in the Black freedom struggle worldwide. It was not long before she became an officer of the day and minister of education, and found herself in meetings with the male-dominated grassroots leadership of the local group.[19]

Martin's rapid ascendancy within the Panther ranks was due in part to her childhood activist experiences in Clinton, Louisiana. Her parents, both educators, often housed James Farmer and other activists from the Congress of Racial Equality (CORE) during the group's Freedom Now campaign. Although only fourteen or fifteen, Martin received training in nonviolence from CORE activists and became active in the local struggle against White supremacy, participating in demonstrations in support of Black cashiers and tellers and for an end to petty apartheid. Police tear-gassed and then arrested her and other activists during one such demonstration. She remained in an adult jail in West Baton Rouge Parish after police found a copy of the *Communist Manifesto* in her book bag. Ironically, a college student activist had given her the book prior to the arrests because he mistakenly thought that Louisiana authorities would not arrest her because of her young age. Martin not only weathered her ordeal, but went on to attend Southern University, where she was an active member of "The Soul," a campus political organization.[20]

Almost from the start, Martin noticed that the leaders of the local Panther chapter were "from the grassroots, born and reared in the state of Georgia." A group of Georgia Panthers led by Alton DeVille and Thomas Freeman traveled to Oakland to study the workings of the national office. Meanwhile, the national Panther leadership dispatched Ron Carter, a "veteran" at twenty-three, to the Kirkwood office following Newton's visit. In time Carter became a well-respected fixture among Black activists in the city. The five offices of the Georgia State Chapter also served as way stations in a manner similar to the Atlanta SNCC office, with Panthers staying in the city en route to offices in New Orleans, North Carolina, and other places throughout the region.[21]

Yet, that did not mean that Panther activists in Atlanta were free of difficulties. Martin recalled that police often arrested or otherwise harassed Party members who sold the Black Panther newspaper. Furthermore the mainstream media projected an image of the Panthers that suggested they were "hoodlums, 'they're a gang.'" The group received some support from more privileged Blacks in the city who requested anonymity. A handful of companies, including Atlanta Dairies and Big Apple Stores, donated perishables for the breakfast program, as did Whites from a local commune, but Panthers had to be careful with the food since "some was good and some bad." Clearly, though, the most consistent source of revenue was the Black Panther, something police realized nationwide. Gene Ferguson, a grassroots activist and former rank-and-file Panther, recalled that the local BPP "never got to be a dominant force like in California and other places, but there was a small core group of us who sold the Panther newspaper and did a lot of organizing for the national organization."[22]

As was the case nationally, a key drawing card for the Party was the free breakfast program for children. The Vine City office distributed leaflets announcing the establishment of the program in that neighborhood, "something that Ware and Bethune Schools should have dealt with long ago." The Vine City center prepared lunch for neighborhood children, seven days a week beginning in 1972. "We need guidance as well as cooperation," the leaflet alerted parents in the neighborhood. "The more children we feed, the more donations come in. So bring or send your children so that we can deal with

Grassroots neighborhood activist Gene Ferguson in 2003. Ferguson was an active rank-and-file member of the local Black Panther Party. Photo by the author.

lunch too." Ferguson, who spent most of his time at the Summerhill center, fondly recalled that at breakfast "there was never a time that we didn't have a full house."[23]

The free breakfast program was one of several survival programs the Atlanta Panthers operated. With the help of churches and professionals, the BPP organized a mobile medical clinic, busing to prisons, pest control, and a day care center—all at no charge to community residents. Having launched the programs, the Panthers contended that at some point neighborhood residents would manage each of them. In this regard the BPP sought support from local businesses. "Your participation in the People's Survival Programs is greatly needed. Survival through service to the people." Panther leaders recognized that some radical Black activists condemned the programs as hopelessly reformist. The Kirkwood office countered, however, with a statement linking internal domestic colonialism to U.S. imperialism abroad, saying the programs provided "the basic necessities for survival until the masses of the people reach the level of awareness necessary to transform the social conditions that we are forced to live under in this fascist Amerikkkan society."[24] As early as summer 1969, when it coordinated the First National Conference for a United Front Against Fascism, the BPP national office explicitly had placed U.S. political repression within a broader international human rights context.

A typical day at the Kirkwood office began at about five-thirty in the morning, as two people from the ten-person staff prepared breakfast for the adults. After everyone ate, all members of the Party staff prepared for the stream of children that reached the door just after seven o'clock. Panthers who had newspaper duty received their assignments to particular sites throughout the area. The officer of the day then began a day on and off the telephone to maintain the lines of communication with the Oakland office and the four subordinate Atlanta branches. In addition to keeping the office running, as minister of education Jean Martin also was responsible for organizing lesson plans for the Party's after-school tutorial and Saturday freedom school. Pastor W. J. Stafford and the congregation of Free For All Baptist Church donated their facilities and money to the Kirkwood office for the Panther survival programs, local evidence of the engagement of several Black churches. The Institute of the Black World, which according to Martin "had a lot of resource materials, pamphlets, booklets," donated its resources as well.[25]

From time to time Martin received telephone calls she would have rather avoided. Whenever a Panther activist had been killed or incarcerated, the national office informed her. "Looked like every time you turned around there was somebody who was killed," she recalled. "That could be depressing on you, too. You just talked to that person on the phone, or you just heard about them. And next time, that person's dead. That affected all the local chapters." Those calls interrupted but did not halt the rhythm of a given day, primarily because of the presence of the children. Once the children arrived in the afternoon, Panthers led a series of chants that began with the familiar refrain made popular by Party chairman Bobby Seale: "Black Power for Black People, Brown Power for Brown People, White Power for White People, All Power to the People!"[26]

Martin began each class with her own creation, a Black alphabet that began "A is for Africa, B is for Black . . ." that energized her as well as the students. These young people, some of whom were "rearing themselves," had drawn Martin to the Panthers in the first place. "They wanted that hug from the brothers and sisters," she remembered, smiling. "And the brothers were genuine role models." The Party formed youth sections at some of the Atlanta branches to attract teenagers to the group in a more substantive way. Columbus Ward joined the youth auxiliary at the Summerhill center, participating in several Panther programs there. His involvement with the Panthers also led him to join the black-and-gold-clad Soul Patrol, an informal youth group that patrolled Summerhill and Peoplestown and enjoyed the respect of neighborhood residents. Ward and other young people had been attracted to the Panthers primarily as a result of the group's grassroots programs. The glamour associated with the BPP at the national level, including the trademark black berets and leather jackets, was nowhere near as pronounced in Atlanta.[27]

Although local Panthers had renounced violence except in self-defense—in keeping with the Newton line—government officials sharpened their focus on Party activities in the latter half of 1972. Local, state, and federal police agencies moved swiftly on the Georgia Panthers for three reasons. First, police agencies continued to perceive the Panthers to be a threat in the Deep South, even though the national organization was in disarray by this time. Intense police scrutiny may have been one reason for the national leadership's final decision not to relocate to Atlanta. Second, violent confrontations between local police and members of the underground Black Liberation Army in 1971 helped draw the combined attention of local, state, and federal authorities on the Georgia BPP.[28]

The third, and perhaps most significant, reason for the marked increase in repression against the group was that the grassroots organizing of the five Panther centers throughout the city had proven successful. In addition to launching its survival programs, Panther activists spoke out against the unrelenting police presence in African American neighborhoods, a hallmark of Party activism nationwide. In August 1972 the Kirkwood office issued a six-point press release condemning police activity: One, the Party called for the elimination of super velocity, dum-dum, hollow point, and flat head bullets. Two, the BPP called for the removal of the police department's special weapons and tactical team, asserting that its members were "occupation troops within the black community." Three, the Panthers demanded that all police on foot patrol "keep on the move, since they have been put there to prevent crime, and not to look at women."[29] The fourth demand called for Atlanta authorities to provide anyone who sold newspapers on the streets of the city with all ordinances governing the sale of publications. Given the constant harassment of Panther activists selling the *Black Panther*, this demand resonated with practical importance. The fifth demand asked that "a representative from each militant organization address cadets in the police academy on the objectives of such organization." Finally, the sixth Panther demand called for the establishment of a community review board with the power to dismiss police officers "who commit crimes against the people." Their demands noted, the Panther leadership punctuated the press release, "*SO LET IT BE DONE.*"[30]

The police offensive began on 23 August following an announcement by Panther spokesman Kouson Oliver that the BPP was demanding fifty thousand dollars in cash, food, buses, and gasoline from three area grocery chains. Oliver made the demands of Kroger, Big Apple, and Colonial, contending that "we have asked in a very nice way for some money to support our food program because our people are the ones who support them." The following day police chief John Inman indicated that the BPP may have been in violation of several city ordinances requiring permits for solicitation of services. Furthermore, Inman asserted, if threats accompanied the Panther demands, Panther activists could be charged with extortion. On 28 August local Panther leaders Ron Carter, Sam Lundy, and Kouson Oliver met with Inman and assistant police chief J. H. Amos, and discovered that the city required such permits.[31]

The following week the political atmosphere in the city became even more highly charged. Clayton Powell, a Black Republican and staunch supporter of President Richard M. Nixon, contended that he had received phone calls from Panther leaders warning him that the group intended to place a fifteen-hundred-dollar bounty on his head. In a statement released to the press, the Party denied the allegations and asserted that Sam Massell and "his running dog John Inman" would not prevent them from obtaining materials for their survival programs. The Panthers also noted that the A&P store chain had been added to their list. No matter the number of stores, Panther activists would need the approval of the Atlanta Fund Appeals Review Board, Aldermanic Police Committee, Aldermanic Board, and the mayor in order to receive a solicitation permit. Realizing there was virtually no possibility for that to occur, Carter did his best to reassure municipal officials. The Panthers were against violence and "gangsterism," he said, preferring "war without bloodshed."[32]

The Panther leader's remarks did little, however, to allay the suspicions of authorities at both the local and federal level. L. Patrick Gray, III, acting director of the FBI, announced on 14 September that the agency had launched a "fully preliminary investigation" to determine whether or not the BPP was guilty of extortion, a federal offense in violation of the Hobbs Act. Gray also expressed dismay at a recent Atlanta rally on behalf of Emily Butler, a local Internal Revenue Service employee on trial for the murder of her White supervisor. Radical Black feminist scholar and former political prisoner Angela Davis spoke at the rally, co-sponsored by the Panthers and SCLC, as the city's Black activists contended that the racism of Butler's supervisor "pulled the trigger." The acting FBI director thought otherwise, asserting that it "is a developing phenomenon in today's society to try to create the impression that a lawless act is nothing more than a political expression."[33]

Of course, Jean Martin and other officers of the day were quite careful about what they said over the telephone because of the possibility of surveillance. Yet, even they may have been surprised by the revelation that the Atlanta Police Department had issued an internal report targeting ten local organizations and nine individual activists. Inman denied the existence of such a report, but attorneys from the American Civil Liberties Union (ACLU) claimed that the BPP and Atlanta Peace Action Coalition topped the list, and that the nine activists named in the report were African American. Meanwhile, the Atlanta Constitution applauded news of the FBI investigation, noting simply that the Panthers "tend to scare people."[34]

The fortunes of the Georgia BPP deteriorated in the coming weeks. Behind two months' rent, a group of Panthers including Oliver found themselves on the street after their landlord, a Black man named J. E. Jordan, evicted them from a six-room apartment in late October. Jordan claimed that the group had "turned that place into a real honky-tonk." Two weeks later, on 9 November, the group suffered another, more major setback, when local and federal authorities raided the English Avenue office. Agents from the Treasury Department's Bureau of Alcohol, Tobacco and Firearms joined the local SWAT unit in a well-coordinated raid that netted guns, explosives, a deactivated hand grenade, and several arrests. Ostensibly, the police action had been undertaken to locate a lone automatic pistol used to wound police officer Daniel Smith during a routine traffic stop the previous week. It was not clear whether the person who shot Smith was indeed a Panther, and police did not find the gun in question. "Look at me," Carter told reporters as police escorted him away in handcuffs. "My face is not bleeding now, but it may be soon."[35]

Local authorities charged the activists with possession of explosives and stolen goods as dozens of supporters filled the courtroom. Panther attorney Al Horn countered by contending that the search warrant had "zero probable cause." Police and federal officials maintained, however, that they had obtained the warrant on the grounds that markings on the spent cartridge found at the scene of the October shooting matched those on cartridges at the Kirkwood center. Municipal Court Judge Robert E. Jones bound Carter and Alton DeVille over for trial but freed the others. Jones also precluded Horn from "eliciting testimony" concerning the validity of the warrant. As dubious as the warrant and raid had been, Panther activists realized that local police and federal authorities already could claim a partial victory. They had found a pretext to disrupt Party activities and remove two of its leading activists, if only temporarily. "The issue was clearly not the legal shotgun in our community center, but our politics," Carter noted shortly after Atlanta authorities all but acknowledged they had no case. "And our successful defense has been due to the united front of progressive groups coming to our defense, not legal technicalities."[36]

Although not accustomed to the level of legal repression waged against Panther offices elsewhere, the Atlanta activists pressed forward with Party activities, including a free Thanksgiving dinner at Memorial Methodist Church. The police raids continued, however, including one on 5 December that netted six additional arrests and a pound of marijuana that Panthers contended had been planted by authorities. Yet, as the number of Panther activists in the city's jails began to increase, so did the resolve of their supporters. Joseph Boone, the veteran activist minister who played a pivotal role during the student sit-ins of the early sixties, happened upon Panther Sam Lundy during one of his regular visits to see inmates. He reluctantly offered Lundy communion. "I didn't feel the cat was gonna take communion. He's a Black Panther and I got this old crazy stuff in me too, you know, that maybe this cat might not understand me as a Christian minister," Boone recalled. "When I finished there were tears in his eyes and in the other cats' eyes and in my eyes. And then we joined hands and we sang a hymn, a hymn that was meaningful to them, 'We Shall Overcome.' "[37]

The police raids and arrests—several conducted while children were present for breakfast or tutoring—took a toll on the organization's morale and finances. There were internal problems as well. A small group of rogue Panthers, most of whom were members from outside Atlanta who had joined the BPP during the volatile period of the Newton-Cleaver schism, had been involved in drug dealing and use in the Atlanta area. The Atlanta leadership purged them, but several chose to remain in the city.[38] On a summer day in 1973—the specific date has been erased from Jean Martin's memory—two members of this rogue group entered the Kirkwood center as she and another woman taught a Saturday freedom school session. Still familiar with the BPP calendar, the ousted Panthers were aware that other activists were away for the weekend. After escorting her out of the sight of the children, one of the men placed a pistol at Martin's temple and ordered her to open the office lock box. "And I told him I wasn't opening it. I said, 'You can just go on and shoot me if you want to get it.' " One of the gunmen finally proceeded to shoot the padlock off the cash box. "They were really hoodlums in a way," she recalled. "But I knew them all, and so I had no fear."[39]

Apparently, one of the children present also displayed no fear as he bolted for the exit before the gunmen could stop him. Soon a number of neighbors gathered outside the Atlanta headquarters demanding to know what had transpired. The former Panthers released the children and then pressured Martin and the other officer of the day to explain that there simply had been a misunderstanding. It had become clear by now that the gunmen had intended to hold the women hostage in the community center, perhaps to send a retaliatory message to others in the local Panther leadership for being purged. If a White supporter of the group had not arrived on Sunday, the ordeal may have been prolonged. Sensing that something was not quite right, the woman called the national headquarters in Oakland, and Huey Newton ordered the immediate release of the hostages. Respectful of Newton's authority, the

Longtime activist and local Black Panther Party official Emma Jean Martin, in 2003. Martin, who joined the Party while in graduate school, had been active in the Black struggle for human rights since doing frontline work in her native Louisiana as a teenager. Photo by the author.

ousted Panthers obeyed. On the Monday following the incident, Carter and Lundy flew to Oakland to meet with Newton, and the national leadership supported the Atlanta purge.[40]

Although she was not frightened at the time, the impact of the experience became embedded in Martin's psyche. Her captors may not have intended to do her or her comrade bodily harm, but that did not matter either. "At that point, that's when I finally said, 'You're trying to help, but is it worth it?' " Martin remained with the BPP through the remainder of 1973, clearly for the sake of the children she served, but left the group after that. "I just couldn't deal with it, because you never knew. It was a frightening experience to see your own people turning on you." Perhaps the Kirkwood incident was a harbinger. The Georgia State BPP was beset by infighting among the branches for the remainder of the year as the number of children who attended the various centers began to decline. Certainly, the children present at the Kirkwood center would not soon forget what they saw that day, no matter what any adult told them. "My heart was broken from it," Martin noted. "I think I worked because of the youth. I had to wean them off of us being there. And after that it just started going downhill, downhill."[41]

PROGRESSIVE BLACK ELECTORAL POLITICS

The Black Power phase of the Black struggle for human rights was significant for often infusing electoral politics with the advocacy of economic and social justice. On 27 September 1971, two hundred and fifty demonstrators, the majority of them students from the Atlanta University Center, seized the House Appropriations Committee room at the state Capitol and blocked chairman James H. Floyd at the entrance, to commemorate the deadly uprising by Black and Latino inmates at New York state's Attica Prison. Led by Rick Reed, regional representative of the Black Workers Congress (BWC), members of the group met with state representatives Benjamin Brown and Julian Bond. Floyd requested that state police forcibly remove the contingent, but Governor Jimmy Carter overruled him.[42]

The Attica prison massacre touched off condemnation among Blacks nationwide. Atlanta's vice mayor, Maynard Jackson, situated Attica within the context of the larger discussion of the "urban crisis." He asserted that "there is no more an urban crisis as such than there was a prison crisis at Attica. It is at bottom a racial crisis and has to do with the immoral arrogance with which white men wield power over black." The vice mayor continued by boldly noting that Blacks had the power to exercise two options in the face of such a predicament: "open politics or open rebellion."[43] In April 1972 Jackson employed the militant tone of his Attica statement in an address before the Hungry Club of the Butler Street YMCA. In this instance, Jackson was highly critical of Jimmy Carter's 1971 approval to redistrict the city between the Fourth, Fifth, and Sixth Congressional districts, a move that would lessen Black electoral political clout.

The governor contended that Blacks would do better to have their "aspirations realized" by having the ear of several leaders, not a lone member of Congress. Jackson fired back that Carter should "advise Mayor Massell to give up his seat to a qualified black man in the best interests of the *white* people of Atlanta." The vice mayor stressed the need for the city's African American community to wield power on its own terms, no doubt a theme his grandfather, Republican stalwart John Wesley Dobbs, advanced in earlier Hungry Club speeches. "It is time for us to avoid letting our lives be bossed by those whose false liberalism is slickly packaged for black consumption," Jackson asserted. "It is time for us to see that those who jailed us yesterday will not free us tomorrow." He cautioned, however, that Atlanta's "talented tenth" could not selfishly pursue its own narrow interests, but that the leadership of the city's "total black community" and "truly concerned" Whites would have to carry the day. Jackson denied any interest in running for Congress, stating instead that he would "continue the campaign here in Atlanta for a new politics, the politics of unbought and unbiased social change."[44]

Jackson's remarks were a reflection of the larger concern with activist electoral politics. At the March 1972 National Black Political Convention in Gary, Indiana, convened by Congressman Charles Diggs, Gary mayor Richard Hatcher, and Imamu Amiri Baraka, of the Congress of African People, delegates endorsed a platform that asserted that the "American system does not work for the masses of our people, and it cannot be made to work without radical fundamental change." The convention also succumbed to the patriarchal contradiction of the period when it failed to endorse the candidacy of New York Congresswoman Shirley Chisholm. As historian Paula Giddings has noted, Chisholm could not help but see the irony that Black male activists considered her a "captive of the women's movement," this despite the reluctance of key White feminists to support her candidacy wholeheartedly.[45]

The delegates in Gary failed to follow the wise counsel political analyst Chuck Stone had offered in an influential 1969 essay in *Black Scholar*. Stone, who chaired the National Conference on Black Power, declared that Blacks "have gotten hung up on militant rhetoric that is a marvelously emotional bowel movement, but a non-fulfilling nourishment for life." Paraphrasing Mao Zedong, he stressed a diverse and patient approach to the acquisition of community control, proportionate access to government decision-making, and the assurance of survival. Realizing these objectives required "political power," which he defined as "government control or the ability to decide who shall control."[46]

Whether through a third party or as what he termed an "oscillating" third force to offset White consensus politics, Stone insisted that Blacks in the United States could achieve more than a modicum of political power. As significantly, however, he asserted that Black elected officials who demonstrated a commitment to "us," such as Chisholm and California's Ronald Dellums, should be supported. The only national Black political group with a majority-male leadership that took this advice—and Chisholm's uncompromising record—to heart was the Black Panther Party, an organization that continued to witness an internal challenge to organizational patriarchy led by female activists.[47]

Chisholm may have been disappointed by the lack of support from the vast majority of male Black activists, but she certainly was not surprised by it. She maintained for some time that most of the obstacles she had encountered during her career were due to her sex, not her race. Furthermore, she contended that anti-feminism was as pernicious as racism. "America has been sufficiently sensitized as to whether or not black people are willing to both fight and die for their rights as to make the question itself asinine and superfluous," she wrote in an influential essay that appeared in *Black Scholar* two years before she sought the Democratic presidential nomination. Chisholm continued, however, "America is not yet sufficiently aware that such a question applied to women is equally asinine and superfluous."[48] Without question, though, there were Black elected officials in Atlanta other than Maynard Jackson who embraced Chisholm's feminist critique and support of women's interests. Earlier in the year, when the local chapter of the NWRO staged a two-week vigil in the freezing rain to protest further decreases in welfare benefits, State Representative Henrietta Canty purchased blankets for the group, then joined them. "I'll never forget what she did for us," recalled Atlanta NWRO president Ethel Mathews.[49]

■ ■ ■

In 1969 Jackson had become Atlanta's first Black vice mayor. That campaign had been marked by careful analysis on the part of scholars at Atlanta University and the newly established Institute of the Black World, as well as by current elected officials including state legislator and former SNCC activist Julian Bond. Thanks in large part to the organizing of Mack Jones, chair of the AU political science department, the school hosted the first annual meeting of the National Conference of Black Political Scientists in May 1970. Two years later, Bond did not hesitate to write William Strickland, of the IBW, to encourage his participation in the delegate selection process for the national convention of the Democratic Party.[50]

Many Blacks wanted Jackson to run for mayor in the fall 1973 election. A poll conducted by Cambridge Survey Research during the first week in March of more than six hundred residents indicated Jackson enjoyed a two-to-one edge over incumbent Sam Massell. Among Whites surveyed, many of whom considered the mayor to be dishonest and linked with organized crime in some way, Jackson was even with Massell.[51] Nearly a month after the release of the independent survey Jackson announced—"in large part" because a broad range of people suggested he do so—that he would run for mayor. He stressed that he would address the specific concerns of the electorate, namely restoring confidence in municipal government, upholding honesty, providing basic services, and halting crime. His position on crime reflected a progressive politics. Jackson asserted that while some people committed crimes of greed, "all too often there are those who turn to crime because of the marginal existence of their daily lives." He discussed the need to move beyond incarcerating people and to explore causes of crime such as drug abuse and unemployment. Nevertheless, he still maintained that as the leader of the city "I shall bust the pusher." Furthermore, Jackson was shrewd and had been well advised by campaign manager and veteran civic leader Jesse Hill. He made a point of saluting the informal pipelines formed during the Hartsfield era between established Black leaders and the city's White power brokers, asserting that his campaign would represent the fruitful cultivation of such "harmonious relationships."[52]

It would be a mistake, however, to categorize Jackson as a moderate cross-over politician, a term that dominated the campaigns of several Blacks throughout the following decade. To a significant extent, he embodied the politics of the National Black Political Assembly and other groups born of the Black Power era, even if he did not do so explicitly. Furthermore, he enjoyed a close relationship with the activist intellectuals of the Institute of the Black World. On 13 June, Vincent Harding sent Institute colleague William Strickland an insightful note regarding the text of a Jackson campaign speech the two scholars had been writing and revising for the past three weeks. Harding was grappling with a paragraph in which Jackson refers to his personal experiences as a Black man. In the end, Harding told Strickland the passage should remain because the discussion of race could prove constructive. Indeed, Harding argued, "our Blackness has been a uniquely humanizing experience."[53]

The spirit of hopefulness that resonated throughout the Jackson mayoral campaign found as welcome a home with the intellectuals at the Institute as it did in the beauty salons and barber shops of Auburn Avenue and Cascade Road. The past few months had been very difficult for local radicals. On the national level many radical Black activists had gone underground or into exile. Almost at the precise point when Black mayors began governing the cities of the industrial Northeast, the cities entered into crises of debt and unemployment. Yet, for Harding, ever hopeful, Jackson's campaign represented an unprecedented opportunity. "We can become mired in the ruts of other cities, or we can blaze new paths," he wrote Strickland. "We can work at being a pitiful carbon copy of New York or we can develop an entirely new mural of urban life."[54]

Two days later Harding and Strickland sent a memorandum to Jackson informing him that they had completed "the speech." In fact, the IBW activists had prepared two essays, a lengthy reference document as well as the shorter "speech version." They sought to "write a statement of significance and integrity," they told Jackson, while being careful to couch the speech so that it "fits comfortably and logically within your own campaign strategy and winsome personality." They also endeavored to locate the essays within the broader national political context of the Watergate scandal that torpedoed the Republican Party. "The speech uses Watergate as a take-off point and thus has the potential, we feel, of attracting national attention if it is presented at the right time, before the right audience and given the right kind of promotion."[55]

Clearly, though, if the tenor of the Jackson mayoral campaign heartened those at the IBW, it disturbed quite a few others, including most members of the Fraternal Order of Police. R. T. Roland, second vice president of the organization, argued that no one in municipal government "has ever been so outspoken against the police officer" as Maynard Jackson. Perhaps he believed that White policemen such as himself were synonymous with the term "police officer." Nevertheless, the underlying issue for Roland was race. He acknowledged the need for Black police, conceding that "they are definitely an asset to the force." But he contended that Jackson "would be happy to see every white officer fired and the entire Police Department composed entirely of blacks."[56]

Meanwhile, Black college students were doing some campaigning of their own for Jackson at the Atlanta University Center. One of the leading campus organizations was the University Movement for Black Unity (UMBU). Michael E. Fisher, the group's acting coordinator, wrote a "Dear Brothers and Sisters" letter to students on 13 August 1973 updating them on the campaign and notifying them of an upcoming UMBU meeting at Rush Memorial Church, a gathering site for student activists since the 1960 sit-ins. Fisher wrote that Jackson had won by a "very substantial landslide margin" over his closest competitor, state legislator Leroy Johnson, in a mock election during the spring. The most tangible way for the members of UMBU to "re-confirm our support," he said, would be to organize one thousand volunteers in the coming days.[57]

The campaign also garnered the support of women and women's organizations throughout the city, partly the result of specific outreach efforts by Jackson and his staff. The 1 September issue of the *Maynard Jackson Journal* featured an article by an unidentified campaign volunteer entitled "Maynard Recognizes Women's Rights." The volunteer asserted that Jackson "knows that the woman on welfare is often humiliated because of her economic dependency and how the divorced suburban housewife is discriminated against trying to obtain credit." The author of the newsletter article also contended that the vice mayor had an appreciation of history, celebrating in August the fifty-third anniversary of the passage of the Nineteenth Amendment. Finally, the volunteer linked the upcoming election to the prospect of more equitable gender relations in City Hall. "In Maynard Jackson's administration women will not 'just make the coffee,' " the volunteer promised, but "will help make the policy as well."[58]

Maynard Holbrook Jackson won the 16 October 1973 run-off election against Massell, getting just over 59 percent of the vote. In doing so, the thirty-five-year-old lawyer became the first African American mayor of a major Deep South city and the sixth nationally since Carl Stokes's surprise 1967 victory in Cleveland. A reporter for the *Atlanta Constitution* noted that Jackson's victory was due to a "crushing black majority with a surprisingly strong showing among white voters." He owed the most to those in the grassroots, for voters in the city's Black districts threw between 90 and 95 percent of their ballots his way. White liberals on the city's North Side did not disappoint Jackson either, with some districts handing him 25 percent of their votes. The victorious candidate proclaimed the election "a resounding affirmation of the principles of unity and brotherhood that have helped make Atlanta truly a city too busy to hate, and we are that city."[59]

Black politicians throughout the state in 1972 had formed the Georgia Service Center for Elected Officials, which soon became the Georgia Association of Black Elected Officials (GABEO), as an explicit way of organizing their resources to better serve their constituents. In May 1972 the group worked with the University of Georgia School of Social Work to conduct public hearings on welfare in the state. After the Jackson victory, GABEO officials began focusing on political districts in the state "where black potential is good" for increased numbers in the legislature. At the same time, however, GABEO members noted that the "intent is not to compete with SCLC, or any other organization," but to simply lend its resources and technical support.[60]

As active as Black elected officials had been at the state level, Atlanta activists also played a role in national politics. In 1974 a number of Black elected officials nationwide pledged their support for the liberation struggles in Southern Africa. Charles C. Diggs, the activist Michigan congressman, wrote Vincent Harding urging IBW support for a drive by the Congressional Black Caucus (CBC) to repeal the Byrd Amendment, under which the United States imported chrome from the white supremacist government in Rhodesia. Of course, the work of Black elected officials in this arena was due in large part to the solidarity work of radical Black activists in organizations such as the African Liberation Support Committee (ALSC). Founded in 1972, the ALSC was a largely Marxist umbrella group that launched "key educational and agitational programs" concerning the struggles against Portuguese colonialism in Mozambique and Angola, the campaign to repeal the Byrd Amendment, and the drive to impeach President Nixon in the wake of Watergate. The ALSC also supported local struggles in the South involving repression and prison reform.[61]

The ALSC had been beset almost from the start, however, by serious and often volatile ideological struggles. The group was at the flash point of the mid-seventies debate—particularly among the leading radical Black male activists—over whether to advance a Marxist-Leninist or nationalist political line. Dawolu Gene Locke, ALSC international chairperson, contended that certain "extreme right-wing nationalists" had refused to adopt the group's statement of principles, this despite approval of the document by international governments and organizations. Although it was doubtful that Black elected officials had been guided by the debate among radical Black activists of the period, they continued to be influenced by the general spirit of African solidarity raised by the activists themselves. The Congressional Black Caucus manifested that spirit in December 1975 when it called for an end to U.S. covert intervention in support of the Portuguese in Angola. Members of the liberal CBC also had been disturbed by the "special implications" of intervention into Angola by the South African Defense Force.[62]

On a more moderate front, the year also marked the incorporation of the Georgia Association of Black Elected Officials, a tangible indication of the increased presence of Black politicians throughout the state. Ed McIntyre, founder and first president of the four-year-old group, sought to define its major objectives. First, GABEO would continue to organize seminars and meetings to give "minority elected officials" information on proposed state and federal legislation. Second, the organization intended to examine issues "peculiar to minority elected officials" and develop their management skills. And third, GABEO would study on a "non-partisan basis" various ways to eradicate poverty and racism and obtain human rights for each of the state's African American citizens.[63]

GABEO also was an important cog in the state machinery that helped organize the successful presidential campaign of Jimmy Carter, even though the state's Black politicians certainly did not see eye-to-eye with the former governor on every issue. Indeed, President Carter saw fit to reward state representative and former student activist Benjamin Brown for his efforts by procuring him a post as vice chair of the Democratic National Committee. At the state level, Atlanta city council president Carl Ware and Macon councilwoman Delores Brooks advanced the notion of a "State of Black People in Georgia" position paper to accompany the governor's annual "State of the State of Georgia" address before the Legislature. Ideally, the position paper would benefit from input from GABEO politicians, IBW scholars, and a Clark

College group called the Southern Center for Studies in Public Policy. In honor of the Atlanta mayor, GABEO members also drafted a resolution proclaiming 7 May 1977 to be "Maynard Holbrook Jackson Day."[64]

Fall 1977 brought with it an ambitious conference organized by GABEO and IBW activists, "Black Politics in Georgia: New Responsibilities, New Challenges," held in Americus. Conference panelists included a number of scholars, among them Columbia University political scientist Charles V. Hamilton, Tuskegee University historian Manning Marable, Clark College political scientist Nathaniel Jackson, Morehouse historian Alton Hornsby Jr., and Atlanta University political scientists Alex Willingham and Robert Holmes. Panelists outside the academy included Albany, Georgia, attorney Mary Young and state representative David Scott. Some panels confronted the problem of Black elected officials who had failed to be responsive to their constituencies. Other sessions analyzed whether the increase in Black political representation had ushered in an "improvement of the overall social, economic, and political conditions" of African American communities throughout the state. Another panel was simply titled "Black Power in America: History and Status."[65]

On 19 November, David Scott delivered the conference's keynote speech. The state representative from Atlanta predicted that the state of Georgia would produce one Black U.S. senator and two Black U.S. representatives within the next eight years. However, Scott maintained that the only way for this to happen would be through establishing interracial coalitions. He asserted, then, that Black elected officials "must be smart enough and shrewd enough and have sense enough to build solid and positive relationships with the many good and decent white people of this state." But Scott did not end there, contending that successes in the years to come would have to be "tied hand-in-hand and cheek-to-cheek with white political power." To the apparent dismay of some in the audience, he concluded his speech by reiterating that "there is no separate black road to political power and fulfillment. There is no future for black politics in a state of isolation, through going it alone."[66]

Even if some who attended the conference took exception to Scott's rejection of independent Black politics at any level, most agreed that the future necessitated a multi-dimensional approach, and that meant elevating the role of economics. Charles Hamilton spoke on the need to join the two spheres so that politicians and theorists could enter into a discourse concerning political economy. Willie Woods, the GABEO official who coordinated the conference along with IBW executive director Howard Dodson, asserted that the conference itself represented that very linkage. "You see, we moved from civil rights to politics to economics."[67]

Woods and Dodson could also take heart from the commendatory response they received from those who attended the sessions. John A. Brown, president of Georgia Southwestern College, wrote the IBW a letter of thanks, as did the leader of the Concerned Citizens of the Black Community Organization, a relatively new group formed in Americus. One of the most thoughtful letters Dodson received came from a GABEO member, Atlanta City Council President Carl Ware. Ware noted that the number of "renowned speakers was indeed impressive and I've heard nothing but positive reactions towards the entire program." He concluded by noting that it was an "understatement to say that our goal and yours are compatible and we look forward to continuing cooperative progress in the future."[68]

BLACK WOMEN-CENTERED ACTIVISM

As the presidential bid of Shirley Chisholm vividly illustrated, the burgeoning discussion of gender in the African American community—so often obscured by a singular focus on race—was long overdue. In early 1972, Georgia State University hosted a symposium on "The Black Woman and the Liberation Struggle." Speakers included elder activist Queen Mother Audley Moore, founder of the Universal Association of Ethiopian Women; Denise Oliver, editor of a New York City magazine called *Babylon*; and Emma Darnell, intergovernmental programs coordinator for the City of Atlanta. As was the case nationally, panelists at the Georgia State forum tended to be more critical of class and white skin privilege in the women's liberation movement than they were of sexism in the Black freedom struggle. "Nobody ever cared for you but your momma and your woman. Better get straight with them," Darnell advised Black men. But she also counseled Black women to "comfort, teach, and instruct your man. It's hard, I know it's hard. . . . But we've got to work together."[69]

A November 1972 forum at the Women's Resource Center at Clark College provided a somewhat sharper assertion of a Black feminist perspective. "It's not the black woman who has castrated her man, but white society who has," argued Barbara Fouche, a local fashion model. Paulette Novel, associate director of the Black women's employment program of the Southern Regional Council, concurred with Fouche and added that the "freedom of the black male is intimately related to the liberation of the black female." She further contended that Black women faced "double jeopardy" on a daily basis because they were "discriminated against as a black and as a woman." Therefore, Novel stressed the need for male activists to confront their sexism. "Black men must realize that upward movement for black people cannot be achieved by asking black women to step back."[70]

At the same time, Novel's intraracial critique of sexism challenged the reticence on the part of a significant number of Black women to embrace an explicitly Black feminist analysis of their lives and was part of a growing effort to complicate and transcend the prevailing understanding of the larger Black struggle for human rights. This understanding was inextricably bound to the process of developing a Black feminist consciousness. Spelman College professor Beverly Guy-Sheftall had come to appreciate just how transformative this process could be, both personally and for students in her literature courses. Guy-Sheftall had developed "no consciousness around feminism" as an undergraduate at Spelman during the mid-1960s. However, things began to change when she studied for a year at Wellesley College, where she enrolled in a "Women and Drama" course. The more decisive moments came for Guy-Sheftall as a graduate student at Atlanta University when she began attending weekly consciousness-raising sessions organized by Sandra Hollin Flowers, a local Black feminist. Although "I had been very preoccupied with race," Guy-Sheftall said, she recalled that the informal discussions, which included "regular Black women and some students," were instrumental for her in terms of "coming into Black feminism."[71]

Conducted in the privacy of Flowers's apartment over the course of six months in 1972, the consciousness-raising sessions provided a safe space for frank discussions about Black womanhood. Flowers came to Atlanta from Yuma, Arizona, where she had come of age in a "very political household," her father being president of the local NAACP chapter. Economic issues provided a key impetus for her activism. "It started actually as a pragmatic sort of thing for women: 'Look at how we're paid. Look at how we fare in the work world,'" she recalled. "It wasn't academic. It wasn't at all abstract. It wasn't at all esoteric. It was just, 'This is what we're living. Do you like it? What's wrong with it? And how does it make you feel?'" Together with her friend Connie Banks, Flowers organized the two-hour consciousness-raising sessions as informal roundtable discussions focusing on the lived experiences of the ten to twenty women present. Flowers recalled that "it was an awakening, that we were sitting around talking about things that were happening in our ordinary lives and that we just took to be our own private problems, when in fact they were shared by nearly everybody there, in one way or another."[72]

Misogyny in all of its forms was a problem that sparked discussion and reflection. While in the hospital for surgery, Flowers roomed with a Black woman whose husband beat her so severely with a belt that the buckle pierced her skin, requiring a blood transfusion to ward off infection. Their hospital conversations helped to confirm for Flowers the need for group discussions of such violence at the hands of Black men. By the second session many women revealed that men in their lives had assaulted them—evidence of a widespread problem. Flowers recalled telling victims of domestic violence that they did not have to "put up with that," but she also realized that it was "hard to tell that to a person who's economically dependent on the person who's abusing them. That was a feminist issue, and it became an organizing premise for us." Soon those who attended the consciousness-raising sessions began making connections between misogynist violence and aspects of Black popular culture that demeaned Black women. Flowers remembered that it was "very disturbing" when the group analyzed popular songs of the period like "Cheaper to Keep Her," or when it discussed the manner in which the Fred Sanford character continually demeaned the Aunt Esther character in the situation comedy Sanford and Son. "We were just objects. We were jokes," Flowers recalled. As was the case for women of the Atlanta Project in SNCC, those who participated in the informal sessions confronted issues of self-perception. Flowers did note, however, that discussion and reflection in a private setting "helped us to raise our own self-esteem."[73]

Publicly, an increasing number of Black women called attention to the need to confront their own ambivalence toward raising gender issues. Grace Towns Hamilton, state representative and former head of the Atlanta Urban League, noted in 1973 that Black women benefited from the women's liberation movement. Nevertheless, she asserted that they "are so used to dealing with racial inequalities that sexism is not the cutting edge." Martha Gaines, a Black feminist and member of the local chapter of the National Organization for Women (NOW), elaborated on Hamilton's remarks. "Black women who are activists usually are going to be primarily working in the black movement," Gaines asserted. "That's their first priority, although they support the women's movement." Flowers later noted that the ambivalence often concerned issues of movement loyalty. "If you were a political Black woman, was it O.K.

to be concerned about feminist issues, or did all of your loyalty belong to the civil rights movement—that is to say, aligned with Black men? And being aligned with Black men at that time did not always play out to the issues that you had as a Black woman with being suppressed and oppressed."[74]

The absence of an explicit discussion of gender also was evident at the Institute of the Black World during the early seventies. Vincent Harding, the IBW's founding director, recalled that discussion and analysis of "gender exploitation and Black patriarchy was often hidden under the mountain of the struggle that we were carrying on for freedom in relationship to White America." He contended that "often this was an unintentional burying. Sometimes, more than was healthy, this was an intentional burying." Although there were several women on the IBW office staff, Joyce Ladner was the lone female research staff member during the think tank's early years, and she had been there for only one year before traveling to Tanzania. Furthermore, Institute documents such as its statement of purpose and program revealed no substantive treatment of issues specific to Black women. As a result, Harding noted, IBW scholars simply did not approach discussions on intraracial gender issues "in the same way that we would have carried them out ten, fifteen, twenty years later."[75]

Fortunately, though, Black women in Atlanta had other venues for launching such discussions. On 29 January 1976, state representatives Betty Clark and Mildred Glover joined Dorothy Bolden of the National Domestic Workers Union (NDWU) in a Hungry Club forum on the "Plight of the Black Woman," held at the Butler Street YMCA. All three panelists took exception with the title of the event, as did sociology professor Anna Grant, who moderated the program. "Black women are ahead of the game," Grant contended. "We have had to prove ourselves because history forced us to do this." Glover and Bolden argued that the strategy employed by most White feminists to gain passage of the Equal Rights Amendment (ERA) alienated Black women. Glover added that many Black women had been concerned that the ERA fight would push specific African American concerns aside somehow, although she did not elaborate.[76]

Without question, though, the most intriguing critique at the Hungry Club panel was an intraracial class one. Bolden, who founded the NDWU in Atlanta in 1968 to press employers for better wages and working conditions, criticized the aloofness of certain college- educated Black women. The NDWU president did not mince her words, exhibiting a frankness in the discussion of class and generational issues that was often absent in the male-centered politics and discourse of the Black Power era. "We must get rid of the attitude of 'I got my degree and I can't deal with that scrubwoman,'" Bolden insisted. "But that scrubwoman is the one who is going to hold you up on that ladder."[77]

■ ■ ■

Unbeknownst to Bolden, perhaps, a clandestine group mostly comprising Black professional women had been active in confronting racial and sexual discrimination in Atlanta and in drawing attention to international issues. Named for the abolitionist and suffragist Sojourner Truth, Sojourner South included within its ranks writer Toni Cade Bambara, Beni Ivey of the Atlanta Black United Fund, IBW activists Jan Douglas and Pat Daly, AU School of Social Work research director Jualynne Dodson, and a woman who would become mayor of the city, Shirley Franklin. The driving forces behind the underground organization were Ivey and Douglas. Ivey had been involved in the groundbreaking effort to launch Black Studies at San Francisco State and regularly attended meetings of both the Black Panther Party and US Organization. She had worked in the Atlanta and New York City offices of SNCC, traveled to Tanzania in 1970, and then returned to Atlanta in 1972 to work with Maynard Jackson and Andrew Young. A professor in the Atlanta University School of Social Work, Douglas headed the city's Community Relations Commission in 1975. "They were forefront women," Dodson noted of Douglas and Ivey. "They were breaking ground."[78]

The organizational structure of Sojourner South helped its eclectic mix of activists mobilize their constituencies. Douglas had spoken at events sponsored by Black Women for Political Action, a California organization, and discussed the possibility of launching a similar group in Atlanta. "Nobody had time to manage and develop another organization, so we came up with a really good plan," Douglas recalled. "We got fifteen women together, and all these women had constituents." The core group met regularly, and when mobilization on a given issue was necessary, each core Sojourner South member contacted as many as twenty other women, who in turn contacted others. Its members included political figures, professors, and influential sorority members. "We all had a real commitment to fight racism, to fight for social change, and for women's empowerment," Ivey said. Yet, due largely to the prominence of its core members, Sojourner South members remained clandestine, with the exception of Douglas. "I was very public, so I was kind of the public spokesperson," she noted. "But for a lot of the stuff, we used to say, 'Those who say don't know, and those who know don't say.' We kept our membership secret."[79]

Sojourner South first targeted employment discrimination in Atlanta. A local television station came under fire for the treatment of a Black anchorwoman. When the station's Black spokesman proved unhelpful, Sojourner South activists launched a behind-the-scenes assault that included a complaint to the Federal Communications Commission and a public campaign with picketing in front of the station. A second target was the Metropolitan Atlanta Regional Transportation Authority (MARTA). In order to make their case, members of Sojourner South who worked for MARTA obtained data that supported the group's contention that the transportation agency discriminated against Blacks. Armed with the information, Sojourner South activists "totally unrelated" to those who had done the research entered into successful negotiations with MARTA officials. Much in the tradition of the late-nineteenth- and early-twentieth-century Black club women's movement, Sojourner South activists had challenged institutional racism by coalescing around both formal and informal networks of professional women.[80]

A rare public display of activism by Sojourner South activists involved African solidarity work, revealing the continuing significance of a broader international Black human rights perspective. The most recent campaign of repression conducted by the South African government against Black activists, which began with the 16 June 1976 massacre of student freedom fighters in the township of Soweto, had sparked protests worldwide. Relying on financial support from several prominent Blacks, including entertainment attorney David Franklin, Sojourner South activists paid for dozens of billboards condemning the Pretoria regime in the wake of the massacre. Although the group financed the billboards for only thirty days, many in poorer neighborhoods remained for several months since no business or group provided the funds for new ones. Sojourner South activists paid for a "full-fledged" anti-apartheid billboard in front of the Coca-Cola building to call attention to the Atlanta company's presence in South Africa, a move that anticipated the divestment movement of the next decade.[81]

Members also helped organize a downtown march and rally one week after the Soweto Massacre. The primary sponsor of the rally, in front of the Federal Reserve Bank of Atlanta, was the Atlanta Coalition Against Repression in South Africa (ACARSA). Atlanta University professor Muriel Tillinghast, spokeswoman for the Black coalition group, asserted that she was "dissatis-fied and gravely concerned" by Congressman and former SCLC activist An-drew Young's rather tepid call for Secretary of State Henry Kissinger to be "tough" on South African leader John Vorster in their meetings overseas. ACARSA protesters carried signs that read "Stop the Murders, End Apartheid Now" and chanted "Imperialists, hands off the African land!" Like a number of African American activists, Douglas saw parallels between the situations in South Africa and the United States, which propelled her solidarity activism.[82]

The women of Sojourner South felt compelled to address their relation-ships in the movement with both Black men and White women. Jan Douglas noted that women in the organization had grown frustrated with Black male activists' failure to acknowledge them. "It's very interesting," she said. "Men tend to take everything women do for granted," so organizing explicitly as Black women—even within a largely submerged context—"gave us a lot more clout." Women in the group enjoyed the financial support of those Black men, including spouses of certain Sojourner South members, who respected the group's decision-making autonomy. Douglas recalled that this was certainly the case for one prominent Black man who contributed to Sojourner South's coffers. "We would usually pay him back, and if we didn't, he didn't worry about it."[83]

The relationship between Sojourner South activists and White feminists in Atlanta had been far more contested, however, and some Black women were ambivalent about adopting an explicit feminist moniker. "These were very strong Black women. And one of the problems in terms of using the word 'feminist' is that it had to do with middle-class White women's views," Doug-las said. "We had a huge argument on ERA with White women. We said 'we're ready to go to bat with ERA,' and we turned a lot of Black votes in the Legislature. But when we said, 'we want you on AFDC because that is femi-nist,' they're like, 'I beg your pardon?'" Sojourner South activists considered the refusal by White women to accept a feminist agenda that seriously con-fronted the specific needs of welfare recipients to be a manifestation of both class and white skin privilege. "They had this trickle-down theory that didn't work," Douglas asserted. "It was working for some White women, and so the racism was the problem. You've got women saying, 'We've got prosecutors now, oh great, we're making progress.' But they're racist."[84]

In fall 1977, Jualynne Dodson, who was splitting her time between the AU School of Social Work and the IBW, began organizing a conference on Black women and their relationship to the Black freedom struggle. In her proposal to federal and state funding organizations she stressed the need for outreach to groups ranging from Sunni Muslims and Black Christian nationalists to the Revolutionary Workers' Party and National Welfare Rights Organization. Dodson's conversation with Joy Rogers, a Black activist with the predominantly White Feminist Action Alliance, made her and the IBW staff realize the "necessity to incorporate a discussion topic on Black women and the organized women's movement."[85]

Having obtained a grant from the Georgia Committee for the Humanities and co-sponsorship from the Women's Task Force of the Atlanta Community Relations Commission and the IBW, Dodson was able to finalize the details of the 9–10 December conference, called "Black Women, Black Freedom Struggle: Past, Present, Future." Minister Barbara King gave the invocation as over two hundred "community activists, citizens, and scholars" began the weekend conference at the John F. Kennedy Community Center. The conference—which provided free registration and child care for all attendees—offered panels and workshops, as well as keynote addresses in the evenings. Programming also featured the performances of cultural activists such as Mari Evans, poet and professor of Afro-American Studies at Indiana University. The keynote speaker on Friday was Toni Cade Bambara, the Black feminist writer-editor.[86]

Cade Bambara influenced profoundly the burgeoning Black women's movement in Atlanta from her arrival there in 1974. She and Douglas had established a friendship when they taught together at Livingston College in New Jersey, part of the Rutgers University system. Clark College in Atlanta offered Cade Bambara a teaching position, but when she arrived with her daughter, "they had no job for her," Douglas recalled. Douglas acted quickly, enlisting the help of her cousin, Spelman College president Donald Stewart. Stewart and English professor Michael Lomax arranged for Cade Bambara to become an artist-in-residence at Spelman. The residency proved productive, for it was during this period that Cade Bambara completed her final book, *The Salt Eaters*. "Toni would get really crazy and I'd get a call from the school saying, 'Toni hasn't picked up Karma,'" Douglas recalled of moments when her friend became so absorbed in her writing that her daughter remained at pre-school. "So she spent a lot of time over at my house when her mom was writing." Her friends played another important role as well. "Toni was wonderful because a lot of the stuff in her book reflected our real-life situations. She was always saying, 'There's no connection between the stories I'm writing and real people,' " Douglas laughed. "But there was!"[87]

Cade Bambara's significance rested not only with her writing but also with the way that she led her life. Beverly Guy-Sheftall had been touched by this facet of Cade Bambara when she interviewed her for the groundbreaking book Guy-Sheftall co-edited, Sturdy Black Bridges: Visions of Black Women in Literature. She had already come to know the power of Cade Bambara's humanistic approach to fiction, as well as her political work, including efforts to establish a Black women's union in the United States. Yet, "what struck me was that this was the first time that I had been in close contact with a person who was an activist, a writer, a person who was clearly—from my little vantage point as a person who mostly had been around women who had chosen fairly normative lives—she wasn't married, she had this child, and she lived a totally unconventional life," Guy-Sheftall recalled. "This was a woman who had decided she could live the life she wanted to live totally free of any kind of normative script."[88]

Without question, then, Cade Bambara was one of the most influential Black feminists of the period. In 1970 she edited the anthology The Black Woman—arguably the most powerful textual challenge to the sexism and organizational patriarchy of the Black Power movement. In it, Cade Bambara wrote an essay of her own that elaborated on the question of gender roles vis-à-vis the Black liberation struggle. "Perhaps we need to let go of all notions of manhood and femininity and concentrate on Blackhood," she asserted. "It perhaps takes less heart to pick up the gun than to face the task of creating a new identity, a self, perhaps an androgynous self, via commitment to the struggle." During her conference keynote speech, "Black Women in the Black Freedom Struggle: History and Status," Cade Bambara focused on the need for Blacks to emulate Zora Neale Hurston's tenacious and unrelenting embrace of African American folk culture. She further asserted that Hurston's ability to cultivate the grassroots had meaning for the movement. "The degree to which we ignore our true role models is the degree to which we surrender ourselves up to our enslavement."[89]

Myrian Richmond, news director and commentator at radio station WAOK-AM, delivered the second keynote address, "Role Alternatives for Black Women." Richmond called for the elaboration of common political goals among Black women and the African American community in general. She also stressed the need to develop a global African approach to educating and rearing Black children. The most provocative aspect of Richmond's speech, however, involved her assertion that Black women needed to take an uncompromising position in favor of their reproductive rights. She correctly noted that a "significant number of women who will go to the butchers and back alleys for abortions if the practice is deemed illegal, or the existing laws are not changed, will be Black."[90]

Fully aware of the anti-abortion and anti-birth control arguments raised by a number of nationalists, both male and female, Richmond further asserted that "it is not a question of Black genocide, it is a question of how are they going to feed another mouth with no money and no prospects of any." The pressing concern for her was how such poor and working-class women would "maintain their sanity with another responsibility added to the already overwhelming burdens." Ultimately, Richmond argued, what Blacks desperately needed was clarification and education on the issue of abortion. "Admittedly, abortion is a touchy subject," she noted, "but it will simply remain so without a concerted effort on the part of Black women and men to deal with the subject on a rational, rather than an emotional, level."[91]

The conference came to a close Saturday with the keynote address of Jualynne Dodson, "The Role of Black Women in the Future of American Society." Dodson spoke first of the historic role of the Black woman as the principal community developer throughout the global African world. In focusing on the lives of African American women specifically, she argued that they held the keys that would unlock the door to fundamental change. Indeed, she asserted, their experiences had provided them with the "clarity of knowing the institutional errors of American society." For that reason, Dodson declared, "we take up the responsibility of developing the humanistic characteristics of those who would struggle for the transformation of this sin-sick society." Dodson cautioned her audience, however, against falling prey to certain external and internal factors—most centered around the quest for material gain— that could undermine the freedom struggle. "Out of that kind of orientation comes individualism, opportunism, and a whole slew of other isms, all of them oriented to profit—'how much can I get for me?' "[92]

■ ■ ■

During the next year it appeared as though movement-minded Blacks in the city had followed the advice of Dodson. Women-centered activism around individual and personal wellness issues led to the formation of the National

Black Women's Health Project (NBWHP) in the city in 1978. Black elected officials in Atlanta and statewide continued to expand their ranks as the membership of the Georgia Association of Black Elected Officials grew to nearly three hundred. Yet, in other key ways, it seemed as though an increasing number of folks in what had become Atlanta's multiple African American communities had lost sight of Dodson's message. As Maynard Jackson began his second term as mayor, the city's Black middle class continued to grow and prosper—out into the suburbs. In the meantime, its poor, working majority continued to grow and suffer. The early 1960s direct action campaigns against segregation exposed the fraudulent image of Atlanta as the city too busy to hate. In much the same way, the late 1970s–early 1980s struggle to make sense of the sudden disappearance of dozens of poor Black children would come to symbolize in a most painful way the contradiction inherent in Atlanta's new image as the country's quintessential Black Mecca.

f ever a series of events marked a sobering turning point in the life of an entire city, the tragic murders of twenty-nine poor young Blacks in Atlanta, most of them male children, from summer 1979 to spring 1981, had precisely that effect. As a bewildered city tried to come to terms with the senseless slayings, parents of the murdered and missing young people became increasingly dissatisfied with the response of local, state, and federal authorities to their concerns. Desperate to secure safety for their children, some of the most marginalized citizens in the city organized grassroots groups such as the Committee to Stop Children's Murders (STOP) that unapologetically confronted Mayor Maynard Jackson and other Black political leaders. Led by Camille Bell, whose gifted nine-year-old son Yusef had been murdered, STOP organizers demanded that value be given to each victim's life. "We, the mothers of Atlanta's slain children, share a bond with the parents of missing and murdered children everywhere in this country," Bell affirmed. "We know that our children were not hoodlums or hustlers, but were ordinary children engaged in ordinary children's pursuits."[1]

The highly publicized arrest and eventual conviction of a self-described talent scout, Wayne Bertram Williams, a twenty-three-year-old Black man, for the murder of two adult victims raised some eyebrows just as it settled the matter for authorities. Even if many working-class and poor Blacks acknowledged that Williams was probably guilty of several of the murders, they felt as if the other cases had been closed prematurely in order for power brokers to rush forward with business as usual. "This is untidy," acclaimed author James Baldwin observed in the wake of Williams's trial. "It also establishes a precedent, a precedent that may lead us, with our consent, to the barbed wire and the gas oven."[2]

Yet, just as the disappearance and murder of so many young people came to symbolize the continued marginalization of poor Blacks in Atlanta, the subsequent growth of predominantly African American suburbs spoke to the vitality of its Black middle class. This more privileged group included a steady stream of Northern Black professionals who returned to the South and away from the often hard, cold, and impolite life of places like New York City and Philadelphia. For these Blacks, Atlanta represented the best of both worlds, a cosmopolitan city still framed to a large extent by the slower pace and soothing rhythms of life in the imperfect yet infinitely more livable South. The CBS television news program *60 Minutes* showcased Black suburban Atlanta in 2002. "It may look like Beverly Hills," said anchor Mike Wallace as a bird's-eye camera panned over lavish homes with swimming pools. "But it is Black suburban Atlanta, a Mecca for many new migrants who are buying homes worth from two hundred thousand to two million dollars."[3]

The television news story highlighted several Black families who were part of this larger migration back to the South. For these proud professionals, moving South was an important act of self-determination. "My father always used to say, 'Stop asking for a piece of the pie. Make your own damn pie.' And this is what we want," Deirdre Burrell asserted. "We're no different from anybody else. We all want nice homes. We all have college degrees. Here all of us have white-collar jobs. Why should we have to settle for anything less than what we have?"[4] Yet, even the *60 Minutes* segment noted that the situation was complex. The majority of the city's Blacks have had as difficult a time economically as in any period since the early sixties. Black power brokers have become as uneasy about the reality of intraracial violent crime and homelessness in Atlanta as earlier White political figures were about the real story concerning race relations in the capital of the New South. Historian Dana White noted that there "have always been, and there exist today, two Atlantas—one white, the other black."[5] The past three decades have also revealed the extent to which there are also two Black Atlantas, one middle-class to affluent and the other working class to destitute.

■ ■ ■

Many middle-class Blacks realize that they owe a tremendous debt to the activists of the 1960s. The mobility and access to resources enjoyed by contemporary professionals were inextricably bound to the demise of key apartheid structures, including the obliteration of petty apartheid in Atlanta and other urban areas of the South. In a telling commentary on the resiliency of the state, it is worth noting that local authorities had not forgotten about earlier Black activism either, particularly that associated with the Black Power phase of the human rights struggle. Atlanta authorities had successfully targeted both radical Black SNCC organizers and members of the Black Panther Party as part of a larger national repressive war against Black activists during the 1960s and 1970s. Yet, what had become striking was the extent to which individuals with even remote associations to radical Black nationalism became targets of political oppression.

One such victim of this was Hajj Malik Womack, an honors graduate of Morehouse College who endured a fourteen-month ordeal at the hands of Fulton County authorities. In December 1995 the Fulton County district attorney's office charged him and several others in a ninety-three-count indictment in conjunction with a series of robberies of local fast-food restaurants. Authorities claimed that Womack, who had begun doctoral work in history at the University of Michigan, was the mastermind behind a plot by several members of the Five Percent Nation of Islam to rob the Atlanta restaurants in order to obtain weapons to overthrow the government. With bond denied the Phi Beta Kappa nominee spent nearly one year in the maximum security section of the Fulton County Jail. The Morehouse community quickly rallied in support of Womack. Alton Hornsby Jr., longtime history department chair and editor of the Journal of Negro History, led the effort to establish the Hajj M. Womack Defense Fund, noting that "I would just as soon think that I committed the crimes before I would believe that Hajj did."[6]

The trial of Womack revealed both change and continuity in terms of state legal repression. In a familiar pattern, the state's key witness was Roy Norwood, a police informant who testified to participation in seventeen of the robberies. Besides Norwood's testimony, the state could rely only on Womack's possession of a legally owned firearm and his collection of Black Power political literature. The gun, which could not be linked to any crime, quickly became a non-issue. That left the issue of books such as CIA Diary and The Spook Who Sat by the Door. "Look, those books are on Dr. Hornsby's bookshelf right there! It's ridiculous," Womack later said. "I'm doing my Ph.D. dissertation on black nationalism, particularly the armed struggle of the Black Power movement. Of course I'd have these books in my apartment." In October 1996 a jury of seven Whites and five Blacks acquitted Womack on ninety counts, remaining deadlocked on three. Ten days later Judge Don Langham finally granted Womack bond, even as individuals such as state legislator Henrietta Canty continued to press for his release. "I think in some ways, myself and others like us—older, professional people—have become more radicalized as a result of going through this," Hornsby noted. "Now I'm far more aware; I'm even a little afraid for myself, because of my association with this case. At a traffic stop, or if I hear a little click on my phone, I have to wonder. It's frightening to have the fear that your government might do that."[7]

The Womack case foreshadowed the arrest and imprisonment of Imam Jamil Abdullah Al-Amin (H. Rap Brown), a onetime leader of the Student Nonviolent Coordinating Committee. Al-Amin has been in the Georgia state prison at Reidsville since being convicted in 2002 for the March 2000 shooting of two sheriff's deputies. The case has garnered international attention as a result of the work of grassroots activists in organizations such as the Jericho Movement and the International Committee to Support Imam Jamil Abdullah Al-Amin. These activists have pointed to fundamental inconsistencies in the case, including trial testimony by the deputy who survived the shootout, that contradicted earlier statements. A convert to Sunni Islam since the early 1970s, Al-Amin was a longtime fixture in the West End neighborhood of Atlanta, owning and operating a grocery store and preaching nonviolent alternatives to the intraracial youth violence that was part and parcel of life in economically depressed neighborhoods. He steadfastly has maintained his innocence. "For more than thirty years, I have been tormented and persecuted by my enemies for reasons of race and belief," Al-Amin asserted. "I seek truth over a lie; I seek justice over injustice; I seek righteousness over the rewards of evil doers; and I love ALLAH more than I love the state."[8]

The imprisonment of Al-Amin speaks both to a longstanding effort to punish those who were once associated with the Black Power phase of the movement, as well as to the U.S. security state's discomfort at the historic relationship between Black radicalism and Islam. Such discomfort has only intensified since September 11, 2001, as both Islam and radical dissent have been persecuted. In a scenario familiar to dozens of political prisoners in the United States associated with the contemporary Black freedom struggle, Al-Amin has been isolated from the general prison population because of his effectiveness as an organizer, spending at least twenty-three hours a day in solitary confinement. Atlanta has served as a symbolic site, then, for the political incarceration of radical Black nationalists from the moment that Marcus Garvey spent time in the federal penitentiary there on trumped-up mail fraud charges during the 1920s.

■ ■ ■

The imprisonment of Al-Amin has served as a key reminder that the Blacks who continue to have the most tangible connection to local struggles are the grassroots neighborhood activists in Atlanta. Ethel Mathews and Columbus Ward, who work at Emmaus House, a community center in Peoplestown funded by the Episcopal Church, have spoken of the continuing needs and frustrations of most Blacks. A full-time activist at Emmaus House who has organized a number of programs in the Peoplestown and Summerhill neighborhoods, Ward suggested that what might be needed is the return of organizations such as the Black Panther Party. "It's really kind of sad that the Panthers went out of business, because they were one of the few groups that I think had some type of significant role in our community," Ward noted in 1997, himself a participant in several Panther programs as a teenager in Peoplestown. "That might be what we need as an awakening now, something that Black people can identify with again to bring about some changes."[9]

Mathews continues to head the local chapter of the National Welfare Rights Organization. In addition to work with the NWRO, Mathews and fellow Peoplestown residents led an unsuccessful bid to block construction of the new stadium for the 1996 Summer Olympic Games, taking on the combined forces of the Atlanta Committee for the Olympic Games and the city's biracial power structure. As one of the first tenants to be evicted from rental property to make room for the old Atlanta-Fulton County Stadium in 1965, the bitterness was heightened for her by the fact that some of the most prominent Blacks in the city had championed the building of the new stadium. She has participated in the annual Poor Peoples' Day at the state Capitol, a February event bringing progressive and radical grassroots organizations to Atlanta under the umbrella of the Up and Out of Poverty Now Coalition.

As part of the February 1998 Poor Peoples' Day, the group organized a public hearing that addressed issues of human dignity. The hearing at the state Capitol, "The Working Poor Deserve More," focused on the demand that the state minimum wage be doubled to approximate an actual living wage. Due to a combination of legitimate scheduling conflicts and utter disdain on the part of legislators, however, only two state senators appeared at the hearing. One prominent Black legislator noted privately that colleagues "just don't pay attention to this type of activity anymore." Mathews and other grassroots activists seemed to sense this much. "This is a slap in the face!" she told those in attendance. "I am sick, I am just sick."[10]

Nevertheless, the biggest blow to the prospects of the city's working poor did not come from politicians. According to Mathews, privileged Blacks delivered that blow on a daily basis through their disregard and neglect. "We look at the next Black person. They are more against us than the White man is now. They discriminate against us, the next Black person," she asserted while volunteering her time at Emmaus House. "You don't have to worry about the White man. White man used to beat you, used to would kick you, used to would kill you. He don't do it now. He's scared to bother you now. But the Black man is going to do it, and the White man sits back and look at what the Black person do to the next Black person. And it's sad, you hear me."[11] As the continued marginalization of poor Blacks and the reality of political imprisonment revealed, the notion that white supremacy no longer impacted the lives of Blacks in a fundamental way was a mistaken one. After over forty years of frontline activism, Mathews not only had become troubled by the absence of solidarity across intraracial class lines, but also by the critical issue of economic inequality and limited access to resources during successive Black-led municipal administrations.

The elder activist sought answers in the wisdom of the Alabama sharecroppers who were her parents. "My parents, they taught me what some of the White folks would do to you. They taught me what some of them would do to you. They never sat down and say, 'Ethel Mae, you gotta watch the next Black person.' They never did tell me that," she recalled. Echoing the sentiments of countless grassroots activists, Mathews contended that the abandonment of a fundamental human rights agenda by far too many Blacks amounted to a cruel betrayal. Her parents, she said, "always told me that the next Black person is good, good, good, good, *good*. They didn't tell me that they would hurt you. They didn't tell me, 'Ethel Mae, the next Black person would hurt you.' They didn't tell me, 'The next Black person would step on you to get where they want to get, and discriminate against you.' They didn't tell me all of that," Mathews noted bitterly. "They used to hang people in Alabama. They used to hang them. They used to hang Black men—cut off their penis. Wake up the next morning, they're hanging in your yard. Wake up the next morning, they be done drug him out the house and burn him up. I knew all of that. But I didn't know what the next Black person would do to me."[12]

NOTES

PROLOGUE

1. Borders quoted in Marion Gaines, "Negroes Acclaim Bus Integration." *Atlanta Constitution*, 21 January 1959. The contrast between the desegregation efforts in Montgomery and Atlanta could not have been more obvious. The effort in Montgomery was as much a woman-centered Black working-class movement as one centered around a charismatic young preacher. In Atlanta, however, the effort was thoroughly male, top-down, fairly informal, and calculatingly passive. For a far more detailed discussion of elite Black activism in Atlanta during the first half of the twentieth century consult the following: Davis, *A Clashing of the Soul*; Rouse, *Lugenia Burns Hope*; Kuhn, Joye, and West, *Living Atlanta*; Spritzer and Bergmark, *Grace Towns Hamilton and the Politics of Southern Change*; Dittmer, *Black Georgia in the Progressive Era, 1900–1920*; Martin, *The Angelo Herndon Case and Southern Justice*; and Grady-Willis, "A Changing Tide," esp. 10–54.

2. Margaret Shannon, "Atlanta Negro Leadership Emerges with a New Look," *Atlanta Journal*, 28 February 1960; Atlanta Committee for Cooperative Action, *A Second Look*, foreword, Facts on Film, Southern Educational Reporting Service, N10 196.

3. *A Second Look*. As part of a regional trend, local officials enforced de jure residential segregation for a brief period beginning in 1913; de facto segregation continues nationally. See Massey and Denton, *American Apartheid*, 41 and passim.

4. *A Second Look*.

5. With the notable exception of Komozi Woodard and Nikhil Pal Singh, scholars have been reticent in their written work to use the term *apartheid* in the U.S. context. George Fredrickson, in his groundbreaking 1981 comparative study of race relations in the United States and South Africa, noted that in spite of "some resemblances in practice and a good deal of similarity in ideology and spirit," fundamental differences existed between the nature of the oppression of Blacks in the United States and Africans under "separate development" and apartheid in South Africa. Fredrickson argued that U.S. Blacks had been "more influenced by white culture" than their African counterparts and furthermore that "southern blacks were theoretically citizens of a democratic nation, and not conquered aliens." Nevertheless, he asserted that the situation of African Americans in the Jim Crow South did parallel that of the so-called Cape Colored population, since

both groups experienced emancipation from enslavement only to lose fundamental rights because of a white supremacist backlash. See *White Supremacy*, esp. 240–57. Apartheid structures were elaborated in the most sophisticated and yet crudest form in South Africa, where, as historian Leonard Thompson has noted, they "developed from a political slogan into a drastic, systematic program of social engineering." I contend, however, that some of the most striking features of South African apartheid, including disfranchisement, arbitrary racial categorization, segregation, pass laws, and terrorist violence, were in place in the United States as well, and that scholars tend to downplay the institutionalized nature of white supremacy during the Jim Crow era. However, scholars have been more willing to embrace the term *apartheid* in their analysis of residential segregation in contemporary U.S. history. Sociologists Douglas Massey and Nancy Denton have argued that this country is similar to South Africa in that it provides a "firm basis for a broader system of racial injustice" through residential segregation. "The geographic isolation of Africans within a narrowly circumscribed portion of the urban environment—whether African townships or American ghettos—forces blacks to live under extraordinarily harsh conditions." Komozi Woodard framed his discussion of the battle over the proposed Kawaida Towers project in Newark within this context, noting that "it was the politics of American apartheid, involving the caste arrangements, both violent and institutional," that kept Blacks confined to the ghetto there. See Thompson, *A History of South Africa*, 189–90; Lapping, *Apartheid*, 105–6; Massey and Denton, *American Apartheid*, 15; Woodard, *A Nation within a Nation*, 236–44 and 270; see also Singh, *Black Is a Country*, 222. An important text for studying the relationship of the two countries during the fifties is Borstelmann, *Apartheid's Reluctant Uncle*.

6. Carol Anderson has made an important contribution in this regard, noting that human rights, "especially as articulated by the United Nations and influenced by the moral shock of the Holocaust, had the language and philosophical power to address not only the political and legal inequality that African Americans endured, but also the education, health care, housing, and employment needs that haunted the black community." See Anderson, *Eyes off the Prize*, 2. Framing the discussion of the contemporary Black freedom struggle in terms of human rights not only provides a wider canvass for investigation but also helps to situate it within a broader international context. "For decades, researchers confined Afro-American subjects to lines of inquiry that conformed to an American-exceptionalist world view," historian Brenda Gayle Plummer has noted. "An essentialist perspective on race, combined with the belief that the United States has little in common with

other mixed societies, limited the kind of questions that historians and other social scientists were likely to ask about race relations." See Plummer, *Rising Wind*, introduction. Foregrounding the issue of self-determination within the context of the Black freedom struggle further complicates the discussion of human rights activism. Historian Kenneth Cmiel has asserted that the term *human rights* "developed an aura around it" during the 1970s, but that it was a contested one. "While it conjured up civil and political freedom in most 1970s United States human rights organizations, a unified and articulate Third World bloc in the United Nations was at that time deriding such concerns, arguing instead that economic rights, a nonracist environment, and self-determination were the fundamental human rights." See Cmiel, "The Emergence of Human Rights Politics in the United States," 1231–50.

7. Crimmins, "The Atlanta Palimpsest," 13–32.
8. See Anderson, *Eyes off the Prize*, esp. introduction and chapters 1–2.
9. Jan Douglas, telephone interview by author, 23 May 2004, tape recording.
10. See Gwendolyn Brooks, "I Am Black," in *In Montgomery and Other Poems*, 85–86. I capitalized the word *Black* as a teenager until I took a journalism class in high school back home in Denver. In a moment that remains vivid in my memory, Ms. James chastised me for doing so, noting that "black is simply a color, Winston, but Negro refers to race." I did not begin capitalization again until chastised a second time, in this instance by my master's thesis adviser, James Turner, founding director of the Africana Studies and Research Center at Cornell.

CHAPTER 1: THE COMMITTEE ON APPEAL FOR HUMAN RIGHTS

1. Lonnie King, telephone interview by author, 29 May 2004, tape recording. Had King been assigned to the USS *Midway*, he would have found himself in a controversy when South African authorities restricted the movements of Black and Asian American crew members. See Plummer, *Rising Wind*, 238; Borstelmann, *Apartheid's Reluctant Uncle*, 51, 129.
2. King interview. Azza Salama Layton, a political scientist, has asserted that certain initiatives undertaken by President Harry S. Truman and his administration to end segregation "represented a calculated measure aimed at containing Communism" as much as they were responses to domestic pressures. Yet the overseas experiences of Black students and servicemen reinforced the belief that institutionalized racism in the United States, not communism, needed to be confronted. See Layton, *International Politics and Civil Rights Policies in the United States, 1941–1960*, 7, 75–106.

3. Posey and Fuller, "Protest Drug Counter Discrimination," *Crisis*, December 1958, 612–13; "Negroes Call Off Store Sitdowns," *Daily Oklahoman*, 2 June 1958, Facts on Film, SERS, J6 2682.

4. The best account of the Greensboro movement remains William H. Chafe's community study, *Civilities and Civil Rights*. The states with lunch-counter demonstrations in February 1960 were Alabama, Florida, Kentucky, Maryland, North Carolina, South Carolina, Tennessee, and Virginia.

5. Benjamin Brown, interview by author, 15 December 1997, Atlanta, tape recording; King interview.

6. King interview; Fort, "Atlanta Sit-In Movement," 131–32; Walker, "Sit-Ins in Atlanta: A Study in the Negro Revolt," *Atlanta, Georgia, 1960–1961*, ed. Garrow, 65; Kiker, "Rich's Tells 7 Negroes about Separate Grills," *Atlanta Journal*, 8 March 1960. On 7 March a group of eight students from Atlanta University complicated this backstage process when they requested service at the segregated Barbecue Grill restaurant in Rich's Department Store. Store officials told the student contingent to enter the adjacent Hunter Room, where food and service were supposed to be identical. All eight students left without incident. Vincent Fort has noted that the students who participated in the 7 March protest appear to have been affiliated with a second student group, one advised by Lonnie Cross, chair of the Atlanta University Math Department. Lonnie King argued persuasively for unity under one group, however, and AU President Rufus Clement agreed. As a result the better organized All-University Student Leadership Group prevailed.

7. "An Appeal for Human Rights" appeared as a full-page advertisement in the 9 March 1960 *Atlanta Daily World*, *Atlanta Constitution*, and *Atlanta Journal*. President Clement, serving as an unofficial emissary, delivered the appeal and a check to each newspaper after obtaining the necessary funds. A representative of each of the affiliated Atlanta University Center schools signed the document: Willie Mays, president of the Dormitory Council at Atlanta University; James Felder, president of the Student Government Association at Clark College; Marion D. Bennett, president of the Student Association at Interdenominational Theological Center; Don Clarke, president of the Morehouse College Student Body; Mary Ann Smith, secretary of the Student Government Association at Morris Brown College; and Roslyn Pope, Spelman College Student Government Association president. Pope was the principal author of the appeal.

8. Atlanta Committee for Cooperative Action, *A Second Look*, foreword.

9. "Appeal for Human Rights."

10. Wright quoted in Fort, "The Atlanta Sit-In Movement, 1960–61," *Atlanta, Georgia*,

1960–1961, ed. Garrow, 125; Herschelle [Sullivan] Challenor, telephone interview by author, 25 May 2004, tape recording. Several historically Black colleges and universities established international programs during the 1930s and 1940s. Spelman College's exchange program brought several Kenyan women to Atlanta, and Kenyan nationalist Tom Mboya spoke there in 1959. See Plummer, *Rising Wind*, 33; Fleming, *Soon We Will Not Cry*, 48–49.

11. "Appeal for Human Rights."

12. Walker, *An Appeal to the Coloured Citizens of the World, but in Particular, and Very Expressly, to Those of the United States of America*, 89; Patterson, *The Man Who Cried Genocide*, 181–82; Layton, *International Politics and Civil Rights Policies in the United States*, 49–58; Horne, *Black and Red*. For an excellent discussion of the NAACP's early human rights agenda, see Anderson, *Eyes off the Prize*.

13. King interview. In *Eyes off the Prize*, Anderson has argued for the significance of a human rights frame.

14. Vandiver and Hartsfield quoted in Gene Britton, "Vandiver, Hartsfield Differ On Negro Students' Appeal," *Atlanta Constitution*, 10 March 1960.

15. Editorial, "College Students Issue Their Manifesto," *Atlanta Daily World*, 10 March 1960; Margaret Long, "Appeal for Human Rights Was Intelligent and Moving," *Atlanta Journal*, 17 March 1960.

16. A. D. King quoted in Marion Gaines, "Negro Sitdowns Planned Carefully by Students Alone, Leader Says," *Atlanta Constitution*, 16 March 1960; "Negro Students 'Sit Down' at Nine Eating Places Here," *Atlanta Journal*, 15 March 1960; "77 Negroes Arrested in Student Sitdowns at 10 Eating Places Here," *Atlanta Constitution*, 16 March 1960.

17. "77 Negroes Arrested in Student Sitdowns at 10 Eating Places Here"; Douglas Kiker, "Legal Huddle Called to Map Sit-In Defense," *Atlanta Journal*, 16 March 1960; Walker, "Sit-Ins in Atlanta," 69; King interview; Challenor interview. The Committee on Appeal for Human Rights established a steering committee with three members from each of the six affiliated schools, plus Lonnie King as chair. When Herschelle Sullivan returned from Paris, she became co-chair of the Committee. Larry Fox recalled that practically no one referred to the organization by its acronym, choosing either to say the entire name or "the Committee." Larry Fox, telephone interview by author, 20 March 2004, tape recording.

18. Unidentified students quoted in Kiker, "Bright, Bitter Negroes," *Atlanta Journal*, 13 March 1960.

19. Challenor interview; Fleming, *Soon We Will Not Cry*, 113; Chafe, *Civilities and Civil Rights*, introduction.

20. Fleming, *Soon We Will Not Cry*, 44–48; Challenor interview.

21. Unidentified student quoted in Kiker, "Bright, Bitter Negroes." I tend to agree with the contention by Jack L. Walker and other scholars of the sit-in movement that college students and established leaders had similar class aspirations. Walker further argued that what set them apart was not only tactical differences but the reliance of older leaders upon Whites for financial support. "In fact, to a large extent, the power of the conservatives depends on their influence in the white community." While this was true to a point, I contend that established Black leaders—especially clergy—wielded what power they had primarily because of the respect accorded them by the members of the Atlanta Black community. See Walker, "The Functions of Disunity," *Atlanta, Georgia, 1960–1961*, ed. Garrow, 23.

22. Editorial, "The Sit-Downs Hit Here," *Atlanta Daily World*, 16 March 1960. A week after the *Daily World* editorial a group of 139 White college students, primarily from Emory University, signed a petition supporting the Appeal for Human Rights. "Whites Pledge Support of Negro Drive," *Atlanta Journal*, 23 March 1960; "139 White Students Back Negro Appeal," *Atlanta Constitution*, 23 March 1960.

23. Howard University president quoted in Lerone Bennett Jr., "What Sit-Downs Mean to America," *Ebony*, June 1960, 40; Douglas Kiker, "Clement Sees Hope for End to Sitdowns," *Atlanta Journal*, 22 March 1960; Mays quoted in Fort, "Atlanta Sit-In Movement," 160; Horace M. Bond, letter to the editor, *Atlanta Daily World*, 17 March 1960. The Congress of Racial Equality offered to pay the tuition of certain students expelled from Historically Black Colleges and Universities. Press release, Eighteenth Annual Convention, CORE, 29 June 1960, Facts on Film, SERS, M9 453; press release, Eighteenth Annual Convention, CORE, 30 June 1960, Facts on Film, SERS, M9 455.

24. "Lunch Counter Jim Crow," *Crisis*, March 1960; press release, 17 March 1960, NAACP, Facts on Film , SERS, M9 641; Challenor interview with author.

25. Press release, 24 March 1960, NAACP, Facts on Film, SERS, M9 645.

26. Kelley quoted in "83 Charged on 3 Laws in Sitdowns," *Atlanta Constitution*, 16 April 1960; "Negroes March at 2 Food Stores Here," *Atlanta Journal*, 22 April 1960.

27. "Negro House Dynamited in White Neighborhood Here," *Atlanta Journal*, 14 April 1960; "Crosses Burned in Yard of Martin Luther King," *Atlanta Journal*, 27 April 1960; Douglas Kiker, "Negroes Press Boycott," *Atlanta Journal*, 25 April 1960.

28. Editorial, "Talks Begin, Now Let Pickets End," *Atlanta Daily World*, 5 May 1960; Berry quoted in "Atlanta Picked as Center for Sitdowns," *Atlanta Journal*, 16 May 1960. The *Journal* article made no mention of the involvement of Baker in organiz-

ing the inaugural meeting of SNCC. The most substantive discussion by far of Baker's pivotal connection to SNCC can be found in Ransby, *Ella Baker and the Black Freedom Movement*; see also Branch, *Parting the Waters*, chap. 7, esp. 292–93; Garrow, *Bearing the Cross*, 131–33.

29. King interview.

30. King interview; "Negroes Arrange 'Pilgrimage' to Capitol to Dramatize Fight," *Atlanta Constitution*, 16 May 1960; "March Peaceful; Hartsfield proud," *Atlanta Journal*, 18 May 1960; King quoted in Margaret Shannon, "Jenkins Halted March, King Says," *Atlanta Journal*, 23 May 1960; Fox interview. While there may have been a possibility that the second group was a maverick contingent, it appears more likely that it wandered toward the Capitol because of a simple breakdown in communication. E. L. Edwards, Grand Dragon of the Ku Klux Klan, was among the White spectators at the Capitol.

31. King and Borders quoted in Gene Britton and Bruce Galphin, "Negro Marchers Diverted to Church," *Atlanta Constitution*, 18 May 1960; Claude Sitton, "Negro Marchers Halted in Atlanta," *New York Times*, 18 May 1960.

32. Douglas Kiker, "Negroes Raise $2,000 for Sitdown Defense," *Atlanta Journal*, 24 May 1960.

33. Lonnie King, Borders, Williams, and Martin Luther King Sr. quoted in ibid.; "Negro [*sic*] Deny Split, Pledge to Support College Protests," *Atlanta Constitution*, 24 May 1960; Walker, "Sit-Ins in Atlanta," 73. Walker attributed John Mack's quote to Clark College student leader Benjamin A. Brown.

34. "An Endorsement in Support of Human Dignity" appeared in the Atlanta *Constitution*, *Atlanta Daily World*, and *Atlanta Journal*, 30 May 1960; "Adults Back Sitdowns of Students," *Atlanta Constitution*, 30 May 1960; Walker, "Sit-Ins in Atlanta," 73; Brown interview. Organizations that officially endorsed the statement included the ACCA, Atlanta Voters League, Fulton County Democratic Club, Gate City Republican Club, NAACP, and several ministerial groups.

35. King and Rich quoted in "Negroes Start Sit Drive on Big Store Eating Places," *Atlanta Journal*, 24 June 1960; "Sitdowners Launch New Atlanta Drive," *Atlanta Constitution*, 24 June 1960.

36. Editorial, "Let's Take It Easy," *Atlanta Journal*, 24 June 1960; Editorial, "Are Repeated Demonstrations Necessary?" *Atlanta Daily World*, 26 June 1960.

37. Challenor interview; King interview; Bickers quoted in Walker, "Sit-Ins in Atlanta," 76. The Empire Real Estate Board and the *Atlanta Daily World* managed to work out their differences by August.

38. Cochrane quoted in Walker, "Sit-Ins in Atlanta," 77.

39. Julian Bond, letter to the editor, *Atlanta Constitution*, 12 July 1960; Fleming, *Soon We Will Not Cry*, 56.

40. King interview.

41. Ibid. King said that students placed the charge cards in a safe deposit box and that when the boycott ended, they returned the cards to their owners. "Could you imagine giving up your charge card so willingly to some college student today?"

42. Bennett, "What Sit-Downs Mean," 37; Louis E. Lomax, "The Negro Revolt against 'the Negro Leaders,'" *Harper's*, June 1960, 42–47. Historian August Meier later noted that despite losing some of its influence over the freedom movement, the NAACP weathered the rise of student activism fairly well. See Meier, "Negro Protest Movements and Organizations," *Journal of Negro Education*, 437–43, Facts on Film, SERS, N8 6346. Henry Lee Moon, the NAACP's public relations director, disputed Lomax's claims in a letter to the editor in the August issue of Harper's. Moon labeled Lomax's essay an "abundant misrepresentation . . . and a kind of fantasy." The NAACP official noted that 80 percent of the organization's funding came from its Black membership. Moon also argued that the sit-ins could not be classified as a repudiation of his group when the Oklahoma City and Wichita, Kansas, protests of the late 1950s had been organized by NAACP youth groups. Lomax responded to Moon in the same issue, standing by his contention that the national Black leadership had been financed by White liberals, although he mustered no evidence to support the assertion.

43. Fort, "The Atlanta Sit-In Movement," 140; Gordon Roberts, "Big Demonstration Set by Negroes," *Atlanta Journal*, 17 October 1960; Lawson quoted in Gordon Roberts, "Jail, Not Bail, Welcome, Sit-In Leader Says Here," *Atlanta Journal*, 17 October 1960.

44. Challenor interview. An excellent account of the fall demonstrations is Lincoln, "The Strategy of a Sit-In," *Atlanta, Georgia, 1960–1961*, ed. Garrow, 95–103; students and White customer quoted in "Negroes Sit-In at 8 Stores," *Atlanta Journal*, 19 October 1960.

45. Challenor interview; Brown interview; Joseph E. Boone, interview by author, 13 August 1997, Atlanta, tape recording. The Ebenezer co-pastor made it clear he was no organizer of the Atlanta protest. "I am not the leader," he correctly stated. "It was student planned, student originated and student sustained." Indeed, the COAHR leadership requested Martin Luther King Jr.'s participation only after a lengthy debate over whether he would overshadow the student effort. King quoted in Galphin and McCartney, "King, 51 Others Held in New Sit-In Push Here,"

Atlanta Constitution, 20 October 1960; Tait quoted in Lincoln, "Strategy of a Sit-In," 100–102; "2-Way Radio Car Directing Sit-Ins," *Atlanta Journal*, 9 December 1960. Apparently, one of the radio operators was Bernard Lee, an Atlanta resident expelled from Alabama State College for his activism.

46. Galphin and McCartney, "King, 51 Others Held"; King quoted in Loudon Wainwright, "Martyr of the Sit-Ins," *Look*, 7 November 1960, 123.

47. Brown interview; Margaret Shannon, "Sit-In Group Faces Jail Wait of 4 to 6 Weeks Before Trial," *Atlanta Journal*, 20 October 1960; Schley quoted in Eddie Barker, "Three, Then Four . . . Then Nine—Well-Dressed, Well Organized," *Atlanta Constitution*, 21 October 1960.

48. Brown interview.

49. Galphin and McCartney, "26 More Arrested in Sit-Ins; Many Counters Closed Here," *Atlanta Constitution*, 21 October 1960; Webb and Andrews quoted in Galphin and McCartney, "Negro Picketing Continues but Sit-Ins Decline Sharply," *Atlanta Constitution*, 22 October 1960.

50. Borders quoted in "Negroes Agree to Halt Sit-Ins for 30 Days Here," *Atlanta Journal*, 23 October 1960.

51. Walker, "Sit-Ins in Atlanta," 81–82.

52. Borders quoted in Galphin, "Negroes Resume Sit-Ins, End Truce," *Atlanta Constitution*, 26 November 1960; "Sit-Ins Resume; Counters Close," *Atlanta Journal*, 26 November 1960.

53. "Klan, Negroes Picket Here Peacefully," *Atlanta Journal*, 27 November 1960; YWCA officials quoted in "Five Negroes Eat at White Cafeteria," *Atlanta Journal*, 1 December 1960.

54. "Negro Diners Turned Away from YMCA," *Atlanta Journal*, 3 December 1960; "Wide Support for Sit-In Cited," *Atlanta Journal*, 22 December 1960; letter to the editor, *Atlanta Journal*, 26 December 1960.

55. Reg Murphy, "Vandiver Orders Patrol to Remove Negroes after Wild Demonstration," *Atlanta Constitution*, 12 January 1961; "Negroes Suspended after Campus Riot," *Atlanta Journal*, 12 January 1961; "Four Negroes Bound Over for Sit-In Here," *Atlanta Journal*, 11 January 1961; "Prolonged Sit-In Held in Drugstore," *Atlanta Constitution*, 22 January 1961. Hunter and Holmes registered for classes without serious incident in March. See "Negroes Enroll Again at a Calm University," *Atlanta Constitution*, 21 March 1961.

56. William O. Smith, "11 Negroes Refuse to Make Bond in Sit-In Arrests," *Atlanta Journal*, 8 February 1961; Brown quoted in "31 Negroes in Atlanta Sit-In Refuse Bail, Face Long Wait," *Atlanta Journal*, 9 February 1961.

57. Shannon and Gaines, "6 Negroes Arrested at 2 Restaurants," *Atlanta Journal*, 10 February 1961; Greene quoted in Fred Powledge, "Sit-In Group Studies at Jail," *Atlanta Journal*, 10 February 1961; "Sit-Ins Here to Continue, Leader Says," *Atlanta Journal*, 13 February 1961; Mays quoted in Fort, "Atlanta Sit-In Movement," 147–48.

58. Boone interview; Margaret Shannon and Orville Gaines, "8 Ordered Bound Over in Terminal Sit-In," *Atlanta Journal*, 16 February 1961; Williams quoted in Walker, "Sit-Ins in Atlanta," 84.

59. Editorial, "The Old Campaigner," *Atlanta Inquirer*, 7 January 1961, quoted in Walker, "Sit-Ins in Atlanta," 84.

60. Walker, "Protest and Negotiation," *Atlanta, Georgia, 1960–1961*, ed. Garrow, 31–33; Borders quoted in Galphin, "Negroes at Rally Cheer Call for More Support," *Atlanta Constitution*, 20 February 1961.

61. Johnson quoted in Galphin, "Negroes at Rally Cheer Call for More Support"; King quoted in Margaret Shannon, "Rev. Martin Luther King Sr. Warns Politicians," *Atlanta Journal*, 20 February 1961.

62. Joseph Baird, "Atlanta Negro Adults Join 'Sit-Ins,'" *Christian Science Monitor*, 21 February 1961; Walden quoted in "52 Sit-Ins Post Bail in Switch of Tactics," *Atlanta Constitution*, 24 February 1961; "Sit-In Trials Slated to Begin in 2 Weeks," *Atlanta Journal*, 24 February 1961.

63. Chafe, *Civilities and Civil Rights*, 155; King interview.

64. King interview; Galphin, "Merchants and Negroes Agree, Ending Sit-Ins," *Atlanta Constitution*, 8 March 1961; Walker, "Sit-Ins in Atlanta," 87–88. The press reported that the students signed the agreement, which they did not.

65. King interview; Challenor interview.

66. King interview; Challenor interview; Julian Bond, *Atlanta Inquirer*, 14 January 1961, 2; Holman quoted in Fort, "Atlanta Sit-In Movement," 163; Walker, "Sit-Ins in Atlanta," 88–90.

67. King interview; Nation of Islam activists quoted in Newsom and Gorden, "A Stormy Rally in Atlanta," *Atlanta, Georgia, 1960–1961*, ed. Garrow, 106.

68. Brown quoted in ibid.

69. Walden quoted in Walker, "Sit-Ins in Atlanta," 89.

70. Brown quoted in ibid.; Wilburn quoted in Newsom and Gorden, "Stormy Rally," 107; Wilburn also quoted in "Diner Integration Certain, Says Negro," *Atlanta Constitution*, 11 March 1961; Brown interview.

71. King interview; Challenor interview.

72. King quoted in Walker, "Sit-Ins in Atlanta," 90; King quoted in Newsom and Gorden, "Stormy Rally," 110.

73. King quoted in Newsom and Gorden, "A Stormy Rally in Atlanta," 111; Claude Sitton, "Atlanta Accord Arouses Dispute," New York Times, 12 March 1961.

74. Challenor interview; King interview.

75. Older leader quoted in Walker, "Functions of Disunity," Atlanta, Georgia, 1960–1961, ed. Garrow, 24; Walker, "Protest and Negotiation," 36.

76. King quoted in Walker, "Sit-Ins in Atlanta," 91–92.

77. Galphin, "Negro Vote of 50,000 Urged Here," Atlanta Constitution, 30 June 1961; Martin Luther King Jr., "The Time for Freedom Has Come," New York Times Magazine, 16 September 1961. Charlotte Devree was among the Whites who commented on the distinction between Black and White students. Unlike liberal Whites on Northern campuses, Devree contended, Black college activists were "Christian revolutionaries." Charlotte Devree, "The Young Negro Rebels," Harper's, 21 October 1961.

78. Galphin, "Restaurants at Stores Here Are Integrated Peacefully," Atlanta Constitution, 29 September 1961. The thirteen chains and individual stores that signed the agreement were Rich's; Davison's; Sears, Roebuck and Co.; Woolworth's McCrory; Grant; Walgreen; Jacobs; S. H. Kress; S. S. Kresge; H. C. Green; J. J. Newberry; and Lane.

CHAPTER 2: PHASE TWO AND THE FALL OF PETTY APARTHEID

1. Walden quoted in Raleigh Bryans, "Negro Vote Battle Grows," Atlanta Journal, 6 September 1961; Pat Watters, "The Mood of Revolt Is in the Air; Negroes Seek Political Maturity," Atlanta Journal, 8 September 1961; Herman Hancock, "Allen Rolls to Victory over Maddox by a Solid 64,313 Votes to 36,091," Atlanta Constitution, 23 September 1961; Bruce Galphin, "Negro Voters Form 57 Pct. of Turnout in City Election," Atlanta Constitution, 9 December 1961.

2. Pat Watters, "Receiving an Audience Is among Most Important Things He Wants," Atlanta Journal, 5 October 1961; Nash quoted in Kuhn, Joye, and West, Living Atlanta, 243.

3. Edwina Davis, "Grady Pickets Mum on Plans to Continue," Atlanta Journal, 11 November 1961; "Race Group Vows More Grady Action," Atlanta Journal, 13 November 1961; "Students Call Halt to Grady Picketing," Atlanta Constitution, 14 November 1961; William O. Smith, "Better Hospital Care Sought for Negroes," Atlanta Journal, 12 December 1961.

4. COAHR statement quoted in "Negroes Picket Grady Anew," *Atlanta Constitution*, 7 February 1962; Fred Powledge, "23 Demonstrators Arrested at Grady," *Atlanta Journal*, 14 February 1962; Keeler McCartney, "23 Arrested at Grady; Capitol Case Is Heard," *Atlanta Constitution*, 14 February 1962; Forman, *The Making of Black Revolutionaries*, 263–64; Smith quoted in Fleming, *Soon We Will Not Cry*, 92.

5. "Grady Timetable Sought by Negroes," *Atlanta Journal*, 7 March 1962.

6. "Grady Accepts Its First Negro Woman Physician," *Atlanta Daily World*, 20 April 1962; Bruce Galphin, "Total Integration at Grady Is Sought," *Atlanta Constitution*, 20 June 1962.

7. Spottswood quoted in Gloster B. Current, "The 53rd—A Hard-Working Convention," *Crisis*, August–September 1962, 377–92; Wilkins quoted in Jesse DeVore, "The Convention in the News," *Crisis*, August–September 1962, 393.

8. "NAACP Convention Resolutions Cover Voting, Housing, Jobs," NAACP press release, 13 July 1962, Facts on Film, SERS, N19 3599.

9. Joseph Boone, interview by author, 13 August 1997, audiotape; Middleton quoted in Fred Powledge, "Negroes Threaten Boycotts to Open Job Opportunities," *Atlanta Journal*, 30 October 1962, 6; John D. Pomfret, "Negroes Building Boycott Network," *New York Times*, 25 November 1962; SCLC statement quoted in "City Negro Job Drive Meet Slated," *Atlanta Journal*, 6 November 1962.

10. Black newspapers, including the influential *Pittsburgh Courier*, followed the Breadbasket campaign closely. " 'Operation Breadbasket' Moving in Atlanta, 'Target' Selected," *Pittsburgh Courier*, 2 February 1963, 1; "Operation on 'Bread' Pays Off," *Pittsburgh Courier*, 16 February 1963, 1; "Atlanta Ministers Kayo Another Firm," *Pittsburgh Courier*, 9 March 1963, 3; "Ministers Move against Donut Company Here," *Atlanta Daily World*, 5 April 1963, 4.

11. Johnson quoted in Lerone Bennett Jr., "Georgia's Negro Senator," *Ebony*, March 1963, 25–34. January 1963 also marked the desegregation of state Capitol facilities and Hamilton Holmes's acceptance into Emory Medical School. Holmes and Charlayne Hunter desegregated the University of Georgia.

12. Marion Gaines, "Voters Approve All 13 Bond Issues," *Atlanta Constitution*, 16 May 1963; Raleigh Bryans, "Mayor Meets Negro Leaders to Salve Protests on Bonds," *Atlanta Journal*, 17 July 1962; George M. Coleman, "Negro Vote Shows Intelligent Ballot, Readiness for Future," *Atlanta Daily World*, 17 May 1963; Stanley S. Scott, "Some Entered Booth, Didn't Vote at All," *Atlanta Daily World*, 19 May 1963. An analysis of voting in eight Black precincts by activist scholars C. A. Bacote and John D. Reid indicated that Blacks unfamiliar with an item-by-item ballot had wasted thousands of votes on specific bonds. The Atlanta University professors

based their analysis on a comparison of the public counter, which noted each voter entering a given booth, and the actual tally for that precinct. The overall Black turnout was so high, however, that the loss of some votes did not matter in the end.

13. "Negroes Seek Allen's Aid to Curb Police," *Atlanta Journal*, 10 December 1961; pickets quoted in Ted Simmons, "2 Negro Collegians Arrested after Lie-In in Hotel Lobby," *Atlanta Constitution*, 13 March 1963; Benjamin E. Mays, "My View," *Pittsburgh Courier*, 30 March 1963.

14. Mays, "My View"; Marion Gaines, "Negroes March on City Hall, Carry Hotel Protest to Allen," *Atlanta Constitution*, 15 March 1963; Allen quoted in Stanley S. Scott, "Mayor Lauds Students for Orderly Protest," *Atlanta Daily World*, 15 March 1963; "This Is the Southern Christian Leadership Conference," SCLC pamphlet, April 1963, Facts on Film, SERS, N21 5367.

15. Larry Fox, telephone interview by author, 20 March 2004, tape recording. Fox, who chaired COAHR before joining SNCC, noted that "theoretically, there was always a connection" between the two groups, but as SNCC's national office became more coordinated, it made sense that the organizational relationship intensified. "Police 'Manhandling' Charged At Station," *SNCC News*, 26 March 1963, Facts on Film, SERS, N21 5628; "2 Restaurants Refuse Service to Students," *Atlanta Daily World*, 28 April 1963; *SNCC News*, 6 May 1963; Marion Gaines, "Collegians Rebuff Allen, Renew Push," *Atlanta Constitution*, 18 May 1963.

16. Maddox, Moore, and customer quoted in Fred Powledge, "Pickrick Is Picked Out for Biracial Sit-In Try," *Atlanta Constitution*, 19 May 1963.

17. "Restaurant Picketed for 4 Hours," *Atlanta Constitution*, 21 May 1963; Chamber of Commerce statement quoted in Hal Gulliver, "C of C Bd. of Directors Urge Businesses to Desegregate," *Atlanta Constitution*, 30 May 1963.

18. "Cafes Harassed in Day-Long Push," *Atlanta Constitution*, 15 June 1963; "14 Arrested In Protest at Restaurants," *Atlanta Daily World*, 18 June 1963; NAACP officials quoted in "Negro, 15, Slashed at Sit-In Here," *Atlanta Constitution*, 19 June 1963.

19. Allen quoted in Marion Gaines, "14 Hotels Accept Some Integration," *Atlanta Constitution*, 21 June 1963; "14 Atlanta Hotels, Motels Lower Barriers," *Atlanta Daily World*, 21 June 1963; Smith quoted in "Hotel Plans Questioned by NAACP," *Atlanta Constitution*, 22 June 1963; "Hotel Desegregation Statement Questioned," *Atlanta Daily World*, 23 June 1963; Stanley Scott, "Several Downtown Atlanta Restaurants Desegregate," *Atlanta Daily World*, 26 June 1963. White business leaders were no doubt influenced thoughout June by events in Savannah, where grassroots pro-

tests led by Hosea Williams ended with the arrests of more than three hundred Blacks. See "Negroes in March at Savannah, Ga.," *New York Times*, 15 June 1963; " 'Grass Roots' Leaders behind Savannah Drive," *Pittsburgh Courier*, 29 June 1963.

20. Students quoted in "COAHR Continues Encouragement of Fair Employment," *Atlanta Daily World*, 30 June 1963; "March by 250 Negroes Backs Restaurant Strike," *Atlanta Constitution*, 2 July 1963; Harmon G. Perry, "Strike at Dobbs in Second Week," *Atlanta Daily World*, 24 April 1963; Stanley S. Scott, "Shot Fired into Home over Strike," *Atlanta Daily World*, 27 June 1963.

21. Editorial, "Saturday's Leadership Conference," *Atlanta Daily World*, 22 October 1963. The NAACP, SCLC, Operation Breadbasket, SNCC, COAHR, ANVL, ACRC, Ghandi Youth Council, and ACCA came together under the Summit Leadership Conference umbrella.

22. Hal Gulliver, "Negroes Threaten New Protest Nov. 16," *Atlanta Constitution*, 8 November 1963; " 'Don't Buy at Rich's,' Say Civil Rights Groups," *Student Voice*, 21 November 1963, Facts on Film, SERS, N18 1162; Walden quoted in "Leaders to Meet Saturday; Students Hold Demonstrations," *Atlanta Daily World*, 22 November 1963.

23. Abernathy and Fox quoted in "Negroes Halt All Protests, Pay Tribute," *Atlanta Constitution*, 23 November 1963; "Atlanta Negroes Invite Dr. King to Lead Mass Demonstration Sunday," *Atlanta Constitution*, 10 December 1963; Walden quoted in "Negro Leaders Expect 10,000 at Rally," *Atlanta Constitution*, 13 December 1963; "Assembly Sunday on Rights Day," *Atlanta Daily World*, 13 December 1963.

24. Forman and King quoted in "3000 March in Atlanta," *Student Voice*, 16 December 1963.

25. Jim Bentley, "Caroling Protesters Visit Allen," *Atlanta Constitution*, 24 December 1963; "Stand-Ins at City Hall Continue, Say Negroes," *Atlanta Constitution*, 26 December 1963.

26. Coleman and Johnson quoted in "Negroes Here Vote Massive Street Push," *Atlanta Constitution*, 4 January 1964; Stanley S. Scott, "Leadership to Confer on Protest," *Atlanta Daily World*, 5 January 1964; Walter Rugaber, "Negroes to Plan Protests Here," *Atlanta Constitution*, 5 January 1964.

27. Allen and Lewis quoted in Ted Simmons, "150 Teens Sit In at Allen Office," *Atlanta Constitution*, 8 January 1964.

28. Ibid.; editorial, "Action of Students Tuesday Deplorable," *Atlanta Daily World*, 8 January 1964.

29. "Three SCLC Staff Members Go to Jail in Desegregation Attempt in Atlanta," *SCLC Newsletter*, January 1964, Facts on Film, SERS, N18 1044; Krystal sign quoted in "13

Arrested in Atlanta," *Student Voice*, 14 January 1964, Facts on Film, SERS, N18 1172; "8 Demonstrators Arrested after Two Incidents," *Atlanta Daily World*, 12 January 1964; "16 Students Held in Sit-Ins," *Atlanta Constitution*, 14 January 1964; "7 Gets [sic] Suspended Sentences in Demonstrations," *Atlanta Daily World*, 16 January 1964.

30. Forman quoted in Claude Sitton, "Negroes Resume Atlanta Sit-Ins after Sidewalk Clash with Klan," *New York Times*, 20 January 1964; "73 Demonstrators Released on Bond," *Atlanta Constitution*, 20 January 1964.

31. "73 Demonstrators Released on Bond." Carol Anderson has provided the most substantive discussion of the United Nations and the early call for a human rights agenda by Black activists in *Eyes off the Prize*, chaps. 1–3.

32. Editorial, "For a Public Accommodations Law; Against This SNCC-Led Lawlessness," *Atlanta Constitution*, 21 January 1964; letter, " 'Poor Taste' in Demonstration Hit," *Atlanta Daily World*, 22 January 1964.

33. Pickets quoted in Claude Sitton, "Atlanta Pickets Greet U.N. Panel," *New York Times*, 26 January 1964; B. D. Ayres Jr., "U.N. Group Sees Atlanta Rights March," *Washington Post*, 26 January 1964; Walter Rugaber and Paul Valentine, "Negroes, Klansmen Taunt and Battle," *Atlanta Constitution*, 26 January 1964.

34. COAHR activists and Craig quoted in "Negroes, Klansmen Taunt and Battle."

35. Allen quoted in "84 Are Arrested, 6 Injured, In Downtown Cafe, Inn Picketing," *Atlanta Constitution*, 27 January 1964; Claude Sitton, "Atlanta Seizes 70 in Racial Protest," *New York Times*, 27 January 1964.

36. Sitton, "Atlanta Seizes 70 in Racial Protest."

37. Herschelle Challenor, telephone interview by author, 25 May 2004, tape recording; Fleming, *Soon We Will Not Cry*, 67. Fleming wrote, the "movement had taken over their lives. They suffered flashbacks, anxiety, and insomnia."

38. Hall quoted in *This Far by Faith*, a Public Broadcasting Service documentary on the African American religious experience. Martin Luther King Jr. noted that Hall was such a powerful speaker that she was the only individual whom he dreaded following on a program. It should come as no surprise that Hall went on to become a leading theologian and Baptist preacher. The transcript can be found at http://www.pbs.org/thisfarbyfaith/people/prathia_hall.html.

39. Ted Simmons, "100 Arrested as Race Pickets March 8 Hours," *Atlanta Constitution*, 28 January 1964.

40. Venable quoted in ibid.; "Atlanta Arrests 40 More Pickets," *New York Times*, 28 January 1964; editorial, "Disorder Developing from Demonstrations," *Atlanta Daily World*, 28 January 1964.

41. Cox quoted in Ted Simmons, "4 Sit-Ins Arrested in Mass Rights Push," *Atlanta Constitution*, 29 January 1964; Hall quoted in Stanley S. Scott, "Group Marches to City Hall; Talks to Mayor," *Atlanta Daily World*, 29 January 1964. For the most part, the White reporters who covered the direct action campaigns of the early 1960s for all three Atlanta dailies—as well as Claude Sitton of the *New York Times*—took pains to be thorough and as objective as possible. Stanley S. Scott, of the *Atlanta Daily World*, deserves specific mention, however, for both his attention to detail and his interest in providing depth in his stories beyond the lead paragraphs.

42. Hall quoted in Scott, "Group Marches to City Hall"; FBI Field Report, 20 March 1964, microfilm, Scholarly Resources, MFL-026, Auburn Avenue Research Library on African-American Culture and History (Atlanta-Fulton Public Library System). The original concern of the FBI was to document "Communist infiltration" of SNCC, but the lack of substantive evidence soon led to a broader preoccupation with "fact finding." See FBI Field Report.

43. Boyd quoted in "Solicitor Gen. Calls for End of All Demonstrations," *Atlanta Daily World*, 28 January 1964; Stanley S. Scott, "Mayor Schedules City Wide Leadership Meeting Today in Face of Demonstrations," *Atlanta Daily World*, 29 January 1964; Allen quoted in Claude Sitton, "Atlanta Stiffens Stand on Protest," *New York Times*, 30 January 1964. Allen invited individuals from the following organizations to the 29 January meeting: Atlanta Board of Aldermen; Fulton County Commission; Fulton and DeKalb County state legislative delegations; Chamber of Commerce executive committee; Retail Merchants Association; Atlanta Convention Bureau; Greater Atlanta Council of Churches Southern Regional Council; Atlanta University Center presidents; and Atlanta Summit Leadership Conference steering committee. There also were policemen, lawyers, and bankers present.

44. Forman quoted in Sitton, "Atlanta Stiffens Stand on Protest"; Borders and Brawley quoted in Stanley S. Scott, "Allen Asks 'Cooling Off Period' with Program to 'Guarantee Racial Harmony,'" *Atlanta Daily World*, 30 January 1964; editorial, "Mayor Allen's Suggestion Relative to Demonstrations Points Way to Solution," *Atlanta Daily World*, 31 January 1964.

45. Cox quoted in Don McKee, "Atlanta's Racial Image Dims," *Charlotte Observer*, 29 January 1964, Facts on Film, SERS, J7 3496; Martin Luther King Jr., "The Negro Revolution in 1964," *SCLC Newsletter*, January 1964, N18 1050.

46. ACRC endorsement quoted in "Molested in Jail, Girl Protesters Say," *Atlanta Constitution*, 31 January 1964.

47. Claude Sitton, "Racial Situation Eases in Atlanta," *New York Times*, 31 January 1964; Hill quoted in Claude Sitton, "Atlanta's Mayor Bars Negro Truce," *New York Times*,

2 February 1964; Walter Rugaber, "Mayor Refuses Aid to Jailed Negroes," *Atlanta Constitution*, 2 February 1964.

48. Sitton, "Atlanta's Mayor"; students quoted in Rugaber, "Mayor Refuses."

49. Emory students quoted in "Atlanta Whites Ask End of Segregation," *New York Times*, 3 February 1964; Paul Valentine, "White Man Fells Race Demonstrator," *Atlanta Constitution*, 9 February 1964.

50. Walker did obtain bail, but with "unencumbered" property. The U.S. Supreme Court overturned her conviction in May 1965. Jack Strong, "Coed's Jail Charges to Be Probed Here," *Atlanta Constitution*, 14 February; "Georgia Jails R.I. Girl," *Providence Journal*, 21 February, Facts on Film, SERS, J7 3504; "Coed's Release in $15,000 Bail Expected Today," *Providence Journal*, 22 February 1964, Facts on Film, SERS, J7 3504; editorial, "Final Act in Miss Walker's Ordeal," *Atlanta Constitution*, 25 May 1965.

51. Martin Luther King Jr., "The Danger of a Little Progress," *SCLC Newsletter*, February 1964, Facts on Film, SERS, N18 1062.

52. Lewis quoted in Harmon G. Perry, "Town Meeting Hears Demonstrations Aired," *Atlanta Daily World*, 15 February 1964; physicians quoted in Stanley S. Scott, "Medics, Dentists Lead Saturday March," *Atlanta Daily World*, 16 February 1964.

53. Stanley S. Scott, "Federal Court Asked to Take Over Jurisdiction of Anti-Trespass Cases," *Atlanta Daily World*, 13 March 1964; Achsah Posey and Jack Strong, "Fulton Jail Releases Last of 58 Sit-Ins on Judge Sloan's Orders," *Atlanta Constitution*, 24 March 1964; Achsah Posey, "Trespass Ban Upheld by U.S. Judge," *Atlanta Constitution*, 9 May 1964; ASLC statement quoted in Ted Simmons, "Comply in Peace, Both Races Urge," *Atlanta Constitution*, 3 July 1964.

54. Maddox and Lebedin quoted in Harmon G. Perry, "Lester Maddox, Leb Restaurants Make Protests of Laws," *Atlanta Daily World*, 4 July 1964.

55. Paul Valentine, " 'Pickrick Drumsticks' Sell Like Hotcakes for Maddox," *Atlanta Constitution*, 16 August 1964; Al Kuettner, "Shouting Lester Shoves 4; Faces Contempt Hearing," *Atlanta Daily World*, 29 September 1964; "Maddox Closes Cafeteria after Negro Appears," *Atlanta Constitution*, 8 February 1964.

CHAPTER 3: BRIDGES

1. "Don't Waive [sic] the Red Flag in the Pasture Unless You Want to Fight the Bulls," editorial, *Atlanta Daily World*, 7 July 1964; "Racist Terrorists and Murderers Must Be Caught and Punished," editorial, *Atlanta Daily World*, 15 July 1964.

2. Mukasa Dada (Willie Ricks), interview by author, 3 November 1997, Atlanta, tape recording.

3. Gene Roberts, "From 'Freedom High' to 'Black Power,'" *New York Times Magazine*, 25 September 1966, Facts on Film, SERS, J3 424; Bond quoted in Stoper, *The Student Nonviolent Coordinating Committee*, 277. The most exhaustive accounts of the grassroots character of the Black freedom struggle in Mississippi include Payne, *I've Got the Light of Freedom*; Dittmer, *Local People*; Lee, *For Freedom's Sake*; and Mills, *This Little Light of Mine*.

4. Gwendolyn Zoharah Simmons, telephone interview by author, 30 July 2004, tape recording.

5. Ibid.

6. Ibid.

7. Black feminist scholars Johnetta Cole and Beverly Guy-Sheftall chronicle the "Amazon Project" in *Gender Talk*, 90–92; Zoharah Simmons interview.

8. Zoharah Simmons interview

9. Max Stanford, "Revolutionary Action Movement (RAM)," 76; Michael Simmons, interview by author, 19 April 1998, Philadelphia, tape recording. According to Stanford, the various ideological and organizational tributaries that flowed into what would become the Revolutionary Action Movement began to converge in the summer of 1961. Students for a Democratic Society (SDS), a predominantly White organization of college students, held a conference as part of a larger meeting of the National Student Association in Madison, Wisconsin. A small group of Black SDS members, including Donald Freeman of Case Western Reserve College in Cleveland and several students from Central State College in Wilberforce, went to the conference with hopes of ending Robert Williams's days in exile.

10. Stanford, "Revolutionary Action Movement," 87–88, 165, 77–79, 85, also 40; Martin, *Race First*, preface and 210n.

11. Mukasa interview; Stanford, "Revolutionary Action Movement," 89–91. Donald Freeman, "Black Youth and Afro-American Liberation," *Black America*, Fall 1964, 15–16, Archives of the Martin Luther King Center for Nonviolent Social Change, Black Power File. Scot Brown has shown that one of the most troubling manifestations of the culture/politics binary, the distinction between cultural nationalism and so-called "revolutionary" nationalism, permeated the conflict between the Black Panther Party and the US organization in the late 1960s. See Brown, *Fighting for US*, chap. 5, esp. 113–20.

12. Stanford, "Revolutionary Action Movement," 111–12; Roland Snellings, "The Long Hot Summer," *Black America*, Fall 1964, 13, Archives of the Martin Luther King Center for Nonviolent Social Change, Black Power File.

13. Stanford, "We Can Win," *Black America*, fall 1965, 1–2 and 22, Archives of the Martin Luther King Center for Nonviolent Social Change, Black Power File.

14. Ibid., 21; Robert F. Williams, "Solidarity Speech," *Crusader*, March 1965, Facts on Film, SERS, N10 3077; Robert F. Williams, "USA: The Potential of a Minority Revolution," *Crusader*, August 1965, Facts on Film, SERS, N10 3077.

15. Stanford, "Revolutionary Action Movement," 146–47; Malcolm quoted in Breitman, ed., *Malcolm X Speaks*, 160.

16. *Selected Works of Mao Tse-tung*, 1:29–30. See also Stanford, "Revolutionary Action Movement," 148. The excerpt from Mao's solidarity statement is quoted in Luce, *Road to Revolution*, 164. Robin Kelley has asserted in his recent discussion of RAM that it "might loosely be called the first black Maoist-influenced organization in history." See Kelley, *Freedom Dreams*, chap. 3, esp. 72–90. Kelley's insightful discussion serves as a reminder that further scholarly work on RAM—work that amplifies and complicates Max Stanford's master's thesis—is essential, especially given the organization's foundational connection to later, better-known groups such as the Black Panther Party.

17. Stanford, "Revolutionary Action Movement," 11; Blair, *Retreat to the Ghetto*, 113–14; see also Self, *American Babylon*, chap. 6.

18. Williams quoted in "Appeal and Statement on Race Terror in USA," *Black America*, 9, Archives of the Martin Luther King Center for Nonviolent Social Change, Black Power File. Ironically, the growing tension between Fidel Castro and Che Guevara, and between Maoists and the Soviets, resulted in Robert Williams's being denied observer status at the Tri-Continental Conference in Havana in January 1966. He and his family left for China that year. See Stanford, "Revolutionary Action Movement," 66.

19. Michael Simmons, interview by author, 19 April 1998, Philadelphia, tape recording.

20. The best accounts of the rise to prominence of the Nation of Islam remain Essien-Udom, *Black Nationalism*; Lincoln, *The Black Muslims in America*; and Muhammad, *Message to the Blackman in America*.

21. William Sales has contended in his significant and insightful book that prominent Blacks in New York City such as Ossie Davis and Ruby Dee, along with King attorney Clarence Jones, tried to establish "off-the-record contacts" between Malcolm X and King to reach an informal accord. Sales Jr., *From Civil Rights to Black Liberation*, 125. Malcolm X sent the 1 August 1963 letter to: Martin Luther King Jr., SCLC president; Roy Wilkins, NAACP executive secretary; Gardner C. Taylor, pastor of Concord Baptist Church of Christ, in Brooklyn; Congressman Adam Clayton

Powell; Larry Farmer, CORE leader; A. Philip Randolph, Brotherhood of Sleeping Car Porters; Joseph H. Jackson, president of the National Baptist Convention, USA; and James Forman, SNCC executive secretary. Gallen, ed., *Malcolm X: The FBI File*, 31 and 34; Garrow, *Bearing the Cross*, 275–76.

22. Malcolm X, *The Autobiography of Malcolm X*, 289; Gallen, ed., *Malcolm X*, 34; Martin Luther King Jr., "The Time for Freedom Has Come," *New York Times Magazine*, 16 September 1961; Mukasa interview. Some rank-and-file members of the Nation of Islam did participate in other organizations, such as Philadelphia activist John Churchfield, a field secretary with SNCC. The NOI was not the first Black nationalist organization to enter into talks with Klan leaders. Marcus Garvey of the UNIA did so in the 1920s. See Martin, *Race First*.

23. Williams, *Negroes with Guns*, 110 and 122. The definitive book on Williams is Tyson's *Radio Free Dixie*; "Malcolm X: 'Power in Defense of Freedom Is Greater Than Power in Behalf of Tyranny,'" *Militant*, 25 January 1965, Facts on Film, SERS, N15 4820.

24. "Peacemakers or Apostles of Revenge," editorial, *Atlanta Constitution*, 30 July 1964; Clarke, ed., *Malcolm X*, introduction.

25. Malcolm quoted in Breitman, ed., *Malcolm X Speaks*, 89; Malcolm quoted in Perry, ed., *Malcolm X*, 87.

26. Malcolm X, "Our Struggles Will Merge," *Black America*, fall 1965, 10, Archives of the Martin Luther King Center for Nonviolent Social Change, Black Power File; Stanford, "Revolutionary Action Movement," 99 and 102. Stanford claims that RAM had a national leadership well into the summer of 1964, which aided the group's clandestine activities. According to him, the organization's international spokesman was Malcolm X. Robert F. Williams, though exiled, served as the group's international chairman. Stanford was national field chairman, Donald Freeman executive chairman, and James Boggs ideological chairman. "The OAAU was to be the broad front organization and RAM the underground Black Liberation Front of the U.S.A." An FBI report after Malcolm's assassination mentioned his "affiliation with the Revolutionary Action Movement." The FBI report focused on a four-page memorandum written by a RAM official in New York City titled "Malcolm Lives: Analysis of the Assassination." See Gallen, ed., *Malcolm X*, 431–32.

27. Activist historian William Sales has argued convincingly in his groundbreaking study of the OAAU that a key explanation for why Malcolm X established contact with activists in the South was to spread the group's human rights agenda. See Sales, *From Civil Rights to Black Liberation*, 128–29.

28. Hamer and Malcolm quoted in Ed Smith and David Herman, "Meetings in Harlem Hear Malcolm X and Fannie Lou Hamer," Militant, 28 December 1964, 1, Facts on Film, SERS, N15 4785; Gallen, ed. Malcolm X, 41; Dittmer, Local People, 411 and passim.

29. Hamer and Malcolm quoted in Smith and Herman, "Meetings In Harlem," 1; Malcolm quoted in Breitman, ed., Malcolm X Speaks, 133 and 135; Gallen, ed., Malcolm X, 41; Malcolm quoted in Perry, ed., Last Speeches, 95; see also Mills, This Little Light of Mine, 139–44. Activist scholar Angela Y. Davis has offered an intriguing exploration of Malcolm's possible interaction with feminism. See Davis, "Meditations on the Legacy of Malcolm X," Malcolm X, ed. Wood, 36–47.

30. Malcolm quoted in Breitman, ed., Malcolm X Speaks, 137–46, especially 145.

31. Malcolm quoted in "Malcolm X: Power in Defense of Freedom," 5.

32. Malcolm quoted in "Radio Interview with Malcolm X," Militant, 8 February 1965, 3, Facts on Film, SERS, N15 4835.

33. Malcolm quoted in Sales, From Civil Rights to Black Liberation, 125 and 127; Baldwin, "Malcolm and Martin," Malcolm X, ed. Gallen, 267.

34. Forman, The Making of Black Revolutionaries, 406–11. The SNCC delegation included James Forman, John Lewis, Bob and Dona Moses, Julian Bond, Ruby Doris Robinson, Donald Harris, William Hansen, Prathia Hall, and Matthew Jones.

35. Ibid., 406; Lewis and Harris quoted in Carson, In Struggle, 135–36.

36. Silas Norman, telephone interview by author, 22 July 2004, tape recording.

37. Fay Bellamy Powell, interview by author, 31 March 1998, Atlanta, tape recording; Malcolm quoted in Clark, ed., February 1965, 21.

38. Norman interview; Powell interview.

39. Powell interview; Mukasa interview; Malcolm quoted in Clark, ed., February 1965, 24.

40. Malcolm quoted in Clark, ed., February 1965, 25; Powell interview.

41. Powell interview; Gallen, ed., Malcolm X, 41–42; Malcolm quoted in Clark, ed., February 1965, 28.

42. Malcolm quoted in King, My Life with Martin Luther King, Jr., 258; Powell interview; Norman interview; Sales, From Civil Rights to Black Liberation, 103. According to Sales, the week of Malcolm X's assassination his itinerary called for him to return to Mississippi "to further investigate the ways that the OAAU might more effectively join with the popular struggle for freedom in that state."

43. "Violence Begets Violence," editorial, Atlanta Daily World, 24 February 1965; "Let Us All Be Prepared to Expose Violence," Atlanta Daily World, 24 February 1965.

44. Henry Lee Moon, "The Enigma of Malcolm X," Crisis, April 1965, 226–27. In

January 1965 the public relations department of the NAACP assumed editorial control of the publication.

45. King, *My Life with Martin Luther King, Jr.*, 258; Martin Luther King quoted in Clayborne Carson, "A 'Common Solution,' " *Emerge*, February 1998, 51.

46. Zoharah Simmons interview.

CHAPTER 4: THE ATLANTA PROJECT

1. Michael Simmons, interview by author, 19 April 1998, Philadelphia, tape recording; Gwendolyn Zoharah Simmons, telephone interview by author, 30 July 2004, tape recording.

2. Michael Simmons interview; SNCC statement quoted in FBI Field Report, 4 February 1966, microfilm, Scholarly Resources, MFL-026, Auburn Avenue Research Library on African-American Culture and History (Atlanta-Fulton Public Library System); Lewis quoted in Bill Shipp, "Defiance of Draft Call Urged by SNCC Leader," *Atlanta Constitution*, 7 January 1966.

3. Lewis quoted in Shipp, "Defiance of Draft Call"; SNCC statement quoted in FBI Field Report, 4 February 1966.

4. Michael Simmons interview; Bond quoted in Shipp, "Defiance of Draft Call."

5. Lane quoted in Sam Hopkins, "House Declines to Seat Bond, 184–12, And Viet Critic Plans U.S. Court Appeal," *Atlanta Constitution*, 11 January 1966; Michael Simmons interview; Smith quoted in Dick Hebert, "An Apology Called Bond's Lone Hope," *Atlanta Constitution*, 11 January 1966.

6. Moore and Bond quoted in Hopkins, "House Declines"; Hebert, "An Apology Called Bond's Lone Hope"; Hopkins, "Bond Case Boosts Colleagues' Image," *Atlanta Constitution*, 17 January 1966.

7. Shipp, "Troopers Repel Pickets Trying to Rush Capitol," *Atlanta Constitution*, 15 January 1966; Michael Simmons interview; King quoted in "King Seen Breaking with SNCC," *Atlanta Constitution*, 15 January 1966.

8. Shipp, "Troopers Repel Pickets"; Michael Simmons interview.

9. King quoted in Shipp, "Troopers Repel Pickets"; SCLC aide quoted in "King Seen Breaking Away."

10. Shipp, "Bond Asks U.S. Court to Seat Him," *Atlanta Constitution*, 14 January 1966; Michael Simmons interview.

11. Michael Simmons interview; Carson, *In Struggle*, 191.

12. Michael Simmons interview; Zoharah Simmons interview. Philadelphians Michael Simmons and Dwight Williams served on the Atlanta Project along with veteran organizers from the South such as Willie Ricks, Donald Stone, Larry Fox,

and Bob Moore. Local residents John Bell and Johnny Wilson joined the Project as full-time organizers, as did several student volunteers from Spelman College including Cissy Breland, Connie Henderson, and Margaret Mills. White SNCC workers including Mendy Samstein and Cathy Archibald also served on the Project.

13. The most comprehensive scholarly treatment of the Atlanta Project has been that of Clayborne Carson, who chronicled the group in In Struggle, esp. 189–201 and 236–42. Although largely critical of the "Atlanta separatists," Carson did assert that some of the early theoretical contributions of the group "set forth many of the basic themes that would dominate black politics during the late 1960s." An underlying theme of Carson's critique was that Project activists could claim few concrete accomplishments as SNCC activists. This chapter, which is largely based on interviews with former Project activists as well as on a larger body of archival materials than Carson had available to him, challenges the notion that Project workers evidenced "limited accomplishments as community organizers." It should be noted, however, that more recent studies of SNCC—which are groundbreaking in other key ways—such as Fleming's Soon We Will Not Cry and Payne's I've Got the Light of Freedom, also treat the Atlanta Project less substantively than Carson.

Male activists associated with the SNCC executive committee have been very critical of the Project, in part a reflection of the contentious organizational relationship between them. See Forman, The Making of Black Revolutionaries; Carmichael, Ready for Revolution; and Sellers, The River of No Return.

14. "Prospectus for an Atlanta Project," SNCC–Vine City Project papers, State Historical Society of Wisconsin, box 1, folder 6.

15. Clayborne Carson has noted that many SNCC workers "soon realized that their previous victories in the deep South had exaggerated their sense of power to confront the entrenched, resilient institutions responsible for the social problems of urban, industrial society." See Carson, In Struggle, 168; Zoharah Simmons interview.

16. Untitled affidavit, SNCC–Vine City Project papers, State Historical Society of Wisconsin, box 1, folder 6.

17. Ibid.

18. King quoted in "Dr. King Views Atlanta Slum Areas," SCLC Newsletter, January–February 1966, 3, Facts on Film, SERS, N17 9488. The King visit had been organized after a White slumlord evicted a Black woman from rental property in the area. Harmon, "Beneath the Image," 397.

19. Untitled affidavit; Carson, In Struggle, 238; David Andrew Harmon, "Beneath the

Image: The Civil Rights Movement and Race Relations in Atlanta, Georgia, 1946–1981" (Ph.D. diss., Emory University, 1994), 365–73 and 397–402; Michael Simmons interview; Michael Simmons, electronic correspondence to author, 26 February 2004.

20. Fay Bellamy Powell, interview by author, 31 March, 1998, Atlanta, tape recording; Zoharah Simmons interview.

21. Zoharah Simmons interview; Michael Simmons interview; see also Fleming, Soon We Will Not Cry, 170–72.

22. Zoharah Simmons interview; Michael Simmons interview.

23. Zoharah Simmons interview.

24. Larry Fox, telephone interview by author, 20 March 2004, tape recording. Three such papers remain extant from the turbulent March 1966 staff meeting, and can be found in the papers of the Institute of the Black World Records, Manuscripts, Archives and Rare Books Division, Schomburg Center for Research in Black Culture, New York Public Library, Astor, Lenox, and Tilden Foundations. The IBW Papers are being catalogued. (The position paper that appeared in the 5 August 1966 issue of the New York Times was a composite of the three earlier papers, with some revisions.) Black Consciousness Paper I, a six-page essay with an accompanying preface, appears to be the paper that figures most prominently in the SNCC discussions. While there is quite a bit of repetition among this paper and the other two papers (Black Consciousness Papers II and III), three- and five-page essays respectively, the shorter papers focus a bit more on international issues. Since it was likely that all three circulated and sparked debate among staff members, I have chosen to discuss all three. In a lengthy editorial note in Stokely Carmichael's autobiography, Ekwueme Michael Thelwell offers a blistering critique of the composite draft printed in the Times. See Carmichael, Ready for Revolution, 567–71. The full draft of the composite position paper printed in the Times can be found in Van Deburg, ed., Modern Black Nationalism, 119–26.

25. Michael Simmons interview; Black Consciousness Paper I, 2, Institute of the Black World Records, Manuscripts, Archives and Rare Books Division, Schomburg Center for Research in Black Culture, New York Public Library, Astor, Lenox, and Tilden Foundations. In her critique of the Black Power movement, historian Elisabeth Lasch-Quinn refers to the "increasing focus on the issue of white participation" in the Black human rights struggle on the part of activists. The general thrust of Lasch-Quinn's critique is problematic, however, as she reduces the Black Power phase of the Black freedom struggle to a destructive "black identity movement." See Lasch-Quinn, Race Experts, Prologue.

26. Black Consciousness Paper III, 2, Institute of the Black World Papers, Manuscripts, Archives and Rare Books Division, Schomburg Center for Research in Black Culture, New York Public Library, Astor, Lenox, and Tilden Foundations; Black Consciousness Paper I, 4, Institute of the Black World Papers, Manuscripts, Archives and Rare Books Division, Schomburg Center for Research in Black Culture, New York Public Library.

27. Black Consciousness Paper I, 3, Black Consciousness Paper III, 1, Institute of the Black World Papers, Manuscripts, Archives and Rare Books Division, Schomburg Center for Research in Black Culture, New York Public Library, Astor, Lenox, and Tilden Foundations; Malcolm quoted in Perry, ed., *Malcolm X*, 95.

28. Black Consciousness Paper I, 5, Institute of the Black World Papers, Manuscripts, Archives and Rare Books Division, Schomburg Center for Research in Black Culture, New York Public Library, Astor, Lenox, and Tilden Foundations.

29. "The Necessity for Urban Organizing," SNCC–Vine City Project papers, State Historical Society of Wisconsin, box 1, folder 8.

30. "Poor People's Housing Proposal Program," SNCC–Vine City Project papers, State Historical Society of Wisconsin, box 1, folder 8. See also Williams, *The Politics of Public Housing*; Hirsch, *Making the Second Ghetto*.

31. "The Nitty Gritty: The Reasons Why," SNCC–Vine City Project papers, State Historical Society of Wisconsin, box 1, folder 8. Atlanta Project activists also proposed the creation of a "freedom radio station," a citizens' band station that would broadcast within a ten-block radius. The station would be utilized as "an entertainment station with local people as M.C.'s, but it would be free to broadcast an honest news presentation as well as carry many programs of community interest." This idea never came to fruition.

32. Michael Simmons interview; Forman, *The Making of Black Revolutionaries*, 446 and 451–52; Sellers, *The River of No Return*, 185–87; Carson, *In Struggle*, chap. 13.

33. Jim Van Etten, undated letter to Bill Ware, and Dennis Hale, letter to Bill Ware, 17 November 1966, SNCC–Vine City Project papers, State Historical Society of Wisconsin, box 1, folder 3.

34. Miriam Wasserman, letter to Bill Ware, 2 August 1966, SNCC–Vine City Project papers, State Historical Society of Wisconsin, box 1, folder 3.

35. Zoharah Simmons interview.

36. Biko, *I Write What I Like*, xi and 1–2. Peniel E. Joseph has correctly observed that a "comprehensive historical framework for the Black Power movement must focus on the dynamic relationship between local, national, and international political organizations, leaders, intellectuals, and cultural workers." See Joseph, "Black

Liberation without Apology," *Black Scholar* 31, nos. 3–4 (fall–winter 2001): 14. Discussing Biko's writings is a worthwhile enterprise, despite important differences between the South African and U.S. contexts. In a country with an overwhelming Black majority, Biko and other Black Consciousness Movement activists struggled within majority-White NUSAS, then eventually established an autonomous Black group, SASO. On the other hand, Atlanta Project activists, who were members of a national minority, sought to make SNCC an all-Black organization rather than simply leave it, since it had always been majority-Black—indeed, overwhelmingly so, in its earliest days. The transcendent thread that allows for a comparative discussion is the effort by Black activists in both contexts to grapple with and attempt to understand fundamental issues of self-determination, as well as the ways in which white skin privilege posed a threat to that understanding.

37. Biko, *I Write What I Like*, xvi–xvii.

38. Ibid., 22.

39. Ibid., 23 and 21.

40. Mandela, *Long Walk to Freedom*, 486. The politics of Robben Island reflected the movement tensions in the larger country, as imprisoned ANC, BCM, and PAC activists engaged in sometimes violent clashes over influence. See pages 484–88 and 501.

41. Mandela, *Part of My Soul Went with Him*, 121–22.

42. Biko, *I Write What I Like*, 28–29. In their introduction to the book, Malusi and Thoko Mpumlwana acknowledge that contemporary readers "may be appalled at the way in which Biko's writing and speech is totally insensitive to his exclusion of women in his Black Consciousness campaigns as he stands up for 'the black man' and 'his manhood'! Biko is a product of his time."

43. Powell interview.

44. "SNCC Turns Its Back," editorial, *Atlanta Constitution*, 2 June 1966; Gene Roberts, "From 'Freedom High' to 'Black Power,' " *New York Times Magazine*, 25 September 1966, 120 and 124, Facts on Film, SERS, J3 424.

45. Michael Simmons interview; Sellers, *River of No Return*, 185–87.

46. Ware quoted in Freedom School Meeting Minutes, 25 April 1966, SNCC–Vine City Project papers, State Historical Society of Wisconsin, box 1, folder 12. Unfortunately, a full transcript of meeting minutes does not exist because "the tape ran out!"

47. Williams quoted in ibid.

48. Ware quoted in ibid.

49. Reed Jr., *Stirrings in the Jug*, 16–17. According to Reed, the concept "the masses" is "a homogenizing mystification; it is a category that has no specific referent in black institutional, organizational, or ideological life. . . . The masses do not speak; someone speaks for them." He notes that the term "underclass" poses a similar problem, and is "fundamentally pejorative."

50. Stone and Bell quoted in Freedom School Meeting Minutes, 25 April 1966, SNCC–Vine City Project papers, State Historical Society of Wisconsin, box 1, folder 12.

51. Robinson quoted in ibid.

52. Donald Stone is listed as a teacher "among his many other duties," in an untitled protest leaflet distributed after his arrest at the Atlanta Induction Center, SNCC–Vine City Project papers, State Historical Society of Wisconsin, box 1, folder 9. Michael Simmons, letter to Black publishers, 15 May 1966, SNCC–Vine City Project papers, State Historical Society of Wisconsin, box 1, folder 3; Anell Ponder, memorandum to Robert Green and Bill Ware, 27 May 1966, SNCC–Vine City Project papers, State Historical Society of Wisconsin, box 1, folder 3; Robert Green, memorandum to Donald Stone, 11 July 1966, SNCC–Vine City Project papers, State Historical Society of Wisconsin, box 1, folder 3.

53. Fox interview; letter of invitation, 9 August 1966, SNCC–Vine City Project papers, State Historical Society of Wisconsin, box 1, folder 9.

54. Ibid.

55. Ibid.

56. "What Would You Do with $40 Million Dollars Each Day?" leaflet, SNCC–Vine City Project papers, State Historical Society of Wisconsin, box 1, folder 9.

57. Ibid.

58. "Did Your SON Do This?" leaflet, SNCC–Vine City Project papers, State Historical Society of Wisconsin, box 1, folder 9.

59. Atlanta Project literature quoted in "20 Negroes Hinder New GIs," *Atlanta Constitution*, 18 August 1966; Michael Simmons interview; Fox interview; White bystanders quoted in *Atlanta's Black Paper*, 25 August 1966, SNCC–Vine City Project papers, State Historical Society of Wisconsin, box 1, folder 9.

60. Atlanta Project literature quoted in "20 Negroes"; Michael Simmons interview; Fox interview; *Atlanta's Black Paper*, 1–2.

61. Michael Simmons interview.

62. Ibid.; Fox interview; Dick Hebert, "12 Negroes Jailed after Picket Fight," *Atlanta Constitution*, 19 August 1966.

63. Fox interview.

64. Ibid.

65. Don Howard, letter to Bill Ware and Gwendolyn Robinson, 27 August 1966, SNCC–Vine City Project papers, State Historical Society of Wisconsin, box 1, folder 9.

66. Michael Simmons, letter to Connie Henderson and Project staff, 4 October 1966, SNCC–Vine City Project papers, State Historical Society of Wisconsin, box 1, folder 9.

67. Hebert, "12 Negroes Jailed"; Michael Davis, "Negro Bound Over as Insurrectionist," *Atlanta Constitution*, 19 August 1966; Michael Simmons interview; Zoharah Simmons interview. Moore got charges dropped against Johnny C. Wilson and Donald Stone on a technicality.

68. Fleming, *Soon We Will Not Cry*, 179; Zoharah Simmons interview. See Ransby, *Ella Baker and the Black Freedom Movement*; Lee, *For Freedom's Sake*; Collier-Thomas and Franklin, eds., *Sisters in Struggle*; and Springer, ed., *Still Lifting, Still Climbing*.

69. Zoharah Simmons interview.

70. Accounts of the meeting can be found in several autobiographies, including Forman, *The Making of Black Revolutionaries*; Sellers, *The River of No Return*; and Carmichael, *Ready for Revolution*; and in secondary sources that include Carson, *In Struggle*; Fleming, *Soon We Will Not Cry*; and Ransby, *Ella Baker and the Black Freedom Movement*. The most scathing critique of the Project can be found in editorial remarks by Thelwell in the Carmichael autobiography (570–71). On the controversial vote to expel Whites from policy-making positions, he writes, "what is beyond dispute are the facts. . . . If we consider that before the attrition set in, the meeting had begun with better than a hundred, the percentage carrying that vote approaches that of George W. Bush's percentage of the national election" in November 2000.

71. "From Kingston Springs to Peg Leg Bates," SNCC–Vine City Project papers, State Historical Society of Wisconsin, box 1, folder 11. The formal agenda for the retreat was packed, especially on the first day, and did not allow for a great deal of flexibility.

72. Bill Ware, "Some Comments on the Staff Meeting and Why White People Should Be Excluded from the Meeting," SNCC–Vine City Project papers, State Historical Society of Wisconsin, box 1, folder 11.

73. Carmichael, *Ready for Revolution*, 567; Forman, *Making of Black Revolutionaries*, 475.

74. Carmichael, *Ready for Revolution*, 192 and 565–66; Forman, *Making of Black Revolutionaries*, 452; Zoharah Simmons interview.

75. Zoharah Simmons interview.

76. Ibid.

77. Fleming, *Soon We Will Not Cry*, 116; Zoharah Simmons interview.

78. Carmichael, *Ready for Revolution*, 299–301; Zoharah Simmons interview. Anderson-Bricker provides an important analysis of changes in SNCC's organizational culture in " 'Triple Jeopardy,' " Springer, ed., *Still Lifting, Still Climbing*, 49–69.

79. Michael Simmons interview; Powell interview; Sellers, *River of No Return*, 186; Fleming, *Soon We Will Not Cry*, 158; Mukasa interview; Forman, *Making of Black Revolutionaries*, 478–79; Ransby, *Ella Baker and the Black Freedom Struggle*, 345–47; Fox interview.

CHAPTER 5: NEIGHBORHOOD PROTEST

1. Eisinger, *The Politics of Displacement*, chap. 3; *Report of the National Advisory Commission On Civil Disorders*, 53. Bayor, "Roads to Racial Segregation," *Journal of Urban History* 15 (November 1988): 3–21; Hein, "The Image of 'A City Too Busy to Hate,' " *Phylon* 33, 3 (1972): 205–21; *Atlanta Inquirer*, 3 August 1968. *Central Issues Influencing Community-School Relations in Atlanta, Georgia* (Washington: National Education Association Commission on Professional Rights and Responsibilities, 1969), 13–14. Samuel L. Adams, a Black journalist and former director of research for the Southern Regional Council, noted that Atlanta had a large concentration of Black millionaires, a "sizeable Negro bank," and several Black-owned real estate businesses. Nevertheless, such influence "has not kept whites from controlling land inside and outside the Negro community and developing most of the Negro housing (close to 90% according to some key real estate leaders)." See Adams, "Blueprint for Segregation: A Survey of Atlanta Housing," *New South*, spring 1967, 2, SNCC vertical file, Atlanta University Center, Robert W. Woodruff Library.

2. Residents quoted in Stanley S. Scott, "Summer Hill Housing Plight Hurts," *Atlanta Daily World*, 3 March 1963; Stanley S. Scott, "Blocks of Slums in Summer Hill, Vine City, Buttermilk Bottom, House Minority," *Atlanta Daily World*, 6 March 1963. Scott correctly noted in this series of articles that the well-publicized 1962 struggle to have the city remove a concrete barricade approved by Mayor Ivan Allen in the Peyton Forest subdivision marked a victory for middle-class Blacks on the West Side, but had practically no impact on the lives of the vast majority of Blacks throughout the city. See also Baylor, "Roads," 12–13. A full discussion of the city's urban renewal efforts can be found in Stone, *Economic Growth and Neighborhood Discontent*.

3. Ethel Mae Mathews, interview by author, 10 February 1998, Atlanta, tape recording. Mathews was a community representative on the Model Cities Board. How-

ever, she soon found herself organizing protests against the program's Atlanta office when residents learned that bureaucrats had hidden a dozen empty trailers behind the Atlanta Federal Penitentiary. For an overview of the Model Cities Program in Atlanta consult Harmon, *Beneath the Image*, 429–32.

4. "Klan, SNCC Hold Rallies in City Area," *Atlanta Journal*, 4 September 1966; Harold Martin, "Vine City Was a Place Apart, with Its Yards and Flowers," *Atlanta Journal*, 4 September 1966. The Chicago housing movement receives extensive coverage in Garrow, *Bearing the Cross*, esp. 500–530; "Guardsmen Group for Rights March," *Atlanta Journal-Constitution*, 4 September 1966.

5. Alton Hornsby Jr., "The Negro in Atlanta Politics, 1961–1973," *Atlanta Historical Bulletin* 21 (spring 1977): 7–33.

6. Williams quoted in Wayne Kelley, "Summerhill Was Likely Spot for Trouble When It Came," *Atlanta Journal*, 7 September 1966.

7. Marjorie Prather quoted in untitled affidavit, SNCC vertical file, Atlanta University Center, Robert W. Woodruff Library; Columbus Ward, interview by author, 21 January 1997, Atlanta, tape recording. Ward, Prather's nephew, did not witness the shooting. Tom Dunkin, "73 Arrested in Melee in Area Near Stadium," *Atlanta Journal*, 7 September 1966. Witnesses to the shooting included Harold Louis Prather's stepbrother Emmit Boyd, 26, as well as Willie Frank Alfred, 43, and Tom Bush, 40, both of whom were passengers in the car Prather drove. According to Dunkin's reporting of the incident, all three men confirmed that Harris warned Prather before firing. Ward asserted, however, that neighborhood residents claimed that his mother begged police not to open fire. Prather's criminal record receives mention in "15 Injured as Hundreds of Negroes Riot, Toss Rocks at Police, Smash Cars Here," *Atlanta Constitution*, 7 September 1966; Sellers, *The River of No Return*, 180–81.

8. Marjorie Prather affidavit; Fay Bellamy Powell, interview by author, 31 March 1998, Atlanta, tape recording; Michael Simmons, interview by author, 19 April 1998, Philadelphia, tape recording; Dunkin, "73 Arrested."

9. Residents and Allen quoted in "15 Injured."

10. SNCC worker and Allen quoted in ibid.; Dunkin, "73 Arrested"; Paul Hemphill, "Pop Bottles, Bricks Fly in Troubled Area Here," *Atlanta Journal*, 7 September 1966. Allen told reporters after the rebellion that "the city's highest office commands some degree of respect." He further claimed that "I was never pushed or jostled," yet almost contradicted himself when he complained, "I saw plenty of brutality but it was all directed towards the Atlanta police and the mayor." See Raleigh

Bryans, "Found Respect to a Point—Allen," *Atlanta Journal*, 7 September 1966; some of the most powerful images of the Summerhill protest can be found in "Perspective on the Atlanta Rebellion," a sixteen-page pamphlet published by SNCC with photographs by Rufus Hinton, Julius Lester, and Jimmy Lytle, in SNCC vertical file, Atlanta University Center, Robert W. Woodruff Library.

11. Ward interview; Ethel Mae Mathews, interview by author, 29 April 1996, Atlanta, tape recording (subsequent Mathews citations will be to this interview). Columbus Ward noted that he continues to wear a beard in large part for political reasons. Historian William L. Van De Burg has studied the cultural significance of the Black Power phase of the African American liberation struggle in two significant works: *New Day in Babylon* and *Black Camelot*, esp. 62–83.

12. Dunkin, "73 Arrested."

13. Borders, Williams, and police officer quoted in ibid.

14. Ibid.; Bill Winn, " 'You Should've Seen It Man . . . It Was a Bad Scene,' " *Atlanta Journal*, 7 September 1966.

15. Williams and SNCC worker quoted in David Nordan, "Black Power Vies with Nonviolence," *Atlanta Journal*, 7 September 1966.

16. Ralph McGill, "Story of a Man and of SNCC," *Atlanta Constitution*, 8 September 1966.

17. Ibid. Ralph McGill noted that Victor Rabinowitz, a White attorney from New York City, dismissed SNCC lawyer Charles Morgan shortly after the organization ran into financial trouble in the fall of 1965. Rabinowitz had registered himself with the federal government as an agent of Fidel Castro's government in Cuba. Thus, McGill's claim that SNCC might be funded by Cuba. See also "Who Runs This City?" *Atlanta Journal*, 8 September 1966.

18. Arnall quoted in "Arnall Rips KKK, SNCC, Birchers," *Atlanta Journal*, 8 September 1966; Byrd quoted in "Byrd Turns Guns on SNCC Leader," *Atlanta Journal*, 8 September 1966; Carter quoted in John Askins, "Carter Commends Mayor, Police," *Atlanta Journal*, 8 September 1966.

19. Allen and Jenkins quoted in "Allen and Jenkins Blame SNCC; Children Hurl Rocks at 2 Cars," *Atlanta Journal*, 7 September 1966; Kelley, "SNCC 'Nonviolent' in Name"; Carmichael quoted in Robert Coram and Tom Dunkin, "Carmichael Riot Charge Goes to Fulton Grand Jury," *Atlanta Journal*, 9 September 1966.

20. Powell interview.

21. Unidentified resident quoted in "Defendants in Riot Cases Fined in Municipal Court," *Atlanta Journal*, 7 September 1966.

22. Williams quoted in Kelley, "SNCC 'Nonviolent' in Name"; McDaniel quoted in Raleigh Bryans and Wayne Kelley, "Negro Leaders Put Blame on SNCC," *Atlanta Journal*, 8 September 1966.

23. Davis, Smith, Borders, Hunter, and Williams quoted in Bryans and Kelley, "Negro Leaders Put Blame on SNCC."

24. McDaniel quoted in ibid.; Ward interview.

25. Martin Luther King Jr., SCLC press release, 14 October 1966, Facts on Film, SERS, N15 7593.

26. King Jr., *Where Do We Go from Here*, chap. 2, esp. 41 and 44. James H. Cone has provided an insightful analysis of King's assessment of Black Power in *Martin and Malcolm and America*, 227–35.

27. Foster Davis, "Carmichael Given Edge in 'Black Power' Debate," *Atlanta Constitution*, 10 February 1967; Carmichael and Hamilton, *Black Power*, preface. Six years later Hamilton wrote *The Black Experience in American Politics*, in which he observed that there were five distinct themes in Black political thought: constitutionalism, sovereign nationalism, plural nationalism, leftist thought, and pan-Africanism. The unifying element for Hamilton was "continuity of influence."

28. King, *My Life with Martin Luther King, Jr.*, 208 and 293. Cone, *Martin and Malcolm and America*, 235–43; Garrow, *Bearing the Cross*, 550–64; Martin Luther King Jr., "Why I am Opposed to the War in Vietnam," undated sermon at Ebenezer Baptist Church, Atlanta, tape recording, in author's possession. Cone has asserted that King's "Beyond Vietnam" speech was "his greatest hour" with regard to "moral courage." Coretta King's recollection of speaking at the largest antiwar rally the country had yet witnessed, on Thanksgiving weekend in 1965, is instructive in that she wrote of a conversation she had with activist physician Benjamin Spock about the need for her husband to speak out on the war. Yet, she did not discuss her own address.

29. King, "Why I Am Opposed to the War in Vietnam"; Garrow, *Bearing the Cross*, 576–77; Daniel H. Watts, "Rev. King and Vietnam," editorial, *Liberator*, May 1967, Facts on Film, SERS, N12 4499.

30. *Report of the National Advisory Commission*, 53–54. Atlanta Police Department Chief Herbert Jenkins was one of the most active members of the eleven-member commission headed by Governor Otto Kerner of Illinois that studied the wave of violent Black protests throughout the United States from 1964 through 1967. *New York Times* columnist Tom Wicker wrote in the introduction to the report that "Jenkins, the policeman, surprised other members with his acute sensitivity . . . and his progressive and compassionate approach." Nevertheless, the report's

coverage of the four-day Dixie Hills protest and the pivotal Summerhill protest should be viewed critically. The report went so far to state that the "dramatic ghetto appearance" of Mayor Allen actually "averted a riot" in September 1966.

31. Mukasa Dada (Willie Ricks), interview by author, 3 November 1997, Atlanta, tape recording; Margaret Hurst and Frank Wells, "Carmichael, 4 Arrested as 500 Gather at Northwest Shopping Center Here," *Atlanta Constitution*, 19 June 1967; "Police Riot in Atlanta," *SNCC Newsletter*, June–July 1967, 3, Facts on Film, SERS, N20 8241; Johnson and residents quoted in Joe Brown and Keeler McCartney, "Dixie Hills Negroes Hurl Bricks, Bottles," *Atlanta Constitution*, 20 June 1967; *Report of the National Advisory Commission*, 54–55.

32. "Police Riot in Atlanta," 3; Carmichael quoted in Brown and McCartney, "Dixie Hills Negroes"; Hurst and Wells, "Carmichael, 4 Arrested."

33. Carmichael quoted in Brown and McCartney, "Dixie Hills Negroes"; *Report of the National Advisory Commission*, 54–55.

34. *Report of the National Advisory Commission*, 54–55; Hurst and Wells, "Carmichael, 4 Arrested"; Brown and McCartney, "Dixie Hills Negroes."

35. Brown and McCartney, "Dixie Hills Negroes," 55–56 and 156; Mukasa interview; Boesel and Rossi, eds., *Cities under Siege*, 145; "Police Riot in Atlanta."

36. Johnson, Featherstone, Ricks and Brown quoted in Joe Brown and Duane Riner, "Negro Killed, 3 Shot in Dixie Hills; Mayor Declares Emergency," *Atlanta Constitution*, 21 June 1967.

37. Accounts of the 20 June police shooting differ with regard to what precipitated the incident. According to the Kerner Commission, police responded to a cherry bomb in the street, not a Molotov cocktail that exploded on the roof of the Verbena Shopping Plaza. "Police Riot in Atlanta," 3; Boesel and Rossi, eds., *Cities under Siege*, 145; *Report of the National Advisory Commission*, 56; unidentified relative of victim quoted in Brown and Riner, "Negro Killed, 3 Shot in Dixie Hills."

38. Allen quoted in Brown and Riner, "Negro Killed, 3 Shot in Dixie Hills"; *Report of the National Advisory Commission*, 55–56.

39. "Carmichael, 4 Arrested"; Vine City residents quoted in Alfred Johnson, "Vine City Rejects SNCC Campaign," *Atlanta Journal*, 8 September 1966.

40. ACCA activists quoted in Margaret Hurst and Remer Tyson, "Negro Leaders Urge Action on Projects to Stem Violence," *Atlanta Constitution*, 22 June 1967; Joe Brown and Duane Riner, "Dixie Hills Quiet under Late Curfew," *Atlanta Constitution*, 22 June 1967. Black moderates and conservatives did share certain specific concerns with radical activists. Like SNCC activists, members of both the moderate ACCA and the more conservative Atlanta Summit Leadership Conference became in-

creasingly frustrated by Allen's refusal to lift the curfew in the neighborhood. In addition to Johnson and Davis, those in attendance at the emergency ACCA meeting were: Alderman Q. V. Williamson; Clarence D. Coleman, of the Southern regional office of the National Urban League; Horace Tate, Atlanta School Board; Vernon Jordan, Voter Education Project of the Southern Regional Council; Franklin Thomas, Butler Street YMCA; John Cox, Atlanta Youth Council; and Ben Lewis, National Urban League.

41. SNCC worker quoted in "15 Injured"; "Pop Bottles, Bricks Fly."

42. Hornsby, "Negro in Atlanta Politics," 21; Ward interview. Several scholars have debunked the long-held notion that the Black Power phase of the larger Black freedom struggle was without Southern roots. See Umoja, "Eye for an Eye"; Tyson, *Radio Free Dixie*; and Hill, *The Deacons for Defense*. Political scientist Clarence N. Stone, in the preface to *Regime Politics*, has argued that absolute racial polarization did not come to dominate Atlanta life because "a biracial coalition formed and became an integral part of the city's governing regime."

43. "SNCC Adopts Policy Statement," *Freedom Information Service Mississippi Newsletter*, 2 June 1967, 2, SNCC vertical file, Atlanta University Center, Robert W. Woodruff Library.

44. "Document Calls for Black Revolution," *Detroit News*, 1 August 1967, Facts on Film, SERS, J3 142.

45. Ibid. Cooks later organized and headed the African Nationalist Pioneer Movement, based in New York City. Cooks called for Blacks in the United States to take up arms against Italy when the army of Benito Mussolini's fascist regime invaded Ethiopia in 1935.

46. Ibid. See also *Black America*, summer–fall 1965, 10, Black Power files, Martin Luther King, Jr. Center for Nonviolent Social Change; Maxwell C. Stanford, "Revolutionary Action Movement (RAM)," passim.

47. King quoted in "Target Areas Chosen for Protest Recruiting," *Washington Post*, 17 December 1967; Jose Yglesias, "Dr. King's March on Washington, Part II," *New York Times Magazine*, 31 March 1968, 30; "Marching to a Different Tune," editorial, *Atlanta Constitution*, 6 December 1967.

48. "Marching to a Different Tune"; Michael Simmons, interview by author, 19 April 1998, Philadelphia, tape recording; Mukasa interview; Bond quoted in David Llorens, "Julian Bond: 'Down by the Lake, Shootin' Fish,'" *Ebony*, May 1969, 68.

49. Mathews interview.

50. "Biography," George Wiley Papers, State Historical Society of Wisconsin; Jackson, "Welfare Mothers and Black Liberation," *Black Scholar*, 34–35.

51. Mathews interview.

52. Ibid.; "Metropolitan Atlanta Conference on Hunger and Malnutrition, Public Hearings, Georgia House of Representatives," schedule and agenda, 10–11 July 1969, George Wiley Papers, State Historical Society of Wisconsin, box 25, folder 1.

53. Brown interview; John Neary, "Close-up: Julian Bond, a Militant inside the System," *Life*, 8 November 1968, 43–48; Bond quoted in Llorens, "Julian Bond," 58–67; "Mrs. Henrietta Canty Seeks 7th Ward Seat," *Atlanta Daily World*, 21 September 1969.

54. The weekly Black newspaper the *Atlanta Voice*, which played an activist role similar to that of the *Atlanta Inquirer* in the early 1960s, followed the tenants' movement at Bolton Garden Apartments closely. George Coleman, "Rent Withheld From Landlord," *Atlanta Voice*, 9 November 1969, Facts on Film, SERS, N10 349; Coleman, "Idea of Tenants Union Spreading," *Atlanta Voice*, 16 November 1969; Coleman, "Bolton Tenants Protest Ruling," *Atlanta Voice*, 18 January 1970.

55. As tensions between the police department and Atlanta Blacks continued to escalate, the city's Black police officers organized a chapter of the Afro-American Patrolmen's League. King quoted in George Coleman, "Brutality Real, Atlantans Say," *Atlanta Voice*, 9 November 1969, 1, Facts on Film, SERS, N10 344; Brooks quoted in "Second Woman Charges White Police Beat Her," *Atlanta Voice*, 16 November 1969, Facts on Film, SERS, N10 351.

56. Mathews interview.

57. Rhonda Y. Williams noted that while grassroots Black women activists in Baltimore "probably would not characterize themselves as Black Power advocates or even civil rights activists, their activism was influenced by the larger political milieu that shaped militant black freedom fighting organizations." See Williams, " 'We're Tired of Being Treated like Dogs,' " *Black Scholar*, 31–41, and esp. 39; see also Williams, *The Politics of Public Housing*, esp. chaps. 5 and 6; Mathews interview; Ward interview; Mukasa interview. Both Mathews and Ward embrace the term "activist," which is significant, for they place a premium on doing the often mundane work necessary to bring about change in their communities.

58. Mathews interview. The connection between Black churches and the female foot soldiers of the human rights movement has been well documented. See Lee, *For Freedom's Sake*; Collier-Thomas, *Daughters of Thunder*; Giddings, *When and Where I Enter*, 52–53, 64, and 284; Jones, *Labor of Love, Labor of Sorrow*, 215, 279–83. Robin D. G. Kelley offers an important theoretical discussion of religion and the culture of opposition in his study *Hammer and Hoe*.

59. Mathews interview. The spelling of Charlie as "Chahlie" represents anthropolo-

gist John Langston Gwaltney's use of the word in his study of "core black culture," *Drylongso*, glossary.

CHAPTER 6: BLACK STUDIES

1. Vincent Harding, "No Turning Back?" *Renewal* 10, no. 7 (October–November 1970): 10. *Renewal* was a publication of the National Committee of Black Churchmen, an important body of activist clergy based in New York City. Institute of the Black World Records, Manuscripts, Archives and Rare Books Division, Schomburg Center for Research in Black Culture, New York Public Library, Astor, Lenox, and Tilden Foundations, William Strickland Series, folder 5. The archivists of the Schomburg are still in the process of organizing and cataloguing the extensive collection of the Institute of the Black World.

2. Ibid.; David Massey, "Black Studies: A Volatile Issue," *Atlanta Constitution*, 29 June 1969.

3. Although a series of bloody clashes between police and a Black-led student contingent in 1968 did prevent Columbia University from building a gymnasium in a nearby Harlem park, the demand for a Black Studies program did not materialize until the mid-1980s as a direct result of the spring 1985 anti-apartheid student protests in support of university divestment organized by the Coalition for a Free South Africa (CFSA). A student-faculty committee led by historians Hollis Lynch and Eric Foner oversaw the process of establishing an interdepartmental program in African American Studies. Prior to 1985 Barbara Ransby and Danny Armstrong played pivotal roles as CFSA organizers. Later CFSA student activists included Tanaquil Jones, Tony Glover, Whitney Tymas, and Rob Jones.

4. Student demands quoted in Hugh Gloster to Morehouse Board of Trustees, Sanford S. Atwood Papers, Special Collections Department, Robert W. Woodruff Library, Emory University, box 63; Mukasa Dada (Willie Ricks), interview by author, 3 November 1997, Atlanta, tape recording; Sellers, *The River of No Return*, chap. 5.

5. Philip Gailey, "Davison Tells of Demands by Students," *Atlanta Constitution*, 11 March 1969.

6. George M. Coleman, "Did Not Use Guns Student Heads Say," *Atlanta Voice*, 1, Facts on Film, SERS, N9 1407; "Dissidents Hit at Morehouse," *Atlanta Constitution*, 26 April 1969; Gloster quoted in "Dr. Gloster Opposed to Meet under Duress," *Atlanta Voice*, 27 April 1969; "Morehouse Trustees Nullify Agreements during Lock-In," *Atlanta Voice*, 27 April 1969.

7. Taylor quoted in "Dissidents Hit at Morehouse"; "Firebomb at AUC Described," *Atlanta Constitution*, 25 April 1969.

8. Virgil Hartley, "Four Days in May," *Emory Magazine*, May–June 1969, 16–22, EU-FAC, box 6, folder 1, series 9: Afro-American Studies Subcommittee 1969, Special Collections Department, Robert W. Woodruff Library, Emory University; "The History of Afro-Americans at Emory," Division of Campus Life, Special Collections Department, Robert W. Woodruff Library, Emory University.

9. "The History of Afro-Americans at Emory"; Christena Bledsoe, "Students, Administrators Make Emory Concessions," *Atlanta Journal*, 28 May 1969; Lee Simowitz, "Compromise Ends Strife at Emory," *Atlanta Constitution*, 29 May 1969; special edition, *Emory Wheel*, 27 May 1969, Sanford S. Atwood Papers, Special Collections Department, Robert W. Woodruff Library, Emory University, box 63.

10. Bledsoe, "Students, Administrators"; Simowitz, "Compromise Ends Strife."

11. Lee quoted in "Morehouse President Is Silent on Report of 15 Expulsions," *Atlanta Constitution*, 25 June 1969; Coleman, "Action of Morehouse Board Shows Lack of Charity," *Atlanta Voice*, 6 July 1969.

12. Robert LaPrince, "A.U. Serve [sic] Summons on Trustees," *Atlanta Voice*, 27 July 1969; Colonized Objectors quoted in ibid.; Robert DeLeon, "ITC Head Answers Student Manifesto," *Atlanta Constitution*, 21 November 1969. The five people named in the injunction were Quenton Griffin, John Holmes, Willie Ricks, Harvey B. Smith, and Bill Ware.

13. "Emory Faculty Approves Black Studies Program," *Atlanta Daily World*, 4 May 1970; Aldridge quoted in "Emory Women," *Emory Magazine*, October 1989, 5, Special Collections Department, Robert W. Woodruff Library, Emory University; Black Studies brochure, Special Collections Department, Robert W. Woodruff Library, Emory University, Academic Departments—Black Studies, box 146:1.

14. Aldridge quoted in Winston Grady-Willis and Scott Switalla, "African American Studies and Emory," *Fire This Time* (Emory University), spring 1994; Rena M. Price to Sanford S. Atwood, 14 July 1969, EUFAC, box 6, folder 1, Series 9: Afro-American Studies Sub-Committee, 1969, Special Collections Department, Robert W. Woodruff Library, Emory University.

15. Vincent Harding, interview by author, 7 March 1997, Denver, tape recording; August Meier and Elliott Rudwick have discussed the shift toward nationalism in Harding's activism and scholarship in *Black History and the Historical Profession, 1915–1980*, 207–11.

16. Harding interview.

17. Ibid. Stephen Ward has written an important essay that also focuses on the early years of the IBW. See Ward, "Scholarship in the Context of Struggle," *Black Scholar*, 42–53.

18. Ibid.; Meier and Rudwick, *Black History and the Historical Profession*, 209.

19. Harding interview; Thomas A. Johnson, "Institute Studies 'Black Humanism,'" *New York Times*, 8 December 1969.

20. Institute of the Black World, "Statement of Purpose and Program," fall 1969, Institute of the Black World Files, Special Collections, Robert W. Woodruff Library, Atlanta University.

21. Institute of the Black World, "Program of Work," Institute of the Black World Papers, Manuscripts, Archives and Rare Books Division, Schomburg Center for Research in Black Culture, New York Public Library, Astor, Lenox, and Tilden Foundations.

22. For a discussion of Stuckey's influences, see Meier and Rudwick, *Black History and the Historical Profession*, 176 and 206–7.

23. Joyce Ladner, telephone interview by author, 28 May 2004, tape recording.

24. Ibid.

25. Ibid.

26. Ibid.

27. Ibid.; William Strickland, telephone interview by author, 20 June 2004, tape recording.

28. Harding interview; Vincent Harding, "Black World without End. Amen," *Renewal* 10, no. 7 (October–November 1970): 3.

29. Bennett quoted in Johnson, "Institute Studies"; and in Harding, "Black World without End."

30. Ladner interview; see also Davis, *A Clashing of the Soul*; Rouse, *Lugenia Burns Hope*.

31. Harding, "Black World without End," 3; Ladner interview.

32. Strickland quoted in Johnson, "Institute Studies"; Ladner interview.

33. Strickland quoted in Johnson, "Institute Studies"; Harding interview.

34. Vincent Harding to Coretta Scott King, 17 November 1969, Institute of the Black World Papers, Manuscripts, Archives and Rare Books Division, Schomburg Center for Research in Black Culture, New York Public Library, Astor, Lenox, and Tilden Foundations, box 7, folder 2; Mack H. Jones to colleagues, 25 November 1969, Institute of the Black World Papers, Manuscripts, Archives and Rare Books Division, Schomburg Center for Research in Black Culture, New York Public Library, Astor, Lenox, and Tilden Foundations, box 7, folder 2.

35. Harding interview.

36. Ibid.; Strickland interview; Harding, "Black World without End," 3.

37. "Towards a Black Agenda," 23 March 1970, Institute of the Black World Papers, Manuscripts, Archives and Rare Books Division, Schomburg Center for Research in Black Culture, New York Public Library, Astor, Lenox, and Tilden Foundations. No individual staff member was credited with authorship of the document, yet it was apparent that one person, most likely William Strickland or Vincent Harding, wrote it.

38. Ibid.

39. Center for African and African-American Studies, Summer Study Abroad 1970 brochure, Facts on Film, SERS, N10 262. The complete course offerings that summer were CAAS 410, African Tradition in the Caribbean; CAAS 420, Peoples of the Caribbean; CAAS 430, African Tradition in Latin America; CAAS 450, Arts of West Africa; CAAS 460, Survey of Contemporary Black African Culture; and CAAS 470, Peoples of West Africa. The instructors who joined Richard Long were George Roberts, professor of comparative cultures at the University of California, Irvine; Roy Glascow, professor of international relations at Bowie State in Maryland; James E. Lewis, professor of art, Morgan State in Baltimore; George Roberts, professor of comparative cultures at the University of California, Irvine; and the Panamanian-born sociologist Roy Bryce-Laporte, director of the Afro-American Studies program at Yale.

40. "AU jointly calls for united front against oppression," *Atlanta Voice*, 31 May 1970, 1, Facts on Film, N10 503.

41. Jualynne Dodson, interview by author, 5 March 1997, Boulder, tape recording.

42. Ibid.; hooks, *Talking Back*, 55–61.

43. Dodson interview.

44. Ibid.; Harding interview.

45. Dodson interview. Jualynne Dodson recalled that she and her husband had a "major confrontation" over whether to return to graduate studies. Howard Dodson had become thoroughly engrossed in the activities of the institute during their stay in Atlanta. The two of them returned to the IBW in 1972, and Howard Dodson would succeed Vincent Harding as IBW director in 1973. After completing her doctoral work, Jualynne Dodson became research director at the Atlanta University School of Social Work, doing collaborative work with the Institute on occasion.

46. Forman quoted in "Manifesto Demands Church Reparation," *National Observer*, 12 May 1969, 3, Facts on Film, SERS, J11 192.

47. Jenkins quoted in Diane Stepp, "Church Is Silent on Black Demands," *Atlanta*

Constitution, 24 May 1969; Stepp, "Church Vetoes Black Demands," *Atlanta Constitution*, 25 May 1969.

48. National Committee of Black Churchmen, press release, 25 June 1970, Institute of the Black World Papers, Manuscripts, Archives and Rare Books Division, Schomburg Center for Research in Black Culture, New York Public Library, Astor, Lenox, and Tilden Foundations, box 6, folder 5. The NCBC leadership included Herbert Bell Shaw, NCBC president; M. L. Wilson, Council of Churches of the City of New York; J. Metz Rollins, executive director of NCBC; Wendell Foster, Black Clergy Coalition; and Sam Holder, president of the Inter-Faith Clergy Association of Queens.

49. Vincent Harding, "No Turning Back?" *Renewal* 10, no. 7 (October–November 1970): 7, Institute of the Black World Papers, Manuscripts, Archives and Rare Books Division, Schomburg Center for Research in Black Culture, New York Public Library, box 6, folder 5.

50. Ibid., 8–13; NCBC report of the Workgroup on the Black Declaration of Independence, 19 November 1970, Institute of the Black World Papers, Manuscripts, Archives and Rare Books Division, Schomburg Center for Research in Black Culture, New York Public Library, Astor, Lenox, and Tilden Foundations, box 6, folder 5. Harding also criticized the absence of any discussion of the Vietnam War in the Black Power statement, though he said the failure to do so was understandable.

51. Harding interview.

52. Institute of the Black World Papers, Manuscripts, Archives and Rare Books Division, Schomburg Center for Research in Black Culture, New York Public Library, Astor, Lenox, and Tilden Foundations, box 6, folder 4; see also Wilkins, "Belly of the Beast." Blacks in Canada had a long history of launching independent institutions. They established newspapers, refashioned troubled schools, sought community autonomy, and founded fraternal and benevolent societies throughout the nineteenth century. The churches were an important foundation for antislavery activism. Ministers such as William A. White and William Oliver were committed spokesmen for the Black community in Canada. Canadian Blacks led by J. W. Montgomery (Toronto) and James Jenkins (London, Ontario) formed the Canadian League for the Advancement of Colored People in 1924. See Winks, *The Blacks In Canada: A History*.

53. Georgia inmate to IBW staff, 5 December 1971, Institute of the Black World Papers, Manuscripts, Archives and Rare Books Division, Schomburg Center for Research in Black Culture, New York Public Library, box 6. The best-known

writings by and about prisoners concern the California state penal system. Two significant primary sources are radical Black inmate George Jackson's *Blood in My Eye* and *Soledad Brother: The Prison Letters of George Jackson*. See also Angela Y. Davis et al., *If They Come in the Morning*. Independent scholar Eric Cummins has written an insightful book, *The Rise and Fall of California's Radical Prison Movement*.

54. Tampa activist to IBW staff, 29 January 1972, Institute of the Black World Papers, Manuscripts, Archives and Rare Books Division, Schomburg Center for Research in Black Culture, New York Public Library, box 6; Ft. Benning soldier to IBW staff, February 1972, Institute of the Black World Papers, Manuscripts, Archives and Rare Books Division, Schomburg Center for Research in Black Culture, New York Public Library, Astor, Lenox, and Tilden Foundations, box 6, William Strickland Series.

55. Strickland interview.

56. William Strickland to IBW research staff, no date, Institute of the Black World Papers, Manuscripts, Archives and Rare Books Division, Schomburg Center for Research in Black Culture, New York Public Library, box 6; Cruse, *The Crisis of the Negro Intellectual*, part III, esp. 206–24, and passim.

57. George Dugan, "Black Action Unit Takes Aim at Bias," *Washington Post*, 19 March 1972, Institute of the Black World Papers, Manuscripts, Archives and Rare Books Division, Schomburg Center for Research in Black Culture, New York Public Library, Astor, Lenox, and Tilden Foundations, box 6, IFCO folder.

58. IBW-IFCO letter of agreement, 9 October 1972, Institute of the Black World Papers, Manuscripts, Archives and Rare Books Division, Schomburg Center for Research in Black Culture, New York Public Library, box 6, IFCO folder; Strickland to IFCO-COTI participants, 9 October 1972, Institute of the Black World Papers, Manuscripts, Archives and Rare Books Division, Schomburg Center for Research in Black Culture, New York Public Library, box 6, IFCO folder. According to an IFCO brochure, COTI developed "Training of Community Organizers in the Liberation Arts." The core curriculum of the institute comprised Systems Analysis, History of Struggle, International Studies, and Administration and Management.

59. William Strickland to COTI participants in Cuba, 9 February 1973, Institute of the Black World Papers, Manuscripts, Archives and Rare Books Division, Schomburg Center for Research in Black Culture, New York Public Library, Astor, Lenox, and Tilden Foundations, box 6, IFCO folder.

60. Janet L. Douglas to Jerry Vallery and Phil Littlejohn, no date, Institute of the Black World Papers, Manuscripts, Archives and Rare Books Division, Schomburg Center for Research in Black Culture, New York Public Library, Astor, Lenox, and

Tilden Foundations, box 6, IFCO folder; Jan Douglas, telephone interview by author, 23 May 2004, tape recording.

61. Vincent Harding to IBW planning committee, 14 February 1973, Institute of the Black World Papers, Manuscripts, Archives and Rare Books Division, Schomburg Center for Research in Black Culture, New York Public Library, Astor, Lenox, and Tilden Foundations, box 6, folders 8 and 9.

62. William Strickland to Charles Spivey, General Secretariat, Programme to Combat Racism, World Council of Churches, 1972, Institute of the Black World Papers, Manuscripts, Archives and Rare Books Division, Schomburg Center for Research in Black Culture, New York Public Library, Astor, Lenox, and Tilden Foundations, box 6, folder 10.

63. Baldwin Sjollema to Vincent Harding, 29 January 1973, Institute of the Black World Papers, Manuscripts, Archives and Rare Books Division, Schomburg Center for Research in Black Culture, New York Public Library, Astor, Lenox, and Tilden Foundations, box 6, folder 10.

64. IBW brochure, "Black People and the International Crisis: Where Do We Go from Here?" Institute of the Black World Papers, Manuscripts, Archives and Rare Books Division, Schomburg Center for Research in Black Culture, New York Public Library, Astor, Lenox, and Tilden Foundations.

65. Harding interview.

CHAPTER 7: THE MULTI-FRONT BLACK STRUGGLE

1. Mathews quoted in "NWRO Gets Visitor: The Man from Welfare," *Atlanta Constitution*, 22 March 1970. Burson drew fire from conservative politicians during state hearings on the status of the program. See also Kornbluh, "Black Buying Power: Welfare Rights, Consumerism and Northern Protest," Theoharis and Woodard, eds., *Freedom North*, 199–222; Tait, "'Workers Just like Anyone Else,'" Springer, ed., *Still Lifting, Still Climbing*, 299–303; see also West, *The National Welfare Rights Movement*; Kotz and Kotz, *A Passion for Equality*; Williams, *The Politics of Public Housing*, esp. chap. 6.

2. Boyd Lewis, "City Workers Strike; Wage Demands Unmet," *Atlanta Voice*, 22 March 1970, 1, Facts on Film, SERS, N10 453.

3. Evans and Bradford quoted in ibid.; George Coleman, "What's behind Mail and Garbage Strikes?" *Atlanta Voice*, 29 March 1970, 1, Facts on Film, SERS, N10 456; Boyd Lewis, "5 Weeks Jobless Hurting Garbage Workers, Families," *Atlanta Voice*, 19 April 1970, 1, Facts on Film, SERS, N10 472.

4. Mathews quoted in "Atlanta Mothers Hit Check Cuts," *Welfare Fighter* (National

Welfare Rights Organization), May 1970, 8, Facts on Film, SERS, N22 3621; Abernathy quoted in George Coleman, "Abernathy Ready to Aid Atlanta Garage [sic] Strikers," *Atlanta Voice*, 5 April 1970, 1, Facts on Film, SERS, N10 463.

5. "Union Men March on Downtown," *Atlanta Voice*, 12 April 1970, 1, Facts on Film, SERS, N10 466; hecklers quoted in Lewis, "5 Weeks Jobless," 1.

6. Boyd Lewis, "Garbage Strike Over; but Wage Hike Slighted," *Atlanta Voice*, 26 April 1970, 1, Facts on Film, SERS, N10 477; "Vice Mayor Jackson Ask Judge Panel on Increases," *Atlanta Voice*, 26 April 1970, 1, Facts on Film, SERS, N10 477; Boyd Lewis, "Rats Flourish in City," *Atlanta Voice*, 3 May 1970, 1, Facts on Film, N10 481.

7. Williams quoted in Lewis, "Rats Flourish in City," 11; Brown quoted in "More History of Blacks Urged for State Schools," *Atlanta Constitution*, 1 April 1970.

8. Mathews quoted in "Atlanta Mothers," 8. The base of operations for the local NWRO chapter was Emmaus House, a community center in Peoplestown funded by the Episcopal Church and headed by pastor Austin Ford, a liberal White minister. Mathews and Columbus Ward conducted their work with a greater degree of autonomy than some radical Black activists were willing to acknowledge at the time. Fellow grassroots activists recognized the power and influence of Mathews, however, and sometimes sought to challenge it. See Boyd Lewis, "Hot Arguments Sear MC Mass Convention," *Atlanta Voice*, 25 January 1970, 1, Facts on Film, SERS, N10 410.

9. Howard quoted in Portia Scott, "Where Is the Black Support?" *Atlanta Daily World*, 30 April 1970.

10. Carmichael quoted in "Stokely Returns," *Atlanta Voice*, 26 April 1970, 1, Facts on Film, SERS, J2 905.

11. Carmichael quoted in ibid. The development of Stokely Carmichael's neo-Marxist pan-African politics eventually led him to change his name to Kwame Ture and to found the All-African People's Revolutionary Party. For an extended discussion of the AAPRP within the context of the politics of the period, consult Alkalimat et al., *Introduction to Afro-American Studies*, 309–12.

12. "Stokely Returns," 1.

13. "3 Die, 50 Hurt in Augusta Riots; Guards, State Troopers Called In," *Atlanta Constitution*, 12 May 1970; Phil Gailey, "Augusta Dead Shot in Back," *Atlanta Constitution*, 14 May 1970; "Tense Augusta Seeks Means to Restore Peace after Riot," *Atlanta Daily World*, 14 May 1970; Maddox quoted in Bill Shipp, "Maddox Says Rioting Sparked by Panthers," *Atlanta Constitution*, 13 May 1970.

14. Smith quoted in "Sen. Smith Lashes Tech Panther Rally," *Atlanta Constitution*, 17 February 1970.

15. "Rall Interrupted by Augusta Blacks," *Atlanta Constitution*, 22 September 1969; Newton quoted in Aaron Taylor, "Panthers Moving HQ to Atlanta—Newton," *Atlanta Constitution*, 9 September 1971.

16. Although most chapters of the Black Panther Party remained in line with Huey Newton, significant exceptions, particularly the New York Panthers, supported Eldridge Cleaver in the often violent internecine struggle between the factions fueled by the FBI's counterintelligence program. For a more substantive discussion of state repression against the party at the national level from 1969 until 1971, see Grady-Willis, "The Black Panther Party," Jones, ed., *The Black Panther Party Reconsidered*, esp. 374–76; see also Scot Brown's discussion of state repression in *Fighting for US*.

17. Young quoted in Taylor, "Panthers Moving"; Abernathy quoted in "Abernathy Welcomes Panthers," *Atlanta Constitution*, 11 September 1971; Massell and Maddox quoted in "The Panthers Are Coming," editorial, *Macon Telegraph and News*, which appeared in the *Atlanta Constitution*, 19 September 1971.

18. Grady-Willis, "The Black Panther Party," 374–76.

19. Emma Jean Martin, interview by author, 26 March 1998, Atlanta, tape recording.

20. Ibid. Martin maintains that many of her current respiratory problems date back to her inhalation of the tear gas.

21. Ibid.

22. Ibid.; Gene Ferguson, interview by author, 15 August 1997, Atlanta, tape recording.

23. Leaflet, Georgia State Chapter of the BPP, February 1972, author's possession; Ferguson interview; "People's Survival Programs," Georgia State Chapter of the BPP, no date, author's possession. The propaganda apparatus of the Atlanta group was much less sophisticated and polished than that of the national office and established party chapters in cities such as Chicago, Los Angeles, and New York City, yet every bit as effective.

24. "People's Survival Programs." The local Panther leadership acknowledged that business owners could not shoulder the burden themselves. "We realize that the community businessman's survival depends on whether the people of the community support his business. Likewise, the people of the community need the help of the businessmen in making their People's Survival Programs a success."

25. Martin interview.

26. Ibid.

27. Ibid.; Columbus Ward, interview by author, 21 January 1997, Atlanta, tape record-

ing. Jean Martin noted that members of the Georgia group wore their "traditional uniforms" for special events, such as a speaking engagement by Angela Y. Davis.

28. Several members of the Black Liberation Army (BLA)—an armed underground group of former Panther activists—left their New York base in August 1971 headed for Atlanta, apparently because "it got too hot" in the Northeast. Fulton County authorities implicated the BLA in the murder of policeman James Richard Greene. According to police, the Atlanta group engaged in weapons and survival skills training in preparation for a mission to return exiled Panther leader Eldridge Cleaver from Algeria. See Keeler McCartney, "Policeman's Murder a Militant Ceremony," *Atlanta Constitution*, 30 September 1972; for a more sympathetic treatment of the BLA consult Shakur, *Assata*.

29. Georgia State Chapter of the BPP, press release, August 1972, in author's possession.

30. Ibid.; Ferguson interview.

31. Oliver quoted in Jim Stewart, "Store Chains Get Demands of Panthers," *Atlanta Constitution*, 24 August 1972; Keeler McCartney, "Police Will Investigate Black Panthers' Demands," *Atlanta Constitution*, 25 August 1972; "Chief Says Panthers Need Permits to Solicit Funds," *Atlanta Constitution*, 29 August 1972.

32. Panther statement quoted in Nick Taylor, "Panthers Deny Threat against Powell," *Atlanta Constitution*, 5 September 1972; Carter quoted in Alex Coffin, "Panthers to Continue Efforts," *Atlanta Constitution*, 6 September 1972.

33. Gray quoted in Nick Taylor, "FBI Eying Panther Money Demand Here," *Atlanta Constitution*, 15 September 1972.

34. Keeler McCartney and Tom Linthicum, "Shoot-to-Kill Intent Is Denied by Inman," *Atlanta Constitution*, 15 September 1972; "Black Panthers," editorial, *Atlanta Constitution*, 16 September 1972.

35. Jordan quoted in Jim Stewart, "Panthers Get Heave-Ho from Apartment," *Atlanta Constitution*, 21 October 1972; Carter quoted in Barry Henderson, "Arms Seized by Police in Panther Raid," *Atlanta Constitution*, 10 November 1972.

36. Horn quoted in Bill McNabb, "Black Panther Hearing Postponed to Tuesday," *Atlanta Constitution*, 11 November 1972; Jones quoted in Barry Henderson, "2 Are Bound in Panther Case," *Atlanta Constitution*, 15 November 1972; Carter quoted in Joe Cole, "Atlanta Panthers describe cop harassment," *Militant*, 12 January 1973, 15.

37. Barry Henderson, "Six Arrested in Drug Raid," *Atlanta Constitution*, 6 December 1972; Joseph Boone, interview by unidentified Interdenominational Theological

Seminary student and transcribed by Fay Bellamy, 17 October 1974, Institute of the Black World Papers, Manuscripts, Archives and Rare Books Division, Schomburg Center for Research in Black Culture, New York Public Library, Astor, Lenox, and Tilden Foundations. Boone incorrectly referred to Sam Lundy as "Charles Lundy" in the ITC interview.

38. Martin interview. Martin was reluctant to mention by name any of the members of this criminal group within the Party. However, her account of what occurred at the Kirkwood office, given both during an informal interview and the formal taped session, was consistent with respect to other details. An excellent analysis of the party's internal weaknesses can be found in Johnson, "Explaining the Demise of the Black Panther Party," in Jones, ed., *The Black Panther Party Reconsidered*, 391–414.

39. Martin interview.

40. Ibid.

41. Ibid. Martin remained in Atlanta after leaving the Panthers. She completed her master's degree and worked as a French teacher with Exodus Academy and at Southside High School. She continues to work as an educator and minister in Decatur, a majority-Black suburb of Atlanta.

42. Beau Cutts, "250 Blacks Seize Room at Capitol, Bar Floyd," *Atlanta Constitution*, 28 September 1971. Adolph Reed Jr. has noted that activists of the Black Power era were ill-equipped to deal with "mundane" everyday politics. See Reed, *Stirrings in the Jug*, introduction.

43. Maynard Jackson, press release, September 1971, Institute of the Black World Papers, Manuscripts, Archives and Rare Books Division, Schomburg Center for Research in Black Culture, New York Public Library, Astor, Lenox, and Tilden Foundations, box 6, folder 3.

44. Carter quoted in Duane Riner, "Carter Okays Redistricting," *Atlanta Constitution*, 13 September 1971; Maynard Jackson, speech to the Hungry Club of the Butler Street YMCA, 5 April 1972, Institute of the Black World Papers, Manuscripts, Archives and Rare Books Division, Schomburg Center for Research in Black Culture, New York Public Library, Astor, Lenox, and Tilden Foundations, box 6, folder 3.

45. Roger Wilkins, "The National Black Political Convention in Gary—and How It Went about the Job of Achieving 'Unity without Uniformity,'" *Washington Post*, 16 March 1972, reprinted in *IFCO News*, March–April 1972, 11, Institute of the Black World Papers, Manuscripts, Archives and Rare Books Division, Schomburg Center for Research in Black Culture, New York Public Library, Astor, Lenox, and

Tilden Foundations, box 6; platform quoted in Alkalimat et al., *Introduction to Afro-American Studies*, 258; Chisholm quoted in Giddings, *When and Where I Enter*, 337–40. The best account of Chisholm's experiences can be found in her autobiography, *The Good Fight*. For a fuller discussion of the convention and its broader context, see Woodard, *A Nation within a Nation*.

46. Stone, "Black Politics," *Black Scholar*, 8–13.

47. Ibid.; Giddings, *When and Where I Enter*, 339; Jones and Jeffries, " 'Don't Believe the Hype': Debunking the Panther Mythology," Jones, ed., *The Black Panther Party Reconsidered*, 32. An excellent analysis of gender struggles within the party can be found in the same volume: Matthews, " 'No One Ever Asks What a Man's Role in the Revolution Is," 267–304.

48. Chisholm, "Racism and Anti-Feminism," *Black Scholar*, 40.

49. Ethel Mae Mathews, interview by author, 29 April 1996, Atlanta, tape recording.

50. William Strickland to Mack Jones, September 1969, Institute of the Black World Papers, Manuscripts, Archives and Rare Books Division, Schomburg Center for Research in Black Culture, New York Public Library, Astor, Lenox, and Tilden Foundations, box 7, folder 2; Julian Bond to William Strickland, 25 February 1972, Institute of the Black World Papers, Manuscripts, Archives and Rare Books Division, Schomburg Center for Research in Black Culture, New York Public Library, Astor, Lenox, and Tilden Foundations, box 7, folder 2.

51. Election survey, 2 March 1973 (Cambridge, Mass.: Cambridge Survey Research), Institute of the Black World Papers, Manuscripts, Archives and Rare Books Division, Schomburg Center for Research in Black Culture, New York Public Library, Astor, Lenox, and Tilden Foundations, box 7, folder 2.

52. Maynard Jackson, "Candidacy Speech," 28 March 1973, Institute of the Black World Papers, Manuscripts, Archives and Rare Books Division, Schomburg Center for Research in Black Culture, New York Public Library, Astor, Lenox, and Tilden Foundations, box 7, folder 2; Jackson quoted in Sharon Bailey, " 'Bring the City Together,' " *Atlanta Constitution*, 17 October 1973.

53. Vincent Harding to William Strickland, 13 June 1973, Institute of the Black World Papers, Manuscripts, Archives and Rare Books Division, Schomburg Center for Research in Black Culture, New York Public Library, Astor, Lenox, and Tilden Foundations, box 6, folder 2.

54. Ibid.

55. Vincent Harding and William Strickland to Maynard Jackson, 15 June 1973, Institute of the Black World Papers, Manuscripts, Archives and Rare Books Divi-

sion, Schomburg Center for Research in Black Culture, New York Public Library, Astor, Lenox, and Tilden Foundations, box 6, folder 2.

56. R. T. Roland, editorial, "FOP Newsletter," Institute of the Black World Papers, Manuscripts, Archives and Rare Books Division, Schomburg Center for Research in Black Culture, New York Public Library, Astor, Lenox, and Tilden Foundations, box 6, folder 2.

57. Michael E. Fisher to students, 13 August 1973, Institute of the Black World Papers, Manuscripts, Archives and Rare Books Division, Schomburg Center for Research in Black Culture, New York Public Library, Astor, Lenox, and Tilden Foundations, box 6, folder 2.

58. Volunteer quoted in "Maynard Recognizes Women's Rights," *Maynard Jackson Journal*, 1 September 1973, Institute of the Black World Papers, Manuscripts, Archives and Rare Books Division, Schomburg Center for Research in Black Culture, New York Public Library, Astor, Lenox, and Tilden Foundations, box 6, folder 2.

59. Tom Linthicum, "Jackson Leading in Mayor Race; Fowler Sets Pace for President," *Atlanta Constitution*, 3 October 1973; Jackson quoted in Tom Linthicum, "City Elects First Black Mayor; Fowler In as Council President," *Atlanta Constitution*, 17 October 1973. An editorial in the same edition entitled "The New Team" applauded the victory of "the proud black son of a distinguished family."

60. Bob Rohrer, "New Face of Atlanta's Government," *Atlanta Constitution*, 17 October 1973, 12-A; Willie Woods to Institute of the Black World, 15 May 1972, Institute of the Black World Papers, Manuscripts, Archives and Rare Books Division, Schomburg Center for Research in Black Culture, New York Public Library, Astor, Lenox, and Tilden Foundations, box 6, folder 3; GABEO officials quoted in GABEO meeting minutes, 23 March 1974, Macon, Georgia, Institute of the Black World Papers, Manuscripts, Archives and Rare Books Division, Schomburg Center for Research in Black Culture, New York Public Library, Astor, Lenox, and Tilden Foundations, box 6, folder 3.

61. Charles C. Diggs to Vincent Harding, 12 February 1974, Institute of the Black World Papers, Manuscripts, Archives and Rare Books Division, Schomburg Center for Research in Black Culture, New York Public Library, Astor, Lenox, and Tilden Foundations; Dawolu Gene Locke, "A Few Remarks in Response to Criticisms of ALSC . . ." (Lynn Eusan Institute, August 1974), Institute of the Black World Papers, Manuscripts, Archives and Rare Books Division, Schomburg Center for Research in Black Culture, New York Public Library, Astor, Lenox, and Tilden Foundations; Alkalimat et al., *Introduction to Afro-American Studies*, 335.

62. Locke, "A Few Remarks"; Congressional Black Caucus, press release, 17 December 1975, Institute of the Black World Papers, Manuscripts, Archives and Rare Books Division, Schomburg Center for Research in Black Culture, New York Public Library, Astor, Lenox, and Tilden Foundations.

63. Ed McIntyre, draft, "History and Purpose of GABEO, Inc.," no date, Institute of the Black World Papers, Manuscripts, Archives and Rare Books Division, Schomburg Center for Research in Black Culture, New York Public Library, Astor, Lenox, and Tilden Foundations. The group's second president was state representative and former COAHR activist Benjamin Brown.

64. Carl Ware and Delores Brooks, draft resolution, "State of Black People in Georgia," 7 May 1977, Institute of the Black World Papers, Manuscripts, Archives and Rare Books Division, Schomburg Center for Research in Black Culture, New York Public Library.

65. Willie Woods and Howard Dodson, "Final Project Report," IBW to the Committee for the Humanities in Georgia, 19 December 1977, Institute of the Black World Papers, Manuscripts, Archives and Rare Books Division, Schomburg Center for Research in Black Culture, New York Public Library, Astor, Lenox, and Tilden Foundations.

66. Scott quoted in "Black Politics Not Enough, Officials Told," *Atlanta Journal and Constitution*, 20 November 1977.

67. Woods quoted in Lee May, "Black Power in Politics?" *Atlanta Constitution*, 23 November 1977.

68. John A. Brown to IBW, November 1977, Institute of the Black World Papers, Manuscripts, Archives and Rare Books Division, Schomburg Center for Research in Black Culture, New York Public Library, Astor, Lenox, and Tilden Foundations; Concerned Citizens of the Black Community Organization to IBW, November 1977, Institute of the Black World Papers, Manuscripts, Archives and Rare Books Division, Schomburg Center for Research in Black Culture, New York Public Library, Astor, Lenox, and Tilden Foundations; Carl Ware to Howard Dodson, 6 December 1977, Institute of the Black World Papers, Manuscripts, Archives and Rare Books Division, Schomburg Center for Research in Black Culture, New York Public Library, Astor, Lenox, and Tilden Foundations.

69. Darnell quoted in Cathy Yarbrough, "Black Men, Women 'Have to Work Together,'" *Atlanta Constitution*, 8 February 1972. Paula Giddings has asserted that a binary opposition has impinged upon the way Blacks frame the discussion of gender, race, and class. "It is no wonder that the issues of intraracial sexuality and

gender have long been tabooed in public discourse." See Giddings, "The Last Taboo," Morrison, ed., *Race-ing Justice, En-gendering Power*, 442.

70. Fouche and Novel quoted in Colleen Teasley, "Black Male-Female Roles Are Explored," *Atlanta Constitution*, 11 November 1972.

71. Beverly Guy-Sheftall, telephone interview by author, 16 June 2004, tape recording.

72. Sandra Hollin Flowers, telephone interview by author, 19 February 2005, tape recording.

73. Ibid. bell hooks has written several books that treat issues of Black feminist politics and their relationship to self-esteem, including *Rock My Soul* and *Sisters of the Yam*. Historian Darlene Clark Hine has discussed Black women's responses to violence in a white male supremacist society in "Rape and the Inner Lives of Southern Black Women," 177–89.

74. Hamilton and Gaines quoted in Cathy Yarbrough, "Feminist Leaders Note Movement's Progress," *Atlanta Constitution*, 26 August 1973. This article appeared in the society section of the newspaper; Flowers interview.

75. Vincent Harding, interview by author, 7 March 1997, Denver, tape recording; Joyce Ladner, telephone interview by author, 28 May 2004, tape recording.

76. Grant quoted in Tina McElroy, "Panel Looks at 'Plight' of Black Women," *Atlanta Constitution*, 30 January 1976.

77. Bolden quoted in ibid.

78. Jualynne Dodson, interview by author, 5 March 1997, Boulder, tape recording; Beni Ivey, telephone interview by author, 21 May 2004, tape recording; Jan Douglas, telephone interview by author, 23 May 2004, tape recording.

79. Ivey interview; Douglas interview.

80. Douglas interview; Ivey interview. The mobilization model employed by Sojourner South activists brings to mind the detailed organizational framework developed by Lugenia Burns Hope and the activists of the Neighborhood Union in Atlanta during the early 1900s. See Rouse, *Lugenia Burns Hope*. For a discussion of Black women's mobilization within the context of contemporary anti-misogyny activism, see White, "Talking Black, Talking Feminist," in Springer, ed., *Still Lifting, Still Climbing*, 189–218.

81. Dodson interview; Ivey interview; Douglas interview. For a brief but important discussion of Black female antiapartheid activists in a policy-making context, see Culverson, "From Cold War to Global Interdependence," in Plummer, ed., *Window on Freedom*, 226, 237n.

82. Dodson interview; Tillinghast quoted in Bill King, "S. Africa Talks Protested

Here," *Atlanta Constitution*, 24 June 1976; Douglas interview; see also Culverson, "From Cold War to Global Interdependence," 222–24.

83. Douglas interview.

84. Ibid.

85. Jualynne Dodson, program proposal to the National Endowment for the Humanities and Committee for the Humanities in Georgia, fall 1977, Institute of the Black World Papers, Manuscripts, Archives and Rare Books Division, Schomburg Center for Research in Black Culture, New York Public Library, Astor, Lenox, and Tilden Foundations. Dodson was able to rely on an informal network of contacts throughout the city: Juanita Love, coordinator of women's activities at Wheat Street Baptist Church; Gay Cobb, regional director, Women's Bureau; Penny Gibson, producer, television station WXIA; Gloria Walker, chair of communications, Clark College; and Barbara Whitaker, director of student-community affairs, Atlanta Public Schools.

86. Program, "Black Women, Black Freedom Struggle: Past, Present, Future," Institute of the Black World Papers, Manuscripts, Archives and Rare Books Division, Schomburg Center for Research in Black Culture, New York Public Library, Astor, Lenox, and Tilden Foundations; IBW press release, "Role Alternatives for Black Women: Where To from Here?" December 1977, Institute of the Black World Papers, Manuscripts, Archives and Rare Books Division, Schomburg Center for Research in Black Culture, New York Public Library; "Key Women Participate in Workshop at JFK," *Atlanta Daily World*, 15 December 1977. The *Daily World* provided only general coverage of the conference, offering no in-depth reporting or analysis.

87. Douglas interview.

88. Guy-Sheftall interview. Beverly Guy-Sheftall noted, "it was the first interview I had ever done. If you read that interview, it was clear in retrospect that I already knew that I was a feminist." See Guy-Sheftall, "Commitment: Toni Cade Bambara Speaks," Bell et al., eds., *Sturdy Black Bridges*, 230–50.

89. Cade, "On the Issue of Roles," Cade, ed., *The Black Woman*, 103; Cade quoted at conference in IBW press release, "Role Alternatives for Black Women."

90. Program, "Black Women, Black Freedom Struggle"; Richmond quoted in press release, "Role Alternatives for Black Women."

91. Richmond quoted in ibid.

92. Program, "Black Women, Black Freedom Struggle"; Dodson quoted in press release, "Role Alternatives for Black Women."

EPILOGUE

1. The murders took place within a context of growing disaffection for Mayor May-nard Jackson among working-class and poor Blacks. In a telling about-face from his principled support for municipal workers during the protracted 1970 strike, for instance, the mayor stood in opposition to the American Federation of State, County, and Municipal Employees. Jackson deftly worked to undercut support for a second strike by arguing that the White leadership of AFSCME was out to destroy his administration. These maneuvers garnered the administration support from business leaders, but served to frustrate a growing number of Blacks. Adolph Reed has provided an important critique of the Jackson administration in *Stirrings in the Jug*, esp. 5 and 177. Camille Bell quoted in Headley, *The Atlanta Youth Murders and the Politics of Race*, 56. Headley's study is the most comprehensive scholarly discussion of the tragedy.

2. Baldwin, *The Evidence of Things Not Seen*, 98. Baldwin did note that "anything is possible, and the man may be guilty, but I smell a rat; and it is impossible to claim that his guilt has been proven, any more than it can be proven that the murders have ceased." Bernard Headley said of Baldwin's essay that it "turned out to be not much more than a far-flung, disassociated polemic." See Headley, *Atlanta Youth Murders*, prologue.

3. Wallace quoted in "Going Home," *60 Minutes*, 27 October 2002, CBS News.

4. Burrell quoted in ibid.

5. White, "The Black Sides of Atlanta," *Atlanta Historical Journal*, 199.

6. Hornsby quoted in Winston Grady-Willis, "Hajj Womack: Atlanta's Political Pris-oner?" *City Sun*, 16–23 October 1996, 7.

7. Womack and Hornsby quoted in Greg Land, "5 Percent Solution: Accused More-house Graduate Hajj Womack Tells His Side," *Creative Loafing*, 19 April 1996, 1 and 25.

8. Justin Bachman, "Who Is Al-Amin? From Radical H. Rap Brown to Religious Leader to Murder Charge," *Detroit News*, 24 May 2000; Al-Amin statement quoted in International Committee to Support Imam Jamil Abdullah Al-Amin Web site, http://www.geocities.com/icsijaa/index.htm

9. Columbus Ward, interview by author, 21 January 1997, Atlanta, tape recording.

10. Mathews quoted in author's notes, 12 February 1998, Atlanta.

11. Ethel Mae Mathews, interview by author, 29 April 1996, Atlanta, tape recording.

12. Ibid.

BIBLIOGRAPHY

INTERVIEWS BY AUTHOR

Benjamin A. Brown, 15 December 1997, Atlanta, audiotape.

Joseph E. Boone, 13 August 1997, Atlanta, audiotape.

Herschelle Challenor (Herschelle Sullivan), telephone interview, 25 May 2004, audiotape.

Beverly Guy-Sheftall, telephone interview, 16 June 2004, audiotape.

Mukasa Dada (Willie Ricks), 3 November 1997, Atlanta, audiotape.

Jualynne Dodson, 5 March 1997, Boulder, audiotape.

Jan Douglas, telephone interview, 23 May 2004, audiotape.

Gene Ferguson, 15 August 1997, Atlanta, audiotape.

Sandra Hollin Flowers, telephone interview, 19 February 2005, audiotape.

Larry Fox, telephone interview, 20 March 2004, audiotape.

Vincent Harding, 7 March 1997, Denver, audiotape.

Beni Ivey, telephone interview, 21 May 2004, audiotape.

Lonnie King, telephone interview, 29 May 2004, audiotape.

Joyce Ladner, telephone interview, 23 May 2004, audiotape.

Emma Jean Martin, 26 March 1998, Atlanta, audiotape.

Ethel Mae Mathews, 29 April 1996 and 10 February 1998, Atlanta, audiotape.

Silas Norman, telephone interview, 22 July 2004, audiotape.

Fay Bellamy Powell, 31 March 1998, Atlanta, audiotape.

Gwendolyn Zoharah Simmons (Gwendolyn Robinson), telephone interview, 30 July 2004, audiotape.

Michael Simmons, 19 April 1998, Philadelphia, audiotape.

William Strickland, telephone interview, 20 June 2004, audiotape.

Columbus Ward, 21 January 1997, Atlanta, audiotape.

MANUSCRIPT SOURCES

Atlanta, Georgia

    Auburn Avenue Research Library on African-American Culture & History

        FBI File on Student Nonviolent Coordinating Committee

    Martin Luther King Center for Nonviolent Social Change

        Black Panther Black Community News Service

Black Power Movement Files

Student Nonviolent Coordinating Committee Papers

Atlanta University Center, Robert W. Woodruff Library

Institute of the Black World Files

SNCC Vertical File

Emory University, Robert W. Woodruff Library

Black Student Movement Files

Sanford S. Atwood Papers

Madison, Wisconsin

State Historical Society of Wisconsin

SNCC–Vine City Project Papers

George A. Wiley Papers

New York, New York

Schomburg Center for Research in Black Culture

Black Power Movement Kaiser Files

Institute of the Black World Papers

NEWSPAPERS, MAGAZINES, ORGANS, AND OFFICIAL JOURNALS

Atlanta Constitution

Atlanta Daily World

Atlanta Inquirer

Atlanta Journal

Atlanta Voice

Black America

Black Panther

Charlotte Observer

Chicago Defender

City Sun

Creative Loafing

Crisis

Crusader

Ebony

Emerge

Emory Magazine

Emory Wheel

Fire This Time

Harper's

Macon Telegraph

Militant

New South

New York Times

New York Times Magazine

Nitty Gritty

Providence Journal

Renewal

SCLC Newsletter

Student Voice

Washington Post

Welfare Fighter

ARTICLES, BOOKS, PAMPHLETS, AND PUBLISHED PROCEEDINGS

Alkalimat, Abdul, and others. *Introduction to Afro-American Studies: A Peoples College Primer*, 6th ed. Chicago: Twenty-First Century Books and Publications, 1986.

Allen, Ivan, in collaboration with Paul Hemphill. *Mayor: Notes on the Sixties.* New York: Simon and Schuster, 1971.

Allen, Robert L. *Black Awakening in Capitalist America: An Analytical History.* Garden City, N.Y.: Anchor, 1969.

Anderson, Carol. *Eyes off the Prize: The United Nations and the African American Struggle for Human Rights, 1944–1955.* Cambridge: Cambridge University Press, 2003.

Anderson-Bricker, Kristin. " 'Triple Jeopardy': Black Women and the Growth of Feminist Consciousness in SNCC, 1964–1975." *Still Lifting, Still Climbing: African American Women's Contemporary Activism*, ed. Kimberly Springer, 49–69. New York: New York University Press, 1999.

Atlanta Committee for Cooperative Action. *A Second Look: The Negro Citizen in Atlanta.* Atlanta: Allied Printing, 1960.

Bacote, C. A. "The Negro in Atlanta Politics." *Phylon* 16 (1955): 333–50.

Baldwin, James. *The Evidence of Things Not Seen.* New York: Henry Holt, 1985.

Bayor, Ronald H. "Roads to Racial Segregation: Atlanta in the Twentieth Century." *Journal of Urban History* 15 (November 1988): 3–21.

Biko, Steve. *I Write What I Like: A Selection of His Writings*, ed. with a personal memoir by C. R. Aelred Stubbs. London: Bowerdean, 1996.

Biondi, Martha. *To Stand and Fight: The Struggle for Civil Rights in Postwar New York City.* Cambridge: Harvard University Press, 2003.

Black, Earl, and Merle Black. *Politics and Society in the South.* Cambridge: Harvard University Press, 1987.

Blair, Thomas L. *Retreat to the Ghetto: The End of a Dream?* New York: Hill and Wang, 1977.

Blauner, Bob. *Black Lives, White Lives: Three Decades of Race Relations in America.* Berkeley: University of California Press, 1989.

Bloom, Jack M. *Class, Race and the Civil Rights Movement.* Bloomington: Indiana University Press, 1987.

Blumberg, Rhoda Lois. *Civil Rights, the 1960s Freedom Struggle.* Boston: Twayne, 1991.

Boggs, James. *The American Revolution: Pages from a Negro Worker's Notebook.* New York: Monthly Review, 1963.

——. *Racism and the Class Struggle: Further Pages from a Black Worker's Notebook.* New York: Monthly Review, 1970.

Borstelmann, Thomas. *Apartheid's Reluctant Uncle: The United States and Southern Africa in the Early Cold War.* New York: Oxford University Press, 1993.

Bozzoli, Belinda. *Women of Phokeng: Consciousness, Life Strategy, and Migrancy in South Africa, 1900–1983.* Portsmouth: Heinemann Educational, 1991.

Bracey, John H., Jr., August Meier, and Elliott Rudwick. *Black Nationalism in America.* Indianapolis: Bobbs-Merrill, 1970.

Branch, Taylor. *Parting the Waters: America in the King Years, 1954–63.* New York: Simon and Schuster, 1988.

——. *Pillar of Fire: America in the King Years, 1963–1965.* New York: Simon and Schuster, 1998.

Breitman, George, ed. *Malcolm X Speaks.* New York: Grove, 1966.

Brisbane, Robert H. *Black Activism.* Valley Forge: Judson, 1974.

Brown, Elaine. *A Taste of Power: A Black Woman's Story.* New York: Anchor, 1994.

Brown, Scot. *Fighting for US: Maulana Karenga, the US Organization, and Black Cultural Nationalism.* New York: New York University Press, 2003.

Burman, Stephen. "The Illusion of Progress: Race and Politics in Atlanta, Georgia." *Ethnic and Racial Studies* 2, 4 (October 1979): 441–54.

Burner, Eric. *And Gently He Shall Lead Them: Robert Parris Moses and Civil Rights in Mississippi.* New York: New York University Press, 1994.

Bush, Rod. *We Are Not What We Seem: Black Nationalism and Class Struggle in the American Century.* New York: New York University Press, 1999.

Button, James W. *Blacks and Social Change: Impact of the Civil Rights Movement in Southern Communities.* Princeton: Princeton University Press, 1989.

Cade, Toni, ed. *The Black Woman.* New York: Mentor, 1970.

Campbell, Horace. *Rasta and Resistance: From Marcus Garvey to Walter Rodney.* Dar es Salaam: Tanzania Publishing, 1985.

——. *Reclaiming Zimbabwe: The Exhaustion of the Patriarchal Model of Liberation.* Trenton: Africa World, 2003.

Carmichael, Stokely, and Charles V. Hamilton. *Black Power: The Politics of Liberation in America.* New York: Vintage, 1967.

Carmichael, Stokely, with Ekwueme Michael Thelwell. *Ready for Revolution: The Life and Struggles of Stokely Carmichael (Kwame Ture).* New York: Scribner, 2003.

Carson, Clayborne. *In Struggle: SNCC and the Black Awakening of the 1960s.* Cambridge: Harvard University Press, 1981.

Carter, Dan T. "From Segregation to Integration." *Interpreting Southern History: Historiographical Essays in Honor of Sanford W. Higginbotham,* ed. John B. Boles and Evelyn Thomas Nolen, 408–33. Baton Rouge: Louisiana State University Press, 1987.

——. *Scottsboro: A Tragedy of the American South.* Baton Rouge: Louisiana State University Press, 1979.

Carty, Linda, ed. *And Still We Rise: Feminist Political Mobilization in Contemporary Canada.* Toronto: Women's Press, 1993.

Central Issues Influencing Community-School Relations in Atlanta, Georgia. Washington: National Education Association Commission on Professional Rights and Responsibilities, 1969.

Chafe, William H. *Civilities and Civil Rights: Greensboro, North Carolina, and the Black Struggle for Freedom.* New York: Oxford University Press, 1980.

Chisholm, Shirley. "Racism and Anti-Feminism." *Black Scholar,* January–February 1970.

——. *The Good Fight.* New York: Bantam, 1974.

Churchill, Ward, and Jim Vander Wall. *Agents of Repression: The FBI's Secret Wars Against the Black Panther Party and the American Indian Movement.* Boston: South End, 1988.

Clark, Steve, ed. *February 1965: The Final Speeches: Malcolm X.* New York: Pathfinder, 1992.

Clarke, John Henrik, ed., assisted by A. Peter Bailey and Earl Grant. *Malcolm X: The Man and His Times.* New York: Macmillan, 1969.

Cleaver, Kathleen, and George Katsiaficas. *Liberation, Imagination, and the Black Panther Party: A New Look at the Panthers and Their Legacy.* New York: Routledge, 2001.

Cmiel, Kenneth. "The Emergence of Human Rights Politics in the United States." *Journal of American History* 86, 3 (December 1999): 1231–50.

Cock, Jacklyn. *Maids and Madams: A Study in the Politics of Exploitation.* Johannesburg: Ravan, 1980.

Cole, Johnnetta, and Beverly Guy-Sheftall, eds. *Gender Talk: The Struggle for Women's Equality in African American Communities.* New York: One World, 2003.

Collier-Thomas, Bettye. *Daughters of Thunder: Black Women Preachers and Their Sermons, 1850–1979.* San Francisco: Jossey-Bass, 1998.

Collier-Thomas, Bettye, and V. P. Franklin. *Sisters in the Struggle: African American Women in the Civil Rights–Black Power Movement.* New York: New York University Press, 2001.

Cone, James H. *Martin and Malcolm and America: A Dream or a Nightmare.* Maryknoll, N.Y.: Orbis, 1991.

Crawford, Vicki L., et al., eds. *Women in the Civil Rights Movement: Trailblazers and Torchbearers, 1941–1965.* Brooklyn: Carlson, 1990.

Creel, Margaret Washington. *A Peculiar People: Slave Religion and Community Culture among the Gullahs.* New York: New York University Press, 1988.

Crimmins, Timothy J. "The Atlanta Palimpsest: Stripping Away the Layers of the Past, 1870–1970." *Atlanta Historical Journal* 26, 2–3 (summer–fall 1982): 13–32.

Cruse, Harold. *The Crisis of the Negro Intellectual.* New York: Quill, 1967.

Cummins, Eric. *The Rise and Fall of California's Radical Prison Movement*. Stanford: Stanford University Press, 1994.

Davies, Carol Boyce. *Black Women, Writing, and Identity: Migrations of the Subject*. London: Routledge, 1994.

——, ed., with Meredith Gadsby, Charles Peterson, and Henrietta Williams. *Decolonizing the Academy: African Diaspora Studies*. Trenton: Africa World, 2003.

Davis, Angela Y. *Angela Davis: An Autobiography*. New York: Random House, 1974.

——. *Blues Legacies and Black Feminism: Gertrude "Ma" Rainey, Bessie Smith, and Billie Holiday*. New York: Pantheon, 1998.

——. *If They Come in the Morning: Voices of Resistance*. New York: Third Press, 1974.

——. "Meditations on the Legacy of Malcolm X." *Malcolm X: In Our Own Image*, ed. Joe Wood, 36–47. New York: St. Martins, 1992.

——. *Women, Race, and Class*. New York: Vintage, 1981.

Davis, Leroy. *A Clashing of the Soul: John Hope and the Dilemma of African American Leadership and Black Higher Education in the Early Twentieth Century*. Athens: University of Georgia Press, 1998.

Dittmer, John. *Black Georgia in the Progressive Era, 1900–1920*. Urbana: University of Illinois Press, 1977.

——. *Local People: The Struggle for Civil Rights in Mississippi*. Urbana: University of Illinois Press, 1994.

Du Bois, W. E. B., with introductions by Nathan Hare and Alvin F. Poussaint. *The Souls of Black Folk*. Chicago: A. C. McClurg, 1903. Reprint, New York: New American Library, 1982.

Eisinger, Peter K. *The Politics of Displacement: Racial and Ethnic Transition in Three American Cities*. New York: Academic, 1980.

Ellis, Ann Wells. " 'Uncle Sam Is My Shepherd': The Commission on Interracial Cooperation and the New Deal in Georgia." *Atlanta Historical Journal* 30 (spring 1986): 47–63.

English, James W. *Handyman of the Lord: The Life and Ministry of the Rev. William Holmes Borders*. New York: Meredith, 1967.

Essien-Udom, E. U. *Black Nationalism: A Search for an Identity in America*. Chicago: University of Chicago Press, 1962.

Evans, Sarah. *Personal Politics: The Roots of Women's Liberation in the Civil Rights Movement and the New Left*. New York: Alfred A. Knopf, 1979.

Fanon, Frantz. *The Wretched of the Earth*. New York: Macmillan, 1972.

Findlay, James F., Jr. *Church People in the Struggle: The National Council of Churches and the Black Freedom Movement, 1950–1970*. New York: Oxford University Press, 1993.

Fleming, Cynthia Griggs. *Soon We Will Not Cry: The Liberation of Ruby Doris Smith Robinson*. Lanham, Md.: Rowman and Littlefield, 1998.

Fleming, Douglas L. "The New Deal in Atlanta: A Review of the Major Programs." *Atlanta Historical Journal* 30 (spring 1986): 23–45.

Forman, James. *The Making of Black Revolutionaries*. New York: Macmillan, 1972. Reprint, Washington: Open Hand, 1985.

Fort, Vincent. "The Atlanta Student Sit-In Movement, 1960–61: An Oral Study." *Atlanta, Georgia, 1960–1961*, ed. David J. Garrow, 119–76. Brooklyn: Carlson, 1988.

Fredrickson, George M. *White Supremacy: A Comparative Study in American and South African History*. New York: Oxford University Press, 1981.

Gallen, David, ed., with an introduction by Spike Lee and commentary by Clayborne Carson. *Malcolm X: The FBI File*. New York: Carroll and Graf, 1991.

Garrow, David J., ed. *Atlanta, Georgia, 1960–1961*. Brooklyn: Carlson, 1988.

——. *Bearing the Cross: Martin Luther King, Jr. and the Southern Christian Leadership Conference*. New York: William Morrow, 1986.

——. *The FBI and Martin Luther King, Jr.: From "Solo" to Memphis*. New York: W. W. Norton, 1981.

——, ed. *The Montgomery Bus Boycott and the Women Who Started It: The Memoir of Jo Ann Gibson Robinson*. Knoxville: University of Tennessee Press, 1987.

Gatewood, Willard B. *Aristocrats of Color: The Black Elite, 1880–1920*. Bloomington: Indiana University Press, 1990.

Geschwender, James A., ed. *The Black Revolt: The Civil Rights Movement, Ghetto Uprisings, and Separatism*. Englewood-Cliffs, N.J.: Prentice-Hall, 1971.

——. *Class, Race, and Worker Insurgency*. New York: Oxford University Press, 1977.

Giddings, Paula. *When and Where I Enter: The Impact of Black Women on Race and Sex in America*. New York: William Morrow, 1984.

Grady-Willis, Winston A. "The Black Panther Party: State Repression and Political Prisoners." *The Black Panther Party Reconsidered*, ed. Charles E. Jones, 363–89. Baltimore: Black Classic, 1998.

Guy-Sheftall, Beverly. "Commitment: Toni Cade Bambara Speaks." *Sturdy Black Bridges: Visions of Black Women in Literature*, ed. Roseann P. Bell et al., 230–50. Garden City: Anchor, 1979.

——. *Daughters of Sorrow: Attitudes toward Black Women, 1880–1920*. Brooklyn: Carlson, 1990.

——, ed., with an epilogue by Johnnetta B. Cole. *Words of Fire: An Anthology of African American Feminist Thought*. New York: New Press, 1995.

Haines, Herbert H. *Black Radicals and The Civil Rights Mainstream, 1954–1970.* Knoxville: University of Tennessee Press, 1988.

Harding, Vincent. *Hope and History: Why We Must Share the Story of the Movement.* Maryknoll, N.Y.: Orbis, 1990.

——. *Martin Luther King: Inconvenient Hero.* Maryknoll, N.Y.: Orbis, 1996.

Harmon, David Andrew. *Beneath the Image of the Civil Rights Movement and Race Relations: Atlanta, Georgia, 1946–1981.* New York: Garland, 1996.

Harris, Robert L., Jr. "Coming of Age: The Transformation of Afro-American Historiography." *Journal of Negro History* 67, 2 (summer 1982): 107–21.

—— "The Flowering of Afro-American History." *American Historical Review* 92, 5 (1985): 1150–61.

Harris, William H. *The Harder We Run: Black Workers Since the Civil War.* New York: Oxford University Press, 1982.

Haywood, Harry. *Black Bolshevik: Autobiography of an Afro-American Communist.* Chicago: Liberator, 1978.

Headly, Bernard. *The Atlanta Youth Murders and the Politics of Race.* Carbondale: Southern Illinois University Press, 1998.

Hein, Virginia H. "The Image of 'A City Too Busy to Hate': Atlanta in the 1960's." *Phylon* 33, 3 (1972): 205–21.

Hill, Lance. *The Deacons for Defense: Armed Resistance and the Civil Rights Movement.* Chapel Hill: University of North Carolina Press, 2004.

Hilliard, David, and Lewis Cole. *This Side of Glory: The Autobiography of David Hilliard and the Story of the Black Panther Party.* Chicago: Chicago Review, 1991.

Hine, Darlene Clark. *Black Victory: The Rise and Fall of the White Primary in Texas.* New York: Kraus-Thornson Organization, 1979.

——. "Rape and the Inner Lives of Southern Black Women: Thoughts on the Culture of Dissemblance." *Southern Women: Histories and Identities,* ed. Virgina Bernhard et al., 177–89. Columbia: University of Missouri Press, 1992.

Hine, Darlene Clark, Wilma King, and Linda Reed, eds. *"We Specialize in the Wholly Impossible": A Reader in Black Women's History.* Brooklyn: Carlson, 1995.

Hirsch, Arnold R. *Making the Second Ghetto: Race and Housing in Chicago, 1940–1960.* Cambridge: Cambridge University Press, 1983.

Holt, Len. *The Summer That Didn't End: The Story of the Mississippi Civil Rights Project of 1964.* New York: Da Capo, 1992.

hooks, bell. *Rock My Soul: Black People and Self-Esteem.* New York: Atria, 2003.

——. *Sisters of the Yam: Black Women and Self-Recovery.* Boston: South End, 1993.

——. *Talking Back: Thinking Feminist, Thinking Black.* Boston: South End, 1989.

Horne, Gerald. *Black and Red: W. E. B. Du Bois and the Afro-American Response to the Cold War, 1944–1964*. Albany: State University of New York, 1986.

Hornsby, Alton, Jr. "A City That Was Too Busy to Hate." *Southern Businessmen and Desegregation*, ed. Elizabeth Jacoway and David R. Colburn. Baton Rouge: Louisiana State University Press, 1982.

——. "The Negro in Atlanta Politics, 1961–1973." *Atlanta Historical Bulletin* 21 (1977): 7–33.

Hull, Gloria T., Patricia Bell Scott, and Barbara Smith, eds. *All the Women Are White, All the Blacks Are Men, but Some of Us Are Brave: Black Women's Studies*. New York: Feminist Press, 1982.

Jackson, George. *Blood in My Eye*. New York: Random House, 1972.

——. *Soledad Brother: The Prison Letters of George Jackson*. New York: Coward, McCann, 1970.

Jackson, Larry P. "Welfare Mothers and Black Liberation." *Black Scholar*, April 1970.

James, Joy, ed. *Imprisoned Intellectuals: America's Political Prisoners Write on Life, Liberation, and Rebellion*. Lanham, Md.: Rowman and Littlefield, 2003.

——. *Resisting State Violence: Radicalism, Gender, and Race in U.S. Culture*. Minneapolis: University of Minnesota Press, 1996.

Jones, Charles E., ed. *The Black Panther Party Reconsidered*. Baltimore: Black Classic, 1998.

Jones, Mack H. "Black Political Empowerment in Atlanta: Myth and Reality." *Annals of the American Academy of Political and Social Science* 439 (September 1978): 90–117.

Joseph, Peniel E. "Black Liberation without Apology: Reconceptualizing the Black Power Movement." *Black Scholar* 31, nos. 3–4 (fall–winter 2001): 3–20.

Kaplan, Marshall, et al. *The Model Cities Program: The Planning Process in Atlanta, Seattle, and Dayton*. New York: Praeger, 1970.

Kelley, Robin D. G. *Freedom Dreams: The Black Radical Imagination*. Boston: Beacon, 2002.

——. *Hammer and Hoe: Alabama Communists during the Great Depression*. Chapel Hill: University of North Carolina Press, 1990.

——. *Race Rebels: Culture, Politics, and the Black Working Class*. New York: Free Press, 1994.

Kerber, Linda K. "Separate Spheres, Female Worlds, Woman's Place: The Rhetoric of Women's History." *Journal of American History* 75, 1 (June 1988): 9–39.

King, Coretta Scott. *My Life with Martin Luther King, Jr.* New York: Holt, Rinehart and Winston, 1969.

King, Martin Luther, Jr. *Where Do We Go from Here: Chaos or Community?* New York: Harper and Row, 1967.

King, Richard H. *Civil Rights and the Idea of Freedom*. New York: Oxford University Press, 1992.

Kornbluh, Felicia. "Black Buying Power: Welfare Rights, Consumerism and Northern Protest." *Freedom North: Black Freedom Struggles outside the South*, ed. Jeanne Theoharis and Komozi Woodard, 199–222. New York: Palgrave Macmillan, 2003.

Kotz, Nick, and Mary Lynn Kotz. *A Passion for Equality: George A. Wiley and the Movement*. New York: W. W. Norton, 1977.

Kuhn, Clifford M., Harlon E. Joye, and E. Bernard West, with a foreword by Michael L. Lomax. *Living Atlanta: An Oral History of the City, 1914–1948*. Athens: University of Georgia Press, 1990.

Kytle, Elizabeth. *Willie Mae*. McLean, Va.: EPM, 1958.

Ladner, Joyce A. *The Death of White Sociology*. New York: Random House, 1973.

——. *The Ties That Bind: Timeless Values for African American Families*. New York: J. Wiley, 1998.

Lapping, Brian. *Apartheid: A History*. New York: George Braziller, 1989.

Lasch-Quinn, Elisabeth. *Race Experts: How Racial Etiquette, Sensitivity Training, and New Age Therapy Hijacked the Civil Rights Revolution*. New York: W. W. Norton, 2001.

Lawson, Steven F. "Freedom Then, Freedom Now: The Historiography of the Civil Rights Movement." *American Historical Review* 96, 2 (April 1991): 456–71.

——. *Running for Freedom: Civil Rights and Black Politics in America since 1941*. Philadelphia: Temple University Press, 1991.

Layton, Azza Salama. *International Politics and Civil Rights Policies in the United States, 1941–1960*. Cambridge: Cambridge University Press, 2000.

Lee, Chana Kai. *For Freedom's Sake: The Life of Fannie Lou Hamer*. Urbana: University of Illinois Press, 1999.

Lefever, Harry G. *Undaunted by the Fight: Spelman College and the Civil Rights Movement, 1957–1967*. Macon, Ga.: Mercer University Press, 2005.

Lessons from the Damned: Class Struggle in the Black Community. Washington, N.J.: Times Change, 1973.

Lewis, David Levering. *W. E. B. Du Bois: Biography of a Race, 1868–1919*. New York: Henry Holt, 1993.

Lewis, John. *Walking with the Wind: A Memoir of the Movement*. New York: Simon and Schuster, 1998.

Lincoln, C. Eric. *The Black Muslims in America*. Boston: Beacon, 1961.

Lindemann, Albert S. *The Jew Accused: Three Anti-Semitic Affairs (Dreyfus, Beilis, Frank), 1894–1915*. Cambridge: Cambridge University Press, 1991.

Lipsitz, George. *A Life in the Struggle: Ivory Perry and the Culture of Opposition.* Philadelphia: Temple University Press, 1988.

Luce, Philip Abbott. *Road to Revolution: Communist Guerrilla Warfare in the U.S.A.* San Diego: Viewpoint, 1967.

Malcolm X, with the assistance of Alex Haley. *The Autobiography of Malcolm X.* New York: Random House, 1965.

Mandela, Nelson. *Long Walk to Freedom: The Autobiography of Nelson Mandela.* Boston: Little, Brown, 1994.

Mandela, Winnie. *Part of My Soul Went with Him.* Ed. Anne Benjamin and adapted by May Benson. New York: W. W. Norton, 1984.

Martin, Charles H. *The Angelo Herndon Case and Southern Justice.* Baton Rouge: Louisiana State University Press, 1976.

Martin, Tony. *Race First: The Ideological and Organizational Struggles of Marcus Garvey and the Universal Negro Improvement Association.* Dover: Majority Press, 1976.

Massey, Douglas S., and Nancy A. Denton. *American Apartheid: Segregation and the Making of the Underclass.* Cambridge: Harvard University Press, 1993.

Matthews, Tracye. " 'No One Ever Asks What a Man's Role in the Revolution Is': Gender and the Politics of the Black Panther Party, 1966–1971." *The Black Panther Party Reconsidered,* ed. Charles E. Jones, 267–304. Baltimore: Black Classic, 1998.

Meier, August, and Elliot Rudwick. *Black History and the Historical Profession, 1915–1980.* Urbana: University of Illinois Press, 1986.

——. *CORE: A Study in the Civil Rights Movement, 1942–1968.* Urbana: University of Illinois Press, 1975.

——. "Negro Protest Movements and Organizations." *Journal of Negro Education: The Relative Progress of the American Negro since 1950,* fall 1963, 437–43.

Mills, Kay. *This Little Light of Mine: The Life of Fannie Lou Hamer.* New York: Dutton, 1993.

Moody, Anne. *Coming of Age in Mississippi.* New York: Dell, 1968.

Moraga, Cherríe, and Gloria Anzaldua, eds., with a foreword by Toni Cade Bambara. *This Bridge Called My Back: Writings by Radical Women of Color.* New York: Kitchen Table, Women of Color, 1983.

Morris, Aldon D. *The Origins of the Civil Rights Movement: Black Communities Organizing for Change.* New York: Free Press, 1984.

Morrison, Toni, ed. *Race-ing Justice, En-gendering Power: Essays on Anita Hill, Clarence Thomas, and the Construction of Social Reality.* New York: Pantheon, 1992.

Moynihan, Daniel Patrick. *The Negro Family: The Case for National Action.* Washington: U.S. Department of Labor, Office of Policy Planning and Research, 1965.

Mugo, Micere Githae. *African Orature and Human Rights*. Roma, Lesotho: National University of Lesotho, Institute of Southern African Studies, 1991.

Muhammad, Elijah. *Message to the Blackman in America*. Chicago: Muhammad's Temple Number Two, 1965.

Newsom, Lionel, and William Gorden. "A Stormy Rally in Atlanta." *Atlanta, Georgia, 1960–1961*, ed. David J. Garrow, 106–8. Brooklyn: Carlson, 1988.

Newton, Huey P. *To Die for the People*. New York: Vintage, 1972.

——. *Revolutionary Suicide*. New York: Harcourt Brace and Jovanovich, 1973.

Norrell, Robert J. *Reaping the Whirlwind: The Civil Rights Movement in Tuskegee*. New York: Vintage, 1985.

O'Reilly, Kenneth. *Black Americans: The FBI Files*, ed. David Gallen. New York: Carroll and Graf, 1994.

——. *"Racial Matters": The FBI's Secret File on Black America, 1960–1972*. New York: Free Press, 1989.

Patterson, William L. *The Man Who Cried Genocide: An Autobiography*. New York: International Publishers, 1971.

Payne, Charles M. *I've Got the Light of Freedom: The Organizing Tradition and the Mississippi Freedom Struggle*. Berkeley: University of California Press, 1995.

Perry, Bruce, ed. *Malcolm X: The Last Speeches*. New York: Pathfinder, 1989.

Plummer, Brenda Gayle. *Rising Wind: Black Americans and U.S. Foreign Affairs, 1935–1960*. Chapel Hill: University of North Carolina Press, 1996.

——, ed. *Window on Freedom: Race, Civil Rights, and Foreign Affairs, 1945–1988*. Chapel Hill: University of North Carolina Press, 2003.

Preston, Howard L. *Automobile Age Atlanta: The Making of a Southern Metropolis, 1900–1935*. Athens: University of Georgia Press, 1979.

Ransby, Barbara. *Ella Baker and the Black Freedom Movement: A Radical Democratic Vision*. Chapel Hill: University of North Carolina Press, 2003.

Reed, Adolph, Jr. *Stirrings in the Jug: Black Politics in the Post-Segregation Era*. Minneapolis: University of Minnesota Press, 1999.

Reed, Linda. "Fannie Lou Hamer: New Ideas for the Civil Rights Movement and American Democracy." *The Role of Ideas in the Civil Rights-Era South*, ed. Ted Ownby. Jackson: University Press of Mississippi, 2002.

Reid, Inez Smith. *"Together" Black Women*. New York: Third Press, 1972.

Report of the National Advisory Commission On Civil Disorders. New York: E. P. Dutton, 1968.

Robinson, Armstead L., and Patricia Sullivan, eds. *New Directions in Civil Rights Studies*. Charlottesville: University Press of Virginia, 1991.

Robinson, Cedric J. *Black Marxism: The Making of the Black Radical Tradition*. London: Zed, 1983.

Rouse, Jacqueline Anne. *Lugenia Burns Hope: Black Southern Reformer*. Athens: University of Georgia Press, 1989.

Rudwick, Elliott M. "W. E. B. Du Bois and the Atlanta University Studies on the Negro." *Journal of Negro Education* 26 (1957): 466–76.

Sales, William W., Jr. *From Civil Rights To Black Liberation: Malcolm X and the Organization of Afro-American Unity*. Boston: South End, 1994.

Seale, Bobby. *Seize the Time: The Story of the Black Panther Party and Huey P. Newton*. New York: Vintage, 1970.

Self, Robert O. *American Babylon: Race and the Struggle for Postwar Oakland*. Princeton: Princeton University Press, 2003.

Sellers, Cleveland, with the collaboration of Robert Terrell. *The River of No Return: The Autobiography of a Black Militant and the Life and Death of* SNCC. Jackson: University Press of Mississippi, 1990.

Sernett, Milton C. *Bound for the Promised Land: African American Religion and the Great Migration*. Durham: Duke University Press, 1997.

Shakur, Assata. *Assata: An Autobiography*. Westport: Lawrence Hill, 1987.

Sitkoff, Harvard. *A New Deal for Blacks: The Emergence of Civil Rights as a National Issue*. New York: Oxford University Press, 1978.

Singh, Nikhil Pal. *Black Is a Country: Race and the Unfinished Struggle for Democracy*. Cambridge: Harvard University Press, 2004.

Smith, Barbara, ed. *Home Girls: A Black Feminist Anthology*. New York: Kitchen Table, Women of Color, 1983.

Solomon, Irvin D. *Feminism and Black Activism in Contemporary America: An Ideological Assessment*. New York: Greenwood, 1989.

Springer, Kimberly, ed. *Still Lifting, Still Climbing: African American Women's Contemporary Activism*. New York: New York University Press, 1999.

Spritzer, Lorraine, and Jean B. Bergmark. *Grace Towns Hamilton and the Politics of Southern Change*. Athens: University of Georgia Press, 1997.

Stone, Chuck. "Black Politics: Third Force, Third Party or Third-Class Influence?" *Black Scholar* 1, 2 (December 1969): 8–13.

Stone, Clarence N. *Economic Growth and Neighborhood Discontent: System Bias in the Urban Renewal Program of Atlanta*. Chapel Hill: University of North Carolina Press, 1976.

——. *Regime Politics: Governing Atlanta, 1946–1988*. Lawrence: University Press of Kansas, 1989.

Stoper, Emily. *The Student Nonviolent Coordinating Committee: The Growth of Radicalism in a Civil Rights Organization.* Brooklyn: Carlson, 1989.

Tait, Vanessa. " 'Workers Just Like Anyone Else': Organizing Workfare Unions in New York City." *Still Lifting, Still Climbing: African American Women's Contemporary Activism,* ed. Kimberly Springer. New York: New York University Press, 1999.

Theoharis, Jeanne, and Komozi Woodard, eds. *Freedom North: Black Freedom Struggles Outside the South.* New York: Palgrave Macmillan, 2003.

Thompson, Leonard. *A History of South Africa.* New Haven: Yale University Press, 1990.

Trotter, Joe William, Jr. *Black Milwaukee: The Making of an Industrial Proletariat, 1915–45.* Urbana: University of Illinois Press, 1985.

Turner, James. "Blacks in the Cities: Land and Self-Determination." *Black Scholar,* April 1970.

Tyson, Timothy B. *Radio Free Dixie: Robert F. Williams and the Roots of Black Power.* Chapel Hill: University of North Carolina Press, 1999.

U.S. Congress, Senate. *Book III: Final Report of the Select Committee to Study Government Operations with Respect to Intelligence Activities.* Washington: S.R. No. 94-755, 94th Congress, 2nd Session, 1976.

Van Deburg, William L., ed. *Black Camelot: African-American Culture Heroes in Their Times, 1960–1980.* Chicago: University of Chicago Press, 1997.

———. *Modern Black Nationalism: From Marcus Garvey to Louis Farrakhan.* New York: New York University Press, 1997.

———. *New Day in Babylon: The Black Power Movement and American Culture.* Chicago: University of Chicago Press, 1992.

Vincent, Theodore. *Black Power and the Garvey Movement.* Oakland: Nzinga, 1988.

Von Eschen, Penny M. *Race against Empire: Black Americans and Anticolonialism, 1937–1957.* Ithaca: Cornell University Press, 1997.

Walker, David. *An Appeal to the Coloured Citizens of the World, but in Particular, and Very Expressly, to Those of the United States of America.* Boston, 1829. Reprint, Baltimore: Black Classic, 1993.

Walker, Jack L. "Negro Voting in Atlanta, 1953–1961." *Phylon* 24 (winter 1963): 379–87.

———. "Protest and Negotiation: A Case Study of Negro Leadership in Atlanta, Georgia." *Midwest Journal of Political Science* 7 (21 May 1963): 99–124.

Ward, Stephen. " 'Scholarship in the Context of Struggle': Activist Intellectuals, the Institute of the Black World (IBW), and the Contours of Black Power Radicalization." *Black Scholar* 31, nos. 3–4 (fall–winter 2001): 42–53.

Washington, James M. *A Testament of Hope: The Essential Writings of Martin Luther King, Jr.* San Francisco: Harper and Row, 1986.

Weisbrot, Richard. *Freedom Bound: A History of America's Civil Rights Movement*. New York: W. W. Norton, 1990.

West, Guida. *The National Welfare Rights Movement: The Social Protest of Poor Women*. New York: Praeger, 1981.

West, Michael O. *The Rise of an African Middle Class: Colonial Zimbabwe, 1890–1965*. Bloomington: Indiana University Press, 2002.

White, Dana F. "The Black Sides of Atlanta: A Geography of Expansion and Containment, 1870–1975." *Atlanta Historical Journal* 26 (summer–fall 1982): 199–225.

White, Walter. *A Man Called White*. New York: Arno, 1969.

Williams, Rhonda Y. *The Politics of Public Housing: Black Women's Struggles against Urban Inequality*. New York: Oxford University Press, 2004.

Williams, Robert F. *Negroes with Guns*, ed. Marc Schleifer. New York: Marzani and Munsell, 1962.

Winks, Robin W. *The Blacks in Canada: A History*. Montreal: McGill-Queen's University Press / New Haven: Yale University Press, 1971.

Wood, Joe, ed. *Malcolm X: In Our Own Image*. New York: St. Martins, 1992.

Woodard, Komozi. *A Nation within a Nation: Amiri Baraka (LeRoi Jones) and Black Power Politics*. Chapel Hill: University of North Carolina Press, 1999.

Woodward, C. Vann. *The Strange Career of Jim Crow*, 3rd revised ed. New York: Oxford University Press, 1974.

Year of the Hate Bomb: NAACP Annual Report. New York: National Association for the Advancement of Colored People, 1951.

Young, Andrew. *A Way Out of No Way: The Spiritual Memoirs of Andrew Young*. Nashville: T. Nelson, 1994.

Zinn, Howard. *SNCC: The New Abolitionists*, 2nd ed. Boston: Beacon, 1965.

———. *A People's History of the United States*. New York: Harper and Row, 1980.

DISSERTATIONS, THESES, AND UNPUBLISHED PAPERS

Ambrose, Andrew Marvin. "Redrawing the Color Line: The History and Patterns of Black Housing in Atlanta, 1940–1973." Ph.D. diss., Emory University, 1992.

Carter, David C. " 'Two Nations': Social Insurgency and National Civil Rights Policymaking in the Johnson Administration, 1965–1968." Ph.D. diss., Duke University, 2001.

Grady-Willis, Winston A. "A Changing Tide: Black Politics and Activism in Atlanta, Georgia, 1960–1977." Ph.D. diss., Emory University, 1998.

Harmon, David Andrew. "Beneath the Image: The Civil Rights Movement and Race Relations in Atlanta, Georgia, 1946–1981." Ph.D. diss., Emory University, 1994.

Hazirjian, Lisa Gayle. "Negotiating Poverty: Economic Insecurity and the Politics of Working-Class Life in Rocky Mount, North Carolina, 1929–1969." Ph.D. diss., Duke University, 2003.

Matthews, Tracye. " 'No One Ever Asks What a Man's Role in the Revolution Is': Gender and Sexual Politics in the Black Panther Party, 1966–1971." Ph.D. diss., University of Michigan, 1998.

McGrath, Susan Margaret. "Great Expectations: The History of School Desegregation in Atlanta and Boston, 1954–1990." Ph.D. diss., Emory University, 1993.

Stanford, Maxwell C. "Revolutionary Action Movement (RAM): A Case Study of an Urban Revolutionary Movement in Western Capitalist Society." Master's thesis, Atlanta University, 1986.

Umoja, Akinyele. "Eye for an Eye: The Role of Armed Resistance in the Mississippi Freedom Movement, 1955–1980." Ph.D. diss., Emory University, 1996.

Vanlandingham, Karen Elizabeth. "In Pursuit of a Changing Dream: Spelman College Students and the Civil Rights Movement, 1955–1962." Ph.D. diss., Emory University, 1985.

Wilkins, Fanon Che. "In the Belly of the Beast: Black Power, Anti-Imperialism, and the African Liberation Solidarity Movement, 1968–1975." Ph.D. diss., New York University, 2001.

INDEX

Abernathy, Ralph David, 42, 171, 175
African Liberation Support Committee (ALSC), 192–93
African National Congress (ANC), 95
Afro-American Student Conference on Black Nationalism, 64
Ahmed, Akbar Muhammad (Max Stanford), 63–65, 230 n. 9
Al-Amin, Jamil Abdullah (H. Rap Brown), 131, 209
Aldridge, Delores P., 148
All-Citizens Registration Committee (ACRC), 31
Allen, Ivan, 26, 33–34; Dixie Hills protest and, 132; students and, 39, 47, 50; Summerhill protest and, 117–19, 124, 242–43 n. 10
All-University Student Leadership Group (AUSLG), 5–8
American Federation of State, County and Municipal Employees (AFSCME), 170–72
Anderson, Carol, 214–15 n. 6
Apartheid: resilience of, 114; as term, xvii–xviii, 213–14 n. 5
"Appeal for Human Rights, An" (AUSLG), 5–7, 216 n. 7
Atlanta Coalition Against Repression in South Africa (ACARSA), 200–201
Atlanta Committee for Cooperative Action (ACCA), xiii–xv, 5, 8, 132
Atlanta Constitution: on Malcolm X and Harlem nationalists, 69; on SNCC, 96–97; on student confrontations with Klansmen, 45

Atlanta Daily World: on Black electorate, 38; Empire Real Estate Board on, 15; on sit-ins, 9, 14–15, 42, 44; students on, 13
Atlanta Inquirer, 15
Atlanta Journal, 14, 119
Atlanta Project (SNCC), 83–113; antiwar activism of, 101–9; community freedom schools and, 97–101; formation and significance of, 83–85, 235 n. 13, 235 n. 15; housing activism of, 85–87; white skin privilege and, 86–90. See also Student Nonviolent Coordinating Committee
Atlanta Summit Leadership Conference (ASLC), 42–44, 51–54, 126
Atlanta Welfare Rights Organization. See National Welfare Rights Organization
Attica Prison riot, 186–87
Atwood, Sanford S., 146–48

Baker, Ella J., 11, 112–13
Baldwin, James, 206
Banks, Arthur C., 46
Baraka, Amiri, 159, 187
Bayne, Clarence S., 162
Bell, Camille, 206
Bell, John, 99
Bell, R. C., 34
Bell, Yusef, 206
Bellamy, Fay, 73–76, 96, 106–8, 113, 125
Benjamin, Playthell, 63
Bennett, Lerone, Jr., 17, 143, 151, 154, 162
Berry, Mary Frances, 164, 167

Biko, Stephen, 93–96, 237–38 n. 36, 238 n. 42

Billingsley, Andrew, 158

Black, Charles, 34

Black, Hector, 86–87

Black America, 65, 69

Black Consciousness Movement, 93–96, 237–38 n. 36, 238 n. 42

Black Consciousness Papers (SNCC), 88–90, 236 n. 24

Black feminism, 196–201

Black Liberation Front, 64–65

Black Manifesto, 160–61

Black nationalism: Atlanta and radical aspects of, 173–86; frontline activism and, 59–63; Malcolm X and, 67–78; SNCC and, 87–92; Robert Williams and, 64–68

Black Panther Party (BPP), 84, 158, 174–86, 199

"Black People and the International Crisis" (symposium), 167

"Black Politics in Georgia" (conference), 194–95

Black Studies: at Atlanta University Center schools, 144–48, 157–58; at Emory, 146–48; King assassination and, 143. See also Institute of the Black World

"Black Woman and the Liberation Struggle" (symposium), 195

Black women: in Atlanta, xviii–xix; class and, 108–9; RAM and, 64; self-perceptions of, 111–12, 197; women-centered activism and, 195–205

"Black Women, Black Freedom Struggle: Past, Present, Future" (conference), 202–4

Black Women for Political Action, 199

Black Workers Congress (BWC), 186

Bolden, Dorothy, 198–99

Bond, Horace Mann, 10, 82

Bond, Julian, 15, 24, 61, 80–84, 135–36, 186

Boone, Joseph, 44, 183–84

Borders, William Holmes, xiii, 12–13, 22–23, 50, 119, 126

Bradford, Marvin, 170

Brawley, James P., 4, 50

Brooks, Delores, 193

Brown, Benjamin, 14, 21, 24, 28, 186

Brown, H. Rap, 131, 209

Burrell, Deirdre, 207

Byrd Amendment, 192

Cabral, Almicar, 164

Cade Bambara, Toni, 199, 202–3

Calhoun, John, 26–27

Campbell, Finley C., 46

Canty, Henrietta, 137, 208

Carmichael, Stokely, 91, 125; on Black Power, 127–28, 173–74; in Dixie Hills, 130–32; at Peg Leg Bates retreat, 109–10

Carson, Clayborne, 235 n. 13, 235 n. 15

Carter, Jimmy, 124, 186–87

Carter, Ron, 177, 181–86

Center for African and African-American Studies (Atlanta University), 158

Chafe, William, 26

Challenor, Herschelle (Herschelle Sullivan), 6, 18, 27, 30

Chamber of Commerce (Atlanta), 40

Chisholm, Shirley, 187–88

Civil Rights Act of 1964, 54

Clark, Mark, 158

Class: educated women and, 198–99; fast-food sit-ins and, 46; intraracial class conflict, 172–73, 209–11; students and, 8–9, 16

Clayton, Horace R., 159
Clement, Rufus, 4–5, 10
Cmiel, Kenneth, 215 n. 6
Cochrane, Warren, 15
Coleman, George M., 38, 147, 170
Committee on Appeal for Human Rights
    (COAHR): Klansmen and, 45–48;
    phase one of nonviolent direct action,
    8–27; phase two alliance with SNCC,
    38–55
Committee to Stop Children's Murders
    (STOP), 206
Community Organizing Training Insti-
    tute (COTI), 164–65
Congo crisis, 69, 74–75, 128
Congress of African People, 159
Congress of Racial Equality (CORE),
    176–77
Congressional Black Caucus (CBC),
    192–93
Consortium for Research and Develop-
    ment on the Black Experience, 154
Cruse, Harold, 163–64

Dada, Mukasa (Willie Ricks), 59–61, 82,
    131–32, 144, 147
Daly, Pat, 164, 199
Daniel, Elotse, 85–86
Darnell, Emma, 195
Davis, Albert, 132
Davis, Angela, 182
Davison, Fred, 144
Denton, Nancy, 214 n. 5
DeVille, Alton, 177, 183
Diggs, Charles C., 192
Dixie Hills, 129–33
Dobbs, John Wesley, 187
Dodson, Howard, 158, 194–95
Dodson, Jualynne, 158–60, 199–204
Douglas, Jan, xvii–xviii, xix, 165, 199–201

Drake, St. Clair, 158–60
Du Bois, Shirley Graham, 159
Du Bois, W. E. B., 154

Electoral politics, xv, 17, 33–34, 38, 54,
    124; Black Power era and, 137–39,
    186–95; Julian Bond and, 81–83
Emmaus House, 137, 209–10
Emory Manifesto, 146
Endorsement in Support of Human Dig-
    nity, 13–14
Equal Rights Amendment (ERA), 198,
    201
Epps, Jesse, 170
Evans, Mari, 202
Evans, Tom, 170

Farmer, James, 176
Featherstone, Ralph, 131
Federal Bureau of Investigation (FBI), 50,
    175, 182
Feminism. See Black feminism
Ferguson, Gene, 177–78
Fisher, Michael E., 191
Fleming, Cynthia Griggs, 9, 111–12
Flowers, Sandra Hollin, 196–98
Ford, Austin, 137
Forman, James, 35, 43, 50–51, 72–73,
    110–12, 160–61
Fox, Larry, 12, 42, 103, 106–7, 113
Fouche, Barbara, 195
Franklin, David, 200
Franklin, Shirley, 199
Fredrickson, George, 213–14 n. 5
Freeman, Donald, 64
Freeman, Thomas, 177

Gaines, Martha, 197
Gender: Black manhood constructed, 16,
    89–90, 95–96, 238 n. 42; Black wom-

Gender (continued)
  anhood constructed, 9, 108–12; inter-
    racial relationships and, 65, 111–12;
    misogyny and, 197; sexism of Black
    men, 187–88, 197, 201. See also Black
    feminism; Black women
Georgia Association of Black Elected
    Officials (GABEO), 192–95
Giddings, Paula, 187
Gloster, Hugh M., 144–45
Grant, Anna, 198
Grassroots activism, 136–40, 169–73
Gray, L. Patrick, 182
Gregory, Dick, 48, 51
Guerrero, Gene, 93
Guy-Sheftall, Beverly, 196, 203

Hall, Prathia, 48–50, 227 n. 38
Hamer, Fannie Lou, 70–71, 110
Hamilton, Charles V., 127–28, 194
Hamilton, Grace Towns, 197
Hampton, Fred, 158
Harding, Vincent, 143, 148–51, 198; IBW
    and, 167; Maynard Jackson and, 190–
    91; NCBC and, 160–62;
Hartsfield, William, 7
Health care, 34–35
Henderson, Stephen, 149–50
High school students: Atlanta sit-ins
    and, 41, 44; Oklahoma City sit-ins
    and, 4
Hill, Jesse, 52, 171, 189
Hill, Robert, 155
Hollowell, Donald L., 18, 53
Holman, M. Carl: ACCA and, xiii; Atlanta
    Inquirer and, 15,
Hope, John, 154–55
Hope, Lugenia Burns, 154
Horn, Al, 183
Horne, Etta, 136–37

Hornsby, Alton, Jr., 115–17, 194, 208
Hotel segregation, 37, 39
Housing: segregation and, xiv, 241 n. 1;
    in Vine City neighborhood, 85–86,
    90–91
Howard, Donald, 107–8
Howard, Helen, 172–73
Human rights: Malcolm X on, 70, 72–
    73, 232 n. 27; student protesters on,
    6–7; as term, xvi–xvii, 214–15 n. 6
Hunter, Robert, 126
Hurston, Zora Neale, 203

Incarceration: Atlanta Project activists
    and, 106–8; Black families and, 109;
    harassment of female students during,
    51; sit-in protesters and, 21. See also
    Repression
Inman, John, 181–82
Institute of the Black World (IBW), 148–
    68, 173, 179; electoral politics and,
    189–91, 194–95; founding of, 148–51;
    funding problems of, 155–56, 164–67;
    gender and, 198; prisoners and sol-
    diers and, 163
International Committee to Support
    Imam Jamil Abdullah Al-Amin, 209
Interreligious Foundation for Commu-
    nity Organization (IFCO), 164–66
Isles, Gwendolyn, 39
Ivey, Beni, 199

Jackson, Maynard H., 171, 186–92
James, C. L. R., 155, 158
Jarrett, Thomas D., 147, 158
Jenkins, Herbert, 12, 125
Jericho Movement, 209
Johnson, Benjamin Joseph, 25
Johnson, Leroy, 38, 44, 129–32, 171, 191
Jones, Mack, 156, 167, 189

King, A. D. Williams, 21

King, Barbara, 202

King, Coretta Scott: antiwar activism of, 128, 244 n. 28; Institute of the Black World and, 150, 156–57; on Malcolm X, 76–77

King, Lonnie: attack on, 16; on desegregation compromise, 26–27; early sit-in movement and, 3–4, 7, 11–14; on Martin Luther King, Jr., 30

King, Martin Luther, Jr.: on assassination of Malcolm X, 77; on Black Power, 127; Malcolm X on, 75; on housing in Vine City, 86; Pilgrimage for Democracy, 43; Poor People's Campaign, 135–36; at rally for Julian Bond, 82–83; sit-in movement and, 12, 18, 29–31, 51–53; on Vietnam War, 128–29

King, Martin Luther, Sr., 13, 25–30

Ku Klux Klan, 18, 23, 45–48, 67

Ladner, Dorie, 151, 155

Ladner, Joyce, 151–55, 198

Lebedin, Charles, 40, 47, 54

Legal Aid Society, 172

Lewis, John, 44, 53, 65, 79–80

Locke, Dawolu Gene, 193

Lomax, Louis E., 15

Lomax, Michael, 202

Long, Richard A., 158

Lumumba, Patrice, 69

Lundy, Sam, 181–86

Lynd, Staughton, 61, 149

Maddox, Lester, 33–34, 40, 54–55

Malcolm X, 67–78; post-assassination discussion of, 76–78

Mandela, Nelson, 95

Mandela, Winnie, 95

Mao Zedong, 66

Marable, Manning, 194

Martin, Emma Jean, 176–86

Martin Luther King Community School, 154

Massell, Sam, 171–72, 175

Massey, Douglas, 214 n. 5

Mathews, Ethel Mae, 115, 118, 136–40, 169–72, 209–11

Mays, Benjamin, 4, 10, 12, 39

McDaniel, Robert, 126–27

McGill, Ralph, 124

Metropolitan Atlanta Regional Transportation Authority (MARTA), 200

Minnis, Jack, 92–93

Moon, Henry Lee, 76–77

Moore, Howard, Jr., 53, 81, 107, 125

Moore, Queen Mother Audley, 64, 159, 195

National Association for the Advancement of Colored People (NAACP): Grady Memorial Hospital and, 35; national convention of, 35–37; Nation of Islam and, 37; sit-ins and, 17

National Black Coalition (Canada), 162

National Black Political Convention, 187

National Committee of Black Churchmen (NCBC), 160–62

National Domestic Workers Union (NDWU), 198–99

National Union of South African Students (NUSAS), 93

National Welfare Rights Organization (NWRO), 136–37, 169–72

Nation of Islam, 28, 37, 67–68, 106

Newton, Huey P., 175–76

Nitty Gritty, 91

Norman, Silas, 73–76

Novel, Paulette, 195–96

Oliver, Kouson, 181
Operation Breadbasket, 37–38, 51
Organization of Afro-American Unity
   (OAAU), 68

Parsons, Jonathan, 152–53
Peoplestown, 113–16
Peterson v. City of Greenville, 40
Petty apartheid, xv, xviii
Pilgrimage for Democracy, 42–43
"Plight of the Black Woman" (forum),
   198–99
Ponder, Annell, 101
Poor People's Campaign, 135–36
Poor People's Day, 210
Pope, Roslyn, 5
Prather, Harold Louis, 117, 241 n. 7
Prather, Marjorie, 117
Price, Rena N., 148
Programme to Combat Racism, 166–67
Protests: Attica commemoration, 186–
   87; in Augusta, 174; in Dixie Hills,
   129–33; at Grady Memorial Hospital,
   34–35; at hotels, 39, 44; at induction
   center, 104–6; at lunch counters, 7–8,
   11, 17–26; at Morehouse College
   trustees' meeting, 145–46; during
   1970 municipal workers' strike, 170–
   71; at restaurants, 40–41, 45–55; in
   support of Atlanta Project activists,
   108–9; in Summerhill, 117–27; violent
   neighborhood protests, 133

Radnoss, Michael, 172
Rainwater, Lee, 152
Reagon, Bernice Johnson, 159
Reed, Rick, 186
Repression: of Atlanta Project activists,
   106–8; Atlanta University on, 158; of
   Black Panther Party in Atlanta, 180–

84; Carmichael on, 173–74; Dixie
   Hills protests and, 130–31; of early sit-
   in movement, 10–11; FBI surveillance
   of SNCC, 50; Mississippi violence and,
   61–63; in South Africa, 10, 93–95,
   200–201
Revolutionary Action Movement (RAM),
   63–67
Richmond, Myrian, 203–4
Rich's department store, 14, 15, 16, 17–
   18, 22, 31, 216 n. 6, 233 n. 78
Ricks, Willie, 59–61, 82, 131–32, 144,
   147
Robinson, Gwendolyn, xviii–xviii;
   Atlanta Project and, 83–88, 92–93,
   98–101, 108–12; Laurel, Mississippi
   SNCC project and, 61–63, 79, 113; Mal-
   colm X and, 77–78
Rodney, Pat, 155
Rodney, Walter, 155, 158, 167
Rogers, Joy, 202

Sadaukai, Owusu (Howard Fuller), 164
Sales, William, 231 n. 21, 232 n. 27
Sanders, Beulah, 136
Scott, David, 194
Seale, Bobby, 180
Second Look, A (ACCA), xiii–xv
Sellers, Cleveland, 113, 144
Shapiro, Morton, 170
Simmons, Michael, 91–92, 97, 113: anti-
   war activism of, 105–8; Julian Bond
   and, 80–83; RAM influence on, 67; on
   white skin privilege, 86–88
Simmons, Zoharah. *See* Robinson,
   Gwendolyn
Sjollema, Baldwin, 166–67
Smith, C. Miles, 41, 52
Smith, Ruby Doris, 16, 35, 39
Snellings, Roland, 65, 88–90

Sojourner South, 199–201

South Africa: apartheid in, xvii–xviii; Black Consciousness Movement in, 93–96; economic boycott of, 164, 200–201; Sharpevillle massacre in, 10

South African Students Organization (SASO), 93–94

Southern Christian Leadership Conference (SCLC), 37–38, 101, 135–36, 171, 175

Soweto, 95, 200–201

Southern Regional Council (SRC), 53, 195

Southern Student Organizing Committee (SSOC), 93

Stanford, Max, 63–65, 230 n. 9

Stewart, Donald, 202

Stone, Donald, 88–90, 99–101

Strickland, William, 151–54, 162–66; Maynard Jackson mayoral campaign and, 189–91

Stuckey, Sterling, 151

Student–Adult Liaison Committee (SALC), 14, 27–31

Student Nonviolent Coordinating Committee (SNCC): Julian Bond and, 80–83; COAHR and, 38–53; formation of, 11; Malcolm X and, 70–78; Peg Leg Bates retreat and, 109–12, 240 n. 70; Vietnam war and, 79–80; violent neighborhood protests and, 117–35. See also Atlanta Project

Sullivan, Herschelle, 6, 18, 27, 30

Sullivan, Leon H., 37

Summerhill, 114–27

Tait, Lenora, 18

Taylor, Nelson, 145–46

Thrasher, Sue, 93

Tillman, Johnny, 136

Tillinghast, Muriel, 200–201

Toure, Askia Muhammad (Roland Snellings), 65, 88–90

Toure, Sekou, 72

"Towards a Black Agenda," 157

Towns, Cora, 138

Ture, Kwame. See Carmichael, Stokely

Turner, James, 143–44

United Church of Christ (UCC), 165–66

United Nations, 45–48

University Movement for Black Unity (UMBU), 191

US Organization, 84, 199

Vandiver, Ernest, 7

Vietnam War: Atlanta Project and, 101–9; early SNCC criticism of, 79–83; Coretta Scott and Martin Luther King on, 128–29

Vine City, 85–86, 90–91, 115, 132

Vine City Foundation, 172–73

Vine City Project (SNCC). See Atlanta Project

Walden, A. T., 8, 25–26, 28, 33–34

Walker, Lucius, Jr., 164

Walker, Mardon, 52–53

Walker, Wyatt Tee, 43–44

Wallace, Mike, 207

Walton, Bobby, 117

Ward, Columbus, 118–19, 126, 133, 180, 209–10

Ware, Bill, 83, 88–90, 98–99, 110, 113, 117, 147

Ware, Carl, 193–95

Watts, Daniel H., 128–29

Welfare Fighter, 172

We Want Black Power (SNCC), 134–35

White, Dana, 207

White skin privilege: Atlanta Project
  activists on, 86–90; Biko on, 93–95;
  Sojourner South members on, 201
Wilburn, J. A., 28–29
Wiley, George, 136
Wilkins, Roy, 10, 37
Williams, Clyde, 119
Williams, Dwight, 67, 83, 98, 103–4, 107
Williams, Hosea, 120, 126, 171–72
Williams, Robert F., 64–68
Williams, Roy, 117, 125
Williams, Samuel, 25, 171
Williams, Wayne Bertram, 206

Wilson, Johnny, 106
Winters, Sylvia, 158
Womack, Hajj M., 208–9
Woodard, Komozi, 213–14 n. 5
Woods, Willie, 194–95
World Council of Churches, 166–67
Wright, Marian, 6

Young, Andrew, 175

Zellner, Bob, 110–11
Zellner, Dottie, 110–11
Zinn, Howard, 149

WINSTON A. GRADY-WILLIS
is an associate professor of African American
Studies at Syracuse University.

Library of Congress
Cataloging-in-Publication Data

Grady-Willis, Winston A.
Challenging U.S. apartheid : Atlanta and Black struggles for
human rights, 1960–1977 / Winston A. Grady-Willis.
p. cm.
Includes bibliographical references and index.
ISBN 0-8223-3778-9 (cloth : alk. paper)
ISBN 0-8223-3791-6 (pbk. : alk. paper)
1. African Americans—Civil rights—Georgia—Atlanta
—History—20th century. 2. Civil rights movements—
Georgia—Atlanta—History—20th century. 3. African
Americans—Segregation—Georgia—Atlanta—History—
20th century. 4. Atlanta (Ga.)—Race relations. 5. African
Americans—Georgia—Atlanta—Politics and government
—20th century. 6. Atlanta (Ga.)—Politics and government
—20th century. I. Title.
F294.A89N4387 2006
975.8′23100496073—dc22
2005031753